The
Hendre Ddu
Tramway

Quarrymen toil in Hendreddu no more
No songs from Capel Soar
No sounds but the raven's caw
Green trees over blue stone bore

Looking north along the tramway into Maesygamfa Quarry. The mill sat on top of the lower tips to the left. [Dan Quine]

Front Cover, Top: The short-lived Willys-Overland locomotive built in 1929. Seen hauling empty slab wagons past the locomotive shed at the top of the Brynderwen cutting. [Jonathan Clay]

Lightmoor Press

The Hendre Ddu Tramway

'Blue Stones and Green Trees'

Dan Quine

Telephone and Telegrams:
No. **41**
MELTON MOWBRAY

QUARRIES:
ABERANGELL, N. WALES
Private Sidings at Aberangell Station (G.W.R.)

Directors—W. BOWLEY.
J. H. HARRIS.

Best Welsh Slate Slabs
for
Electrical Switchboards.
Mantel Pieces.
Monumental Headstones.
Kerbing.
Louvres.
Tanks.
Tablet Backs.
Billiard Tables.
Shelving.
Paving.
Lavatory Slabs.

Best Welsh Slate Slabs
for
Divisions.
Blackboards.
Dampcourses.
Skittle Alley Floors.
Dowells.
Window Sills.
Doorsteps.
Columbariums and Numerous Requirements for many Trades.
—— □□ ——
Plain or Finished.

A CORNER OF THE MILL

Where SLABS are produced in all standard thicknesses and any size up to 12 feet long by 6 feet wide.

An advertisement for Hendreddu Slate Quarries Ltd. from between 1927 and 1934. The main picture is the interior of the quarry mill. The many slab products produced at the quarry are listed. [Courtesy Jon Knowles]

Published by LIGHTMOOR PRESS
© Lightmoor Press & Dan Quine 2022
Reprinted 2023
Designed by Jess Taylor

British Library Cataloguing-in-Publication Data. A catalogue record for this book is available from the British Library

ISBN: 9781 915069 15 3

LIGHTMOOR PRESS
Unit 144B, Harbour Road Trading Estate, Lydney, Gloucestershire GL15 4EJ
website: www.lightmoor.co.uk email: info@lightmoor.co.uk

Lightmoor Press is an imprint of Black Dwarf Lightmoor Publications Ltd

Printed in Poland
www.lfbookservices.co.uk

Contents

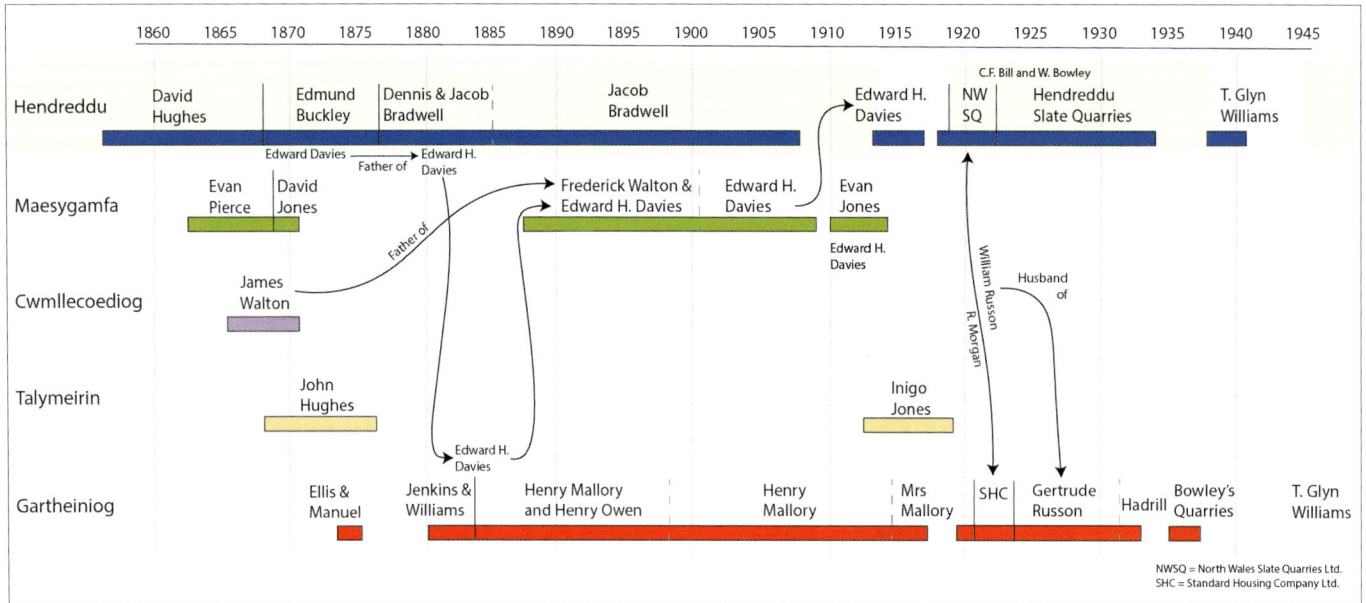

A timeline of the slate quarries around Aberangell, showing the years of operation and their principal owners. The ownership of the quarries in the early 1920s is particularly complex.

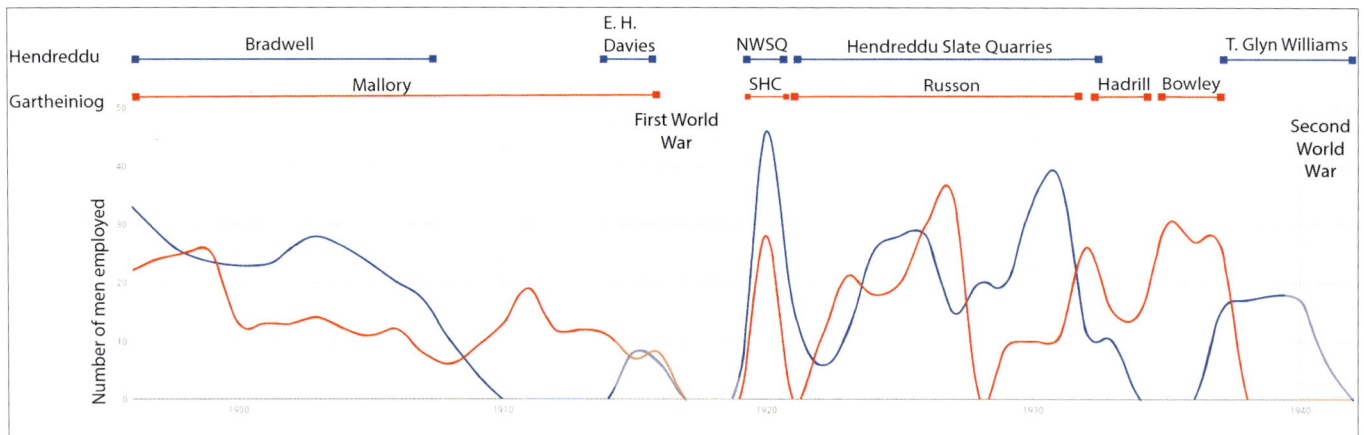

The number of men at Hendreddu and Gartheiniog between 1895 and 1941. These were the only quarries that consistently reported their manning levels, and even these records are incomplete. The decline of employment in the quarries leading up to the First World War can be seen, as well as the extreme swings in employment at both quarries between the wars.

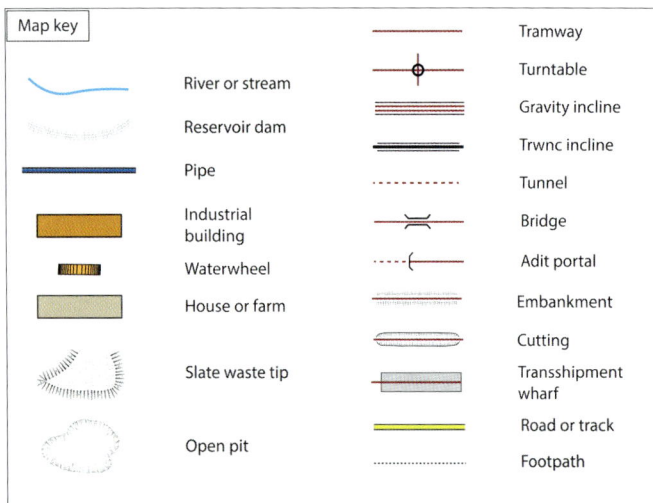

Left: Key to the maps in this book.

Below: The logo of the Hendreddu Slate Quarries. company.

1: Introduction

In 1969, my grandparents bought a cottage deep in the Dyfi Forest. I spent my childhood holidays there, surrounded by mountains and trees and by the narrow gauge railways and the quarries they served. I developed a love of the lines running along the valleys. The quarry waste tips were like vast, grey hands clawing at the landscape. The tiny railways were human-scaled and deeply eccentric. A lifelong fascination with these extraordinary places was born.

The nearest railway was the Hendre Ddu Tramway. It had, by the time I first visited Dyffryn Angell, long been dismantled, but there were still significant remains to be found. Our cottage contained a copy of Lewis Cozens's seminal book on the tramway – a thin, iron way that connected the distant farms and quarries to the tiny village of Aberangell. Over the years, my interest in the Hendre Ddu has been a constant presence. In 2011, I began what I thought would be a modest article about the Hendre Ddu, correcting some of the errors in previously published accounts.

My research began at the National Library of Wales's digital newspaper collection, which proved invaluable, as did the National Archives at Kew. As the research expanded, I was able to speak with several Aberangell villagers, who remembered the people and places so vividly. My fellow railway and quarry enthusiasts proved most generous, supplying me with notes, recollections and photographs.

I was able to access many of the papers and articles written by Bill Breese. He spent decades researching the history of the area around Aberangell and Dinas Mawddwy. As a young man, he had worked in two of the quarries and travelled on the tramway in its last years of operation. His work remains the most extensive and reliable history of the area, though sadly not all of it survives. Finally, I talked to members of several of the families who were connected to the Hendre Ddu Tramway. They helped me uncover many details of the past. It was a privilege to work with them.

Diving into the history of this fascinating tramway and the equally fascinating people involved with it has been a wonderful experience. My original modest article has ballooned into the book you hold now. I hope you enjoy reading it as much as I enjoyed writing it.

Dan Quine
San Francisco, November 2021

The spelling of place names has varied over time. Often these were minor variants like 'Hendre Ddu' and 'Hendreddu'. Sometimes the differences were larger: for example 'Maesygamfa' is sometimes written as 'Maesgamdda'. I have tried to be consistent within the book, so Hendreddu is the name of the quarry, while Hendre Ddu refers to the tramway.

Important note: the quarries described in this book are dangerous places. The surface workings have deep pits with crumbling walls. The underground workings are exceptionally unsafe and suffer from ongoing roof falls and collapses. They are on private property and should not be entered.

Slate Quarrying in Mid Wales

Beds of Ordovician slate run beneath the mountains of Mid Wales. Ice Age glaciers cut deep valleys, exposing the slate at the surface. For hundreds of years these outcrops were quarried on a small scale to provide stones for local buildings.

Commercial quarrying took hold between 1750 and 1800, becoming the major industry of North and Mid Wales. The Industrial Revolution drove a great urbanisation across Britain that resulted in a vast new demand for slate. Industrialists sought their fortunes exploiting the mineral wealth of Wales.

There were four major areas in Mid Wales where slate was commercially worked: Bryn Eglwys quarry, served by the Talyllyn Railway; The quarries along the Dulas Valley around Corris and Aberllefenni, served by the Corris Railway; The quarries of Dyffryn Angell, served by the Hendre Ddu Tramway; and Minllyn Quarry, south of Dinas Mawddwy, served by the Mawddwy Railway. There was also a cluster of smaller quarries near Fairbourne, served by short tramways.

Two veins run from Tywyn to Dinas Mawddwy: the Broad Vein and the Narrow Vein. Bryn Eglwys, the largest slate quarry south of Blaenau Ffestiniog, worked both. Braichgoch mined the Narrow Vein, but Abercwmeiddaw on the opposite side of the valley was on the Broad Vein. The Narrow Vein was worked successfully at Aberllefenni, Cymerau and Ratgoed; though the latter also trialled the Broad Vein.

As the slate progressed inland it generally declined in quality. Bryn Eglwys and Braichgoch produced large quantities of finely grained rock that could be split into thin roofing slates. By the time the vein outcropped at Hendreddu most of the rock, while still of robust quality, was used to produce slabs for flooring, gravestones, billiard tables, cisterns, and similar uses.

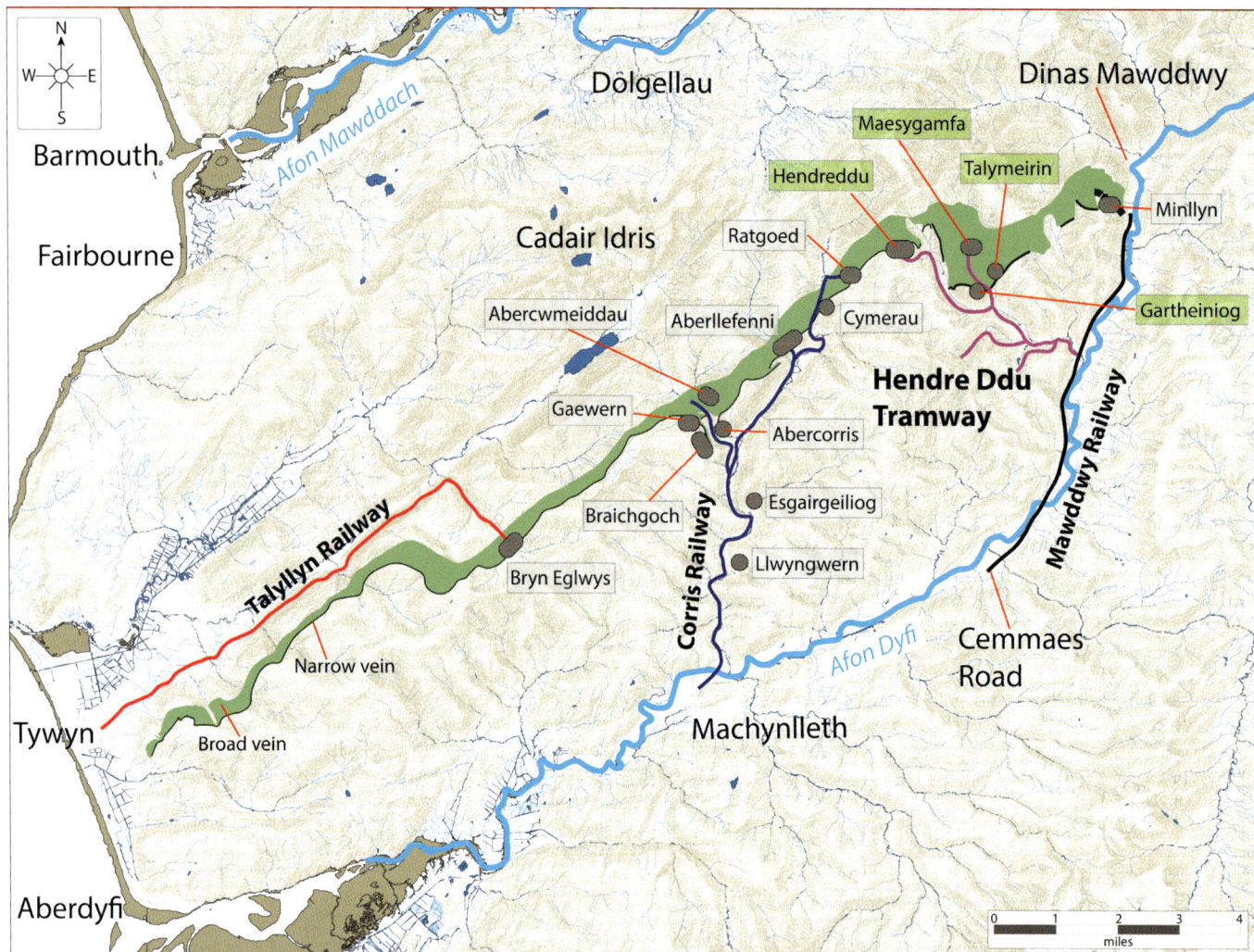

Between the Afon Mawddach in the north and the Afon Dyfi in the south lies the major slate belt of Mid Wales, running from Bryn Eglwys in the west to Minllyn in the east. Almost all worked the Narrow and Broad veins that sweep diagonally across this region, with notable outliers at Esgairgeiliog and Llwyngwern.

The Hendre Ddu Tramway

Of the many railways that traversed the mountains of Wales, the Hendre Ddu Tramway is perhaps the least well known. The main line ran 3 miles and 48 chains (5.8 km) from Hendreddu Quarry to the wharf at Aberangell on the Mawddwy Railway. Over the years, a large number of branches were laid, reaching into the tributary valleys. It was a private narrow gauge railway running through one of the least populated areas of Wales. It was the lifeblood of the local economy, but was hardly known in the outside world.

The valleys to the west of Aberangell crossed the veins, and there were natural outcroppings of the Narrow Vein at Hendreddu, Gartheiniog and Talymeirin. Maesygamfa to the north of Gartheiniog was on the Broad Vein.

As well as slate, these valleys contained rich stands of trees. Miles of tramways were laid to support timber felling between 1914 and the early 1970s. Many, but not all, of these timber tramways were connected to the Hendre Ddu Tramway. There were also various branches from the main tramway to farms and factories along its route.

Though the Hendre Ddu was obscure there are many fascinating connections between Dyffryn Angell and the wider world. Those who lived and worked here were directly connected to:

- The Darracq Car Company of Paris and London
- The invention of Linoleum
- The largest private colliery company in Britain
- Two Members of Parliament for Newcastle-under-Lyme
- Classic counterpoise desk lamps
- The founding of the London Marathon
- The Anti-Bolshevik White Army in the Russian Civil War
- The 'pirate accent' first heard in the film Treasure Island
- The Hartley jam empire
- The oldest pork pie shop in Melton Mowbray
- Oakeley, the largest underground slate mine in the world

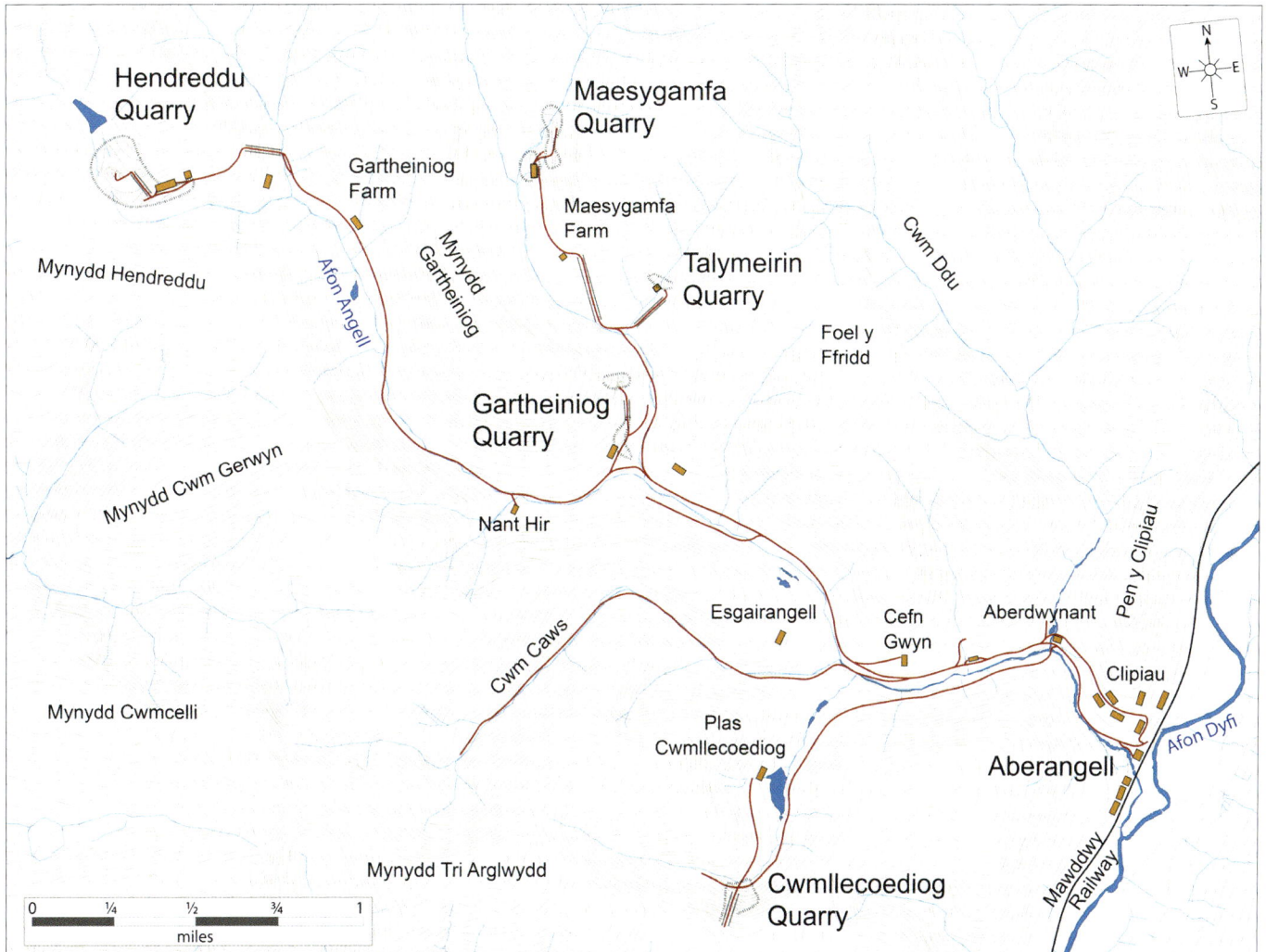

The complex web of tramways west of the village of Aberangell. The lines did not all exist at the same time, and some of them had more than one purpose and life span.

- The Leek and Manifold Light Railway
- The Kerry Tramway, near Newtown
- R.&G. Cuthbert's, Britain's leading seller of packet seeds
- And even, possibly, to Jack the Ripper

Ultimately, the story of the Hendre Ddu is of a particular time, place and people. The Williams, Jones, Breese, Davies and other families were the farmers, blacksmiths, quarrymen and foresters whose work forever changed the landscape.

Into this Welsh world came a wave of English industrialists, determined to make their mark on this isolated valley. These men had built empires in the mills and collieries of the English North West. The Buckleys and the Waltons arrived between 1855 and 1860, buying vast tracts of Welsh mountains to form their grand estates and taking on the title of Lord of the Manor. Sir Edmund Buckley revived slate quarrying in the upper Dyfi valley and constructed the Hendre Ddu Tramway. In the 1870s, the Bradwell brothers from Congleton arrived and purchased much of the Buckley estate, including the Hendreddu quarry and its tramway.

Bill Breese, the pre-eminent historian of Aberangell, put it well:

'For almost a century, industrious minded Englishmen (including Sir Edmund Buckley of Manchester and the Bradwell brothers of Congleton, the well-known silk merchants) had followed one another to (and from) the Angell and Mynach valleys. They came so as to gamble their vast fortunes in an effort to get richer by exploiting the varied resources that lay hidden in those two remote but pleasant 'Cymoedd'. Most unfortunately for them, they forfeited much capital while tangling with such a wily and tough opponent as our Welsh Broad and Narrow slate veins that still zig zag their uninterrupted course over hill and dale in old Merioneth.'

Hendreddu quarry saw success during the 1880s and into the 1890s. The quarries opened at Gartheiniog and Maesygamfa by local quarryman Edward Hurst Davies also did well. Production peaked in 1898 and a long decline set in. Both Hendreddu and Maesygamfa were shut down in 1910 and though both were briefly revived, the First World War soon saw them close again.

The Great War brought many changes to the valley. A large number of young men volunteered early, and as the war ground on, conscription took most of the rest off to war. So many did not return. With one exception, all the slate quarries closed. Colliery owner Henry Sharrock Higginbottom arrived looking for pit props for his mines and he felled many of the forests in the valley.

Another wave of English arrived after the war. They brought with them new ideas about making money from slate and new technologies that they had seen during their wartime service. Major Charles Bill and William Bowley led a revival at Hendreddu, finding first failure and then a period of success. William Clayton Russon brought Gartheiniog back to life, and he too experienced the fickle nature of slate quarrying. In their midst was Roland Morgan, who described himself as a stockbroker, but whose real work was swindling unsuspecting investors.

As the thirties arrived, the short boom in demand for slate turned into a long depression. The quarries struggled and new owners came and went. Gartheiniog sputtered to a halt in 1937, despite investment from a successful London firm. Hendreddu struggled on, revived by T. Glyn Williams, but by 1939 the tramway was out of use, replaced by lorries, and the quarry was barely operating. Its fate was sealed as war once again engulfed the world.

After the war, the Forestry Commission purchased much of the land west of Aberangell to form the Dyfi Forest.

This employed some of the men returning from the fronts. Tramways were installed for timber operations from the late 1940s onwards, with their use finally ending in the 1970s.

All these people were intimately bound together through work, chapel and school. Slate quarrying was, for decades, the major industry of Aberangell. Those who did not labour in the quarries were mostly farmers, indeed many were both and the distinction between farmer and quarryman is blurred.

When these ventures succeeded it was because of the hard work, ingenuity and discipline of the Welsh. Theirs were hard lives and they were determined to thrive. The English brought with them capital and new ideas. Some of them cared deeply for Dyffryn Angell and the people who lived there; too many were looking for a quick profit and, lacking practical experience, lost their money; a few were scoundrels and swindlers of the worst kind.

Today, Dyffryn Angell is quiet once more, returned to the upland farmers and the foresters. It is a place of immense natural beauty. Amongst the trees you can still find lengths of rail, buildings and the tramway trackbed, and if you know where to look, the impressive remains of the slate quarries. Few visit them now, but they stand their lonely vigil in the high hills, monuments to all who toiled amongst the green trees, digging out the blue slate stone.

The Hendre Ddu wharf at the north end of Aberangell station in 1949, showing the GWR's six-ton crane. The section of the platform in the foreground was rebuilt in 1893 to make room for the Mawddwy Railway siding to be extended into a loop. Gwastagoed Farm bridge is in the distance. The Hendre Ddu Tramway had been lifted by this date, but the wharf was being used by the Forestry Commission.
[David Elliot, Dan Quine collection]

2: The Cwmllecoediog Tramroad 1865-1870

The story of the Hendre Ddu Tramway starts with a quarry that was not connected to the tramway at all. Cwmllecoediog is a deep valley running south from Pont yr Hirgwm. It was for many years part of the Cwmllecoediog estate, which extended from Esgairangell in the north and to the banks of the Dyfi in the east.

Cwmllecoediog Quarry* was developed on the south side of the valley in the 1860s. It worked the Caerau mudstone, which was only quarried here and in a small, unsuccessful quarry near Rhayader. There was an internal tramway and circumstantial evidence suggests a tramroad ran from there to Plas Cwmllecoediog. The quarry and tramroad were owned by the Walton family. Cozens and Boyd describe a branch of the Hendre Ddu Tramway running to the quarry, Boyd claiming it was taken up 'sometime before 1900'. But this is almost certainly wrong as the quarry ceased working before the Hendre Ddu Tramway was laid.

The Cwmllecoediog Estate

The Cwmllecoediog Estate was owned for many years by the Astley family. The last of the family to live there was the notorious 'Mad' Jack Astley. He had been a director of the Gwanas slate quarry northwest of Dinas Mawddwy.[1] 'Mad' Jack had a reputation as a playboy and dilettante, but his debts caught up with him and he sold Cwmllecoediog around 1840. By 1842, he was in Fleet debtors' prison in London.[2] After paying off his debts, he emigrated to Canada and died there in 1857.[3]

Cwmllecoediog was purchased by Henry Foskett in 1853.[4] Foskett apparently dug a trial adit looking for copper on his property in 1854: '*It is said that a copper mine was discovered in a place nearby.*'[5] There were several copper mines to the north and east of Dinas Mawddwy at the time, but the Cwmllecoediog copper venture came to nothing.

When the Cwmllecoediog estate was listed for auction in 1859, it was described as a '*freehold estate of 1,134 acres centred with a gentlemanly residence, with ornamental grounds and lake, and enriched with about 278 acres of fine marketable timber… together with a water corn mill*'.[6] Despite the advertisement highlighting the commercial opportunities of the timber and mill, no mention is made of a slate quarry. Given the boom in quarrying at the time, if a quarry had been present or even considered possible, it is likely it would have been mentioned.

James Walton

James Walton was born near Sowerby in Yorkshire in 1802 or 1803.[7] His father Isaac was a successful merchant, but it was James who made the family's fortune. James established a large cloth carding factory at Sowerby Bridge. Carding disentangles and cleans raw cotton fibres in preparation for weaving; it is the small but essential process that makes industrial production of cloth possible.

In 1834, James was granted his first patent for a cloth card with an india rubber back. These cards proved to be substantially cheaper to manufacture than the traditional wooden ones, so there was great demand for Walton's invention and it generated vast profits. He was an early railway investor, including in the West Yorkshire Railway Company[8] – which was amalgamated into the Lancashire and Yorkshire Railway in 1846.

In 1846, James moved to Manchester, establishing a large factory on Chapel Street in Ancoats, next to Manchester London Road (later renamed Piccadilly) Station. The factory was described as '*one of the sights of the cotton industry*'.[7] In 1853, he moved to a new factory in nearby Haughton Dale as the business expanded;[9] it was described as '*the largest establishment of the kind in the world*'. In 1855, the business became James Walton and Sons as Frederick (born 1834[10]) and William (born 1832[11]) joined the family business.[10] James Walton became extremely wealthy and well known during his lifetime:

'James Walton… was remarkable in his inventive genius. Like Brindley and Arkwright and other great leaders of industry who have established the supremacy of England as a manufacturing nation, he was a man of marked individuality of character, of mental vision, strength of will and steadfastness of purpose and he has left behind him a long list of original ideas many of which were carried into practice and assisted greatly in increasing the productive powers of the great cotton spinning trade.'[12]

James Walton, believed to have been taken in the 1850s during his days at Haughton Dale.

---

* Boyd mistakenly calls this quarry Coed y Chwarel

In the late 1850s, James was looking for a country estate to retire to. Cwmllecoediog was ideal and he purchased it from Foskett in 1859.[13] By May 1860, James and his son William were living there.[14] In 1868, James purchased an even larger estate at Dolforgan, near Kerry. He retired there that year, leaving Cwmllecoediog as a residence for his sons.

Cwmllecoediog Quarry 1865-1870

James Walton had seen the profit made in mines and quarries during the early Industrial Revolution. The Welsh slate industry was booming; the horse-worked Corris, Machynlleth & River Dovey Tramroad (later renamed the Corris Railway) had opened four years earlier, proving a real boost for the quarries of the Dulas Valley. Walton wanted to try his hand at this local industry.

Perhaps Walton knew of Foskett's failed search for copper on the estate when he decided to seek slate there. He began quarrying in the valley south of the house probably in 1865 or 1866; certainly, the Cwmllecoediog quarry was working by August 1867, just a month after the first Mawddwy Railway train arrived at Aberangell. In January 1868, Walton was sued by one of his miners:

'Humphrey Pearce, miner, Machynlleth, sued Mr James Walton, Cwmlledwg [sic], Machynlleth, to recover £3 8s 6d. for work done. Mr. G. Jones Williams appeared for the defendant. The case, which occupied a considerable time in hearing, turned upon the correctness of the measurement of some rock which plaintiff and five others had taken as piece work in Mr Walton's quarry in August last.

On behalf of the plaintiff, Richard Jones, a farmer and "freeholder" living near Machynlleth, said that he had measured the work, and handed in his calculation, which differed very materially from that which had been prepared by Thomas Davies, the late Manager of the quarry. In cross-examination, it was elicited that this witness knew nothing of the mining business, and had not been connected with the quarry in any capacity, while the valuer who had been employed for the defendant was a practical man.

For the defendant, a receipt, signed by one of the plaintiff's

Looking uphill into the quarried ravine in the south valley wall in May 2016. The rock here is of extremely poor quality, but at least could have been pried loose without the need for explosives. The incline down to the tramroad would have run up to the right of the photograph. [Dan Quine]

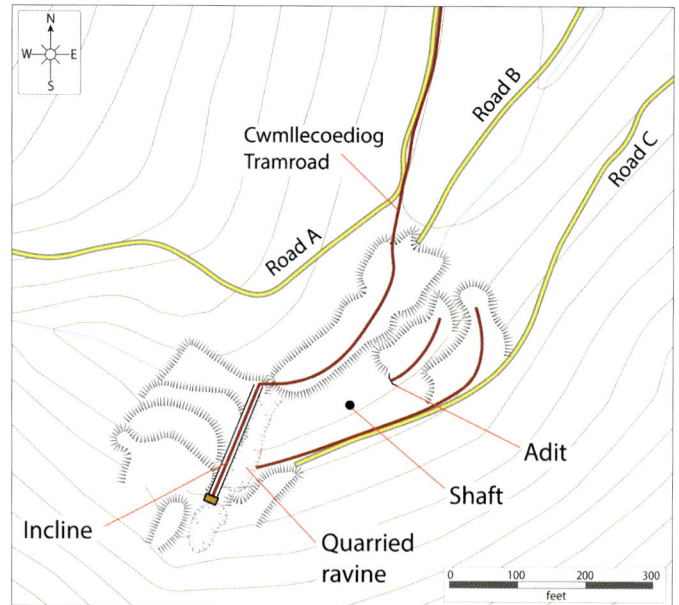

Possible layout of Cwmllecoediog quarry while it was active.

partners in the job, was put in, and this partner in evidence said that he signed the receipt with the concurrence and knowledge of the plaintiff, who was the only one of the six who took the job that had backed out and refused to receive his share. His Honour reserved his decision.'[15]

The quarry was a simple working, with a shallow quarried ravine in the steep south side of the valley, one shaft and a short adit, most likely to a single chamber. The shaft was probably a roofing shaft from the chamber. The quarry was more than a mile south of the main slate veins and must have produced very poor rock. The Caerau mudstones are friable and highly fractured; any slabs produced would have deteriorated quickly in use.

On Friday 31st July 1868,[16] there was a fatal accident at Cwmllecoediog. Several men were excavating rock, when a large fall buried Thomas Pugh of Aberangell, killing him instantly. Given the very steep ground and the soft, fractured nature of the rock, it is not surprising that rockfalls occurred. John Waltman of Darowen broke both legs, one in two places, and Richard George of Commins Coch broke one leg just above the ankle. Waltman and George were treated by Dr Richard Griffiths and are believed to have survived their injuries. Pugh's inquest returned a verdict of accidental death.[17]

Thomas Pugh was just twenty-four when he died. He left a widow, Catherine, and three children. Catherine Pugh struggled financially after the death of her husband, which led her to take the position of caretaker at Hendreddu quarry barracks.[18] Thomas's youngest daughter was Sian Roberts who lived at the family home, Winllan in Clipiau. Her brother-in-law David Roberts was killed in a rockfall at Minllyn Quarry, and her son William Thomas was killed in the Senghenydd colliery disaster in October 1913.[19]

In October 1869, Walton was sued again, in Machynlleth County Court:

'Mr. Davies, plaintiff, for whom appeared Mr. Hughes, claimed from the defendant Mr. Walton, on whose behalf Mr. Woosnam appeared, the sum of £33 14s 5d for goods supplied to a quarry. Defendant alleged that the goods were never ordered; but plaintiff proved that his (defendant's) waggoner took them from the station to the quarry. Judgement for £16 19s was given for the plaintiff.'[20]

The goods referred to was likely machinery for the quarry, hauled in Walton's wagon from Aberangell station to Cwmllecoediog. The goods would be worth around £30,000 in 2018 prices. It is not certain who the plaintiff, Mr Davies was, though one possibility is Edward Davies who was in the process of opening Hendreddu quarry at the time for Sir Edmund Buckley.

The last contemporary account of the quarry comes in July 1870. An otter hunt led by Colonel Pryse pursued their prey into Cwmllecoediog and onto Walton's land. The rather florid report includes this passage:

'The otter knew his stronghold, and there we were at last at the mouth of an apparently endless culvert which drained the waters from some slate quarries above. The question was how was he to be bolted… Mr Apperley, with characteristic pluck, dived into the dark passage and was lost to sight for a long twenty minutes. Indeed, we became nervous about his safety, for the roof of the drain was uncertain and supposed to be fallen in some parts; but signs of life occasionally heard beneath us, and at last he appeared at the far end, having traversed the whole length often knee deep in water, and compelled to go on hands and knees over the rocky bottom, but no signs of the otter except his nest. Again he plunged in with a bit of miner's candle, and succeeded in finding a small branch drain. There the otter must be. An opening was sunk through the roof, the main drain stopped at the junction, another opening made far up the branch drain, dead silence kept, and in five minutes out bolted our long lost friend, his coat as shiny, soft, and bright as silk, in full view up a side hill, and away across country to Mr Walton's lake again.'[21]

From this description, it appears that the quarry had stopped working by this date. The 'culvert' that Mr Apperley traversed carried the Gwern Fraith stream underneath the quarry's waste tips.

Closure

The date of closure of Cwmllecoediog quarry is unknown. it had closed by 1887 when the 6-inch OS map was surveyed.

In 1870, Walton built a new, larger house on his estate called Plas Cwmllecoediog, replacing the original hunting lodge. He also built a new drive and significantly upgraded the path that ran above Allt Ddu. It seems likely that quarrying halted at around the same time that Walton turned his attention to upgrading the estate. Breese gives 1870 as the date of closure for the quarry and this seems highly probable.[22]

Cwmllecoediog Tramroad

The question of whether there was rail transport at Cwmllecoediog quarry in the 1860s remains unanswered. Tramways were likely used within the quarry,

and there is circumstantial evidence for a tramroad from the quarry to Plas Cwmllecoediog, where slate could be loaded onto carts and taken to Aberangell. Boyd and Cozens's claim that the tramroad ran to Aberdwynant is almost certainly incorrect; the Hendre Ddu Tramway was not built until 1874 so there was nothing at Aberdwynant for the speculated tramroad to connect to.

Bill Breese's map shows an incline at Cwmllecoediog quarry. Given the steepness of the slope and the large waste tips, it seems very likely that the quarry had an incline and associated internal tramways. Bill also states that there was no tramway from Aberdwynant to Cwmllecoediog before the First World War.[22]

The map in Cozens's book shows the timber tramway laid during the First World War from Aberdwynant to the bottom of the valley below the quarry. It also shows a branch from the head of the tramway back to Plas Cwmllecoediog, running along the north side of the valley. There is no viable

Part of Bill Breese's hand-drawn map, showing Cwmllecoediog quarry with an incline on the west side of the quarry.
[Courtesy Mike Cowley]

route for this supposed branch as the timber tramway was a long way below the level of the supposed branch, and there was no reason why the timber tramway would have connected to the house.

There is a track running along the hillside connecting Plas Cwmllecoediog and the location of the quarry. This is well made and level and could have been the route of an early tramroad. The track would have connected the quarry to the nearest well-made road, allowing slabs to be transported to Aberangell.

If there was a tramroad from the quarry to Cwmllecoediog Villa, it would have been used in the late 1860s and lifted when the quarry closed around 1870. The gauge is unknown, though most likely a nominal 2ft gauge.

There is one last piece of circumstantial evidence related to the route of the tramway: a 1941 Forestry Commission report says:

'A walk was taken from Cwmllecoediog Hall through the valley where the old tramline used to run, and where road construction will be necessary for timber extraction in the future… Instruction was given to clear the coppice off camp ride where the tramline used to run so as to enable men to move up the valley quickly in the case of fire.'

Right: conjectured route of the Cwmllecoediog tramroad. Evidence for the route and dates of operation is limited and should be taken as a 'best guess'. During the Second World War, the Forestry Commission is thought to have referred to the road from its camp, past the Plas and along the west side of the valley as 'Camp Ride'. This was the presumed trackbed of the Cwmllecoediog tramroad.
[Extract of 1900 map courtesy of Ordnance Survey]

Below left: The track from the quarry to Plas Cwmllecoediog, seen in May 2016 from the far side of the valley. This was a particularly well constructed and level route for a light farm track and is believed to have carried the Cwmllecoediog tramroad in the 1860s.
[Dan Quine]

Below right: Looking north into Cwm Llecoediog from directly above the quarry. The fishing lake is visible in the centre and Plas Cwmllecoediog sits in the deciduous trees to the left of the lake. The Cwmllecoediog tramroad may have run across the open hillside on the near left, where the probable trackbed can just be made out. Dyffryn Angell runs in front of the hills in the distance.
[Dan Quine]

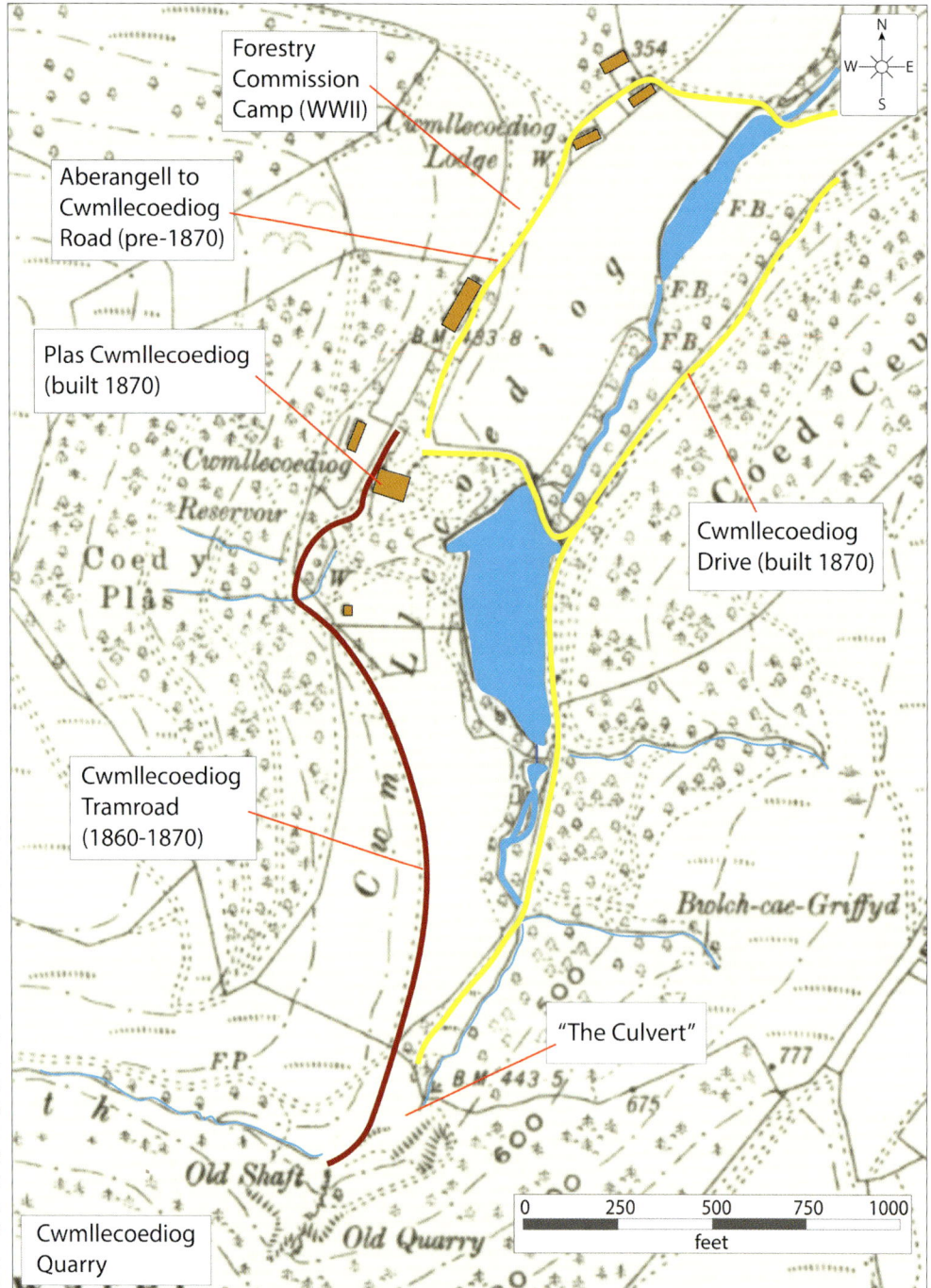

Forestry Commission Camp (WWII)

Aberangell to Cwmllecoediog Road (pre-1870)

Plas Cwmllecoediog (built 1870)

Cwmllecoediog Drive (built 1870)

Cwmllecoediog Tramroad (1860-1870)

"The Culvert"

Cwmllecoediog Quarry

Plas Cwmllecoediog, built in 1870 by James Walton to replace the earlier hunting lodge. This view, probably taken in the early 1920s, shows the house and some of its landscaped gardens. The Cwmllecoediog tramroad of the 1860s is believed to have terminated behind the house. The hillside to the left shows the results of clear-felling during the First World War. [Lilywhite's Postcard]

This reference to the 'old tramline' appears to refer to a line from the quarry to the lodge. Given that the Forestry Commission maintained a camp just north of Plas Cwmllecoediog during the war, 'camp ride' may refer to a direct route from the Plas to the quarry, supporting the existence of this line.

The waste tips that once filled the valley have long since been removed. There are some signs of degraded tips on the southern slopes of the valley, though substantially smaller than those shown on the 1887 map. It is believed that the tips were removed in two phases. During the First World War, the tips blocked access to the forest to the south and west. Material was taken from them to build up the trackbed of the timber tramway and allow it to extend past the remaining tips. The second phase was between 1920 and 1923[24] when further material was removed to resurface Cwmllecoediog Drive — John Breese was one of the estate employees who worked on this project.[18]

References

1   The Gwanas Slate Quarry, *Monmouthshire Merlin*, Sep. 21st, 1839.

2   The Court for Relief of Indolent Debtors, *The London Gazette*, no. 20105, p.1532, Jun. 3rd 1842.

3   Obituaries, *Barrie Herald*, Aug. 19th, 1857.

4   Notice of Sale, *Law Times*, Jul. 16th, 1863.

5   Caradawc o. Lancarfan, *A Portrait of Machynlleth and its Surroundings*. Machynlleth: Adam Evans, 1854.

6   Montgomeryshire, Freehold Estate, *Birmingham Journal*, Mar. 12th, 1859.

7   James Walton: obituary, *Manchester Guardian*, Nov. 8th, 1883.

8   West Yorkshire Railway Company, *Bradford Observer*, Oct. 17th, 1844.

9   George Clement Boase, Walton, James, in *Dictionary of National Biography*, 1899.

10 Ralph Parsons, Linoleum: A Chiswick Invention, *Brentford & Chiswick Local History Journal*, vol.5, 1996.

11 Walton, 1851 England, Wales & Scotland Census, vol. Piece 2219, 1851.

12 *Collections Historical and Archeological Relating to Montgomeryshire and its Borders*. Whiting & Co., 1882.

13 Montgomeryshire: Cwmllecoediog Estate, *Birmingham Journal*, Mar. 19th, 1859.

14 Monthly meeting of the Royal Agricultural Society of England, *The Farmer's Magazine*, May 1860.

15 Pearce vs Walton, *North Wales Chronicle*, p.5, Jan. 25th, 1868.

16 Dinas Mawddwy, *Cambrian News*, p.4, Aug. 1st, 1868.

17 Dinas Mawddwy. — Damwain Angeuol, *Baner ac Amserau Cymru*, p.5, Aug. 1st, 1868.

18 Bill Breese, The old quarrying days in the Angell valley, *Cambrian News*, Jun. 25th, 1976.

19 Bill Breese, Atgofian: Twmplen Mam, *Cambrian News*, Jan. 7th, 1977.

20 Machynlleth County Court, *Shrewsbury Chronicle*, Oct. 30th, 1868.

21 Three days with Col. Pryse's otter hounds, N. Wales, *Oswestry Advertiser*, Jul. 27th, 1870.

22 Bill Breese, Bygone activities within Angell valley, *Cambrian News*, Aug. 6th, 1976.

23 Bill Breese, Notes on local quarrying and quarrymen, *Dolgellau Archive*, vol. ref ZM/6541/9, 1982.

24 Gwyndaf Breese, Hard times on the tramway, unpublished manuscript.

Abergynolwyn village around 1880, much as Sir Edmund Buckley would have known it when planning his housing at Hendreddu. The incline down from the Talyllyn's mineral extension was originally constructed to bring in the slate and other materials needed to build the village. [Francis Frith]

3: The Start of Hendreddu Quarry and Tramway 1868-1875

Sir Edmund Buckley of Ardwick

The early history of the Hendre Ddu quarry and tramway is intricately bound to the Buckley family – wealthy industrialists from Manchester. Edmund Buckley of Ardwick* was born on Christmas Day 1780 and he became one of the most successful industrialists in Manchester. His interests spanned canals, railways, ironworks, collieries, sand quarries and cotton mills. He was a committee member of the Manchester Exchange, the heart of the North West's cotton industry, for thirty years, eventually becoming its chairman.[1] He was described as '*probably the richest man in Manchester*' and served as Conservative MP for Newcastle-under-Lyme, from 1841 to 1847.[2] He was offered a baronetcy by Prime Minister Robert Peel for public service, but he declined.[3]

Buckley was '*the most clubbable of men*' and certainly enjoyed a fine life at a variety of Manchester clubs. He was a leading figure in the delightfully named Scramble Club, which was mainly focused on consuming good food and fine wines. He was a member of the Pitt Club, the Mosley Street Club Room and the Union Club, again mostly for the drinks.[1] He was poet laureate and then president of John Shaw's Club[4] for many years[5] – a social club for Tory Anglicans[6] to which many Manchester mill owners belonged. This club too was not short of occasions for dining and drinking.

Buckley introduced many upcoming businessmen to John Shaw's Club. One of them was James Lillie, a customer of Buckley's ironworks and a mill engineer. Lillie made his name with the contract to fit out McConnel and Kennedy's Sedgwick Mill at Ancoats in the 1820s.[1] It was owned by the McConnel family who thirty years later built the Talyllyn Railway.

Buckley was also a Senior Police Constable and presided over a grand banquet at John Shaw's to celebrate the opening of the Liverpool and Manchester Railway in 1830.[1] He took a great interest in transport, as a board member of the Mersey and Irwell Navigation, an investor in the Erewash Railway, and a director of the Edinburgh and Glasgow Railway.[7]

Edmund of Ardwick never married, but had by his own account at least sixteen children, five of them with his favourite mistress Sarah Peck; clearly, he lived an unconventional life.

---

* Most of the Buckley men in this period had the first name Edmund. For clarity, the place of birth is given for all but Edmund Buckley born in 1834, to distinguish them.

The portrait of Sir Edmund Buckley of Ardwick that hung in John Shaw's Club to celebrate his presidency.

The first of Buckley's children was Edmund Peck, born on April 16th 1834 in Chorlton. A fictitious husband for the unmarried Sarah was concocted for the official account, named Edmund Peck. Edmund Buckley of Ardwick was described as the child's 'uncle'. The *Cambrian News* was a particular perpetrator of this pretence, reporting on Peck's fake 'father' in 1869[8] and again in his obituary in 1910.[9]

In 1856, just after Edmund Peck reached his majority, Edmund of Ardwick purchased the manor of Dinas Mawddwy from John Bird.[8] He paid £35,000 for the estate of 4,000 acres and 8,000 acres of sheepwalks.[10] The estate listing said '*it abounds with minerals and slate, from which an annual income from sleeping rents of nearly £700 is derived*', though it does not specify which mines were then active.

There were many houses on the estate, notably Plas Dinas, the manor house at Dinas Mawddwy. Ownership of the estate also conferred the ancient title of Lord of Mawddwy.

Sir Edmund Buckley, 1st Baronet

Edmund Peck became the agent for his father's Dinas Mawddwy estate and moved into Bryn Hall at Llanymawddwy. He quickly became involved in local affairs, and in 1858 was appointed the Sheriff of Merionethshire.[11]

On October 28th 1859, Buckley of Ardwick wrote to his son Edmund Peck:

'... *your accounts shall all be settled and everything made easy in your mind ...You mentioned my refusing your going into the Army, I did this out of respect to your health, for I was pretty certain in my own mind you could not stand the wet and cold, the wear and tear of what is required. Besides you were always my greatest favourite and I felt much for you, hoping that you would succeed me in everything and stand high in society. You have a strong mind and have had a good education. I think I have refused you nothing that would contribute to your health, comfort and standing in the world.*

You often tell me that I mention the sums that John and you have had. These sums have an effect upon the mind of one who has known the want of a dinner and lived for 6 months upon 7/- per week, struggling hard to maintain a poor mother and a young family in a respectable way, and you are aware that I have had 16 young ones or more to bring up and I hope I have done justice to them. Now as I have said, you shall on my return be clear of everything.

I must have a promise from you to quit the company that you have kept, at least some of them dining at an hotel and spending the afternoons or evenings often, I am fearful, not in a rational manner, and you cannot be comfortable after, or in the morning, when you awake. You can be of very great use indeed in taking the management of the works, but you say I interfere with you. I have interfered very little with the Yorkshire or Fairfield works. I have done so with Collyhurst because we never had such a time, and putting up an engine, it has made me more anxious than usual. If you will take the management and attend to them, I shall not care about going there, unless you wish to have my opinion on any important matter, and these three works are by far the greatest part of our business, and as they may (provided you are right) fall into your hands the sooner you take the management the better, provided you think proper to do so...

My time I am sure will be very short and I wish to have these things settled as well as I can before I go hence ... Now I hope you will consider these matters well, as they hang heavy on my mind, it being much worse with old men than young ones ...You must not think that everything will go on straight. There will be

disappointments and we are not sent here to live for ourselves alone, but to comfort and assist others who are dear to you.

I am Dear Ted, Yours Truly, Edmund Buckley.'

Edmund of Ardwick was concerned about his son's wayward and profligate habits; doubts that would later prove all too well-founded. Where his father was a builder of wealth, Edmund Peck was a prodigious spender, prone to reckless investment in dubious and ill-thought-out schemes.

In March 1860, Edmund Peck married 20-year-old Sarah Rees, daughter of William Rees printer, publisher and Mayor of Llandovery.[12] In 1861, Edmund of Ardwick gifted the Dinas Mawddwy estate to his son,[13] and Edmund Peck became the Lord of Mawddwy. Edmund and Sarah Peck's first son, also Edmund, was born on June 19th 1861.[14] Edmund of Ardwick, pleased that his son was settling, obtained a royal order changing Peck's surname to Buckley. It was granted on April 4th 1864.[15] The new Edmund Buckley took control of the businesses in Manchester, a large house at Ardwick and the family's Grotton Head estate at Saddleworth. He was now an extraordinarily wealthy man.

Edmund set about his grand project: to transform Dinas Mawddwy into a centre of industry. He began clearing and replacing most of the houses in the town, including the ancient manor house. In its place began building the grand neo-Gothic Plas-yn-Dinas. He purchased more land, increasing the estate to more than 40,000 acres.

A key part of his plan was to exploit the mineral wealth beneath his property. To the north of Dinas Mawddwy, he opened metal mines. To the south, he focused on slate, issuing take notes (permission to explore for minerals) to people seeking the slate veins on his land.[8] On Christmas Day 1864, he leased Minllyn quarry to the Merionethshire Slate and Slab Company.* The quarry was overseen by Edward Davies, who would go on to run Hendreddu.[16]

Edward Davies was born in Llanwrin on the 5th April 1822.[17] He was industrious, entrepreneurial and became a highly skilled quarryman. On 27th October 1846,[18] he married Anne Hurst, the lady's maid of Mary Cornelia Edwards the wife of George Vane-Tempest, the 5th Marquess of Londonderry.[19]

Edmund Buckley, in the 1860s, probably at the time he was made a baronet.

---

* Not to be confused with the Merionethshire Slate and Slab Company 1846-1849

The imposing neo-Gothic Plas-yn-Dinas which Edmund Buckley built in 1868.[12] This view dates from the 1900s, not long before the Plas was destroyed in a mysterious fire.

Around 1847, Edward and Anne moved to Georgetown, Tredegar, a 'model town' built for the rapidly developing South Wales coalfields. Following an outbreak of cholera in 1849, the family moved back north to Corris, Edward working in the quarries there.

Edward and Ann had eight children including Matilda Ann born in 1848, Mary in 1851, Hannah in 1853, Edward Hurst in 1855, Elizabeth in 1857, John Weston in 1863 and Margaret Maria in 1868. The family moved to Dinas Mawddwy in either 1862 or 1863, where Edward was a police officer.

In November 1864,[20] Buckley put forward a bill to construct the Mawddwy Railway* which was passed in July 1865.[21] The 6.6 mile-long[22] standard gauge railway connected Dinas Mawddwy and Minllyn quarry, with Cemmaes Road where it joined the main line of the newly-formed Cambrian Railways. Buckley provided most of the £70,000** cost of construction, which began in 1865. On 11th July 1867, the first contractor's train reached Aberangell.[23] The line officially opened on 30th September 1867.[24]

In 1865, Edmund Buckley was elected as Conservative MP for Newcastle-under-Lyme, following in his father's footsteps. Edmund Buckley of Ardwick died on 21st January 1867.[1] In November 1868, Edmund Buckley was made a baronet[25] and became Sir Edmund Buckley, Bart. The baronetcy was conferred for his 'leading part in the Conservative interests in Lancashire, as well as in Merionethshire, and … as a public benefactor to the district in which he resides, by his liberal and judicious expenditure of capital in improving and developing the mineral and other resources of the country'.[3] 'Liberal' was an apt description of Edmund's expenditure of capital; 'judicious' was not.

Opening Hendreddu 1868-1871

One of Edmund of Ardwick's take notes was claimed in 1856 by David Hughes of Pen Pentre, Aberangell.[8] His area included Cwm Hendreddu, where some local quarrying had been taking place since about 1800.[26] Hughes developed these pits and found good slate. Sir

---

* Contemporary documents also use the titles Mowddwy Railway and Dinas Mawddwy Railway

** £15 million in 2018

Edmund Buckley saw the commercial possibilities and in 1864 he began expanding the quarry. In August 1868[27] he officially opened the Hendreddu Slate Quarry, 3½ miles west of Aberangell. By the end of the year, the quarry was employing 140 men.[26]

It is not clear why Buckley chose Hendreddu instead of Gartheiniog, which was also part of his estate and was also covered by a take note. Presumably, Hughes had found high-quality slate at Hendreddu. The only quarries in Dyffryn Angell working before 1868 were Cwmllecoediog and Maesygamdda, neither on Buckley's land.

Buckley appointed Edward Davies from Minllyn as his manager at Hendreddu.[28] The Davies family moved into Brynmynach house in Aberangell, which was likely built for them in 1868. Davies initially worked the open pits dug into the Narrow Vein. A small mill was built in 1868,[29] though details of it have not survived. In early 1869 a huge slab, 9ft long and 4ft thick was extracted at Hendreddu and sent to Minllyn to be tested for durability. In January 1871, it was inspected by Sir Edmund, a Dr Whitehead and William Rees, Buckley's father-in-law; they found it to be of excellent quality. Sir Edmund hoped to make roofing slates at Hendreddu. Experts were brought in from Festiniog and Corris, but the dense narrow vein slate proved too hard to split finely. For the next seventy years, the quarry specialised in slabs.[29]

Gillart's or Tibbot's Incline

In 1870 a long incline was built from the pit level to the mill and an adit was driven east of the head of the incline. Bill Breese records the incline as 'Tibbott's Incline' and adit as 'Tibbott's Level'.[29] James Gillart was the quarry surveyor from 1868 until at least 1873,[27] and is likely to have overseen the construction of the incline and level. It may be that 'Tibbott' is actually 'Gillart', and the name has been misheard over the years.

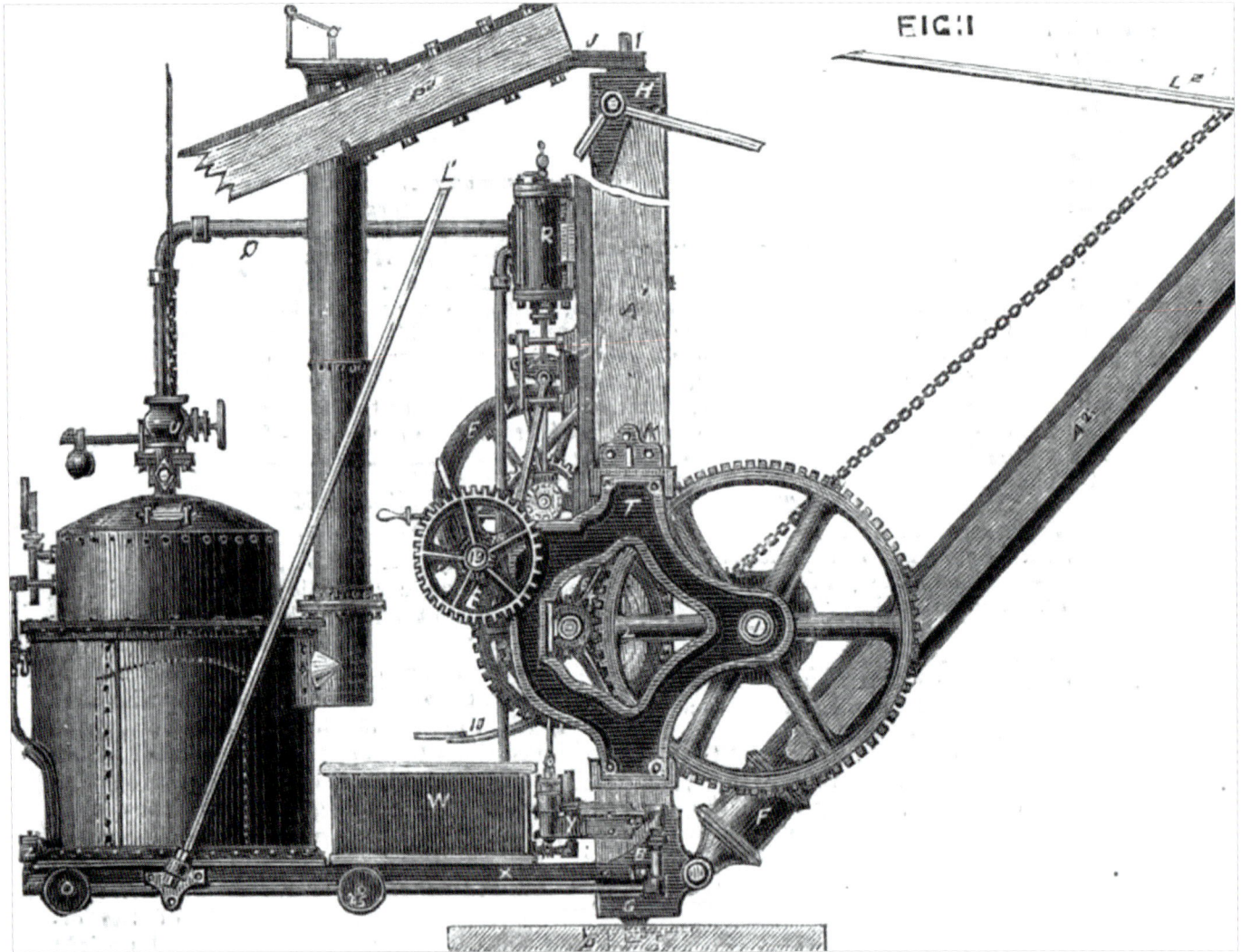

A Joseph Booth & Co. patent steam 'guy crane' of 1864. These were produced into the 1870s and one of this design was supplied to nearby Minllyn quarry and later used at Cae Abaty. The supplier of Hendreddu's 10-ton steam crane is not known.

James Gillart was born in 1830 in Llangadfan and by 1871 he was living at Buckley's Aberhirnant Hall near Bala where he was a land agent and civil engineer. He died in 1880 aged 51, at Dinas Mawddwy and was buried in Mallwyd churchyard.[30] James's older brother Richard was land agent for Earl Vane's estates which included many of the quarries then served by the Corris Railway.[31]

Another possibility is that Tibbott is John William Tibbott, a stonemason and Baptist preacher who lived in Darowen,[32] a hamlet about two miles south of Cemmaes Road. Although no direct connection between J. W. Tibbott and Hendreddu has been established, several men from Darowen are known to have worked at Hendreddu in the early days of quarrying. The name 'Gillart's Incline' is used throughout the rest of this book, with an acknowledgement that 'Tibbott's Incline' might be correct.

In, or shortly after, 1870 the exit incline from the mill level down to the Afon Angell was built.[33] In 1871, there was an accident on the incline, but fortunately no one was hurt:[34]

'Last Saturday two trucks tumbled down the inclines at the quarry, owing to the hooking chain breaking. Twenty minutes

later, two more came down, owing to being sent over the lip before being hooked. The trucks were broken in pieces, and a considerable portion of the incline much damaged.'[35]

Another slate quarry called Hendre-ddu began working in the 1860s. In 1861, Sir William Milman formed the Hendre-Ddu Slate and Slab Quarry Company Limited, issuing 50,000 shares priced at £5 each. This quarry was located in Cwm Pennant, northeast of Porthmadog. This was an entirely separate enterprise that shares the name. There are several share certificates in circulation for the 1861 company, but these are not for the Hendreddu quarry at Aberangell.

Expanding Underground 1872-1874

The pits at Hendreddu were successful, but the quality and accessibility of the slate was limited. On March 5th 1872, the quarry began driving an adit to reach better rock, under the supervision of contractor Thomas Williams. This tunnel was located to the south of, and 200ft below the open pits, running from the mill level northwards towards the vein.[27]

Driving the adit was a huge task. Working with hand tools

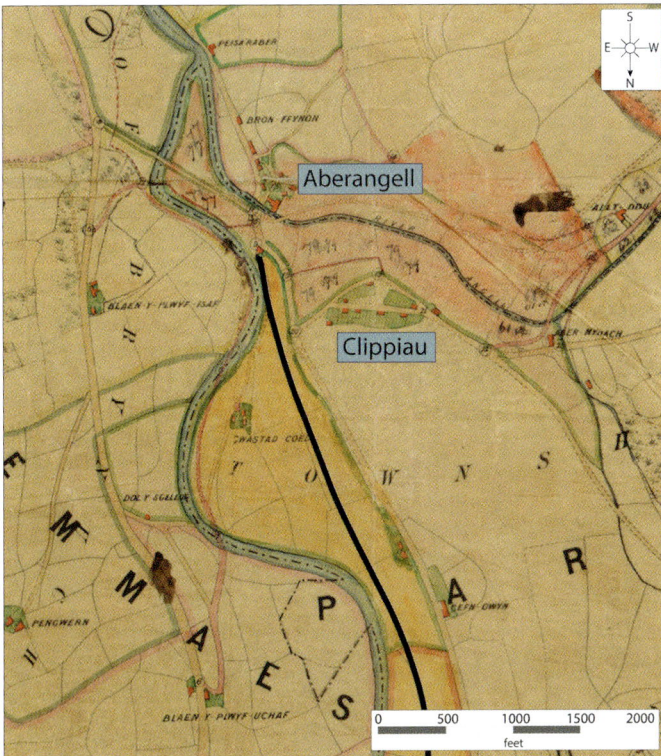

Part of a map of the Cwmllecoediog Estate in 1865, prepared for Walton vs. Mowddwy Railway. Walton's land is shaded in dark pink and Buckely's is in yellow. The Mawddwy Railway approaches from the north. Buckley claimed the right as Lord of the Manor to send his railway across Walton's land and build Aberangell station on it.

only – the quarry did not acquire a gunpowder licence until 1876 – the men drove through 157 yards of hard 'trap' rock. The ground here is heavy with iron and other minerals and the cleavage of the rock is unpredictable, which made for particularly hard tunnelling conditions.

Accidents

Quarry work in those days was dangerous and exacted a significant toll on the workers.

On 3rd February 1873, John Lewis of Ffestiniog was fatally injured. He had been loosening rock in one of the open pits[36] when a large mass of slate fell and trapped his leg, causing serious injuries. The leg was amputated by three local doctors, but his injuries were so severe that he died three days later.[37]

On January 11th 1873, quarryman Absalom Hughes from Abercegir died after a night of drinking in a public house in Cemmaes. He had been working at the quarry for six weeks and was 28 years old. The coroner returned a verdict of accidental death caused by a stroke.[38]

The Adit Breaks Through

On Saturday 12th April 1873,[27] over a year after work began, the adit finally reached the vein. Sir Edmund Buckley threw a party to celebrate. By now, between 50 and 60 men were employed at Hendreddu and the quarry manager Edward Davies pronounced himself pleased that

his 'happy thought' of driving the tunnel had paid off.[27]

A celebratory dinner was held on the Wharf at Aberangell station. Tables were made from slabs, part of an order for billiard tables for London. A large marquee was erected and the celebration chaired by William Williams, with Edward Davies by his side. Many fine toasts and speeches were given and the entire affair gave a sense of good cheer and tremendous optimism:

'Dr. Griffiths arose and said... he trusted the quarry would be largely developed so that a hundred men would be required for each one at present employed... The chairman responded in English, regretting he could not do so in Welsh... He stated that the treat was given by Sir Edmund and not at the suggestion of anyone. In these times of agitation between employers and employed, it was pleasing to see gentlemen of Sir E. Buckley's position endeavouring to promote a kindly feeling between himself and his workmen. Sir Edmund had done much for the benefit of the neighbourhood and his plans embraced much more that was to be done, amongst other things, he had ordered some cottages to be erected for the comfort and convenience of the quarrymen at Hendreddu.

Mr. Williams... stated that quarries ... without workmen were valueless, but with a staff of honest and intelligent workmen, their development was achieved. Masters sought to secure men who would do their duty when their backs were turned as when their eyes were upon them, and such men who brought their intelligence to bear upon their work, not only did well for their employers, but for themselves also. With such a class of men, under the intelligent

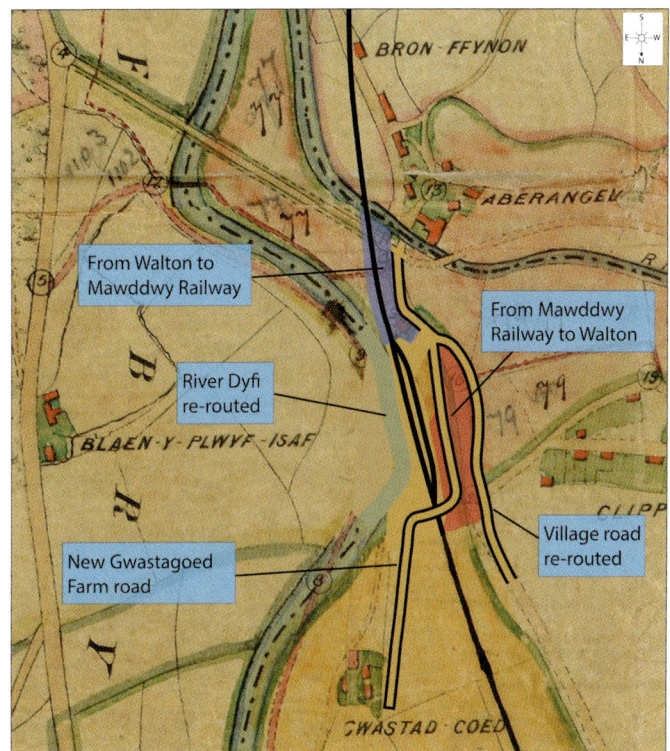

The changes to the course of the Dyfi river and the village road, and the exchange of land necessary to build Aberangell station. Walton gave up the land shaded blue and received the land in red. Walton's ownership of this new parcel would later determine the course of the Hendre Ddu Tramway.

SLATE WORKING MACHINERY

SLATE SAWING MACHINES.   SELF-ACTING SAW-FILING MACHINES.

PLANING MACHINES.

SLATE DRESSERS

TURN-TABLES.

SLATE CARS AND WAGGONS.

WATER WHEELS.

TURBINES.

SHAFTING, PULLEYS, ETC.

TURNER BROS., Cambrian Iron Works, NEWTOWN, NORTH WALES.

Above: An 1895 advertisement for Turner Brothers, listing their wide range of slate working machinery. They supplied the turntable and wagons for the Hendre Ddu Tramway, and probably also the sawing and dressing machines in the Hendreddu Mill. [Board of Trade Journal]

Below: Dyffryn Angell in the early 1860s, before the Mawddwy Railway was built. This shows the major estates, dominated by Buckley's Mawddwy Estate, though his actual ownership of various parts of the land was disputed, notably around Maesygamfa Farm. The road system is shown – the majority of these would be little more than rough farm tracks, and none were metalled. All the river crossings are fords, except Pont Walton, an iron bridge erected by James Walton in the 1860s.

direction of Mr. Davies, he had no fear for the ultimate success of the quarry.

Mr. E. Davies thanked Mr. Williams for the flattering manner he had spoken of him and of the quarry. He was sure every stone would be turned to promote the interests of the quarry, and he had every confidence in its future success. The Rev. J. J. Browne then proposed the health of the agents in the employ of Sir Edmund, coupled with Mr. [James] Gillart's name. He considered they had important duties to perform, and felt sure all the undertakings were successfully carried out. Mr. Gillart returned thanks, and trusted all agents did their duty. He could not see why they should couple his name to a toast, as he was not associated with the work to which the present treat was given. He had only made a few surveys etc.' [27]

Expanding the Quarry

With the adit successfully driven and a large supply of good rock available, Sir Edmund poured substantial capital into developing the quarry. He built a terrace of six cottages by the exit incline for married quarrymen and their families, and a barracks at the quarry for single men.

He also built a substantial mill; likely extending the earlier building. The new mill was generously equipped with machines for slab working: sixteen saw tables, eight planing machines, a water turbine and machinery for saw-sharpening and punching. It had its own smithy for making and repairing ironwork for the quarry, inclines and wagons. [39] The equipment was dragged from Aberangell station to the foot of the exit incline using horses and waggons hired from local farmers. It was then hauled up the incline and trammed to the new mill. [33]

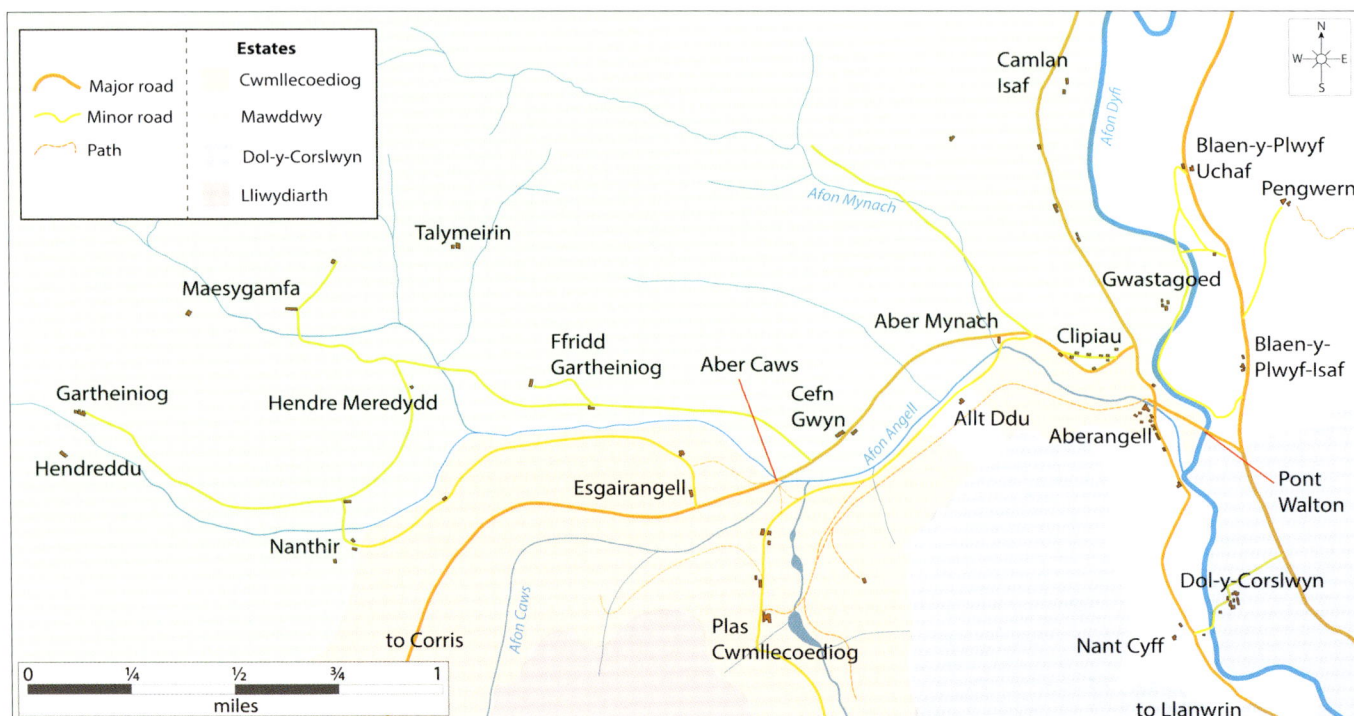

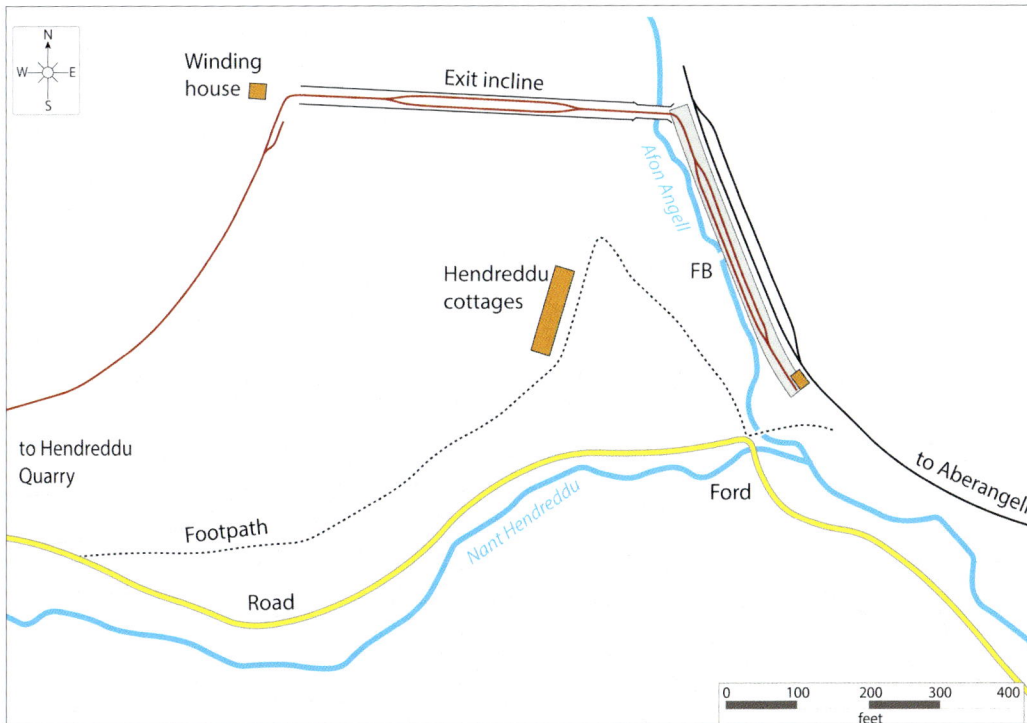

Left: Speculative map of the planned Hendreddu terminus in 1874. The standard gauge branch from Aberangell would have arrived at a simple loop next to the slate embankment at the foot of the exit incline. No contemporary records of the planned arrangement have survived.

Right: In red is the Hendreddu terminus as built in 1874. The exact layout is not known, but this is likely the arrangement. In green is the arrangement for an exit incline to the south. It would run alongside the road up to the quarry, shortening the upper tramway and eliminating the need for an embankment before the line heads south to Aberangell.

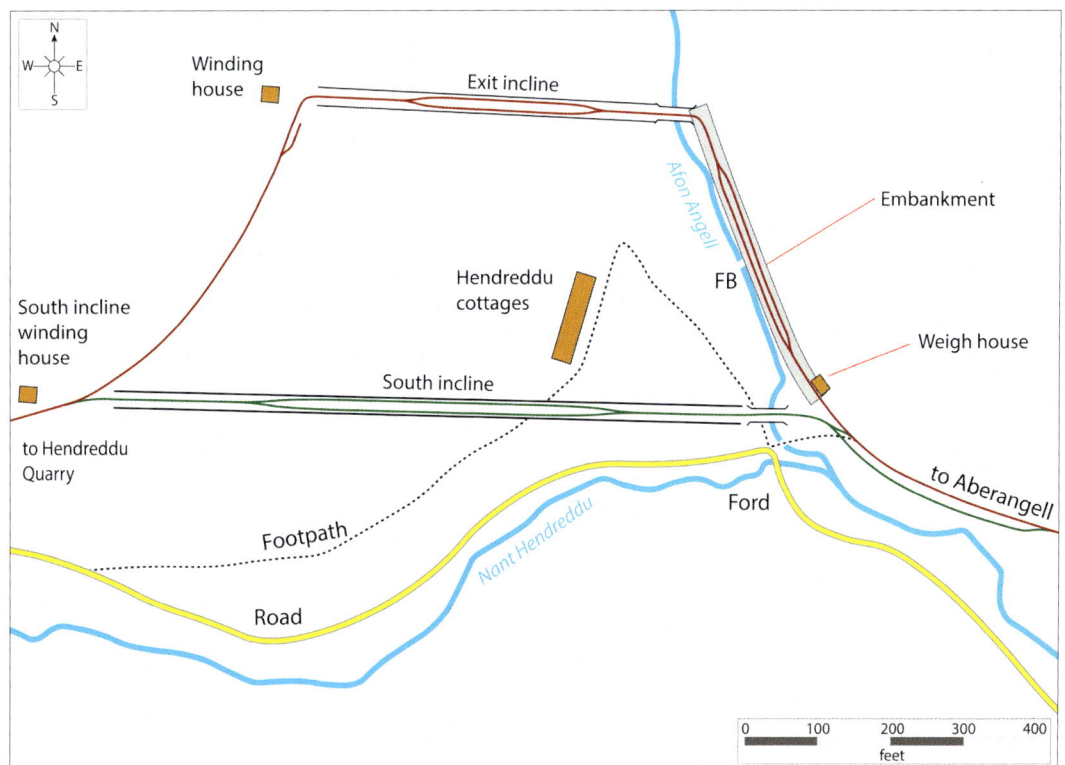

The mill machinery was powered by a 50hp turbine, driven from a new reservoir built above the open pits. Unusually for a quarry of this size, a hospital 'ward' was provided – one room of the Hendreddu cottages set aside for medical purposes.[40] A 10-ton steam crane was installed at the edge of the open pits to lift slabs and rubbish to the tramway running to the top of Gillart's Incline.

Between the Hendre Ddu Cottages and the quarry barracks, a substantial community lived at the quarry. To accompany this new 'village', a Calvinist Methodist chapel was approved in January 1876[41] and opened later that year on land donated by Buckley. Soar Chapel was designed by the Reverend David Williams and could seat up to 100. It not only provided religious services for Hendreddu but also a schoolhouse. The chapel continued in use until around 1899 when it was replaced by the new Capel Bethania in

Aberangell.[42] The derelict Soar Chapel still stands in 2015, just to the south of Hendreddu Farm.

In 1873, Hendreddu was reputed to be producing 150-200 tons of finished slabs per month, though this would represent a significantly higher annual tonnage than the quarry subsequently produced. Whatever the true output, transporting finished slabs by cart through the remote Dyffryn Angell was a significant challenge.

Dispute with James Walton 1865-1868

Edmund Buckley was an enthusiastic promoter of railways and he naturally wanted to use rail transportation for Hendreddu quarry. However, he created a rod for his own back when he became embroiled in a legal dispute with his neighbour James Walton of Cwmllecoediog. In 1865, Walton had sued the Mowddwy Railway over its proposed route through Aberangell. The railway and Aberangell station were to be built on Walton's land. Buckley claimed he had the right, as Lord of the Manor, to use Walton's land as he saw fit. Walton strongly disagreed.

Perhaps Buckley knew of Walton's aversion to courts. In 1875, Richard Williams[43] wrote:

'In 1836, [James Walton] also invented and patented an improved foundation for the backs of wire cards… This invention was contested, and became the subject of long and expensive litigation, the suits of Walton v. Potter & Horsfall, which extended from 1839 to 1843. Mr. Walton then made a vow that he would never afterwards enter a Court of Justice, a vow which he religiously observed even while he was High Sheriff of Montgomeryshire.'

Walton vs Mowddwy Railway was settled in July 1868. The directors of the Mowddwy Railway paid Walton £800* for his land at Aberangell to be paid in instalments. There was also an exchange of land as part of the settlement.[44] The Mawddwy Railway received land for the station and wharf, and Walton got a parcel of Buckley's land between the station and the road. The land Walton received was to cause considerable further trouble.

To make room for the Mawddwy Railway passing loop, the Dyfi river was diverted to the east, and its west bank was raised to form a long embankment. The road between Clipiau and Aberangell was moved west to make room for the station and the new road to Gwastagoed.

The Construction of the Hendre Ddu Tramway 1873-1874

The earliest report of construction of the tramway is from April 1873: '*A tramway is being made between the quarry and the railway station, which will be a great improvement to the shipping at Aberangell.*'[27] Before this, only rough paths and roads led into Dyffryn Angell.

The road to the quarry started at Aberangell, then climbed steeply through Clipiau, before dropping to cross the Afon Mynach by a ford north of Aberdwynant house (then called Aber Mynach). The road climbed again, passing through Cefngwyn Farm, then dropped to Aber Caws (later known as Pont yr Hirgwm). There was a junction here: one road crossed the Afon Angell by a ford, then climbed south of Esgairangell, before heading over the mountains to Aberllefenni. The other road headed west from Aber Caws along the north side of the valley, rising to Ffridd Gartheiniog Farm (commonly known as Ffridd), then dropping again to cross the Nant Maesygamdda. Beyond the ford, the road turned sharply to the south to pass Hendre Meredydd Farm, before swinging westward past Nanthir to the remote Gartheiniog Farm.[45] This road was extended to the foot of the Hendreddu exit incline around 1870, to serve the quarry.

The quarry carts were hauled by horses in both directions. This was a hugely arduous route, with steep uphill and downhill stretches in both directions and multiple fords.

Hendreddu quarry was producing slabs commercially for at least five years before the tramway was built, and needed a facility to load slate onto the Mawddwy Railway at Aberangell station. The Wharf was built around 1868, squeezed into the small triangle of land owned by Buckley between the Mawddwy Railway and the land given to Walton in 1865. This explains the small size of the Wharf; it was designed to handle carts coming by road and there was not room to build anything larger. The tiny Wharf would limit the tramway for the next seventy years.

A Question of Gauge

The exact date the tramway opened is unknown; so too is its precise gauge. Bill Breese quotes it as 1ft 10½in.[46] Rob Pearman, the present owner of Motor Rail 2059 which ran on the tramway in later years, measured the wheelsets of the locomotive at 1ft 11in.[47] There was enough variation in the lightly laid track that both figures could be considered 'correct', and it is clear that it was slightly below the commonly quoted 2ft.

It is surprising that 2ft 3in. was not used, copying the Corris Tramroad less than a mile to the west. Turner Brothers supplied the wagons and other equipment for both concerns so it would have been easy to adopt the same gauge. Sir Edmund was clearly aware that both the older Corris and more recent Talyllyn railways used 2ft 3in. – the Parliamentary Bill for the Mawddwy Railway was a copy of the Talyllyn's bill and originally specified 2ft 3in.[21]

The Hendre Ddu Tramway was originally intended to be a standard gauge branch of the Mawddwy Railway, and the trackbed between the foot of the Hendreddu exit incline and Aberdwynant was built wide enough to use Mawddwy Railway wagons.[36] The Hendre Ddu Tramway may be the only example in mainland Britain of a standard gauge railway being converted to narrow gauge before the 1970s, when several narrow gauge tourist railways were built on standard gauge trackbeds.

It is not surprising that Sir Edmund wanted a standard gauge branch, but it is unclear what route this line would have taken between Aberdwynant and Aberangell Station. The

* £70,000 in 2020

obvious answer was for the branch to cross the Aberangell meadows on the north bank of the Afon Angell. There is a relatively easy downhill gradient and only one road to cross, but the meadows were part of Walton's Cwmllecoediog estate. It seems that once again, Sir Edmund assumed he could use his rights as Lord of the Manor to run his railway wherever he saw fit.

James Walton refused to allow the branch to cross his land. This left Sir Edmund with a significant problem. The only possible route was to skirt the edge of Walton's property, running north of Aberdwynant House, climbing steeply up through Clipiau village, then dropping precipitously along the village road to the Wharf entrance. Both the narrow road and the steep gradients ruled out a standard gauge railway. At the last minute, Buckley told his men to lay the tramway to narrow gauge. Presumably, they used 1ft 11in. because it was the gauge of the quarry tramways.

The Terminus at Hendreddu

The plan to use standard gauge may explain the odd arrangement at the western terminus of the tramway. From the Hendreddu mill, an exit tramway ran east and then turned north and ran along a ledge high above the Afon Angell. The exit incline dropped down the side of the valley and crossed the river on a bridge. At the foot of the incline, the tramway turned sharply to the right and ran south on top of a long, well-built slate embankment, about 3ft high.

The only reason to site the incline so far to the north of the quarry was to make room for the slate embankment on the east side of the Angell. It would have been much easier to build the incline further south, thus eliminating the doubling back of the tramway as built.

There must have been a good reason to incur the extra expense of building the incline to the north. The obvious explanation is that the embankment was planned as a transhipment wharf, where slate was moved from narrow gauge to standard gauge wagons. The embankment has space for a standard gauge line to the east and below it, which would allow slabs to be loaded. This is exactly how the Aberangell Wharf worked. A share offering for the quarry in 1920 described the terminus arrangement as a '*Drumhead with tram lines from quarry to loading up wharf*'[48] – even fifty years later the embankment was described as a wharf.

There are no surviving records of the layout of the standard gauge terminus so this remains speculation, but it does explain the otherwise odd layout. The incline and embankment were built several years before the decision was made to build the main tramway to 1ft 11in. gauge. When the last-minute gauge change was made, the line on top of the embankment was simply extended to the south onto the standard gauge trackbed.

Connections with the Talyllyn Railway

Sir Edmund was familiar with, and inspired by, several local railways when he built the Hendre Ddu. The influence of the Corris Railway has already been mentioned; the other inspiration was the Talyllyn Railway.

Buckley knew William McConnel, the managing director of the Talyllyn Railway. The McConnel family owned several large cotton mills in the north of Manchester (just a few roads over from James Walton's mill) and at least one in Ardwick close to the Buckley family home. The McConnel and Kennedy mill in Ancoats was fitted out by engineer James Lillie, a friend of Edmund Buckley of Ardwick. The McConnel family also dealt with Edmund of Ardwick in his role as chairman of the Manchester Exchange.[1]

Sir Edmund was also a magistrate at the Merionethshire Quarter Session. He regularly dealt with matters related to Tywyn during the 1860s, giving him a ringside seat for the development of the Talyllyn Railway.

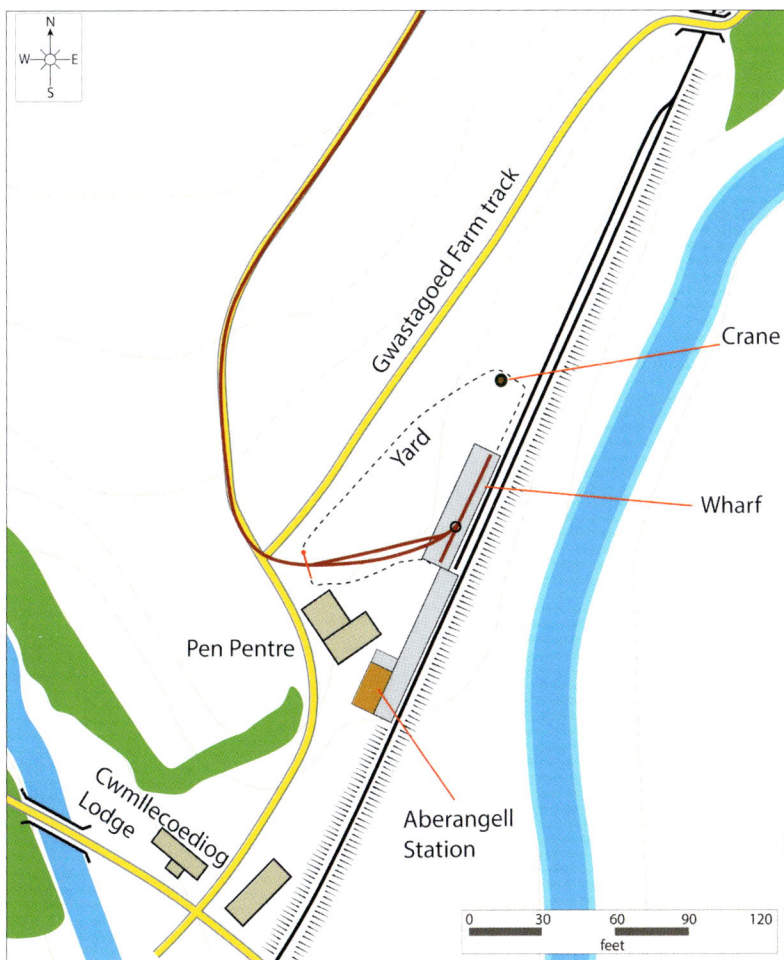

The original layout of the Hendre Ddu Tramway at Aberangell. The tramway descends steeply from Clipiau, ending in a sharp curve onto the Wharf. A passing loop ends at a turntable onto the line running parallel to the Mawddwy Railway siding. The siding was not extended into a loop until 1893.

Perhaps most tellingly, McConnel's Talyllyn Railway and Buckley's Mawddwy Railway shared Howell & Morgan of Machynlleth as their solicitor.[49] The bills for the Talyllyn and Mawddwy Railway that Howell & Morgan drafted were submitted to Parliament on the same day and went through the parliamentary process at the same rate, and both received royal assent on 5th July 1865. They are almost identically worded, indeed they are so similar that it was noted in the contemporary press.[50] It appears that McConnel and Buckley had shared railway plans. In July 1867, Sir Edmund purchased a set of signals second hand, but possibly unused, from the Talyllyn for use on the Mawddwy Railway, paying the exorbitant amount of £176 for them.[44]

Buckley appears to have copied at least two features of the Talyllyn. The Aberangell Wharf bears a strong resemblance to King's Station in Tywyn. Both featured a slate-built wharf beside a standard gauge line, with a triangular layout, and a line running along the wharfside accessed using turntables. Given the constrained space available at Aberangell, Buckley may well have been inspired by King's.

The second influence was Abergynolwyn. In the early 1860s, McConnel transformed a small hamlet consisting of an inn and a few scattered homes into a substantial village for the Bryn Eglwys quarrymen and their families.[51] A long incline was dropped from the mineral extension to the village to allow building supplies to be brought in, and more than 80 new homes were built. In many ways Abergynolwyn was a model village like Saltaire in Yorkshire and it quickly became a vibrant community for the quarry it served.

The success of Abergynolwyn, both as housing for the quarry workers and as a community, may have inspired Edmund Buckley to build the quarrymen's cottages at Hendreddu. Buckley intended to create a lasting community and planned more houses, though his bankruptcy put an end to plans for further expansion.

Aberangell Wharf

The wharf at Aberangell was constructed several years before the tramway was completed. The tramway came into the yard from the west. At the junction of the road to Gwastagoed Farm, it passed through a gate onto the Wharf proper, to the north of Pen Pentre. There was a short passing loop that ended at a turntable. This arrangement was certainly in place by 1887 and is very likely the original tramway layout.

The Route on Opening Day

The tramway opened in 1874.[52] Horses hauled the empties uphill, with loaded trains descending by gravity. The main line was laid in light bridge rail.[53] It passed through the Hendreddu, Gartheiniog, Nant Hir, Ffridd, Cefngwyn, Abermynach and Clipiau farms.[27] Buckley allowed his tenants to use the tramway to carry goods to and from their farms. They were charged 1d per ton. When tenancies changed, charges were gradually increased up to 6d per ton.[45]

There were gates across the tramway where it passed from one farm to another, to prevent livestock straying. The gates were frequently demolished by trains, and just as frequently rebuilt by the tramway's carpenters.[45] From west to east, the gates were at:[54] Cutiau Bach ('the little sheds') where the tramway passed into Gartheiniog Farm, near the south end of the slate embankment; Llidiart Cae Mawr ('the gate at the big field') where it left Gartheiniog, crossing to the west bank of the Angell and entering Nant Hir Farm; Pont y Borfa ('grass bridge') crossing back to the east bank and re-entering Gartheiniog Farm; Llidiart Dwbl ('double gates') east of the bridge across Nant Maesygamfa, where it entered Ffridd farm; and at Aberangell Wharf the entrance to the Wharf was gated.

The tramway had several notable civil engineering features. Two ledges were dug out of the mountainside to allow the track to pass through narrow sections of the valley, one to the west of Pont yr Hirgwm and the second west of Pont y Borfa. The Afon Mynach was crossed on a slate causeway with a stone bridge across the river.[45] A cutting was made at the summit of the climb through Clipiau, to ease the worst of the gradients – the road through the village still uses this cutting. Finally, two large embankments were needed to maintain the grade on the section from Aberdwynant to Cefngwyn.

The original route only had two sections of adverse uphill gradient between Hendreddu and Aberangell. One was a very shallow section below Ffridd farmhouse,[45] the other the steep climb over Clipiau.

The Death of Edward Davies 1874

Edward Davies, the first manager of Hendreddu, had been suffering from diabetes since 1871,[55] a then untreatable condition. His son, Edward Hurst Davies joined him as a quarryman at Hendreddu around this time.

In late summer 1874, aged just 52, Edward Davies fell seriously ill. His health rapidly deteriorated and, despite being attended by the best doctors in the district, he died of kidney failure,[56] a result of his diabetes, on 31st October 1874.[57] His funeral at Dinas Mawddwy was 'one of the largest funerals that has been witnessed for a long time at this place'.[28]

William Williams, the agent for the Buckley estate, took over as manager after Davies died.

Two years after her father's death, Edward Davies's daughter Elizabeth moved to London to take up a position as a lady's maid. She subsequently left service and became a prostitute in a well-known London brothel, noted for its upper-class clientele. In 1885, she disappeared after an extremely short marriage to one Francis Craig. The author Wynne Weston-Davies suggests that she took the name Mary Jane Kelly and resumed her life as a prostitute in Whitechapel. Mary Jane Kelly was the fifth and final victim of the notorious serial killer Jack the Ripper in 1888 and was known to have spoken Welsh.[58] She was killed 800ft from the London office of the Hendre-Ddu Slate & Slab Company at 1 New Street.

Buckley's Failing Finances 1875

Sir Edmund Buckley remained determined to prove his land rights over the entire manor of Mawddwy. His estate ran from Hendreddu Farm in the southwest to the shores of Llyn Vyrnwy in the northeast. However, he considered an even larger area of land to be his property by manorial right.

The case he lost to James Walton in 1865 did not dissuade him from claiming land as his own. In 1875, he sued the owner of Maes-y-gamdda Farm, claiming that the common land surrounding the farm was his. Maes-y-gamdda Farm was owned by Charles Edwards, the Lord of Dolserau Hall and former Liberal MP for Windsor.[59] Edwards claimed the 'sheepwalks' – areas of open mountainside upon which tenant farmers grazed his sheep – were commons and not the property of Buckley.

The case '*excited considerable interest in the Principality*' and came before Lord Chief Justice Coleridge (the great-nephew of Samuel Taylor Coleridge) at the Merionethshire Assizes. Buckley's legal team argued that the Manor of Dinas Mowddwy (sic) was an ancient grant, maintained because '*Courts Baron and Leet had been regularly held, court rolls kept, and the tenants of the manor summoned on juries and fined for non-attendance, waifs and strays had been taken and sold; that the manor, which was about 50,000 acres in extent, and about 30 miles in ambit, embraced many enclosed freehold farms*'.

Buckley's team admitted the enclosed lands were owned and the tenants had rights to use the sheepwalks, but they argued the unenclosed lands were part of the '*waste lands of the Manor*'. In particular, this meant that the Lord of the Manor had the exclusive hunting and mineral rights to these waste lands — this was Buckley's central claim.

Edwards's equally impressive legal team argued that Buckley could not prove his rights over the unenclosed lands and that a *prima facie* case existed that the sheepwalks were commonly owned by the tenant farmers. The case had the potential to set a precedent for ownership of vast swathes of Welsh upland. Lord Coleridge summed up, making it clear that he largely agreed with the defence. A few minutes after the jury retired to consider their verdict, Buckley withdrew his case, to avoid setting the feared precedent.[60]

Buckley was by this time in considerable financial distress. The vast sums he had poured into Hendreddu quarry and

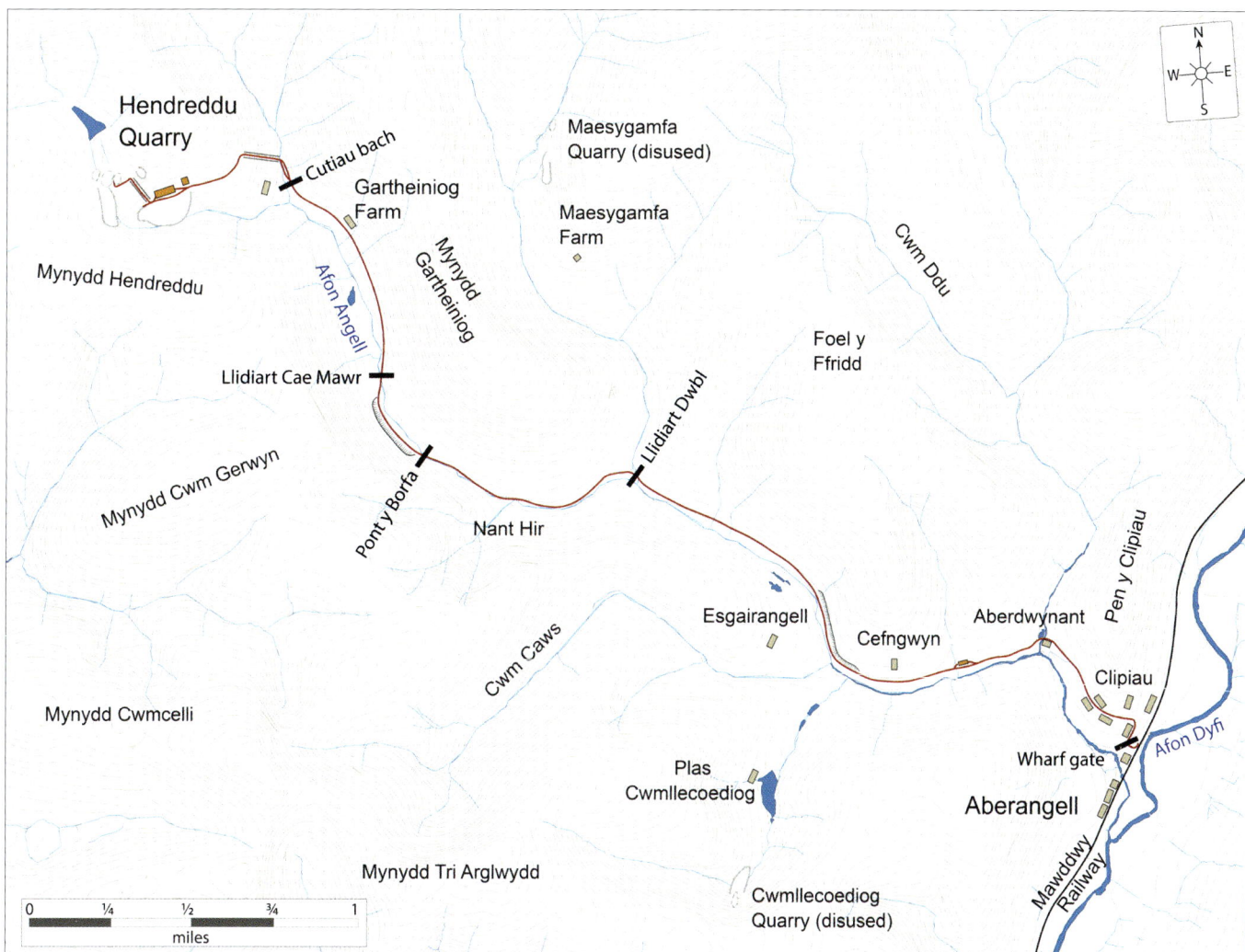

The Hendre Ddu Tramway, as built in 1874, passing through Buckley's Mawddwy Estate for its entire route from Hendreddu Quarry to Aberangell. The gates across the line are shown in black. Maesygamfa and Cwmllecoediog quarries were closed in 1874.

his estate had taken a toll. Perhaps he had pursued the Maes-y-gamdda claim as a last-ditch effort to increase the value of his holdings, in anticipation of selling them. He was certainly aware of the history of slate quarrying there and may have been trying to assert ownership over the quarry. Whatever his intentions, Buckley's finances were spinning out of control, and within a year he was to declare bankruptcy, crushed by staggering debts.

Meanwhile, work at Hendreddu quarry continued. The quarrymen had no idea that Sir Edmund was on the brink of financial calamity. In March 1876,[61] Edward Hurst Davies applied for a gunpowder licence for the quarry, which is probably the date of construction of the gunpowder store built on the west side of Nant Hendreddu, a safe distance from the quarry and mill.

References

1 F. S. Stancliffe, *John Shaw's 1738-1938*. Sherratt and Hughes, 1938.
2 The member's directory. *The History of Parliament*, 2016.
3 Honor where honor is due, *Brecon County Times*, p.5, Dec. 12th, 1868.
4 Rev Jeremiah Finch Smith, *The Admissions Register of the Manchester School*. The Cheetham Society, 1837.
5 John Shaw's Club: A relic of Old Manchester, *Manchester Courier*, May 27th, 1864.
6 Alexandra Mitchell, Middle-Class Masculinity in Clubs and Associations: Manchester and Liverpool, 1800-1914, Doctoral thesis, University of Manchester, 2011.
7 William Atkinson Warwick, *The House of Commons, as Elected to the Fourteenth Parliament of the United Kingdom*. Saunders and Otley, 1841.
8 The Manor of Mawddwy, *The Cambrian News*, Jul. 24th, 1869.
9 The Late Sir Edmund Buckley, *Cambrian News*, Mar. 25th, 1910.
10 Estates in Cheshire and Merionethshire, *North Wales Chronicle*, p.8, Oct. 25th, 1856.
11 Mr. Edmund Buckley, of Manchester, *The Illustrated London News*, p.146, Aug. 19th, 1860.
12 Dinas Mawddwy, *Brecon County Times*, p.8, Dec. 28th, 1867.
13 Manorial Rights in Wales, *Wrexham Guardian*, p.6, Aug. 8th, 1874.
14 Baptisms at Llandingat, Carmarthenshire, 1861.
15 Local Intelligence, *Pembrokeshire Herald*, p.2, May 27th, 1864.
16 Marwolaethau, *Y Goleuad*, p.6, Mar. 9th, 1894.
17 England & Wales Non-conformist births and baptisms.
18 Marriage certificate No. 191317.
19 Private correspondence with Wynne Weston-Davies, 2018.
20 Mowddwy Railway, *London Gazette*, p.5841, Nov. 25th, 1864.
21 Railway Intelligence, *Cambrian News*, p.2, Jul. 1st, 1865.
22 National Archives, Report of Mawddwy Railway meeting with the Board of Trade, Dec. 7th, 1909.
23 Dinas Mawddwy, *Baner ac Amserau*, p.9, Jul. 24th, 1867.
24 Mawddwy Railway, *Wrexham Advertiser*, p.4, Oct. 5th, 1867.
25 The New Baronets, *Northern Standard*, p.3, Dec. 19th, 1868.
26 Bill Breese, Notes on local quarrying and quarrymen, *Dolgellau Archive*, vol. ref ZM/6541/9, 1982.
27 Treat to Hendreddu Quarrymen, *North Wales Chronicle*, p.6, Apr. 6th, 1873.
28 Dinas Mawddwy: Obituary, *Cambrian News*, p.4, Nov. 20th, 1874.
29 Bill Breese, Bygone industrial activities in the Angell valley, *Cambrian News*, Jul. 9th 1976.
30 Deaths, *Eddowes's Journal*, p.10, Sep. 22th, 1880.
31 Machynlleth: Board of Guardians, *Aberystwyth Times*, p.4, Jun. 25th, 1870.
32 England, Wales & Scotland Census, piece 5604, folio 19, p.2, 1871.
33 Bill Breese, The old quarry railway, *Cambrian News*, Jun. 18th 1976.
34 Newyddion Cymraeg, *Y Goleuad*, p.5, Feb. 18th, 1871.
35 Mallwyd: accident, *North Wales Chronicle*, p.3, Feb. 11th, 1871.
36 Bill Breese, The old quarrying days in the Angell valley, *Cambrian News*, Jun. 25th, 1976.
37 Dinas Mawddwy: Serious accident, *Cambrian News*, p.6, Feb. 14th, 1873.
38 Abercegir Coroner's inquest, *Cambrian News*, p.5, Jan. 17th, 1873.
39 Sales by Auction, *Cambrian News*, p.1, Sep. 8th, 1876.
40 Private correspondence with David Gwyn, 2017.
41 Amser Cymdeithasafaoedd Chyfarfodydd Misol, *Y Goleuad*, p.5, Jan. 22nd, 1876.
42 Trefaldwyn Uchaf, *Y Goleuad*, p.14, Oct. 21st, 1908.
43 Richard Williams, *Montgomeryshire Worthies*, Newtown: Phillips & Son, 1894.
44 National Archives RAIL 473/, Minutes of the Board of Directors meetings, Mawddwy Railway 1868-1883.
45 Gwyndaf Breese, The Angell Valley Tramway, unpublished manuscript.
46 Bill Breese, Hen Efail y Chwarel: part II, *Cambrian News*, Jan. 21st, 1977.
47 Private correspondence with Rob Pearman, 2016.
48 National Welsh Slate Quarries prospectus, *The Scotsman*, p.4, Mar. 17th, 1920.
49 Talyllyn Railway, *Cambrian News*, p.2, Nov. 19th, 1864.
50 Talyllyn Railway, *Cambrian News*, p.4, May 13th, 1865.
51 Abergynolwyn: Rejoicing to welcome Mr. and Mrs. McConnel, *Cambrian News*, p.1, Dec. 7th, 1867.
52 Bill Breese, Bygone activities of the Angell valley, *Cambrian News*, Jan. 7th, 1977.
53 Lewis Cozens, R. W. Kidner, Brian Poole, *The Mawddwy, Van and Kerry Branches*, Oakwood Press, 2004.
54 Bill Breese, Hand-drawn tramway map.
55 Death certificate No. 3053480-1.
56 Marwolaeth a chladdedigaeth Mr. E. Davies, Glanafon, Aberangell, *Y Goleuad*, p.7, Nov. 14th, 1874.
57 Dinas Mawddwy, *Aberystwith Observer*, p.3, Nov. 28th, 1874.
58 Wynne Weston-Davies, *The Real Mary Kelly: Jack the Ripper's Fifth Victim and the Identity of the Man that Killed Her*. Bonnier Publishing Ltd, 2015.
59 F. W. S. Craig, Ed., *British Parliamentary Election Results 1832–1885*, London: Macmillan Press, 1977.
60 Manorial rights in Merionethshire, *North Wales Chronicle*, p.3, Aug. 7th, 1875.
61 Explosives Act, 1875, *North Wales Chronicle*, p.7, Mar. 25th, 1876.

4: The Bradwells Take Over 1876-1887

On 27th January 1876, Edmund of Ardwick died. He left the majority of his estate to his eldest son Edmund. Despite this substantial inheritance, Edmund's financial affairs were spiralling out of control, and on May 19th he filed for bankruptcy in Manchester, owing more than £500,000.[*1] The Mawddwy Railway alone had cost him £70,000. His extraordinary expenditure at Dinas Mawddwy, and a series of ill–advised overseas stock investments, had not just run through the considerable Buckley fortune but had left him with overwhelming debts.

The majority of the Dinas Mawddwy estate was put up for auction in October of that year, at the appropriately named 'Great Sale'. Advertisements for the auction appeared in newspapers across the North West of England, as well as Wales, appealing to the wealthy industrialists of that region. Hendreddu quarry and its tramway were the second lot: 'The Hendre-Ddu Slate and Slab Quarries [sic] and the Buildings, Plant, and Machinery, belonging to the same, consisting of one 50-horse turbine, with 500 yards of 8in, 9in, and 10in pipes, two reservoirs, one 10-ton steam crane, tramways, tram wagons, inclines, machine house, sixteen sawing machines, eight planing machines, saw-tiling and punching machines, workshop, smithy, and six newly-built cottages and barracks. The quarry has been working five years, and now produces from 150 to 200 tons of finished slabs monthly. The stock in trade must be taken by the purchaser at a valuation to be produced at the time of Sale. And also all those Farms and Lands, with the Farmhouses and Buildings upon the same, called respectively Hendre-Ddu, Nanthir, and Cwmgerwyn, containing 293 acres, and Sheepwalks over 543 acres, or thereabouts, situate in the parishes of Mallwyd and Tal-y-Llyn, in the respective occupations of Richard Pugh and David Jones, at yearly rents amounting to £126/4.'[2]

The lot included three nearby farms, though not Gartheiniog Farm which was sold separately. A third lot contained 'Cefngwyn, Abermynech [sic], and Ffrydd Gartheiniog' farms. The Gartheiniog and Cefngwyn lots were 'sold subject to a right of the owners for the time being of the Hendre-Ddu Slate and Slab Quarries for ever to maintain upon the said land on its present site, and to use a tramway for the purpose of conveying slates and slabs from their quarry to Aberangell, and at all times of entering upon the said land for the purpose of repairing the said tramway'.

Vast swathes of the upper Dyfi valley were auctioned. The main lot was the 'Manor or Lordship of Mawddwy, in the county of Merioneth, with all the associated Rights, Liberties, and Privileges', with land in the 'absolute ownership, including

the mines and quarries thereon' of the Lord. Included in this lot was Plas-yn-Dinas the 'Gothic Mansion' complete with its 'ornamental Pleasure Grounds, Plantations, Conservatories, Greenhouses, Vineries, Stables, Gasworks, Kitchen Gardens, and Home Farm Buildings'. The Plas contained a central hall, five reception rooms, twenty-four bedrooms, a strong room, a butler's pantry, a 'strong plate room', gun room, servants' rooms, a kitchen, and offices and outbuildings. The grounds covered 100 acres. The lot also contained 'all those Farms, Lands, Tenements, and Hereditaments situate in the parishes of Mallwyd and Llan-y- Mawddwy, and the mountain sheepwalks

THE HOME FARM,
Dinas Mawddwy.
Within half a mile of the Dinas Railway Station.

CATALOGUE
OF AN IMPORTANT SALE OF

FARMING STOCK
Lately the Property of Sir EDMUND BUCKLEY, Bart., M.P.
COMPRISING
FIRST-CLASS DAIRY COWS AND HEIFERS,
GRAND HEREFORD STEERS,
PRIME FAT BULLOCKS & HEIFERS, WELSH & HEREFORD BULLS
POWERFUL DRAUGHT HORSES,
WELL-BRED HACK MARES IN FOAL, HANDSOME HACK
COLTS AND FILLIES, BY "WYNNSTAY,"
A MOST VALUABLE THOROUGHBRED ENTIRE COLT,
EWES WITH CROSS-BRED LAMBS,
SHROPSHIRE AND RADNORSHIRE TUPS, AND AN
ASSEMBLAGE OF THE MOST MODERN FARMING IMPLEMENTS,
6-HORSE POWER PORTABLE STEAM ENGINE,
SETS OF HORSE GEARING, DAIRY UTENSILS, ETC., ETC.
30 TONS OF PRIME MEADOW HAY
TO GO OFF THE PREMISES.

Which will be Sold by Auction

BY MR DANIEL,
AT TANYBWLCH, (THE HOME FARM)
DINAS MAWDDWY,
On THURSDAY, APRIL the 26th, 1877,
Luncheon at the MANSION at 11 30, and the Sale to
commence at 1 o'clock p.m., prompt.
Detailed CATALOGUES may be had at the principal Hotels in the Counties of Montgomery, Cardigan, and Merioneth, and of Mr JAMES BURMAN, Bailiff, Plas-yn-Dinas, Dinas Mawddwy; Mr WILLIAMS, Estate Agent, Salop Road, Oswestry; and of the AUCTIONEER, at Towyn and Machynlleth.
N.B. The Mawddwy Railway Company will run a Special Train from Cemmes-Road Station, on the morning of the Sale, at 11 55, a.m., arriving at Dinas at 12 10, p.m., after the arrival of the Cambrian Train starting from Oswestry at 6 20, a.m., Welshpool, 8 20, p.m., and intermediate Stations—arriving at Cemmes-Road at 11 50, a.m.

ADAM EVANS, PRINTER, MACHYNLLETH.

Unsold lots from the Great Sale were auctioned off piecemeal over the next few years. This is the catalogue for the sale of Home Farm, Dinas Mawddwy in April 1877. A special Mawddwy Railway train was laid on for the occasion. [Dan Quine]

★ £52 million in 2020

thereto belonging, known as Model Farm, Maes-Benddu, Pen-y-Bont, Bwlch, Fron-Goch, and Ffryd-Gilcwm etc., containing together 1,400 acres or thereabouts'.

The remaining fifty-three lots varied from individual cottages – including six in Aberangell – through to substantial farms with hundreds of acres. Not all of the lots sold; those that did raised a total of £93,500. The Hendreddu quarry lot was among those that failed to reach their reserve. By October 1876, serious negotiations were underway for the purchase of the quarry.[3] James Halliday was appointed as the trustee of Buckley's estate while matters were resolved, and he retained William Williams as Hendreddu manager in 1876 and 1877.[4]

In December 1876, Edmund Buckley was sued by several of his uncles and aunts who disputed Edmund of Ardwick's will. They alleged that Edmund had defrauded the family trust to finance his lifestyle at Mawddwy. Edmund admitted he had taken money from the trust to offset some of his losses. A decree was placed against him to recover the missing £180,000 and he was removed from the board of the trust.[5]

Edmund retained some properties at Dinas Mawddwy, but most of the estate was sold off. He withdrew to Manchester, and in 1877 resigned as MP under considerable pressure from his party.[6] For the next few years, the humiliated Edmund stayed away from Wales. In June 1879, his creditors sold off most of his remaining properties.[7] He returned to Wales and resumed his involvement in local affairs, though he never had the same degree of influence. He lived at Plas yn Dinas, which he was allowed to retain.

Buckley had given the Hendreddu quarry and its tramway a spectacular start, though at great financial cost to himself. Buckley was a great enthusiast of steam; if he had continued as owner of the Hendre Ddu Tramway, perhaps he would have turned to Manning, Wardle for one of their early narrow gauge locomotives. But it was not to be, and the Hendre Ddu remained a primitive, horse and gravity-worked tramway for the next forty-five years.

A Terrible Accident 1877

On 10th February 1877, the first recorded accident on the tramway occurred. The manager of the quarry, D.P. Jones, set off with eight workers on two ceir gwyllt – the distinctive four-wheeled gravity carriages used on the line. The quarry stopped work at noon on Saturdays,[8] and the men were trying to catch the 12:30 Mawddwy Railway train from Aberangell. Needing to cover the four miles in half an hour, they let their train

run at significant speed. After about a half a mile they hit the sharp curve coming into Rock Cutting. The cars derailed and the riders were ejected at speed into the cutting wall.[9]

Jones dislocated his shoulder and broke an arm. John Jones, the quarry blacksmith, suffered significant head wounds and a nearly severed ear, losing a great deal of blood. John Ellis Jones, a miner from Aberangell, suffered deep scalp wounds. David Thomas, a *rwbelwyr*, suffered scalp wounds and a badly cut hand. David Owen, a quarry labourer, had less severe scalp wounds. The other four riders, though shaken and bruised, were not seriously hurt and were able to help their stricken colleagues.[10] Despite the best efforts of several local doctors, John Jones did not recover from his injuries and died six days later. At the inquest into his death, the coroner recommended that the tramway stop using the ceir gwyllt. However, despite the obvious risks, these gravity cars continued in use for the next sixty years,[11] and were a distinctive feature of the tramway.

The Bradwell Brothers 1879-1881

Two silk mill owners from Cheshire were enthusiastic bidders at the Great Sale of Dinas Mawddwy. The first was William Bullock of Macclesfield, born in 1816.[12] In 1864 his Merionethshire Slate and Slab Company had leased Minllyn Quarry from Sir Edmund Buckley. Though that company failed, he started another, the Carlyle Slate and Slab Company, which took over the lease at Minllyn.[13] At the Great Sale, Bullock purchased Dugoed Isaf Farm to the east of Mallwyd, and Dolbrodmaeth House opposite Minllyn. The Carlyle company purchased the land on which Minllyn sat.

The second silk mill owner was Dennis Bradwell, the Mayor of Congleton.[14] The Bullock and Bradwell families came from the small village of Prestbury, northwest of Macclesfield. In the 1850s, William Bullock and Dennis Bradwell co-owned the London Silk Mill in Leek, Cheshire.[15] No doubt William told his friend Dennis about the opportunity arising from Buckley's failure. Bradwell made an offer for the entire Buckley estate that was within £1,000 of the reserve price. In the end, he bought two substantial farms on the second day of the auction: Pennant in Llanymawddwy for £1,835 and Blaencowarch for £2,100, together more than 1,000 acres of land.[2]

Dennis Bradwell was joined on his new estate by Jacob, his younger brother. Jacob was born in 1837[16] and spent time in Shanghai representing the family silk mills[17] before returning to Congleton to marry Sarah Bloor on 29th April 1863.[18]

Dennis Bradwell, mayor of Congleton, and owner of the Hendreddu Slate and Slab Company. The photograph was taken around the time he purchased land at Aberangell including the quarry.
[Congleton Museum Trust]

Dane Bridge Mill in Congleton, shortly before it was demolished. The Bradwell brothers owned this successful silk milk for many years. They used the money from selling it to purchase Hendreddu quarry and the tramway. [Courtesy William Jones]

Bloor was the daughter of local merchant William Bloor;[19] their son Dennis William Bradwell was born in 1866.[20]

After the auction, Dennis and Jacob formed a new company, the Hendre Ddu Slate Quarry Co. Ltd and came to a private agreement to purchase the quarry and tramway.[21] The Bradwells had sold their successful Dane Bridge Mill in Congleton in 1875[22] so they had plenty of capital. They took ownership of Hendreddu in April 1879, causing much local excitement: 'Trade report. Everything here is very dead - there is no work anywhere. But this week, we have better prospects than we have had for a long time, because Messrs Bradwell, from Cheshire, decided to re-open the quarry again a short time ago. We hope it comes into operation soon. The quarrymen's gain is also a big gain for the farmers, as they always have a need to feed their stomachs; this will be a big deal, as farm prices have been down.'[23]

D.P. Jones, having recovered from the 1877 accident, was the first quarry manager for the Bradwells, with Owen Parry as mine agent. By late April, Jones was advertising for 'an experienced slate mantle-piece maker and general stone cutter' ready to start work at Hendreddu.[24] In late 1879, Jones was replaced as manager by Edward Donald Nicholson. Nicholson was popular with the workers, but in October 1880 he left and moved to London. The workmen presented him with a purse inscribed: 'You have proved yourself a faithful, honest, and straightforward gentleman. The willingness shown by all who contributed to the testimonial proves how you were esteemed. We should be pleased if the intrinsic value were greater, but believe the contents are free-will gifts of warm and sincere hearts.'[25]

Not all quarry managers were held in such esteem, and Nicholson appears to have been a genuine loss to the district. While he was beloved by the men, he had fallen out with the Bradwells. In early 1883, Nicholson sued them for unpaid wages amounting to £10 1s 9d. He was by then living in Oswestry, working at the Porthywaen Limestone Quarry which he later managed.[26] Jacob Bradwell was due to appear but did not make it to court, his representative claiming he was too ill and asking for the trial to be delayed. The judge was having none of it, and after hearing from several witnesses, he awarded Nicholson the full amount and costs.[27] This was not the last time Jacob Bradwell would be called before a court, nor the last time he would plead

illness in an attempt to avoid appearing.

After Nicholson left, D.P. Jones temporarily returned as manager, though the Bradwells were looking for someone else. They found their man in Edward Hurst Davies, son of the first Hendreddu manager. E.H. Davies had married Margaret Evans on 21st March 1879, at Shiloh Chapel, Aberystwyth.[28] In November 1880, he was appointed as full-time manager at Hendreddu. Davies was a local who had successfully risen to a position of leadership and on his appointment, he 'wished all the workers well, if they honestly fulfilled their tasks for the masters'.[29] Davies was living with his wife and newborn daughter May,[30] at the Black Lion Inn near Strata Florida, which Margaret owned. Presumably, he travelled by train to Aberangell for the week, returning to the Black Lion at weekends.

Sometime between 1879 and 1881, the Bradwells added Cefngwyn Hall to their holdings, and this became their primary residence in the area. The hall provided the brothers with a fine view over their tramway. A short branch was laid from the hall down to Pont yr Hirgwm, allowing farm produce to be shipped out and coal, fodder and other goods to be brought up to the Hall.[31] They also installed a crude telephone system connecting the Hall to the Hendreddu mill which allowed them to listen to the machinery operate and make sure that D.P. Jones was starting promptly each morning. They hired Richard Pugh of Alltddu as their private secretary and Richard Pryce of Winllan as their general duties handyman.[32]

At some point in the early 1880s, E.H. Davies left Hendreddu and became the agent at Gartheiniog. The exact date is uncertain. In the announcement of his second daughter's birth in January 1883, he gives his occupation as 'Hendreddu Quarry Manager'.[33] However, in July 1882 he was fined for keeping gunpowder without a licence as 'Agent at Hendrefredydd'[34] – another name for Gartheiniog. It seems unlikely that the Bradwells would allow their manager to take a role at another local quarry. Perhaps Davies was moonlighting at Gartheiniog to help the new owners? Certainly, he was working full-time at Gartheiniog by the mid-1880s. Davies was replaced as quarry manager by Edward Henry Smith. Originally from London, Smith had moved to Dinas Mawddwy before 1871,[35] following his grandfather who was a Minllyn quarryman. By 1881, he had married a local girl and was station master at Dinas Mawddwy,[36] before becoming Hendreddu manager around 1883.

The early 1880s saw Hendreddu expanding production and employees. The Bradwells added a 'Jenny Lind' polishing machine around this time to expand the range of products they could manufacture at the mill. The Level 2 adit was likely driven around 1881, but the exact date is not recorded.

The 1881 census gives a good sense of the quarry community at Hendre Ddu. Hendre Ddu cottage No. 1 was empty, possibly used as the hospital ward. No. 2 was occupied by slate miner John Jones and his wife Margred. Quarryman Hugh Lewis lived at No. 3 with his wife Cathrin and their son William. Evan James was employed to drive the steam crane at the quarry and lived at No. 4 with his wife Cathrin and five children: Evan, Elizabeth, Ellin, Mary Jane and Richard. At No. 5 was Richard Evans the quarry blacksmith with his wife Margred and son Richard. In No. 6 was quarryman Evan Lewis – originally from Rhostryfan – with his wife Elisabeth, children Elisabeth Jane, Lewis and Joan, and lodger Richard Jones. Richard Jones, was the underground foreman and a well-respected quarryman, though he long held the belief that the main adit should have been dug in a more westerly direction, towards Ratgoed. His three sons, William Evan, Benjamin and John would also become Hendreddu quarrymen. William Evan and Benjamin became known as particularly skilled cutting shed machinists. Richard Jones died on 3rd May 1910.[32]

The quarry barracks above the mill was run by Catherine Pugh, who lived there between 1870 and 1890, with her daughters Jane (born in 1883) and Ellen, and son Hugh. She had a formidable reputation for keeping the men in line and a female barrack boss was unusual in a Welsh slate quarry. Her duties included cleaning the barracks and preparing meals for the twenty-two residents, who worked in rotating eight-hour shifts: 6am to 2pm, 2pm to 10pm and 10pm to 6am. Catherine died on January 10th 1895.[38]

The census also lists the quarry offices, blacksmith's shop and engine house (mill) at the quarry, though none were permanently occupied. Other quarry workers took lodgings in the local farms. Hendreddu was a remote and isolated place at the head of Dyffryn Angell, but it formed a thriving and almost self-contained community.

Industrial Strife 1882-1885

The Bradwells were hard-bitten businessmen and determined to make a success of their new enterprise. They added another adit on Level 3, probably in the early-

An advert for a Jenny Lind stone polishing machine from around 1900. The cast iron polishing head rotates at 300rpm and is pressed lightly onto the surface of the slab, while a stream of water carrying sand or steel grit as a cutting medium is added. The polishing head may be fitted with a carborundum block to give a finer result. Final polishing is done using a felt pad attached to the head, with a tin oxide putty used as the polishing medium.[37] A Jenny Lind like this was installed at Hendreddu in the early 1880s.

Catherine Pugh, the caretaker of the Hendreddu barracks.

to-mid-1880s as they pursued their plan to modernise working practices, to obtain the greatest profits possible. Modernisation led to significant friction with the workforce.

In late 1882, a series of articles appeared in the Welsh language newspaper *Y Dydd*, written by an anonymous Hendreddu quarryman under the pseudonym *Gweithiwr* (Worker). They give a clear sense of the clashes between the English owners and the Welsh workers and offer a fascinating insight into working conditions at Hendreddu at the time.

'Hendreddu... is owned by Messrs Bradwell of Congleton and London, who were said to be successful silk merchants. Whatever the truth of that, they now try to run the quarry like a silk factory, introducing the devil's practice of hourly working. This does not suit the men of Arfon who work in the open quarry for many rainy and windswept days to supply rock to their colleagues in the mill.'[39]

Arfon was the ancient Welsh cantref that included the Gwynedd slate districts around Llanberis and Caernarfon. This suggests a significant number of men had been hired from the north to work in the open pits at Hendreddu. Another of the articles names the 'men of Arfon and Meirion'[40] suggesting the workers were a mix of Merioneth and Caernarvon men, with the local men working underground. The Arfon men likely came from one of the Nantlle quarries, which made extensive use of open pits, unlike the underground workings at nearby Corris or Blaenau Ffestiniog.

Hendreddu had been worked using the traditional bargain system.[41] Each bargain was a section of the quarry let to two or three 'rockmen' – skilled workers who extracted the slate. The rockmen had partners in the mill, who produced slabs from the rock coming from their bargain. These teams set their work hours depending on the weather, the state of the rock and the rate of work of the whole team. They were paid by the amount of finished slab they produced.

SLATE CISTERNS.

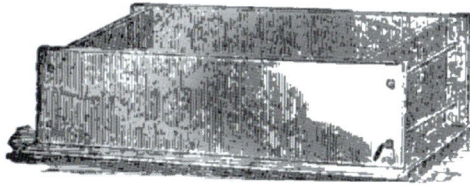

To contain from 10 to 50 gals. 5d. per gal.; 50 to 100 gals. 4d. per gal.; 100 and upwards, 3½d. per gal. Strong Ground Cisterns and Cesspools, of any size, 3½d. per gal. All sizes of Sawn Slabs and Common Flagging supplied to dimensions at special prices. Slabs sawn and planed for enamelling purposes. Billiard-tables, Urinals, Partitions, and for all other purposes to which slate slabs can be adapted.—For particulars of prices and terms apply to **The Hendre-ddu Slate and Slab Co.**, Salop Road, Oswestry, or to T. & J. BRADWELL, 1, New Street, Bishopsgate Street, E. Quarries at Hendre-ddu, Aberangell, near Cemmes, Montgomeryshire.

An 1881 advertisement for The Hendre-ddu Slate and Slab Company.

The Bradwells wanted to change to fixed hours, with tickets used for checking the men into and out of work. The mill workers and quarrymen were to be separated and everyone was to be paid an hourly wage: labourers 4d per hour, rockmen 4½d per hour, and the mill and tramway workers 5d to 6d per hour.[42] The Bradwells first tried to introduce this system in 1879, shortly after they took over. They talked to the workforce and tried to persuade them to try the new system, but were rebuffed.[40] It may be that this dispute led to Nicholson's departure as manager.

In 1882, the Bradwells tried to make the change again, this time imposing the new work practices rather than attempting to negotiate. This did not go down at all well with the Hendreddu workers. They saw the new system reducing them to interchangeable parts, ruled by the clock, rather than skilled workers who judged when and how best to pursue their craft. Matters came to a head on 20th October 1882 when Jacob Bradwell confronted the fifty workers and demanded they work under his new system. The quarrymen refused and told Bradwell they would leave with one week's notice and he could hire a new workforce under his new system.[39]

It appears that the Bradwells got their way and introduced the hourly wage, though whether they had to hire a new workforce is not known. The Bradwells were not well-liked and simmering tensions continued at Hendreddu. As late as 1889, in a heated debate at the Cardiganshire Police Committee, committee member Peter Jones said "*Take Caernarvonshire and Montgomery, for instance … If there is any place where you would anticipate a riot it would be amongst the sturdy quarrymen of Aberangell*".[43] Clearly, unrest remained in the air.

Gweithiwr was also concerned at the possibility of electrical lighting being installed at the mill, which would extend the working day, particularly in winter,[42] though in the end electricity did not come to the quarry until the 1920s.

During this period, Jacob Bradwell was increasingly in control, with his brother Dennis occupying himself elsewhere. In 1884, Jacob took over as the registered owner of Hendreddu, with Dennis withdrawing from running the quarry. On 31st December 1885, the brothers dissolved their business partnership, formed when they took over from their father in 1857.[44] Dennis remained the

sole owner of the Congleton silk business and Jacob took control of the London business that included Hendreddu.[45] Despite giving up involvement in Hendreddu, Dennis did retain an interest in local slate quarries; about the time he dissolved the partnership with Jacob, he lent a substantial amount of money to his old friend William Bullock, in return obtaining a mortgage on the Carlyle Slate and Slab Company, which owned Minllyn quarry.[46]

Jacob Bradwell was an eccentric and rather unpleasant man. In his later years, he kept a private carriage called the 'Old Lady' at Sied Ddu below Cefngwyn, and he would travel up in her to inspect work at Hendreddu. The train was horse-hauled under the supervision of Richard Pryce, one of his servants at Cefngwyn Hall.[31]

Such was the distrust between owner and workers, that Bradwell refused to travel up the exit incline, fearing to put his life in the hands of a quarryman. Instead, he went up the quarry road to the south of Hendreddu cottages. '*He would don a special leather body harness. Then, attached to the traces, he would be borne up, boots scraping for balance, roughly but steadily*'[47] hauled by Richard Pryce's horse. This operation was remembered by Pryce's daughter, Mary Jane Pryce, who served as newsagent at Aberangell for 43 years.[48] It is perhaps for the best that no photograph of this startling operation survives …

Trouble on the Tramway 1886-1887

On 8th January 1887, four local men were caught damaging the car gwyllt owned by quarryman Griffith Roberts. Police Constable Charles Ashton and Jacob Bradwell caught them vandalising the vehicle at night. The ceir gwyllt were left overnight at Aberdwynant, padlocked to the rails. The tramway had suffered from a spate of damage to the cars and at the trial, Bradwell said he wanted to make an example of the perpetrators. The four accused were found guilty, fined and admonished from the bench.[49] One of them was Thomas Lomas aged 18, the younger brother of Abraham Lomas who

SLATE SLABS! SLATE SLABS!

HENDREDDU SLATE AND SLAB COMPANY,
1, NEW STREET, BISHOPSGATE ST., WITHOUT, LONDON,
And Salop Road, Oswestry;
Quarries—Hendreddu, Aberangell, Cemmes, Mont.,

Supply all kinds of SLATE SLABS, any size or thickness, especially suitable for Enamellers, Chimney Piece Makers, and all kinds of SLATE used by Stone and Marble Masons.
BILLIARDS of an exceptional quality supplied to all Table Makers.
Special Terms on all orders over 50 tons weight to the Trade, and for export to hot and other climates.

PRICES ON APPLICATION TO EITHER OF ABOVE OFFICES.

A Hendreddu advertisement placed by the Bradwells in *Skyring's Builders' Prices Catalogue*, 1882.

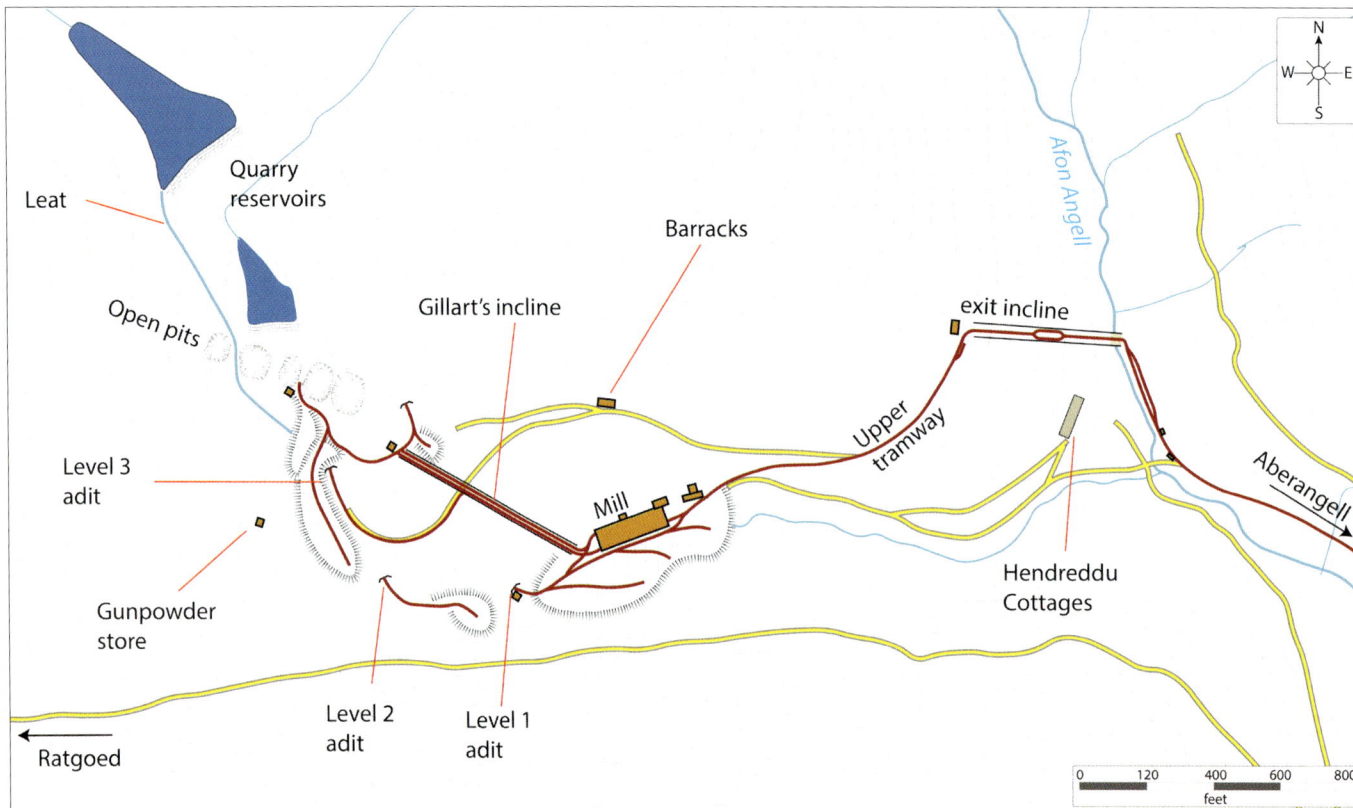

Hendreddu Quarry in the mid-1880s. The tramway bringing rock from the open pits and adits entered the west side of the mill, while finished products were taken out of the east end and on the upper tramway to the exit incline.

a year before had been found guilty of taking a Mawddwy Railway wagon without permission.[50]

In June of 1887, there was a serious accident on the tramway. The seven-year-old nephew of David Owen of Abermynach Cottage had been sent with his sister to fetch milk from Cefngwyn Farm. He returned along the tramway and found three loaded slab wagons next to Sied Wen, waiting to be hauled over Clipiau. The boy removed the rock which held the wagons in place and released the brake. The wagons began to roll downhill towards the Aberdwynant bridge. He attempted to stop them, but slipped and fell under the moving train. One of his legs was seriously fractured, he lost one finger entirely and two more fingers and a thumb were crushed. His leg was amputated by two local doctors though, despite losing considerable amounts of blood, the boy eventually recovered.[51]

References

1   Daily summary, *Greenock Telegraph*, p.2, May 20th, 1876.
2   The Great Sale at Dinas Mawddwy of Sir Edmund Buckley's Property, *Cambrian News*, p.8, Oct. 20th, 1876.
3   The Welsh Estates of Sir Edmund Buckley, Bart, M.P, *Wellington Journal*, p.8, Oct. 28th, 1876.
4   Reports from Commissioners, Houses of Parliament, vol.23, 1877.
5   Alleged fraud by a Member of Parliament, *Western Mail*, p.5, Dec. 5th, 1876.
6   Special telegrams from our London correspondent, *Western Daily Press*, p.8, Feb. 15th, 1877.
7   The bankruptcy of Sir Edmund Buckley, *Morning Post*, p.7, Mar. 21st, 1879.
8   Bill Breese, Damweiniau Llenol, *Cambrian News*, Sep. 19th, 1975.
9   Aberangell, near Dinas Mawddwy, *Cambrian News*, p.8, Feb. 16th, 1877.
10   Dinas Mawddwy, *The Aberystwith Observer*, p.3, Feb. 17th, 1877.
11   Aberangell, near Dinas Mawddwy, *Cambrian News*, p.5, Feb. 23rd, 1877.
12   England, Wales and Scotland Census, piece 2160, folio 524, p.7, 1851.
13   Dinas Mawddwy, Floral and Horticultural Show, *Cambrian News*, p.2, Sep. 7th, 1888.
14   W. B. Stephens, Ed., *History of Congleton*, Manchester University Press, 1970.
15   Agreement of Sale for London Mill, Oct. 14th, 1861.
16   England and Wales Census, Piece 107, Book 6, Folio 15, p.24, 1841.
17   Marriages, *Preston Chronicle*, p 5, May 2nd, 1863.
18   Lancashire, England, Church of England Marriages and Banns, Parish Register, 1863.
19   Marriages, *Blackburn Standard*, p.3, May 6th, 1863.
20   England and Wales Census, Piece 195, Book 16, Folio 37, p.16, 1871.
21   Bill Breese, Tro ar fyd, *Cambrian News*, Jun. 1975.
22   Lyndon Murgatroyd, *Mill Walks and Industrial Yarns*, 2000.
23   Aberangell, *Y Genedl Gymreig*, p.6, Jun. 19th, 1879.
24   To stone cutters: wanted, *Cambrian News*, p.1, Apr. 18th, 1879.
25   Aberangell: presentation, *Cambrian News*, p.6, Oct. 29th, 1880.
26   A carter's sad death, *Shrewsbury Chronicle*, p.11, Sep. 17th, 1909.
27   Claim for wages, *North Wales Chronicle*, p.6, Feb. 24th, 1883.
28   Births, Marriages and Deaths, *Cambrian News*, p.5, Apr. 4th, 1879.
29   Aberangell, *Baner ac Amserau Cymru*, p. 11, Nov. 24th, 1880.
30   Census of England and Wales. Piece 5450, folio 62, p.14, 1881.
31   Gwyndaf Breese, The Angell Valley Tramway, unpublished manuscript.

The three remaining Hendreddu Cottages No's 4, 5 and 6, in 2018. The final curve of the Hendre Ddu Tramway is shown at the bottom of the picture, as it approaches the terminus from the direction of Gartheiniog Farm. The course of the exit incline and the upper tramway to the quarry are also shown.

32   Bill Breese, Bygone industrial activities in the Angell valley, *Cambrian News*, Jul. 9th, 1976.

33   Births, *Cambrian News*, p.8, Jan. 19th, 1883.

34   Llys yr ynadon, *Y Dydd*, p.5, Jul. 14th, 1882.

35   Census of England, Wales and Scotland, piece 5688, folio 24, p.21, 1871.

36   Census of England, Wales and Scotland, piece 5544, folio 18, p.15, 1881.

37   Edmund George Warland, *Practical Modern Masonry*, Donhead Publishing, 1929.

38   Bill Breese, The old quarrying days in the Angell valley, *Cambrian News*, Jun. 25th, 1976.

39   Hendreddu (October 27), *Y Dydd*, p.6, Oct. 27th, 1882.

40   Hendreddu (November 3), *Y Dydd*, p.10, Nov. 3rd, 1882.

41   Dinas Mawddwy: Serious accident, *Cambrian News*, p.6, Feb. 14th, 1873.

42   Hendreddu (November 17), *Y Dydd*, p.11, Nov. 17th, 1882.

43   Cardiganshire Police Committee, *Cambrian News*, p.6, May 31st, 1889.

44   Notices, *London Gazette*, no. 21998, p.1644, May 8th, 1857.

45   Notices, *London Gazette*, no. 25548, p.184, Jan. 12th, 1886.

46   Heavy failure in the silk trade, *Manchester Courier*, p.7, Jan. 13th, 1888.

47   Vanishing Wales, *Country Life*, vol. 160, p.756, Sep. 16th, 1976.

48   Bill Breese, The end of an era, *Cambrian News*, February 20th, 1976.

49   Dolgelley: Petty Sessions, *Cambrian News*, p.5, Jan. 21st, 1887.

50   Trespass on the Mawddwy Railway, *Cambrian News*, Jul. 23rd, 1886.

51   Aberangell, *Aberystwith Observer*, p.4, Jul. 2nd, 1887.

The upper pit at Maesygamfa around 1895. Frederick Walton, on the right, is proudly posing in his quarry. The rails are the northern end of the tramway that leads to the trwnc incline down to the mill level. The bridge rail in the foreground is spiked to sleepers; the rails beyond are laid directly on the ground so they can be slewed left or right to access different parts of the working face. The loaded wagon is a standard Hendre Ddu Tramway box wagon. There is no evidence of compressed air lines in the pit. There are seven men visible in this remarkable photograph. [Gwynedd Archives]

5: Maesygamfa 1862-1914

The Maesygamfa Quarry* is just over a mile north of Llidiart Dwbl. Unlike the other quarries of the area, it worked the Broad Vein, to the north of the Narrow Vein. All the Aberangell quarries were slab producers, but the Broad Vein rock is noticeably harder than the Narrow Vein, making it more difficult to split and work. As a result, Maesygamfa focused its output on larger products; a 1902 advertisement for the quarry boasted that they were '*Acknowledged the best in the district. Makers of Brewer's Tanks, Cisterns, Urinals*'.

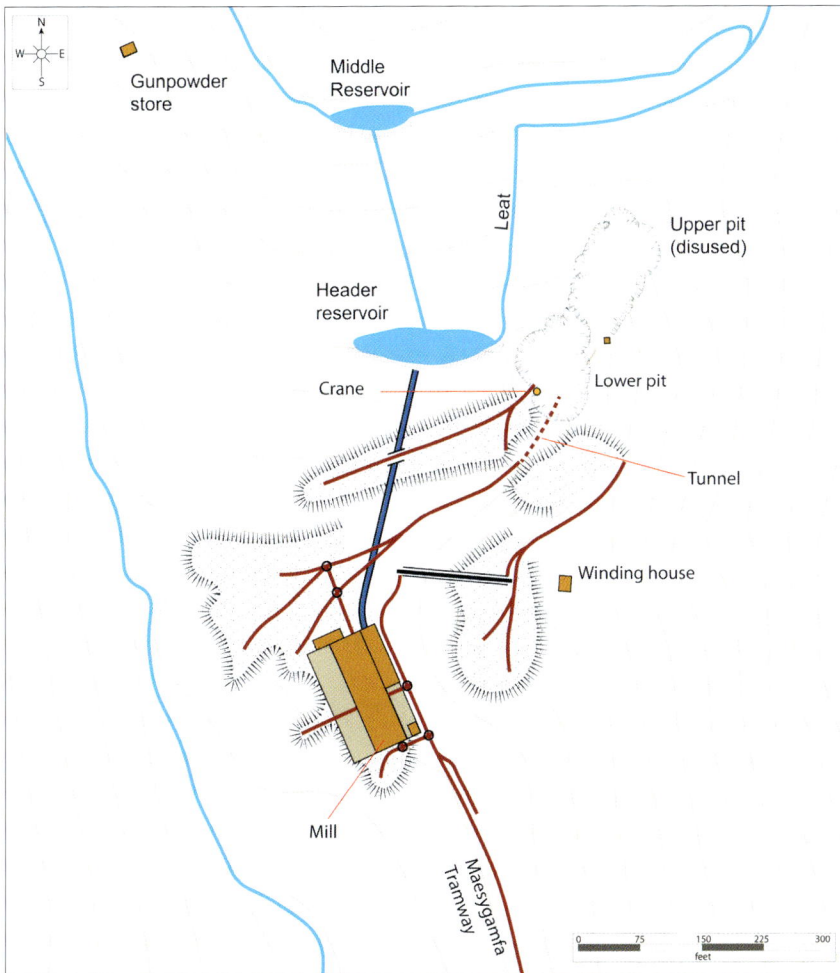

The general layout of Maesygamfa Quarry. The quarry changed considerably during its relatively short life, and this map shows the quarry as it was around 1900.

* Also known as Maes y Gamfa, Maesygamdda and Maesgamdda. Maesygamfa appears to have been the most common spelling for the quarry, especially after about 1880, and is the name used in official returns.

** about £40,000 in 2018.

The Early Years 1862-1870

In August 1861, the 'Dolserry' (aka Dolserau) Estate was bought at auction by Charles Edwards, who had been the Liberal MP for Windsor between 1866 and 1868. The estate included Maesygamfa Farm. In 1862, Edwards began exploring for slate on his land, opening a small quarry to the north of the farm. In 1875, Edwards's use of the sheepwalks surrounding Maesygamfa Farm led to the dispute over manorial rights with Sir Edmund Buckley. The quarry was on the contested land, and Edwards gave the following testimony at the trial:

'*I gave instruction to a man named Evan Pierce to build a quarry at Maesgamdda [sic]. At that time there was a great public interest excited in the matter of slate quarries. I have not been on that quarry myself. Portions of the slate were sent to me in London. They were submitted to other persons in London. Since the year 1862, I spent a considerable sum of money in opening the slate quarry... about £100[1]... I made an agreement with David and Edward Jones [to work the quarry] in either 1868 or 1869.*'**

The mining in 1868/9 by David and Edward Jones was described as '*trials of the slate*' and it lasted '*for some months*', clearly this was little more than a trial pit. The tenant farmer Edward Richards described it being worked '*for a month or six weeks... in the ravine where the blue stone had been cut*'. After this trial period, and by 1870 at the latest, quarrying at Maesygamfa ceased for more than a decade.

Frederick Walton

James Walton's son Frederick was a key player in the revival of Maesygamfa in the 1880s. Frederick worked in his father's business at Haughton Dale from an early age. He wrote of seeing '*a paint pot in the laboratory, and, as usual a skin or surface of dried oil had formed upon it... it occurred to me that I could use it as a... waterproofing material, similar to india rubber.*'[2] This observation was to lead him to great places.

Frederick moved to Chiswick in London and took over an existing factory, the British Grove Works. In September 1861, he applied for a patent for a varnish that could be applied to fabrics to provide waterproofing. In 1863, he produced and patented a hard-wearing flooring product using his waterproofing material. He called this new product linoleum and he was able to mass-produce it much more cheaply than existing flooring solutions.[2] Seeing the potential for linoleum, Walton built a new factory in Staines. Though it took five years to turn the first profit, Walton persevered and opened further factories around the UK, and in Germany and the United States. By the mid-1870s, he had made a considerable fortune. His wealth eventually eclipsed that of his father, who was a rich man in his own right.

On 19th March 1867, Frederick married 27-year-old Alice Ann Scruby in Bushey, Hertfordshire. They had one son Frederick James, and three daughters, Olive, Clarice, and Violet.

In 1868, Frederick moved into Cwmllecoediog after his father retired to Dolforgan. Shortly afterwards, he replaced the existing villa with a much larger house, known as Plas Cwmllecoediog. Built in 1870, it had eleven bedrooms and dressing rooms, three receptions and a billiard room. The grounds had a large coach house, cottages for the coachman and gardener, glasshouses and an ornate fishing lodge on the private lake surrounded by twenty acres of meadows.[3] Like his father, Frederick was interested in developing the estate for commercial use. In 1871, he had 100 acres at Cwmllecoediog planted with larch, spruce, Scots pine and pinus austriaca.[4] This planting was intended for commercial timber production and would pay dividends during the First World War.

Frederick spent two years in America between 1872 and 1874, establishing the American Linoleum Company on Staten Island, New York.[2] He returned to the UK after this, spending much of his time at Cwmllecoediog. His son, Frederick James Walton was born at Cwmllecoediog on 13th November 1876. Frederick Walton retired from his company in 1878, though he remained the majority owner and continued to invent and file patents well into the 1890s.

Frederick Walton the inventor of linoleum, towards the end of this life.

Frederick Walton's second great invention: Walton-Lincrusta. This development of linoleum was a deeply embossed wall covering, which he sold from the 1880s onwards. This example of original Lincrusta was found at the Winchester Mystery House in San Jose California in 2018. [Dan Quine]

Aberangell School 1883

Frederick Walton took a keen interest in local affairs and particularly education. He first proposed building a school in Aberangell in 1880. Before this, the village children had been taught in a small, rather dilapidated church room. Walton donated the land for the school from his estate, paid for its construction and agreed to pay for the first three years of costs, including the teachers' salaries. As a result, education was provided free to local children.

While this was undoubtedly a generous act by Walton, it was not entirely altruistic. It had the intended side effect of ensuring that a compulsory school rate was not imposed and the local gentry could continue to occasionally pay the much lower voluntary rate.[5]

The school opened in February 1883.[6] Situated in the northeast corner of Clipiau, it was a fine building and between 90 and 100 pupils attended each year. In 1892, management of the school was turned over to a school board led by Sir Edmund Buckley and Edward Hurst Davies.[7] The Waltons continued to support the school after it had passed to the school board. They held an annual party from 1883 onwards[6] for the schoolchildren at Plas Cwmllecoediog. The following account from 1887 gives a good sense of these occasions:

'On Friday, August 12th, the children who attend the school at Aberangell were invited by Mrs F. Walton, of Cwmllecoediog, to partake of an excellent tea which had been prepared on the lawn in front of her mansion. The children, about ninety-five in number, formed into a procession at the school at two p.m. and were conducted by the headmaster, Mr H. Lloyd to Cwmllecoediog.

The ladies who presided at the tables were the Misses Hughes, Cemmes; Miss Scruby, Cwmllecoediog; Misses Olive, Violet, and Clarice Walton, Cwmllecoediog; Miss Carver, and Miss Walker. After all had done justice to the good things prepared for

Walton's school building in 2015. The extension on the left is modern, but the fine slate walls in the rest of the building are evident. This is now the village hall. [Dan Quine]

them, several games were organized for their amusement, such as running, jumping, tug-of-war, etc. Then Mrs F. Walton distributed the prizes, which were given by Mrs Henry Walton … The prizes consisted of handsomely bound books and other useful articles.

After the distribution of the prizes the Rev W. Williams (C.M.), Mallwyd, made a few observations in which he thanked Mr F. Walton, Mrs H. Walton, and others of the family for the substantial treat which they gave to the children, which they have done now for several years. The children then sang several hymns under the leadership of Messrs H. Lloyd and Thomas Breese. And after buns and tea were distributed, the National Anthem was sung, which concluded a very pleasant gathering. It is to be regretted that the example of the Waltons, of Cwmllecoediog, is not more universally adopted among our gentry. The school at Aberangell, which is only a very small hamlet, is in a very flourishing condition and that is due to a great extent to the teaching capabilities of the master, but not the least to the encouragement which is constantly given by the members of the Walton family.'[8]

The school consistently won awards for its excellence and sent several pupils on to higher education, at a time when this was a rare opportunity for working-class Welsh children.

Development into Heyday 1886-1900

Edward Hurst Davies, the son of Hendreddu's original quarry engineer, was briefly the manager of Hendreddu under the Bradwells, then worked as the mine agent at Gartheiniog. But he harboured ambitions to run his own quarry. In 1886, Davies obtained a take note for the quarry at Maesygamfa from Charles Edwards, where he quickly established a small quarry, presumably on the site of the earlier trial workings by the Jones brothers.[9] Davies was convinced that the dense Broad Vein rock at Maesygamfa would attract customers, because of the stability and quality of the rock.[10]

Davies persuaded Frederick Walton to join him in a partnership,[11] and together they established the quarry. Davies was the 'practical man' who ran the quarry while

Walton supplied the majority of the money: Davies invested £1,082* and Walton £5,410.[10]** Davies's explorations were fruitful and on 12th October 1888, he signed a long-term lease for the quarry from David Griffiths and John Richards, who had purchased Maesygamfa Farm from Charles Edwards. He was listed as the mine agent at the new Maesygamfa Quarry in 1888.[12]

Davies built a small mill, connected by an internal incline and tramway to the pit.[13] There was a smithy beside the mill, and a gunpowder magazine was built on the hillside to the north. Blocks produced in the mill were used to expand the building to 100ft long[9] in the early 1890s.

A major obstacle stood in the way of the quarry's success. The only practical route to get slate to market was via the Hendre Ddu Tramway. This would require building a long tramway south from the quarry to Llidiart Dwbl, across Jacob Bradwell's land. It also needed Bradwell's permission to run trains over the Hendre Ddu Tramway. Bradwell was under no obligation to provide land and running rights to his competition. The story of how Maesygamfa got permission to use the Hendre Ddu Tramway is told in detail in Chapter 8.

Permission was secured, and Davies surveyed and built a substantial tramway including a particularly long incline south of Maesygamfa Farm. The tramway was built after 1889, most likely opening in 1890 or early 1891.[14] In 1892, the Walton family offered both the Cwmllecoediog and Dolforgan estates for sale.[15] They were not sold, although Cwmllecoediog was leased to Captain St. George between 1895 and 1898.

Davies and Walton invested large amounts of capital in the quarry, equipping it with the best technology then available. The tramway was built to a high standard by the Maesygamfa stonemasons. The mill was equipped with slab planers fitted with shaped blades capable of producing complex carved slate objects.[16]

In January 1892, they spent £125 17s 5d*** on a '*Dori-pen-rhydd*' – a loosehead drill – used to open up a new chamber.[10] The 1898 quarry report by the Inspector of Mines notes that Maesygamfa was one of the first two quarries in Merionethshire to use a rock drill – an '*Ingersoll Sergeant 2¼ inch model, driven by compressed air*'.[17] The cost of the drill, a bar channelling machine and the compressed-air

---

* £500,000 in 2020.

** £2,500,000 in 2020.

*** £55,000 in 2020.

engine to drive it, account for the expenditure. The mill was fitted with a water turbine as well as a conventional water wheel.[18] The turbine drove the compressed-air engine for the drill.

A set of Maesygamfa weighbridge records has survived, showing the weight of rock entering the mill at the end of March and during most of April 1892, when the quarry was at full production.

This shows the quarry working a six-day week, starting on Sunday and running through to the following Friday. It is extremely unlikely that the strongly Methodist workforce would have tolerated working on a Sunday, a practice that happened nowhere in Wales during this period. This discrepancy remains unexplained though possibly the year is a transcription error and these are the figures for 1893. On three days there was not enough water pressure to run the turbine, so no slate was produced. The highest day of production was 21st April when more than 53 tons of rock was weighed in. On average, for every ten tons of rock entering a slab mill, around seven tons is discarded as waste.[19] This ratio means Maesygamfa produced about seventeen tons of finished slab on 21st April, and 150 tons for the month. This results in an annual production of around 1,400 tons – higher than Gartheiniog between 1897 and 1900. Maesygamfa used flat and box wagons holding two tons of slab each, which means three wagons a day were sent down to Aberangell. There would have been inbound traffic as well: coal for the

DATE	TONS	CWT	QTRS
SUNDAY, MARCH 27TH	9	14	0
MONDAY, MARCH 28TH	14	6	0
TUESDAY, MARCH 29TH	12	0	0
WEDNESDAY, MARCH 30TH	NO PRESSURE		
SUNDAY, APRIL 3RD	9	9	0
	8	1	0
MONDAY, APRIL 4TH	NO PRESSURE, MACHINE BROKEN		
TUESDAY, APRIL 5TH	18	19	0
	10	11	2
WEDNESDAY, APRIL 6TH	10	4	0
	9	0	0
THURSDAY, APRIL 7TH	NO PRESSURE		
FRIDAY, APRIL 8TH	4	16	0
	3	0	0
SUNDAY, APRIL 10TH	11	14	0
MONDAY, APRIL 11TH	20	30	0
	9	8	2
TUESDAY, APRIL 12TH	39	7	0
	3	0	0
WEDNESDAY, APRIL 13TH	33	10	0
THURSDAY, APRIL 14TH	25	16	0
	15	0	0
FRIDAY, APRIL 15TH	18	19	0
SUNDAY, APRIL 17TH	12	8	0
	18	0	0
MONDAY, APRIL 18TH	29	2	0
	9	0	0
TUESDAY, APRIL 19TH	19	2	0
WEDNESDAY, APRIL 20TH	14	12	0
	11	11	0
THURSDAY, APRIL 21ST	33	10	0
	20	3	0
FRIDAY, APRIL 22ND	14	1	0
	1	15	2
SUNDAY, APRIL 24TH	13	17	0
	6	0	0
MONDAY, APRIL 25TH	16	12	0
	3	0	0

An Ingersoll-Sergeant compressed air mining drill from the late 1890s. These drills could be mounted on a channelling machine to 'perforate' the footing of a slab. [Maryland Geological Survey]

The drill's work, still evident on the upper waste tips at Maesygamfa in 2015. The scalloped edge of the slab is the result of work with a channelling machine. [Dan Quine]

A mantle plinth scroll recovered from Maesygamfa mill in the 1970s. This was carved at the mill on the slab planers fitted with shaped blades. [Terry Follett]

smithy, explosives, general stores, tools, candles, and lubricants. Possibly the quarrymen would have ridden up in the wagons, though this is not specifically recorded.

In 1893, the quarry was operating under the title Maes-y-gamfa Slate Quarry Company.[20] Peak employment was in 1896 with fifteen men working in the quarry and nine in the mill and on the tramway,[21] the next year the total was down to twenty.

During the 1890s, Walton spent much of his time at his London home, and he grew suspicious that Davies might be defrauding him. He made an unannounced visit to Wales, probably in late summer 1895. When he arrived at the quarry, he started interfering with Davies's work orders. Although Walton found no evidence of financial mismanagement, he remained suspicious, and after returning to London he ordered an independent audit of the quarry books. No impropriety was found.

Brynderwen House 1894-1897

In the early 1890s, Edward Hurst Davies was living at Brynmynach on the edge of Clipiau.[7] His family was growing and he clearly wanted a grander residence. Around

An Ingersoll-Sergeant bar channeller of the type used at Maesygamfa. This example was photographed around 1905 at a marble quarry in New York State. [Ingersoll-Sergeant]

1894, he started to build a new home overlooking the wharf, to be called Brynderwen. He employed the architects F.W. Hipkiss & Bassett of Aberystwyth to design it. The stone for the house, of course, came from Maesygamfa, and a large amount of cut stone was stored in the quarry yard; Walton told Davies to remove the building stones. The ingenious Davies laid a short branch from the top of Brynderwen cutting, along the southern cutting wall and to the construction site for his house. The stones were sent down from Maesygamfa and his house was duly completed in 1897.[10] There are two fine

The smallest of several models of line-driven air compressor made by Ingersoll-Sergeant. The exact model used at Maesygamfa is not known. [Ingersoll-Sergeant]

stone pillars at the east end of the cutting and one bears the inscribed date 1897. It is an extremely grand house, by far the largest in Aberangell at the time, with seven bedrooms over three floors. It is opposite Aberangell Wharf, on the south side of the tramway and gave Davies a view of every train running on the tramway.

After the construction branch was removed, the low wall on the south side of the Brynderwen cutting was extended upwards to provide privacy for the house, and the land behind the wall was excavated to provide a level garden. Two openings were left in the upper wall so that coal could be loaded from tramway wagons into the coal store in the garden. There is some evidence that Davies kept a length of tramway through his garden to move coal from the store to the cellar of the house.

Accidents at the Quarry: 1890s

Sadly, in 1897 there was a fatal accident in the quarry. Richard Edwards, thirty-three,[17] was one of several workers loading a slab at the quarry using a hand crane. The slab had been lowered over the wagon and the men were trying to reposition it, as it was not centred properly. Edwards was standing in front of the crane when the slab unexpectedly dropped, spinning the winding handle. The handle struck him on the forehead and knocked him unconscious. While he recovered consciousness and was taken home, he died a few days later.

The crane had a brake and a catch on the ratchet of the winding mechanism, but the catch was not down when the accident occurred. The rules for operating the crane were printed in English and Welsh and attached to the crane. Evan Jones of Winllan, a fellow worker, reported that Edwards was used to working with the crane – though he had only

been employed at the quarry for six months.[22]

Edward Davies was at the quarry on the day of the accident, and O.R. Jones, the Inspector of Mines, had visited it the previous day. Jones examined the crane after the accident and found it in full working order. He thought that it would have been impossible for the handle to reverse. The jury returned a verdict of accidental death.[23]

There were two further serious accidents involving Maesygamfa workers, sometime in this period, though the exact dates are not recorded. The first victim was William Roberts of Brynawel. He was working in the mill in the mid-late 1890s, making repairs in a confined space. He accidentally knocked out the wedge that was stopping a

Halfway along Brynderwen cutting in 2015, looking towards Aberdwynant. The wall on the shows two distinct layers: the original 1894 wall ran up to the line of grasses growing about halfway up. Above this is the 1897 wall, which is set back slightly and constructed of smaller blocks. This was added to provide privacy for the Davies family. [Dan Quine]

Edward Hurst Davies's substantial house Brynderwen, built in 1895 from Broad Vein blocks cut at Maesygamfa. The Davies family lived here from 1896 until 1926. The Hendre Ddu Tramway ran directly in front of these gates.
[Dan Quine]

to interview Winston Churchill, a family friend.

Herbert was distantly related to the Vivian family who ran the Dinorwic Quarry. He was the co-founder and editor of *The Whirlwind*, a weekly newspaper that had a strongly Jacobite view of the world. He employed his friend the artist Walter Sickert to illustrate the paper. Sickert was an eccentric figure, drawn to underworld subjects; he took lodgings in one of the rooms suspected to have been used by Jack the Ripper and produced a painting titled 'Jack the Ripper's Bedroom'. Three authors have accused Sickert of being the Ripper. So it is possible that Frederick Walton's daughter Olive knew Jack the Ripper, who allegedly killed Edward Hurst Davies's sister.

The Vivians divorced around 1926, as Herbert's monarchist and right-wing political views became more extreme. In later life, he was a vocal supporter of Fascism. He died in 1940.

Edward Hurst Davies was active in the public life of Aberangell and the Dyfi Valley. He regularly served on juries for the local coroner. He was one of the initial members of the Dinas Mawddwy and Aberangell School Board, formed in 1892,[7] and in September 1898 he was voted onto the Unified School Board of Mallwyd and Llanymawddwy, beating out Sir Edmund Buckley amongst others. That same year he was a member of the Dolgelley Board of Guardians[25] and the chairman of Dinas Mawddwy town council.[26] He was a member of the Mallwyd Urban District Council between 1899 and 1902[27] and a magistrate for many years.[28]

Matilda Davies inherited her father's fearless attitude. In 1898, she brought a complaint at the Machynlleth Petty Session against Jane Jones, also of Aberangell, for using threats against her. Jones admitted the offence and was bound over to keep the peace.[29] Not many nine-year-old girls brought and won cases of this sort in late-Victorian Britain.

nearby pulley wheel from turning. The drive ring on the shaft caught his clothing and pulled him. Fortunately his co-worker Tomos Owen saw the accident and rushed to the turbine house to shut down the machinery. Turbines take a long time to spin down, and the mill had no brake system on the drive shafts. Owen was quick-witted enough to kick out the clutch between the turbine and the drive belt – a dangerous thing to do while the machinery was operating but by far the quickest way to shut down the drive shafts. Owen's action undoubtedly saved Roberts's life, though he was severely injured.[10]

Tomos Owen was the victim of the second accident which happened a few years later. Tomos was sitting on the tramway bridge over the Afon Mynach at Aberdwynant. For some reason, a run of loaded Maesygamfa wagons passed by unexpectedly and knocked him into the river below. He also sustained serious injuries. Owen tried to claim compensation from the directors of the Maesygamfa quarry, but they refused, saying the accident had been his fault. The details are hazy, and it appears he may have been in the company of a married woman at the time of the collision. Whatever the circumstances, Owen's actions in saving Roberts were not forgotten. A collection was made amongst the villagers and on 2nd February 1914 he was given £16 0s 9d (£5,000 in 2018).[10]

In September 1897, Frederick Walton's daughter Olive married Herbert Vivian in Brighton.[24] Olive and Herbert published a travel book together, with Olive as photographer and Herbert as writer. Olive became an accomplished journalist, providing photographs to *The Sketch*, *The Royal* and the *Illustrated London News*, and writing dozens of articles for the *Daily Mirror*, *Pall Mall Magazine*, *World Wide Magazine*, *The Strand* and others between 1898 and 1916. Herbert was also a journalist and novelist, and he was the first reporter

Declining Fortunes 1900-1909

The relationship between Walton and Davies deteriorated during the late 1890s,[10] and on 14th November 1900, the partnership between them was formally dissolved,[30] and from then on Davies was the sole leaseholder of the quarry. Walton continued his interest in mining, investing in two

Mexican ventures: the San Jorge Minillas Mining Company in Chihuahua, of which he was a director in 1909[31] and the Alice Santa Eulalia Mining Company.[32]

In 1901, following the closure of the Mawddwy Railway, the workforce was down to seven men working the tramway and mill, and five in the pit.[33] Several of these workers are known: Richard Lewis of Minllyn, Tom Rees Thomas of Aber Cywarch, William Williams from Capel Camlan and his son Wmphre (Humphrey); 'Evan y Gem', Jack Morgan, David 'Defi' Thomas, Tomos Owen of Aberangell, and William Roberts of Brynawel, Aberangell.[10] In July 1901, Davies was part of a deputation of local worthies who met with the leader of the Light Railway Commissioners in London to lobby for the reopening of the Mawddwy Railway – ultimately successfully.[34]

The years after the turn of the century were difficult for the slate industry, and Maesygamfa suffered. The quarry was not working for at least part of 1903, though the exact length of the hiatus is not known. By September 1905, with eight men working[35] Davies was in a position to offer building stones for a new cart bridge at Aberangell '*at half the usual price of 1s 6d a ton, on condition that the bridge would be strong enough to carry the ordinary threshing machines of the district*'.[36]

Bill Breese suspected that Maesygamfa provided some of the rock for the construction of Capel Bethania in Aberangell. The contract for the chapel was let to William Roberts on 6th July 1902, though building did not start until May 1903. The chapel was completed on 10th June 1904, and opened five days later.[37]

In June 1906, Edward Davies's eldest daughter, May, married John Thomas Howell, a 32-year-old solicitor from Bridgend, at Aberangell. Amongst the many gifts the couple received was an inscribed silver afternoon tea kettle on a stand from the Maesygamfa quarrymen. The *Welsh Gazette* covered the wedding and made particular note of Edward Hurst Davies: '*The bride's father is well-known and highly esteemed, being influentially connected with some of the leading slate quarries in the district. He has also taken an active part in local affairs, and has served on the county council and other public bodies.*'[38] The wedding was a significant social event in Aberangell. The *Cambrian News* devoted nearly two broadsheet columns to a detailed account of the nuptials.

John and May Howell had two children: Vivien born in 1910 and John born in 1912. But by 1915, May's health was failing and she died on 29th May 1916, aged 35. She had been the clerk of Bridgend Urban District Council and had lived with her family at a house called Brynderwen on Park Street.[39]

On 16th March 1918, John Howell married May's younger sister Matilda 'Tilly' Davies, in Manchester.[40] They had a son, Anthony, born in 1920.[41] Perhaps coincidentally, Matilda died aged 36 in 1925.[42] John Howell appears not to have remarried.

The severe downturn in the industry following the end of the Penrhyn strike[43] hit Maesygamfa hard. The quarry stopped again for the whole of 1908;[44] it reopened in 1909 with just three men working – two in the mill and one in the quarry – producing less than 30 tons of finished slab by September of that year.[45] These three continued working into 1910, but then the quarry shut for the last time under Davies's ownership.[46] Davies formally relinquished the lease to the quarry on 31st December 1911.[47]

The Final Go 1912-1914

Maesygamfa quarry now returned to the landowner, David Jones of Llwydiarth, who had inherited Maesygamfa Farm from his uncle on 8th March 1908.[47] Jones was deeply troubled that he owned a workable quarry while many local quarrymen were out of work. He let it be known that he would make the quarry available rent-free for a six week trial period. A group of twelve quarrymen[48] eagerly took up his offer and formed the Maes-y-gamfa Slate Co. nominating Richard Lewis of Dinas Mawddwy as their agent.[47] Lewis had been a quarryman at Maesygamfa immediately after the turn of the century and would go on to be the manager of Hendreddu after the First World War and later work at Gartheiniog. Other men included Ifan Jones of Dinas Mawddwy, Twm Tydu, Twm Rhys Tomos of Abercywarch and William Williams of Capel Camlan.[37] Lewis was accompanied by 67-year-old Evan Jones of Dinas Mawddwy, who was the most experienced of the group – he had worked under E.H. Davies at the quarry as early as 1888.[49] They began working the quarry and were able to use the mill and the slab planers that Davies had installed.

This attempt at a revival was, unfortunately, a financial disaster. The men failed to get payment from the dealers for the slab they shipped. The rent-free period was extended, but the end came in January 1914, when Evan Jones died.[50]

Tomos Owen, sitting on the wall beside Cwmllecoediog Lodge, with the Aberangell Mill in the background. This was taken shortly before his death on 27th June 1929.
[Bill Breese collection]

Maesygamfa upper pit in 2020. Although a lot of rock has fallen in the last 125 years, the distinctive vertical slot to the right of the waterfall is recognisable from the 1895 image.
[Keith Whiddon]

Below: Advertisement for the Maesygamfa Quarry, from 1902.

THE MAESYGAMFA
SLATE AND SLAB QUARRY CO.,
ABERANGELL, MERIONETHSHIRE.

THE SLATE and SLAB supplied from the Maesygamfa Quarries are unsurpassed for **Quality**, **Strength**, and **Durability**. Acknowledged the best in the district.

Makers of
Brewers' Tanks, Cisterns,
URINALS.

ALL KIND OF SLATE WORK EXECUTED.

Prices on application to the Manager, Mr. E. H. DAVIES.

Right: These sawn slabs were retrieved from the mill at Maesygamfa. The carving reads 'W.C. Pyx 1913'. No record of anyone by the name of Pyx or with the initials W.C. is associated with the quarry, nor are they in the local 1911 census records. A pyx is also a small round container used to carry the host during Eucharist. The intent of the carving remains unknown.
[Terry Follett]

The rest of the men gave up their effort, and Maesygamfa closed for the last time. John Lewis, the tenant farmer of Maesygamfa, had the sad duty of turning off the turbine that powered the mill. He reused some of the sawn blocks from the mill walls to build new sections of his farm, using a tipping tub to transport them along the upper tramway.

The quarry was dismantled after the outbreak of the First World War. The machinery was removed for scrap, and the tramway was taken up from the quarry to the foot of the Maesygamfa incline. John Lewis arranged for the lower section of the Maesygamfa Tramway to be saved;[47] it was used later in the First World War to serve Talymeirin Quarry.

After the war, the mill was gradually demolished, further stone being reused at Maesygamfa Farm. The lower section of the tramway continued to be used by the owners of the farm to bring coal and other goods up to his farm, and ship wool out;[37] it was not lifted until 1939.

References

1 Manorial rights in Merionethshire, *North Wales Chronicle*, p.3, Aug. 7th, 1875.
2 Ralph Parsons, Linoleum: A Chiswick Invention, *Brentford & Chiswick Local History Journal*, vol.5, 1996.
3 Messrs E. and H. Lumley, *Oswestry Advertiser*, p.1, Jun. 15th, 1892.
4 News, *The Gardener's Chronicle and Agricultural Gazette*, Sep.23rd, 1871.
5 The School Board question - meeting of ratepayers, *Cambrian News*, p.8, Nov. 21st, 1879.
6 Aberangell, Mallwyd, *Montgomeryshire Express*, p.6, Aug. 7th, 1883.
7 Dinas and Aberangell schools - formation of a new School Board, *Montgomeryshire Express*, p.7, Sep. 13th, 1892.
8 Aberangell: school treat, *Cambrian News*, p.6, Aug. 26th, 1887.
9 Bill Breese, Bygone activities within Angell valley, *Cambrian News*, Aug. 6th, 1976.
10 Bill Breese, Notes on local quarrying and quarrymen, *Dolgellau Archive*, vol. ref ZM/6541/9, 1982.
11 Gwyndaf Breese, The Angell Valley Tramway, unpublished manuscript.
12 Great Britain. Mines Department, List of Owners and Openworks, 1888, Mineral Statistics of the United Kingdom of Great Britain & Ireland, 1889.
13 Merionethshire XXXVIII NE, Ordnance Survey, 1887.
14 Gwyndaf Breese, The deviation, unpublished manuscript.
15 Sales by auction, *The Cambrian*, p.5, Jul. 1st, 1892.
16 Gwynedd Slate Quarries: An Archaeological Survey, vol. No. 154. Gwynedd Archaeological Trust, 1994-5.
17 Report of HM Inspector of Mines, Home Department, 1898.
18 Alun John Richards, *Gazetteer of Slate Quarrying in Wales*, Llygad Gwalch, 2007.
19 David Davies, *A Treatise on Slate and Slate Quarrying*, C. Lockwood and Company, 1899.
20 List of Mines in Great Britain and the Isle of Man, 1893. H.M. Stationery Office, 1894.
21 List of Mines in Great Britain and the Isle of Man, 1896. H.M. Stationery Office, 1897.
22 Aberangell: fatal accidents, *Cambrian News*, p.6, Aug. 26th, 1898.
23 Aberangell: adjourned inquest, *Cambrian News*, p.6, Sep. 2nd 1898.
24 Marriage of Mr. Herbert Vivian, *St James's Gazette*, p. 8, Sep. 30th, 1897.
25 Board of Guardians, *Cambrian News*, p.6, Feb. 4th, 1898.
26 Llys yr ynadon, *Y Negesydd*, p.3, May 20th, 1898.
27 Parish of Mallwyd, in Accounts and papers. Montgomery to Wiltshire, vol.77, His Majesty's Stationery Office, 1902.
28 Serious charges against a Postmaster. Alleged theft of letters and stamps, *Cambrian News*, p.2, May 12th, 1899.
29 To keep the peace, *Montgomery County Times*, p.2, Nov. 5th, 1898.
30 Notice is hereby given, *London Gazette*, no. 27251, p.8051, Nov. 27th, 1900.
31 W. R. Skinner, Ed., *Mining Yearbook*, 1909.
32 W. R. Skinner, Ed., *The Mining Manual*, 1912.
33 List of Mines in Great Britain and the Isle of Man, 1901, H.M. Stationery Office, 1902.
34 The Mawddwy Railway, *Barmouth & County Advertiser*, p.5, Jul. 11th, 1901.
35 List of Mines in Great Britain and the Isle of Man, 1905. H.M. Stationery Office, 1906.
36 A new bridge, *Cambrian News*, p.6, Nov. 24th, 1905.
37 Bill Breese, Notebook on tramroad and local quarrying, *Dolgellau Archive*, no. ref ZM/6541/5 , c. 1970.
38 Interesting wedding, *Welsh Gazette*, p. 2, Jun. 28th, 1906.
39 Death, *Glamorgan Gazette*, p.4, Jun. 2nd, 1916.
40 Priodasau, *Y Cymro*, p.3, Mar. 27th, 1918.
41 England & Wales births 1837-2007, vol.11A, p.1968, 1920.
42 England & Wales deaths 1837-2007, vol.11A, p.904, 1925.
43 Jean Lindsay, *A History of the North Wales Slate Industry*, Newton Abbot: David and Charles, 1974.
44 List of Mines in Great Britain and the Isle of Man, 1908. H.M. Stationery Office, 1909.
45 List of Mines in Great Britain and the Isle of Man, 1909. H.M. Stationery Office, 1910.
46 List of Mines in Great Britain and the Isle of Man, 1910. H.M. Stationery Office, 1911.
47 Bill Breese, Bygone activities of the Angell valley, *Cambrian News*, Jan. 7th, 1977.
48 List of Mines in Great Britain and the Isle of Man, 1912. H.M. Stationery Office, 1913.
49 Petty sessions: charge of indecent assault, *Cambrian News*, p.7, May 11th, 1888.
50 Dinas Mawddwy: Gan gwalia, *Y Drych*, p.7, Jan. 8th, 1914.
51 Bill Breese, Relics of the old quarrying days, *Cambrian News*, Jun. 15th, 1975.

6: Gartheiniog Starts 1880-1915

Gartheiniog Quarry was the largest slate producer in Dyffryn Angell after Hendreddu. There may have been local stone extraction there as far back as 1850. Early commercial exploration took place under an 1873 take note from Edmund Buckley, granted to Thomas Ellis and Robert Manuel, both of Aber Cywarch, north of Dinas Mawddwy.[1]

On 1st October 1880, enameller John Jenkins and builder James Williams, both from Aberystwyth, leased the land around Hendre Meredydd farm from Dennis and Jacob Bradwell. They intended to open a quarry, presumably having located the Narrow Vein where it ran near the surface between Hendreddu and Talymeirin.

The companies that worked the quarry were mostly called variations on 'Gartheiniog Slate Quarries', but the quarry itself was commonly known as Hendreferedydd or Hendre Meredydd, after the nearby farm. Between the world wars, the entire operation was often known as Hendre Meredydd locally.

The Early Years 1881-1883

On 16th September 1881, Jenkins and Williams formed the Gartheiniog Slate and Slab Quarry Ltd and eleven days later, on 27th September, it was renamed the Gartheiniog Slate Company Limited. Jenkins and Williams were shareholders in the new enterprise, along with five others, all from London, including the Lambeth slate merchant E.J. Newitt. The company was capitalised with £30,000[2] and they began operations that year.

In March 1882, Henry Owen of Gartheiniog Farm joined as co-owner, and Williams left the company.[3] Owen was born in Caernarfon in 1833,[4] and in 1874 he was the tenant at Gartheiniog Farm[5] when the Hendre Ddu Tramway was built past his front door. Owen would be one of the owners of Gartheiniog quarry for the next fifteen years. By 1882, Edward Hurst Davies, the former Hendreddu manager, was the quarry agent at Gartheiniog. The initial quarry was an open pit, dug into the Narrow Vein. Commercially viable slate was found and, as at Hendreddu, the slate improved in quality as the workings moved deeper.

In July 1882, E.H. Davies was fined at Dolgelley petty sessions for storing 40lbs of gunpowder at the quarry without a licence.[6] In 1883, the company employed nine men and produced a modest 250 tons of finished slab that year.[7]

Mallory and Owen 1884-1898

In 1884, Henry Mallory, a 44-year-old tallow chandler from Warwick, moved to Pier Street, Aberystwyth, following the death of his first wife.[8] He wanted to invest in a business near his new home and towards the end of that year he became the co-owner of Gartheiniog with Henry Owen. Jenkins was not involved after this and Mallory likely bought out Jenkins's interest. This was not Jenkins's last involvement in slate quarrying; in 1883, he took ownership of Cwm Ebol quarry near Pennal.[9]

Mallory injected new life into the company. He and Owen immediately began driving an adit to access the better slate below, and to the southeast of, the existing twll — much as Edmund Buckley had done at Hendreddu more than a decade earlier. In 1885, Owen successfully applied for an explosives licence.[10] Edward Hurst Davies gave up his post, moving on to his own quarry at Maesygamfa, probably in 1886. He was replaced as Gartheiniog quarry agent by William Evans, of Abermynach.

The new adit was completed around 14th December 1886. Following Sir Edmund's example, a celebratory dinner was held, this one at the quarry, catered by Henry Owen's wife who worked at the Pier Hotel in Aberystwyth. A notable guest at the dinner was Jacob Bradwell, who 'spoke very highly of the spirited manner in which the quarry has been carried on, the good it did to the villages about by the employment of so many men'.[11] Bradwell, as landlord of the Gartheiniog Quarry, had a vested interest in its success and clearly relations between him and Mallory and Owen were good. When they approached Bradwell to allow them to run over the Hendre Ddu Tramway he readily agreed and a rail connection was in place no later than the start of 1887.

Gartheiniog

Slate & Slab

Quarry,

Aberangell, Cemmes,

Mont.,

Within 2 Miles of the Aberangell Station on the Mawddwy Railway.

Makers of SLATE SLABS suitable for the manufacture of

Chimney Pieces

etc.

ALSO BEDS OF

Billiard and Bagatelle Tables.

———

Any description of Slabs cut to order.

———

These Slabs are of a Blue colour and are especially adapted for the purpose of Enamelling.

Proprietors—

Owens and Mallory.

Gartheiniog Quarry advertisement from 1892.

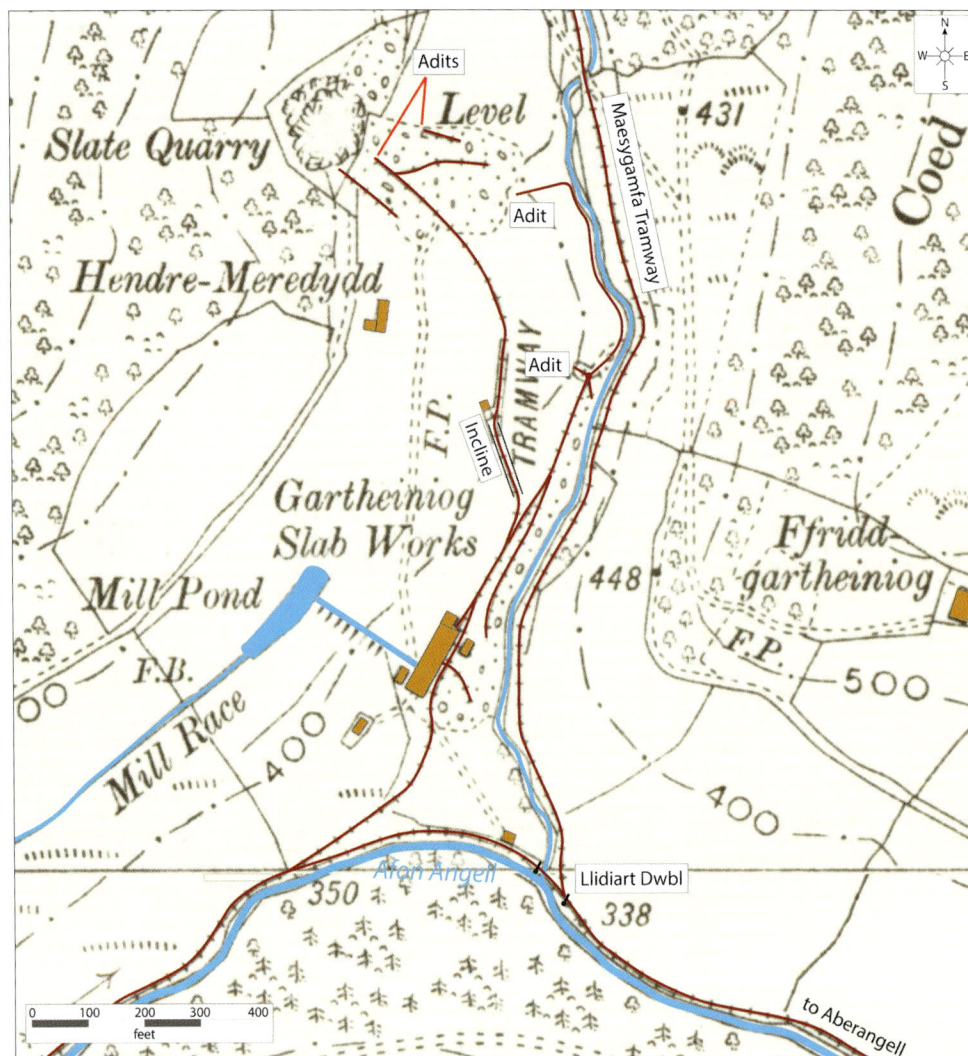

Extract of the 1900 Ordnance Survey map, showing the complex arrangements of tramways at the confluence of the Nant Maes y Gamfa and the Afon Angell. The Gartheiniog Tramway is on the west side of Nant Maes y Gamfa. Hendre Meredydd twll was connected to the mill via a short incline. From the mill, the tramway drops steeply downhill to a junction with the Hendre Ddu to the south and west of the mill. Another tramway runs from the mill north along the banks of the stream, then turning sharply westwards and entering the long adit to the underground workings. Above the mill is the reservoir, fed from a weir above Nanthir Farm, which provided a head of water for the mill turbine. The lower section of the Maesygamfa Tramway runs on the east side of the Nant Maesygamfa, meeting the Hendre Ddu Tramway at Llidiart Dwbl. [Ordnance Survey]

Davies and Walton reached an agreement to connect Maesygamfa quarry with the Hendre Ddu Tramway in October 1887, and the Bradwells wrote Gartheiniog into the contract as well.[12] Around this time, Gartheiniog was supplying slab to the London slate merchant Joseph Brindley & Co. who ran an enamelling works in Bermondsey.[13]

In September 1888, the Gartheiniog Slate Company Ltd was formally dissolved[14] and Mallory and Owen hired John Parry as the new quarry agent. He was to play an interesting role in the story of Hendreddu Quarry after the turn of the century.

Born in 1857,[15] John Parry was the son of Joseph Parry, the quarry supervisor at Abercorris in the 1870s.[16] John followed his father as Abercorris supervisor in the mid-1880s[17] before moving to Gartheiniog, probably in 1886 when Abercorris ran into financial trouble and laid off several men.[18] He married Jane Anne Jones in 1888[19] and they had three children together.[20] At Aberangell he was a noted member of the Temperance movement[21] and along with E.H. Davies was a member of the board of Minllyn School.[22]

The route of the Gartheiniog Tramway was interesting. The mill was close to, but about 50ft above, the Hendre Ddu Tramway. The Gartheiniog Tramway dropped steeply down to the Hendre Ddu, joining it at a junction southwest of the mill. Loaded wagons would be sent down from the mill and would head westwards (uphill) along the Hendre Ddu Tramway. The 'run' would be braked to a halt beyond the junction, the point was switched and the wagons released to run past the junction and on down to Aberangell. It is easy to imagine that this working practice would occasionally go awry.

On 26th February 1890, rockman Isaac Breese of Broad Street, Mallwyd fell to his death at Gartheiniog. Breese, who was 50,[23] had been employed at Gartheiniog for several years and was working on the rock face in the twll, prying slabs free with a crowbar. Around 5:30pm the rock he was standing on gave way. Breese had a rope but had not secured himself to it; he was unable to grab the rope and fell about 80 feet into the pit. He fractured his skull and likely died immediately. Henry Owen was in the quarry on the day of the accident and was on the rock close to Breese; he was one of the witnesses at the subsequent inquest. As usual, a verdict of accidental death was returned with no blame apportioned to the quarry owners. Owen paid for a public funeral for Breese which was

Gartheiniog Mill in 1913. The tramway from the quarry comes in from the right and enters the mill through the door in the end. The building to the left of the mill is the weighhouse. The mill workers stand proudly in front of their place of work. On the left is John Parry, the mine agent. Next to him is Ifan Davis (sawyer) of Nanthir, then Johnnie Jones (plane operator) of Mallwyd, Dafydd Roberts (saw sharpener), Ifan Rhys (plane operator) of Brynhyfryd, and Lewis Rhys (sawyer). [Bill Breese collection]

attended by quarrymen from throughout the district. Breese left a widow and four children.[24]

Owen had a well-deserved reputation for generosity. In 1891, he chaired a concert in Aberangell to raise funds for John T. Jones of Winllan Cottage. Jones was a Gartheiniog quarryman who had been ill for some time. Frederick Walton paid for Jones to undergo surgery at the Middlesex Hospital in London.[25]

In 1892, the Gartheiniog company was admonished by the Dovey, Mawddach and Glaslyn Fisheries Board for allowing dust from their saws to pollute the River Dovey (sic). Salmon had been found with their gills covered in a thick white dust. The company promised to reduce the dust flowing into the Angell and from there into the Dovey.[26]

Another serious accident occurred in April 1894. Four rockmen were working in the quarry, when a large rockfall injured Evan Hughes of Dinas Mawddwy and David Davies of Aberangell. Although their injuries were serious, they both survived.[27]

In 1896, Gartheiniog employed twenty-two men, with six working the quarry and sixteen in the mill, and John Parry was the Mine Agent.[28] That year, a poem appeared in the

Welsh language newspaper *Y Negesydd*. Quarryman William Owen described, rather imaginatively, his journey to work at Gartheiniog:

MY JOURNEY TO WORK
Old Welshman who travels by tramway
To Hendre Feredydd far away,
My rucksack on my shoulders,
A cudgel in my hand;
I get up in the morning
Before the red rooster crows,
Having gone to bed very early,
Around eight o'clock;
I walked for years
For six to seven for sure,
Over hill and hollow, and many streams,
And ditches full of water.
I climb at the Spring
To wave at the blackbird,
Flying with his tenor
singing over our house;
The cuckoo does sweetly sing,

Four Gartheiniog workers. The man on the left is Johnnie Jones, and on the right is Lewis Rhys; the other two are unidentified. Probably also taken in 1913. [Bill Breese collection]

On the thorn bush in the valley,
He may be in the fields, small and large,
Their skins are quite bleak.
I pass Pont yr Hirgwm
And pass Ffridd farm,
Go through Llidiart-Dwbl with my gun,
Ready for Monday.
In the middle of hot days,
A very dry summer,
The sun burning my face brown,
It nearly made me sick.
And when the wind comes in the Autumn,
A 'Sudden shower' on Holy Cross Day,
I was still walking back and forwards
In the company of a great rogue.
In the middle of winter storms,
Rain, ice, snow and cold,
The daily trek through the valley,
In the light of the white moon.
I was desperately tired,
Carrying my white satchel,
There handlebars grow under my hands,
And my head is grey;
I ride an iron horse

Bicycle, then what?
I enjoy this merry riding
Despite the heavy work;
The end of the journey,
Hopefully, soon,
It's novel and it's true.[29]

The 'iron horse bicycle' that Owen refers to is almost certainly one of the pedal-powered ceir gwyllt that ran on the tramway. Owen would have walked to Aberdwynant, then pedalled one of these cars up to Gartheiniog at the start of the day. Clearly, he preferred this method of travel to walking up!

In December 1896, Henry Owen died[4] forcing the sale of both Gartheiniog Farm and, separately, Gartheiniog Quarry.[30] Despite Owen's death, the quarry produced a creditable 700 tons of slate, which sold for £1,925,[31] with John Parry acting as Interim Manager. The auction of the quarry took place on 21st January 1898, in the billiards room of the Wynnstay Hotel, Machynlleth. Included were *'large and commodious Offices, Machine Houses, etc. (now in full operation), with the extensive and modern Valuable Working Plant and Leasehold Lands, containing altogether about 800 acres'*. The auctioneer was David Gillart (nephew of Hendreddu's

Advertising the sale of Gartheiniog.
[*Cambrian News*, 28th October 1904]

James Gillart[32]), who was careful to refer to the '*value of other quarries in the district, viz Braichgoch, Aberllefenni, Ratgoed and Hendreddu which were and had been for generations worked by the same families, a fact that unquestionably… freed it from the suspicion of being of a speculative character*'.[33] That Gillart made such a forceful claim is evidence that 'speculative characters' were already at work in the district, and unfortunately foreshadowed Gartheiniog's fate after the First World War.

Mallory's Sole Ownership 1898-1915

Henry Mallory purchased a 22-year lease of Gartheiniog at the auction for £8,000 and 100s annual rent.[34] He continued as sole owner of the quarry, with John Parry as his agent. By now, the slate industry was in decline, and Gartheiniog struggled financially after the turn of the century. In 1904[35] the quarry was listed for sale, but no buyer was found and Mallory had no choice but to continue with the enterprise.

In 1908, the quarry produced a meagre 221 tons of slate[36] with just two men working below ground and four in the mill. Between 1909 and 1914, the quarry supplied slabs to the enamelling works of Inigo Jones Ltd of Groeslon near Caernarfon, although there were complaints that the rock was so wet it tended to break when enamelled.[37] This contract must have helped the quarry through those lean years and allowed it to struggle through to the Great War.

In July 1915, Henry Mallory died during a visit to Bath, aged 75. He had moved from Aberystwyth to 58 Upperton Road, Eastbourne a few years earlier. His second wife Amelia and his daughter Mabel from his first marriage survived him. Amelia took over the ownership of the Gartheiniog Slate and Slab Quarry.

References

1 Bill Breese, Notes on local quarrying and quarrymen, *Dolgellau Archive*, vol. ref ZM/6541/9, 1982.

2 New companies, *North Wales Express*, p.6, Oct. 7th, 1881.

3 Dissolutions of partnership, *Manchester Courier*, p.7, Mar. 13th, 1882.

4 Aberystwyth: Marwolaeth, *Y Negesydd*, p.1, Dec. 4th, 1896.

5 Cymdeithas amaethyddol Sir Feirionydd, *Y Goleuad*, p.12, May 2nd, 1874.

6 Llys yr Ynadon, *Y Dydd*, p.5, Jul. 14th, 1882.

7 List of Mines in Great Britain and the Isle of Man, 1883. H.M. Stationery Office, 1884.

8 Census of England and Wales, piece 4558, folio 72, p.43, 1891.

9 Pennal, *Cambrian News*, Mar. 16th, 1883.

10 Application for license to keep explosives, *Cambrian News*, p.2, Sep. 25th, 1885.

11 Aberangell, *Aberystwith Observer*, p.5, Dec. 18th, 1886.

12 Gwyndaf Breese, The deviation. Unpublished manuscript.

13 George Roper papers, Denbighshire Record Office, p. GB 0209 DD/RO.

14 Joint stock companies, *London Gazette*, no. 25856, p.5169, Sep. 14th, 1888.

15 Census of England, Wales and Scotland, piece 4641, folio 8, p.7, 1891.

16 Mr. John Parry, *Y Dydd*, p.7, Sep. 7th, 1888.

17 Adgofion o'r amser gynt, *Y Dydd*, p.3, Apr. 9th, 1886.

18 In the High Court of Justice - Chancery Division, *London Evening Standard*, p.6, Nov. 24th, 1886.

19 Merionethshire marriage registry, vol. 11B, p.58, 1888.

20 Census of England, Wales and Scotland, piece 34273, 1911.

21 Mallwyd: Cyfarfod ysgolion, *Y Negesydd*, p.1, Jun. 23rd, 1899.

22 Dinas Mawddwy: School Board election, *Cambrian News*, p.7, Sep. 6th, 1901.

23 Census of England, Wales and Scotland, piece 5688, folio 21, 1871.

24 Aberangell: Inquest, *Cambrian News*, p.4, Mar. 7th, 1890.

25 Aberangell: concert, *Montgomeryshire Express*, p.8, Mar. 10th, 1891.

26 Dovey, Mawddach and Glaslyn Fisheries Board, *Cambrian News*, p.3, Apr. 29th, 1892.

27 Dinas Mawddwy: damwain, *Y Dydd*, p.5, Apr. 13th, 1894.

28 List of Mines in Great Britain and the Isle of Man, 1896. H.M. Stationery Office, 1897.

29 Barddoniaeth, *Y Negesydd*, p.4, Jul. 31st, 1896.

30 Farm to let, *Montgomery County Times*, p.4, Feb. 20th, 1897.

31 List of Mines in Great Britain and the Isle of Man, 1897. H.M. Stationery Office, 1898.

32 England, Wales & Scotland Census, piece 4239, folio 50, p.30, 1861.

33 The sale of Gartheiniog Slate and Slab Company, *Montgomery County Times*, p.5, Jan. 22nd, 1898.

34 Y Golofn Gymreig, *Montgomeryshire Echo*, p.4, Feb. 20th, 1897.

35 For disposal, *Cambrian News*, p.1, Nov. 4th, 1904.

36 List of Mines in Great Britain and the Isle of Man, 1908. H.M. Stationery Office, 1909.

37 Manuscript notes, reference Z/DDJ/46/1101/5, Gwynedd Archives.

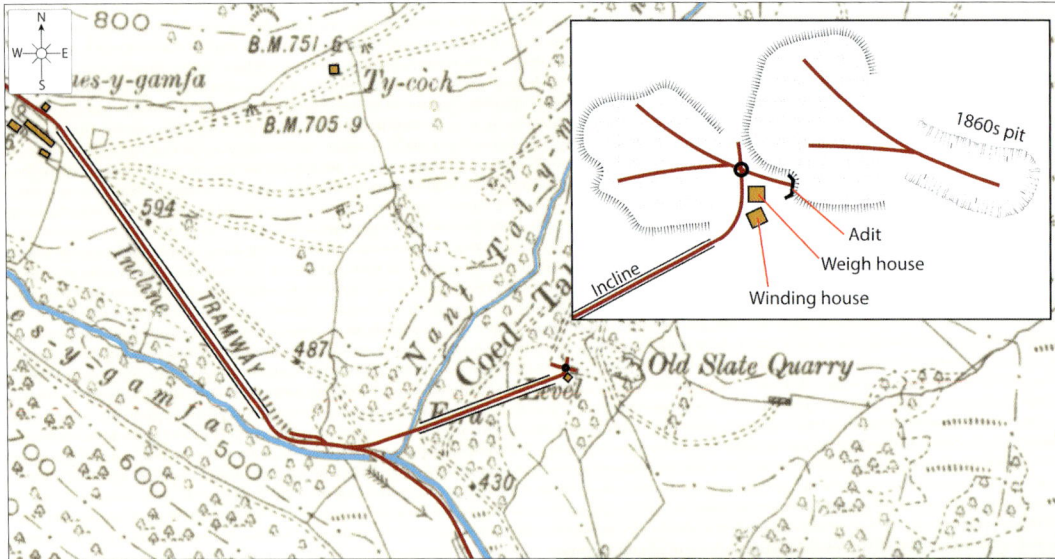

Left: Location of Talymeirin, showing the quarry and exit incline in relation to the Maesygamfa Tramway. The inset drawing shows a possible layout of the top of the incline, based on a brief 2015 ground survey.

Right: The remains of the upper pit in September 2020. [Ken Griffith]

Left: The Talymeirin adit that leads to the chamber used during the Inigo Jones period. Above the adit is the waste tip from the older open-pit working. To the right are the foundations of a weighbridge. [Dan Quine]

7: Talymeirin 1868-1919

About half a mile northeast of Gartheiniog Mill, high above Nant Maesygamfa lies Talymeirin, '*a small quarry, set in a lovely place*' as Bill Breese described it.[1] This Narrow Vein quarry only worked intermittently and with limited success.

The Early Working 1868-1876

Quarrying at Talymeirin started in June 1868, but it was not a success. The following year a legal dispute broke out over the failure of the quarry. The *Aberystwyth Observer* reported that the quarry had been a '*perfect failure*'; but it also noted that a level had been driven.[2] The *North Wales Chronicle* reported:

'*The court was occupied for five hours on Friday in the hearing of a case in which Evan Richards, quarryman, Machynlleth, was sued by John Hughes to recover £60, which had been advanced under misrepresentation as to the taking of a certain quarry known as the Tanymarian (sic) Slate and Slab Quarry, near Mallwyd, Montgomeryshire. His Honour gave judgment, for the defendant, but without costs.*'[3]

Despite this early failure, quarrying restarted on a limited scale and the quarry was active until at least 1870.[4] In April 1876, Talymeirin Farm was offered for sale, consisting of 274 acres of arable farmland and woodland.

'*There is also a Valuable Slate Quarry upon this property, which from its advantageous situation can be worked without the aid of machinery and it is believed from the reports that have been made upon it that the celebrated Aberllefenni and Hendreddu Slate Veins run through the property, and that it only requires a small capital to develop the quarry. There is an abundant supply of water, which can be utilized either for mining or agricultural purposes. The Farm is bounded by property belonging to Sir Edmund Buckley, Bart., Charles Edwards, Esq., and John Parry, Esq.*'[5]

Clearly, the quarry was not operating in 1876. The claim that the quarry could be worked without machinery implies that the cleavage and footing of the slate made it easy to work manually; this feature of the quarry becomes apparent in its later life.

The early workings of the 1860s were mainly in an open pit dug down into the Narrow Vein, with associated waste tips. A trial adit had been driven below the pit to test the vein at a lower level. There is only limited evidence of internal use of tramways, and there was no rail transport from the quarry to Aberangell. The slabs were taken out by horse or cart.[1]

Inigo Jones 1913-1919

The next mention of Talymeirin Farm comes in August 1908. Edward Morgan of Aberdovey was a significant landowner, owning much of the town of Machynlleth and large areas of farmland to the north. When he died, his estate was split up. Amongst his properties was the 'grazing farm' of Talymeirin, which presumably he had purchased in 1876. The farm was sold at auction to David Jones of Llwydiarth for £900.[6] Jones had inherited Maesygamfa Farm from his uncle John Richards in February 1908,[7] so the adjoining Talymeirin was a sensible addition to his holdings. The auction notice in the *Welsh Gazette* described the '*valuable slate veins traversing the lot*'.[8] There is no evidence that the quarry had been worked since 1870.

Late in 1913, Inigo Jones and Co. reported to the Home Office that they had taken a lease on the quarry at Talymeirin. They produced just five tons of dressed slate that year.[9] They ramped up slate production in 1914, just after their contract with Gartheiniog ended. Inigo Jones is a well-known name in the Welsh slate industry, with a long connection to the slab quarries of Mid Wales. It still operates the slate works at Y Groeslon, near Caernarfon.

Looking down the lower half of the Talymeirin incline. In the foreground is the approximate location of the passing loop with the lower section of the incline sitting in a very shallow cutting to maintain an even gradient. Nant Talymeirin can just be made out in the trees at the bottom of the valley; on the right side of the photograph is the ford across the stream. [Dan Quine]

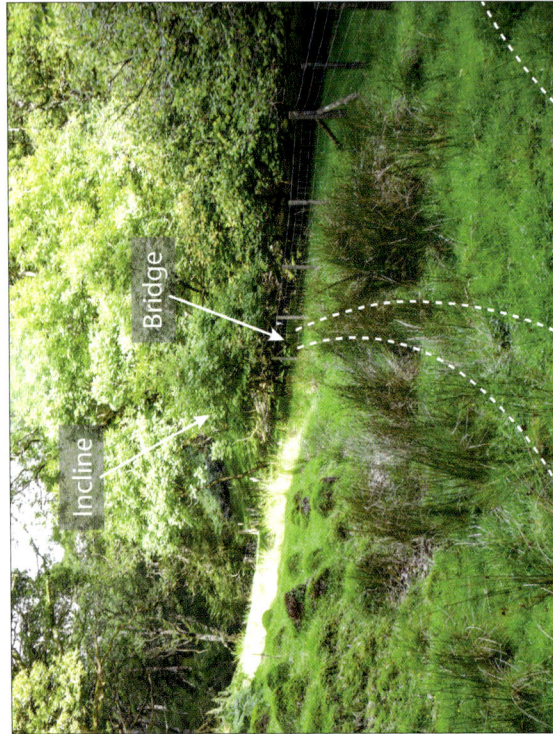

Right: The end of the adit at Talymeirin in 2019. Lying against the right wall are slabs that had been cut but not removed. The small chamber is off to the left at the junction, while the tunnel to the right extends a few dozen yards, and is partly backfilled with waste rock. [Iain Robinson]

Below: The crimp of the Talymeirin incline – the approximate location of the three rails of the incline is shown in red. The adit and winding house are in the bracken to the right of the fence. The incline is quite shallow and runs on a low slate embankment at the top. The waste tips from the Inigo Jones operations are off to the left of the photograph, beyond the incline. [Dan Quine]

Below Left: Looking up into the chamber roof at Talymeirin, showing slot working, in September 2020. Had the quarry continued, it is likely this slot would have been worked up until it met the floor of the pit above. The quarry could then be worked as a twll. This is the same method used to develop the lower twll at Maesygamfa. [Keith Whiddon]

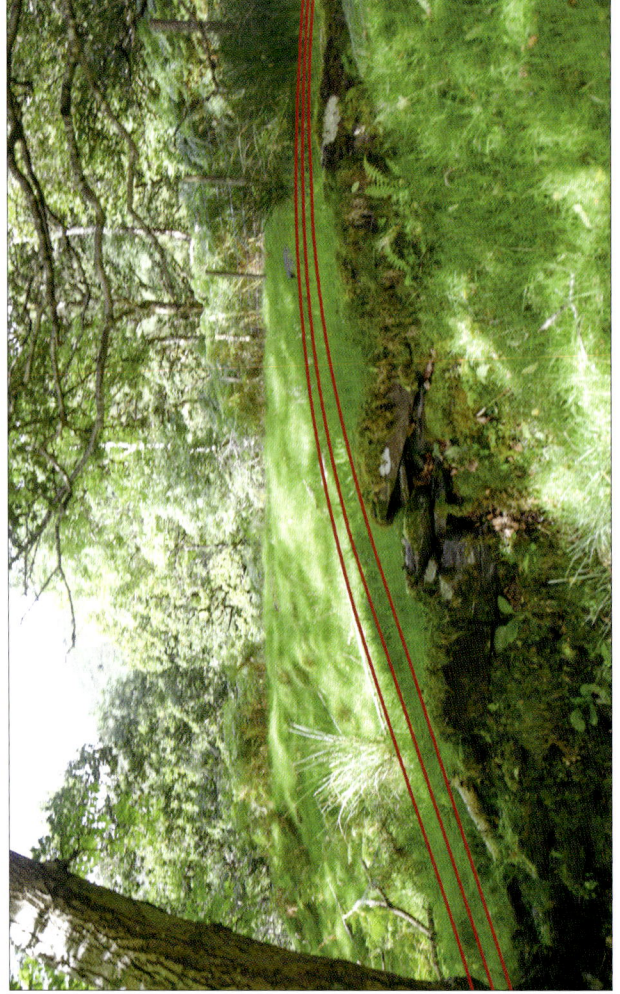

Above: Standing on the north bank of Nant Talymeirin, looking towards the quarry. The Talymeirin exit tramway crossed the stream on a bridge as marked, then joined the Maesygamfa Tramway, which can be seen on the right. The slate abutments of the bridge are still evident, and as late as 1988 at least one timber beam from the bridge was still in the river. The incline climbs away from the photographer into the trees. Wagons coming off the incline would be trammed westwards towards the foot of the Maesygamfa Farm incline and then run down to the Hendre Ddu Tramway by gravity. [Dan Quine]

54

Inigo Jones did not use the 1870s pit, instead working the lower adit, extending it to 159 yards in length,[1] ending about 150 feet below the pit. A start was made to open the end of the adit into a small chamber, working upwards into the vein. Beyond the chamber, a further tunnel was driven in an attempt to find the vein further north. This tunnel was abandoned and partly filled with slate waste from the chamber.

They also added a small dressing shed located near the adit entrance. This held a single sawing table, which was operated by 'Tom Siop' and Richard Williams of Abermynach Farm.[7] A three-rail incline with a small passing loop halfway down was laid down to the Maesygamfa Tramway.[1] Cozens[10] reports that the incline was laid in bridge rail, but flat-bottomed rails found on the site of the incline in 2015 suggest that at least part of it was laid in flat-bottomed rail. Bill Breese was sceptical that the brakesman at the head of the incline would have had a clear enough view of empty wagons waiting to ascend, but he was not able to talk to anyone who had worked the incline to confirm his suspicion. The first slabs sent down the incline were loaded onto wagons by Dafydd Roberts and hauled to Gartheiniog by Williams, where they were tested by John Parry.[1]

There was no production reported during 1915 when the quarry was officially suspended, though it is believed it did operate that year.[11] In 1916, Inigo Jones reported that the were employing five workers[12] at Talmeirin [sic]. All of Inigo Jones's production that year was for munitions work, mostly supplying electrical boxes for the War Office.[13]

As the war drew on, the workforce shrank; by 1918 and through 1919, the only employee was Thomas Thomas, of Tanyfron, who operated the quarry alone. This was a risky and difficult undertaking. Thomas had a reputation for great strength and was an efficient

Thomas Thomas and his wife Kate later in life. After his time at Talymeirin, he served as an officer with the Metropolitan Police in London.

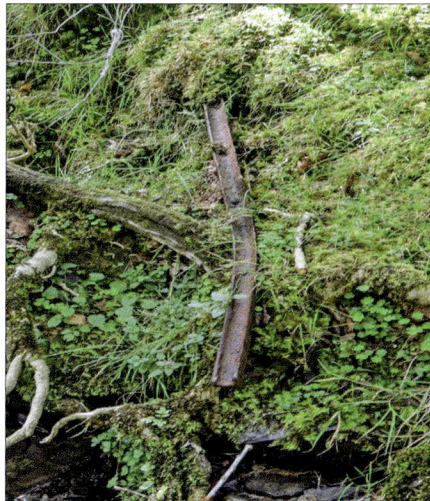

A length of light flat-bottomed rail at the ford across Nant Talymeirin. This is curved upwards and likely formed the foot of the exit incline. [Dan Quine]

machine operator and an excellent rockman. In 2020, the adit at Talymeirin still contained slabs in a variety of sizes.

Talymeirin quarry closed in 1919. Maesygamdda Quarry was still working when Inigo Jones took over Talymeirin, though it closed in 1914. The Maesygamfa Tramway was lifted from the quarry to the foot of the Maes-y-gamfa Farm incline, just north of where the Talymeirin incline joined the tramway. The rest of the tramway was left in place for the use of Inigo Jones, and this section of the tramway survived until the main Hendre Ddu Tramway was lifted in 1939. Slabs from Talymeirin would have been sent down to Aberangell, then shipped to Groeslon on the standard gauge.

References

1 Bill Breese, Notes on local quarrying and quarrymen, *Dolgellau Archive*, vol. ref ZM/6541/9, 1982.
2 Merionethshire: to quarry proprietors, capitalists and others - valuable quarry and freehold estate for sale, *Aberystwith Observer*, p.1, May 6th, 1876.
3 Machynlleth, *North Wales Chronicle*, p.5, Feb. 20th, 1869.
4 Document archive of Mr I. Robertson Williams, reference number 1938148, National Library of Wales.
5 Merionethshire: to quarry proprietors, capitalists and others. Valuable quarry and freehold estate for sale, *Cambrian News*, p.1, May 12th, 1876.
6 Sale of freehold estates at Machynlleth, *Montgomeryshire Express*, p.5, Aug. 4th, 1908.
7 Bill Breese, Bygone activities of the Angell valley, *Cambrian News*, Jan. 7th, 1977.
8 Important freehold sale: estate of the late Mr. Edward Morgan, *Welsh Gazette*, p.5, Jul. 30th, 1908.
9 List of Mines in Great Britain and the Isle of Man, 1913. H.M. Stationery Office, 1914.
10 Lewis Cozens, R.W. Kidner, Brian Poole, *The Mawddwy, Van and Kerry Branches*, Oakwood Press, 2004.
11 List of Mines in Great Britain and the Isle of Man, 1915. H.M. Stationery Office, 1916.
12 List of Mines in Great Britain and the Isle of Man, 1916. H.M. Stationery Office, 1917.
13 Women? Good Scott!, *Liverpool Daily Post*, p.8, Apr. 20th, 1916.

NOTICE.

Mawddwy Railway.

NOTICE is hereby given that pending Repairs to the Permanent Way the

PASSENGER TRAFFIC

will be

DISCONTINUED

as and from this date until further notice.

Chas. E. WILLIAMS,
SECRETARY & MANAGER.

MAWDDWY STATION,
17th April, 1901.

WHITRIDGE, PRINTER, OSWESTRY.

Left: Official notice of closure of the Mawddwy Railway to passenger traffic in 1901.

Below left: Brynderwen cutting, looking east towards the Wharf. The stonework of the walls is very high quality. The line is dropping at about 1 in 25 towards the road. Behind the wall on the right is Brynderwen house, on the left is the Capel Bethania cemetery.
[Dan Quine]

Below right: The deviation crossing Walton's land on a low stone embankment. The fine quality of the stonework is evident, with an identical style and material as the low embankments of the Maesygamfa Tramway.
[Dan Quine]

8: Heyday into Decline 1887-1914

The Bradwells were keen for Gartheiniog to succeed as it was on land leased from them, so they gave the quarry running rights over the Hendre Ddu Tramway. When Davies and Walton were developing Maesygamfa Quarry, they had no such rights. Indeed, E.H. Davies may have fallen out with the notoriously difficult Bradwells in 1882, when he left his post as manager of Hendreddu.

In 1887, Maesygamfa was starting to produce slab and needed a route to market. The best option was a tramway from the quarry to join the Hendre Ddu at Llidiart Dwbl. This would cross Bradwell land, and require running rights over their tramway. This drove the next major development of the Hendre Ddu Tramway.

The Clipiau 'Deviation' 1887-1897
Working the Original Route

By the mid-1880s, the Hendre Ddu Tramway was working well with the notable exception of the approach to Aberangell Wharf. The route over Clipiau was difficult to work, its extreme gradients a result of James Walton's refusal to allow the tramway to cross his land. At Aberdwynant (then known as Abermynach) the tramway passed on a causeway to the north of the house and over the Afon Mynach. It then climbed at a steady 1 in 30 to the summit in the middle of Clipiau and turned due east towards the school, dropping at 1 in 14. South of the school, the line swings sharply to the south[*] and drops precipitously to the wharf – this section has an average gradient of 1 in 9. At the bottom of the drop, the line turns sharply east and enters the wharf.

Working trains over this section was fraught with peril. Loaded wagons from Hendreddu were held in the loop next to Sied Wen until horses were available to work them into Aberangell. The climb to the summit was hard work: a single horse could haul two 1½ ton loaded wagons up the 1 in 30 gradient.[1] The main challenge was the descent to the wharf. The 1 in 14 drop to the school curve may have been possible using the wagon brakes alone, but the long 1 in 9 was not. A breeching strap allowed the horses to be attached to the uphill end of the wagons to help slow the descent,[2] and sprags were used to prevent runaways.[3] This could have been avoided by an incline from the school curve to the north end of the wharf, but the land required had been given to James Walton in the settlement of the 1865 dispute with the Mawddwy Railway.

---

[*] Cozens and Boyd describe a reversing neck south of the school. This is incorrect — contemporary maps show a curve.

Agreeing to the New Route 1887

There was a much better route for the tramway across Aberangell Meadows but these were owned by the Cwmllecoediog Estate. On 6th October 1887, a meeting was arranged between Jacob Bradwell and Davies and Walton of Maesygamfa. Owen and Mallory of Gartheiniog mediated the discussion. Owen and Mallory were apprehensive about their role; they were all too aware that Bradwell controlled half the water flowing into their quarry reservoir.[4]

James Walton had retired to his Dolforgan estate, and his son Frederick was now in charge at Cwmllecoediog. Edmund Buckley no longer owned the tramway, but his dispute of 1865 with James Walton coloured the negotiations. Frederick Walton offered to allow the tramway to be rerouted across the meadows, if Bradwell would allow Maesygamfa running rights over the tramway. Avoiding the expense and difficulty of working over Clipiau must have been very attractive to Bradwell and he readily agreed. Walton and Bradwell would share the cost of a new bridge across the Afon Mynach south of Aberdwynant and Walton would fund the construction of the new route across his land.

Walton's section of the tramway would charge 6d per ton of slate, 1s per month for passengers, 6d per wagon load of stone for construction. Bradwell imposed the same rates for traffic over his section of the tramway.[2] Bradwell agreed to pay £24 per year to Walton in compensation for the loss of land, and Gartheiniog would pay £12 per year. There was no fee for Maesygamfa as Walton was a co-owner of that quarry. These annual fees were payable in two instalments on Lady Day, the 25th March, and on Michaelmas, the 29th September, at Cwmllecoediog Hall. The fees would be reduced for any year in which a quarry was not in production.

Maintenance of the tramway, including the new deviation route, would remain the responsibility of Hendreddu. The extended Walton family and their servants were granted unrestricted use of the tramway. Bradwell agreed to provide two sidings to serve the Cwmllecoediog Estate, at positions to be determined later,[2] though they were never built. Walton insisted that the owners of the tramway could never seek to deny public use of the tramway, nor revoke any part of the agreement. The full agreement was signed by all parties on 5th October 1887.

Around this time Sied Ddu was added. A 150ft-long loop was laid about 1000ft west of Sied Wen and the new shed erected over it. Sied Ddu had 3ft-high stone walls fitted with wall-plates on which was secured a timber frame. The frame was covered with black felt, which explains the shed's name.[5] It was initially used as a workshop for the construction and repair of wagons, allowing the Hendreddu carpenter's shop to be used solely for quarry work.[6]

Building the Deviation 1890-1894

The deviation branched off from the original route west of Sied Wen. The new line ran to the south of the shed and along a new slate embankment to a bridge across the Mynach. On the far side, the line continued on an embankment passing a few feet from the south wall of Aberdwynant house. The siding into Sied Wen was removed when the deviation opened, and the shed appears not to have been used by the tramway after this. The ceir gwyllt were stored in the open.

East of Aberdwynant House, the deviation crossed the road from Clipiau to Allt Ddu and entered Aberangell meadows. A low slate embankment carried the tramway across the open fields, as it headed southeast. After 1000ft, it ran met the north bank of the Afon Angell and ran alongside it. The river drops through a series of weirs and waterfalls as it approaches its confluence with the Dyfi. The tramway held to the north edge of the river, dropping gently until it was about 1,000ft west of the Wharf. Here the deviation enters Brynderwen Cutting which passes through the shoulder of Pen y Clipiau. The tramway descends relatively steeply through the cutting before crossing the main village road and entering the wharf.

Work on the deviation probably started in 1891 or 1892, after the Maesygamfa Tramway was completed. Stone from Maesygamfa was used in the embankment across Walton's meadows. The deviation was completed in 1894, opening for traffic on the 6th June.[7]

Sometime after 1890, responsibility for the Wharf at Aberangell was transferred from the Hendreddu quarry

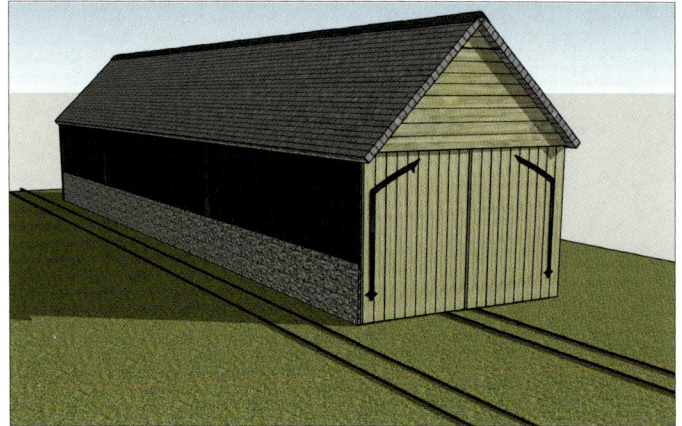

A computer reconstruction of Sied Ddu from the east, based on limited contemporary accounts.

In 1890, with Maesygamfa established, E.H. Davies looked to expand his empire further afield. He took a lease to dig for slate on land at Ffynnon Badarn in Cwm Ratgoed north of Aberllefenni, opposite the adits of Cymerau quarry. He obtained an agreement with R.D. Pryce, the owner of Aberllefenni, to allow a tramway across his land to join with the Ratgoed Tramway.[8] The trial was quickly abandoned and the proposed tramway was never built.

In 1891, Hendreddu advertised looking for 170ft of leather belting for the mill. The advertisement gives the purchasing company as the 'Hendreddu Slate Company, Congleton' reflecting the continued links between Jacob Bradwell and his hometown.[9]

On 1st April 1892, the Mawddwy Railway, the transport link to markets in Britain and abroad, closed without notice. Repairs were required for the bridges and track,[10] and Edmund Buckley was unable to finance them. The impact on the Dyfi valley was immediate and severe. A series of meetings were held to try to find a solution. The railway reopened on 1st August 1892,[11] much to the relief of the quarries, with one of the directors of the Mawddwy Railway loaning the money for repairs.[12]

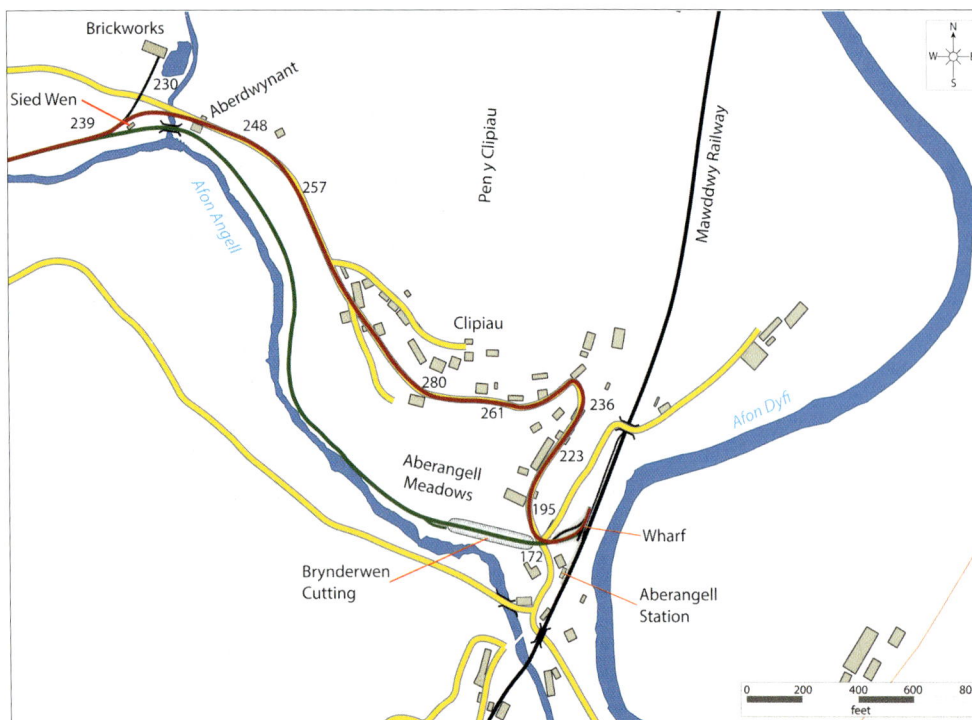

The two routes between Aberdwynant and Aberangell. The original northerly route is red and deviation is green. The original route passed to the north of Aberdywnant, climbed to the summit at 280ft in Clipiau, then dropped 40ft to the village school. Here it turned to the south and descended to the Wharf 70ft below. The numbers along the route are heights in feet above sea level. The deviation route crossing Aberangell Meadows and through Brynderwen cutting is much easier.

The Mawddwy Railway's closure brought it to the attention of the Board of Trade. They noticed that the railway was not in compliance with the Regulation of Railways Act of 1889, requiring interlocking points, and continuous brakes on passenger trains. In January 1893, the company ordered new point mechanisms from Dutton & Co.[12] When these were fitted, the siding at Aberangell station was extended to form a loop. The station platform was shortened at the north end to make room for the loop and was extended southwards along the embankment. The loop was fitted with a catch point at the downhill end.

The Tramway at Its Peak 1893-1900
Tramway Business, 1895-1897

Although Jacob Bradwell was in sole control of Hendreddu in 1895, he still had strong connections to his family business in Congleton. The Bradwell and Bullock families jointly owned a silk mill in the town, and part of the ledger for that mill survives.[13] The Bullocks owned Minllyn Quarry, supported by a mortgage from Dennis Bradwell. There is a page related to Hendreddu quarry in this ledger showing purchases and income from the quarry in 1895. These are the only Hendreddu-related entries in the ledger.

Expenses

		L	S	D
July 1st	W. Transon	£0	1	4
	G&D Sharp	£0	8	6
	Rugby Cement Co.	£0	11	4
July 23rd	E. Eccleston (tools)	£1	1	0
Aug. 3rd	G. Goodwin (trucks etc.)	£2	7	11
Aug. 6th	I. Hedger	£0	1	4
	I. Hodgson	£0	9	6
Aug. 24th	Choularton & ??? (wallpaper)	£1	8	4
Sept. 14th	W. Higginbotham (brushes)	£0	15	0
	I. Hodgson (stencil plate)	£0	4	0
Sept. 25th	Key and Bloor (oilcloth)	£1	3	0
Sept. 27th	J. Towers (templates)	£0	13	3
Sept. 30th	V.S.R. Co. (carriage)	£0	16	9

Income

July 1st	Bromley Hill Co.	£34	9	6

Profit and Loss Account: £1366 2s 3½d

This is Hendreddu at its peak, turning an annual profit of £1,366.*

Key and Bloor was the family firm of Jacob's wife Sarah. The VSR Co. which supplied a 'carriage' has not, unfortunately, been traced, and it is not clear whether the carriage is a road or rail vehicle. The 'trucks etc.' from G.

* about £143,000 in 2016.

Goodwin also remains a mystery; one possibility is this refers to the Leicester engineering company of Goodwin, Barsby & Co. Ltd which was founded in 1875 and specialised in quarry plant.

Trouble and Danger 1897-1900

The 1890s were a time of considerable strife in the Welsh slate industry. The quarrymen were organizing themselves on a wide scale to demand better wages and conditions. In 1891, the Royal Commission on Labour examined conditions in the mines of North Wales. W.J. Parry, the president of the North Wales Quarrymen's Union gave evidence:

'The numbers of persons engaged in [slate quarrying] was about twelve thousand…About one-fourth of the quarry men were unskilled. Wages were regulated by a system of bargaining…Wages were low and had been so for some years, the earnings being from 3s to 5s per day …The hours of labour varied: in winter, the men could only work during daylight. In summer, they worked between eight and a half and nine hours excluding meals. In winter, the average was about seven hours excluding meals; there were no houses or similar privileges provided for the quarrymen. Many of them resided two or three miles from their work and others (who had to go by rail) much longer distances.

When the state of trade necessitated a change in the rate of wages, the quarrymen at each quarry had to deal with their own employers. Lately, there had been only small strikes. In the end of 1885 and the beginning of 1886, there was an important strike in the Dinorwic Quarry. It lasted three months.

As to machinery. there was comparatively little used. In that respect,

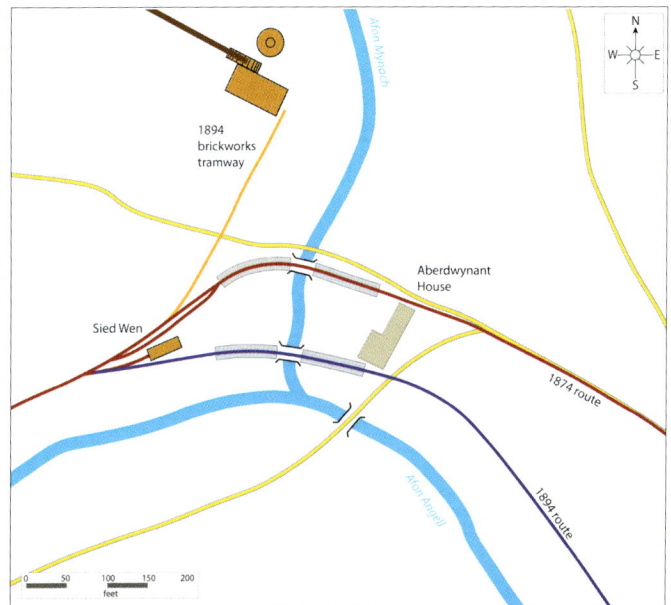

The area around Aberdwynant, showing the three pre-World War One tramway routes. The original line (in red) ran on a slate embankment and bridge across the Afon Mynach, passed north of Aberdwynant house and then climbed towards Clipiau. After 1894 the deviation ran on an embankment south of Sied Wen, over the Afon Mynach, immediately south of Aberdwynant house and across Walton's land to Aberangell. The 1894 brickworks branch used part of the original trackbed before swinging to the north.

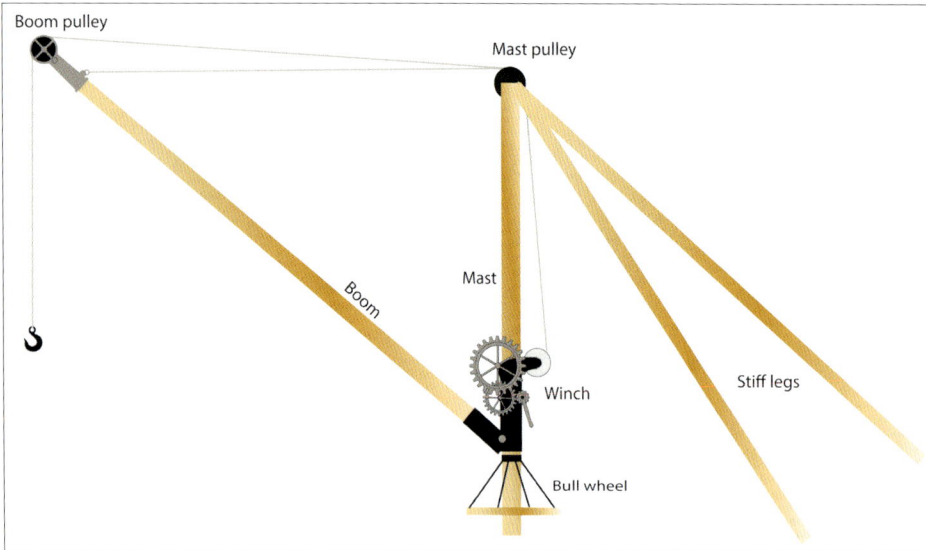

Sketch of the stiff leg derrick crane which was on the Wharf from 1874-1925. The general structure is correct, but the details of the winch are based on contemporary cranes. The bull wheel was turned to move the boom in an arc. The winch could independently raise and lower the boom and hook. The two legs on the right support the mast. The boom pulley is a single wheel, the mast pulley has two.

and fined 10s, with £1 8s 3d costs. The Inspector of Mines highlighted this prosecution in his annual report.[16] Hendreddu produced a record 1,150 tons of slate worth £2,800 in 1897, more than Abercorris and nearly double Minllyn.[17]

slate quarrying was in a more backward condition than most trades. Drilling, sawing, and dressing machines, also locomotive engines, were supplied by the masters. The men wished to see machinery employed more generally to do the hard work. Perhaps some fewer men might be employed; but the change would be good on the whole.'[14]

Relations between the managers and the quarrymen deteriorated throughout the 1890s. This culminated in the 1896 strike at Penrhyn Quarry in Bethesda. The strike lasted almost a year and had the side effect of producing a boom for other slate quarries.[15]

In 1896 Bradwell was prosecuted for failing to adequately fence off dangerous machinery in the mill. He was convicted

Hendreddu manager Edward Smith left the quarry between 1895 and 1898.[18] He had been appointed in 1883 and worked for the Bradwells through difficult times. He was succeeded as manager by Richard Jones, who lived at Hendreddu Cottages.[19]

The dangerous conditions in the quarries are illustrated in a series of accidents at Hendreddu. In April 1897, a large rockfall trapped the leg of quarryman Robert Jones who was seriously injured.[20] On 18th August 1898, miner Richard Roberts, 55, was driving a tunnel underground. The day before there had been a small fall and the men were warned by Richard Jones not to work in the same place until it had been properly examined. Roberts and his partner David Williams were nevertheless drilling there when a much larger fall killed Roberts instantly.[21] Williams, of Darowen, described the accident:

'They had had some stones down on the previous day. They commenced drilling each a hole. Deceased was at the furthest end of the level and witness close by. Deceased was anxious to finish drilling the hole which he had commenced the previous day. Witness told him he thought they had plenty to do to clear what they had already taken down and told the deceased so.

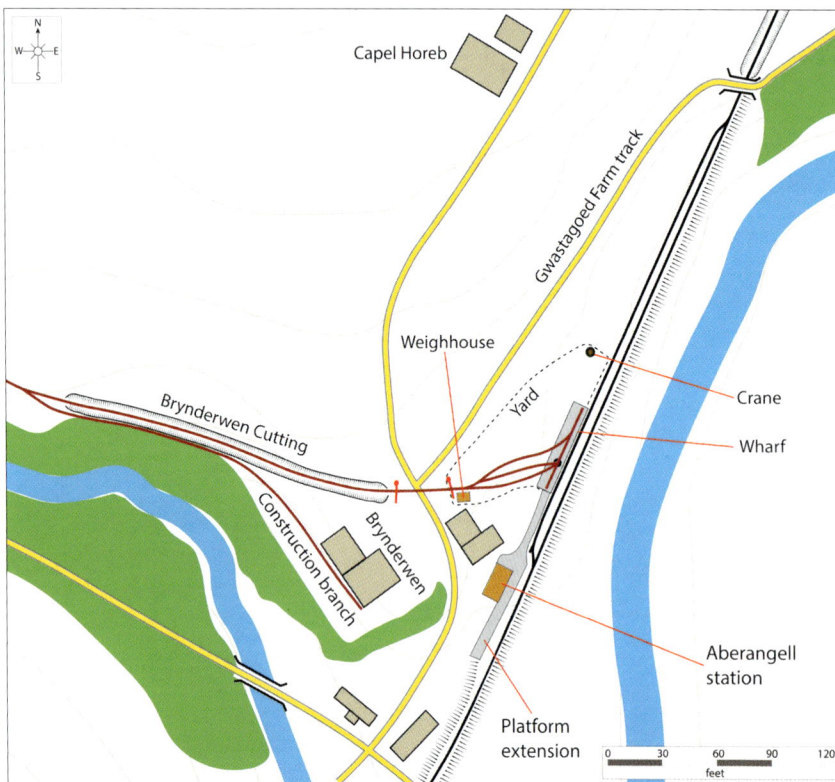

Aberangell in the late 1890s. The Mawddwy Railway was now responsible for the tramway on the Wharf and laid a new siding to the north of the existing loop and built a weighhouse at the entrance. The standard gauge siding was extended to form a passing loop. Capel Horeb was built in 1899, but Capel Bethania was not completed until 1903. E.H. Davies laid a short branch to allow stone from Maesygamfa to be used to build Brynderwen House This branch was probably used between 1895 and 1897. When the branch was lifted a short siding was left at the west end, which was used to hold loaded wagons before they were sent down to the Wharf.

Jack Bradwell's brickworks in 1902, with its impressive waterwheel. The short branch from the Hendre Ddu Tramway passed to the right of the shed. On the hillside behind the works is the edge of Coed Gwynion, which was felled during the First World War.

The remains of Bradwell's brickworks, in May 2016. The stone-lined gully to the left of the trees is the waterwheel pit. In the distance are the flooded clay pits. The Afon Mynach bends behind them. [Dan Quine]

Deceased was about to come away from the spot and had picked his tools up when the rock came down upon him. Witness did not expect the fall and did not consider the place dangerous. He had tested the rock in the usual way with a hammer. When deceased caught his tools up he said "What is there?" [Williams] heard a few small stones falling and immediately the rock fell. They had been blasting with black powder.'[22]

The inquest was chaired by the Merionethshire coroner W.R. Davies, with the Inspector of Mines O.R. Jones present at the coroner's request. The foreman of the jury was Edward Hurst Davies, ex-manager of Hendreddu and current manager of Maesyganfa. Davies was also an eye witness in a second inquest on the same day into a fatal accident at his own quarry. How he could act as an independent jury foreman is unclear, though this was common practice at the time. The inquest returned a verdict of accidental death – as usual in these cases no blame was apportioned to the quarry owners.[19]

In September 1899, there was another fatal accident at Hendreddu. Llewellyn Jones was preparing a bore for blasting when a 20-ton block of slate fell and crushed him against the side of the chamber.[23] The Inspector of Mines again made special mention of Hendreddu in his annual report to Parliament: '*For the last six years, the slate has been got by a method of undercutting which differs somewhat from that generally in vogue in North Wales, and is said by the owners to be more economical, but which, like most innovations, is eyed with suspicion by the ordinary working man*'. The inquest jury found the undercutting 'not satisfactory', but the inspector considered it as safe as other methods and allowed it to continue.[24] Jones left a widow and four children.

Jack Bradwell's Brickworks 1894-1910

Around 1880, Jacob's younger brother John Bradwell, generally known as 'Jack', moved into Cefngwyn Hall.[25] Jacob was spending most of his time at his London home in Ashfield House, Feltham.

Sometime before 1890, a small kiln was installed at Sied

Ddu and clay was dug from the river banks and fired into bricks.[4] In 1894, Jack Bradwell built a brickworks north of Sied Wen.[26] A 25ft-diameter overshot waterwheel drove the brick-making machinery and was fed by a mill race taking water from the Afon Mynach about a mile upstream. Clay was dug from the banks of the Mynach, then crushed, graded and pressed and fired in a kiln on the north side of the shed. The completed bricks were shipped out along a short branch on the Hendre Ddu Tramway, laid in light, chaired rail.

The 1887 deviation agreement was amended in July 1894 to allow Bradwell to move clay, coal, and timber over the tramway. Frederick Walton, not to be outdone, took the same rights under the amendment, but he never entered the brickmaking trade.[2] However, the provision for timber traffic over the tramway was to prove crucial.

The brickworks was operating by 1895 but was a commercial failure. The workers were not able to get the kiln to the right temperature and the bricks were too brittle. The brickworks closed in 1912.

Chapels, Weddings and Englynion 1899-1904

In 1896, Frederick Walton and Jacob Bradwell agreed to build a new Calvinist Methodist chapel in Aberangell. Walton donated the land[27] and Bradwell paid for the construction of Capel Horeb, which was completed in 1899. Horeb was the second chapel in the village, after 1833's Capel Hebron.

In 1900, the Welsh language newspaper *Y Negesydd* published an account of a trip to Aberangell written under the pseudonym 'Londoner'.[28] The writer spent Easter in the Dyfi valley. He met with several '*knowledgeable and funny acquaintances*' in Aberangell and travelled by '*narrow tramroad towards Hendreddu, with five (horses) in front*'. He recalls the valley in winter: '*narrow, cold, long, steep and ugly*'; but in spring he enjoyed travelling with '*the primroses covering the valley, with hundreds of Jackdaws screeching overhead*'. After much '*sweating and toiling (by the horses), I reached the head of the valley about midday. I went up to Hendreddu quarry and had a good cup of tea with the owner'* – Jacob Bradwell.

Jones sat down to lunch with the quarrymen, who took their *'eternal sandwiches and the tea they call Chinese Poison. It is no wonder that the faces of the miners are grey'*. The room for the 'boys' to eat their lunch was provided by Bradwell and *'credit is due to the gentleman for making so comfortable an arrangement for his employees' lunch hour'*. The workings impressed him: *'I have seen the quarry, and there is an inexhaustible wealth of slate in that mountain. Looming over us there were blocks of stone as huge as London Bridge'*.

That night he attended a local eisteddfod at Capel Horeb. He was particularly taken by the poems on the subject of the tramway's ceir gwyllt. He quotes the poem that won the 'highest approval of the majority':

Car gwyllt ydi henw hi
Myn'd lawr drwy y dyffryn heibio dy Ffri,
Drwy y gwynt, chwil di chwali,
Cipio chi ffwrdd 'sna watchiwch chi.

Which roughly translates as:

'Wild car' is your name,
From the peaks, through the valley, past Ffridd farm,
No ordinary thing, but reeling through the wind,
We watch you run noisily past.

Another englyn on this subject, from the same eisteddfod, has also survived:

Trip wibiol tua'r pebyll - tan lywiant
'Hen law' hyf ac anwyllt;
Awn i waered yn orwyllt
O'r creigiau, ar y Car Gwyllt[29]

Which loosely translates as:

An erratic trip to the chapel - on the brake
I am an 'Old hand', bold and furious;
On the wild, flowing descent
From the crags, on the Wild Car.

This probably describes a trip to chapel in Aberangell. 'Pebyll' literally translates as 'tents' but can mean the local chapel, and particularly meetings of the Independent Order of Rechabites, a temperance movement that had many adherents in Dyffryn Angell. 'Lywiant' means 'steering' but in this context likely refers to operating the hand brake. The local enthusiasm for riding the ceir gwyllt was clear. The accident of February 1877 and the warning from the coroner had not dampened that enthusiasm in Dyffryn Angell.

In 1902, the Upper Montgomery Presbytery (the Calvinistic Methodist council) decided to construct a third chapel in Aberangell, along with a schoolhouse.[30] The new chapel, Capel Bethania, was built between Capel Horeb and E.H. Davies's house, Brynderwen. It was completed in 1903 for £1,600.[31]

Around this time, Davies employed schoolboy John Pryce[32] as an occasional carriage driver, to take him from Brynderwen to the Penrhos Arms in Cemmaes. Edryd Pryce recalls his uncle John:

'John was a well-known local figure. Born in Aberangell in 1897, he was a cleaner on the Mawddwy Railway by age 14. He signed on to fight at the start of the First World War, and he was twice sent back from the front in France because he was underage. One time he spent three days hiding in a tree to avoid being sent back. Both times he found his way back to his unit on the front to resume fighting.

After the end of the war, he worked on the Cambrian Railways as a fireman and later driver where he earned the nickname Hellfire Jack. No one could touch him coming down Talerddig. He was a little man, but hard. There were no rules with Jack, he just went flat out all the time.'

With three substantial chapels in a village of little more than 100 inhabitants, religion was alive and well in Aberangell before the First World War.

Frederick Waltons's wife, Alice, was a formidable presence in Aberangell. When she arrived at Aberangell station, villagers were expected to leave the south end of the platform so she could be assisted into the First Class compartment. Under no circumstances were locals allowed to talk to 'Her Ladyship' unless she approached them first. One lad dared

Capel Horeb, when it was just three years old. Both the chapel and Ty Horeb next door, still stand.

Capel Bethania, newly built in 1903. The building is a fine example of the gable entry style of chapel popular at this time. It was constructed by local masons from slate quarried in Dyffryn Angell and opened by David Davies MP on 5th January 1903. Twenty years earlier, loaded slate wagons came down the steep road in the foreground.

Pen Pentre, around 1902 when it was the village store. John Parry was the station agent and the corner of the station building is visible on the right. The Hendre Ddu wharf is on the far side of the house.
[Courtesy Steve Culverhouse]

to speak to her on the platform. She inquired who he was, and learned he was the son of Mrs Jones of Walton Terrace. Word was then put about that none of the local quarries were to offer him work. None of them dared go against Lady Walton, and young Jones was forced to move to South Wales to work in the coalfields.[33]

The Penrhyn Boom and Bust 1900-1908

On the 22nd November 1900, the workforce at Penrhyn quarry began the three-year-long 'Great Strike', the longest in British industrial history. Lord Penrhyn wanted to break the Quarrymen's Union and end the bargain system.[14] In the short term, the strike was a boon for smaller slate quarries: In 1899, Penrhyn had produced nearly 100,000 tons, over 20 per cent of all Welsh production;[35] in 1901, almost nothing. Other quarries increased production to satisfy the demand that Penrhyn was no longer fulfilling.

Second Mawddwy Railway Closure 1901

The Mawddwy Railway was still suffering from a lack of investment. By the turn of the century, the track was unsafe, and the rolling stock was falling to pieces. Matters came to a head in 1901. On 17th April, passenger services were suspended[36] and on 25th May goods services were also stopped.[37] This had an immediate effect on the local quarries who again had lost transportation to their markets. Concerned quarry owners sent a deputation led by Jacob Bradwell, to talk with Sir Edmund.[38]

The Cambrian Railways were approached to take over the Mawddwy, but their Engineer advised against taking on the burden.[39] Solomon Andrews, who ran several quarries near Fairbourne, explored forming a company to take over the

Mawddwy and extend it to Bala,[40] but this came to nothing. In October 1901, goods trains started running three days a week, but these were threatened by the continued deterioration of the track.

At Hendreddu, Jacob Bradwell abandoned the open pits and removed Gillart's Incline. Work focused on the underground chambers accessed from the Level 1 adit.

Frederick James Walton and the Boer War

In February 1900, Frederick Walton's son Frederick James left to serve in the Boer War as a Lieutenant in the Montgomeryshire Yeomanry. More than 300 people were there to cheer him off, including quarrymen from Hendreddu, Gartheiniog and Maesygamfa.[41] His unit was involved in more than seventy engagements, though most were minor skirmishes. During the campaign he was promoted to the rank of Captain.

In June 1901, he returned to Aberangell amidst much celebration. A large dinner was laid on at Plas Cwmllecoediog with the Corris silver band attending, and several hundred well-wishers.[42] Captain Walton's return was treated as the end of a rather jolly adventure, the sort of thing every young man of means should enjoy in his prime. Frederick Walton, speaking at Cemmaes during the celebrations, said:

"*His son undoubtedly thought, when lying on the veldt with the stars above him, of his friends in the Dovey Valley who would come and grip him by the hand when he returned home. He hoped his son had done, as he always knew he would do, his best ... The*

Cemmaes Road celebrating the return of F.J. Walton from the Boer War with a banner which read, 'Welcome home from the seat of war to Lieutenant F. J. Walton. May God bless him for his patriotism'.

implements of war are now getting so terrible that it was quite certain that nations would think twice before they approached each other in conflict. In his opinion, the military engineer who invented the machines of destruction was the most benevolent man of the age and the best promoter of peace, as people would soon be afraid to go to war."[43]

In 1903, shortly after his return, Captain Walton was appointed a Justice of the Peace of Montgomeryshire.[44] He married his cousin Florence Margaret Walton on 10th February 1904.[45] In 1905, Frederick James and Florence had a daughter Margaret, followed in 1908 by a son, Rowland Henry.[46]

Margaret was known by her middle name, Petronella. In 1929, she married the film star Robert Newton, most famous for the 1950 film *Treasure Island* in which he starred as Long John Silver and originated Hollywood's idea of a pirate's accent. The marriage did not last long. Petronella lived at Coed-y-Cae during the Second World War and cooked a daily dinner for the children of Aberangell School throughout the conflict.[26]

Penrhyn Reopens 1902-1906

In 1902, with the Mawddwy Railway operating again and Penrhyn still on strike, Bradwell placed adverts in local papers seeking miners to work at Hendreddu with accommodation at the quarry cottages,[47] an indication of the improving prospects at the quarry. He was granted a patent for '*improvements of machinery for making slate ridge roll used on tops of houses*' in 1902.[48]

In December 1902, a lively debate was held at Aberangell led by Reverend R.W. Jones. The question was 'Which is harder, the life of a farmer or a quarryman?'. Lewis Davies and Richard Pughe put the case for the quarrymen, and they won the debate with four times the votes of the opposing side.[49]

By 1901, John Parry of Gartheiniog had moved to Pen Pentre, the house by Aberangell Station.[50] He had been appointed station agent, a caretaking role for the station and the wharf. Although not employed by the Mawddwy Railway he lived in the house rent-free and was paid a stipend of 2s a week.[51] His wife Jane Ann Parry kept a shop in the corner of the house.[50] Parry

Petronella Walton in the 1920s shortly before her marriage to Robert Newton.
[Courtesy John Lazenbury]

HENDREDDU

SLATE & SLAB COMPANY,

Hendreddu, near Aberangell, Mont·

ESTABLISHED 1864.

MAKERS OF SLATE SLABS
—FOR—

Lavatories, Urinals

CISTERNS,

Chimney Pieces, Billiard Tables,

AND EVERY DESCRIPTION OF

PLAIN SLATE WORK.

There is a Narrow Guage Tramway, 4 miles in length, running from Aberangell Station of the Mawddwy Railway up to the Quarry, through splendid scenery. Arrangements can be made for conveying Tourist parties to and from the Quarry at low fares on previous application being made to the Manager.

There are several easy and beautiful Mountain Walks, amongst them being to Dolgelley 7 miles, Corris 4 miles, and Aberllefenny 3 miles.

A Hendreddu advertisement from 1902. Bradwell was keen to encourage tourist traffic on the tramway, though it is doubtful that many took up the offer, considering the meagre passenger carriages, slow journey times and many local alternatives. The date of establishment of 1864 is incorrect but may indicate when David Hughes started exploring under Edmund Buckley's take-note.

stayed at Pen Pentre until 24th August 1924, when he moved to Corris to live with his daughter Elsie Edwards.[4] He died in Corris early in 1925.[52]

The Penrhyn strike ended in November 1903 and as the largest slate quarry in the world resumed production many of the other Welsh quarries suffered financially. Stockpiles of slate increased greatly in 1904 and 1905, with many quarries moving to short working or closing down.[35] The smaller, less efficient quarries of Mid Wales were particularly badly hit:

'*The unemployment question is prominent around Machynlleth at present and on all hands it is admitted that there are gloomy prospects for the winter months... many people have been thrown out of employment. This depression is particularly felt in the slate quarries. Several of the slab quarries in the Corris district have been closed and workmen have emigrated in large numbers to South Wales... The slackness of trade is attributed to foreign importations which were introduced at the time of the Penrhyn strikes which gave them a footing that is not likely to be lost hold of for some time.*'[53]

A wedding party at Plas Cwmllecoediog, probably for the wedding of Clarice Walton in July 1903.[34] The ceremony took place at Mallwyd church and the party was held at the Plas. Frederick and Alice Walton are in the centre. Clarice and her husband Henry Baird Leete sit in the front row on the right. The man standing on the far right of the group is the notorious Herbert Vivian, husband of Olive Walton.
[Courtesy John Lazenbury]

Hendreddu tried to widen the market for their products. In 1904, the quarry supplied slabs to Messrs Williams and White, who had a contract with Aberystwyth Town Council to supply kerbs and channels for road work and repairs to Aberystwyth Castle.[54] It was not just economic conditions that caused problems. During the first two weeks of August 1904, drought led several quarries in Mid Wales to temporarily stop working, including the Era Slate Quarry at Esgairgeiliog, Llwyngwern and 'some at Aberangell'.[55]

Bradwell's health was failing, and his tendency to be careful with his money became more pronounced in his later years. In October 1906, he was summoned before the Dolgelley Assessment Committee for non-payment of the poor rate.[56] The equipment at Hendreddu was ageing and there were no profits to pay for new machinery. A strike halted production for several months at the end of 1906. The men were upset at pay and working conditions and sent a deputation with their demands. Bradwell advised the men "*to go and pick their daisies elsewhere if not satisfied with the conditions within his quarry*".[5]

Tenders

TO BUILDERS AND CONTRACTORS.

FOR SALE, 1" and 2" slabs suitable for floors, chanelling etc., made into floors, according to plan and particulars. Estimates given for channeling and curbing, also window-sills, steps, linings, grave coverings, and headstones, on application to Hendreddu S. & S. Co., Aberangell, Mont
9c

Despite financial struggles, Hendreddu continued to advertise its products after the turn of the century. This one appeared in the *Welsh Gazette* on 6th. June 1907.

The Death of Jacob Bradwell 1907-1908

On 21st November 1907, Mines Inspector H.G. Williams visited Hendreddu and found the shafts, belts and saw tables in the mill lacked protective fencing. Bradwell said he was unwell and could not meet the inspector on the day, so a letter was sent requiring that the problems be fixed within two weeks. Williams returned to the quarry on 5th December to find that only a small part of the required work had been completed. Bradwell was charged with contravening Section 10c of the Factory Act, 1901 – an almost identical charge to the one that he had been convicted of in 1896.[57]

Bradwell wrote to say his 'precarious health' prevented him from attending the Dolgelley Petty Session in person, but that the work had now been completed. He also claimed that in his twenty-five years associated with the quarry, 'no accident had ever occurred': an untrue claim. Bradwell was fined 10s and costs.[58]

Early in 1908, Jacob Bradwell sued E.H. Davies for trespassing on the tramway and assault. Unfortunately, the details of the case are not recorded.

Bradwell died 17th June 1908. He left £7,685* to his wife Sarah. The Hendreddu quarrymen followed his coffin through Aberangell and on to Mallwyd Church cemetery on the day of his funeral.[59]

The case against Davies was dropped by Bradwell's executors[60] and Hendreddu shut down in June 1908. Some equipment was sold off, including a 'road trolley' which was acquired by the Corris Railway for £4 10s. This was used to transport loaded slate wagons by road from Rhiw'r Gwreiddyn quarry to the Corris railhead at Esgairgeiliog.[61]

* about £2 million in 2020.

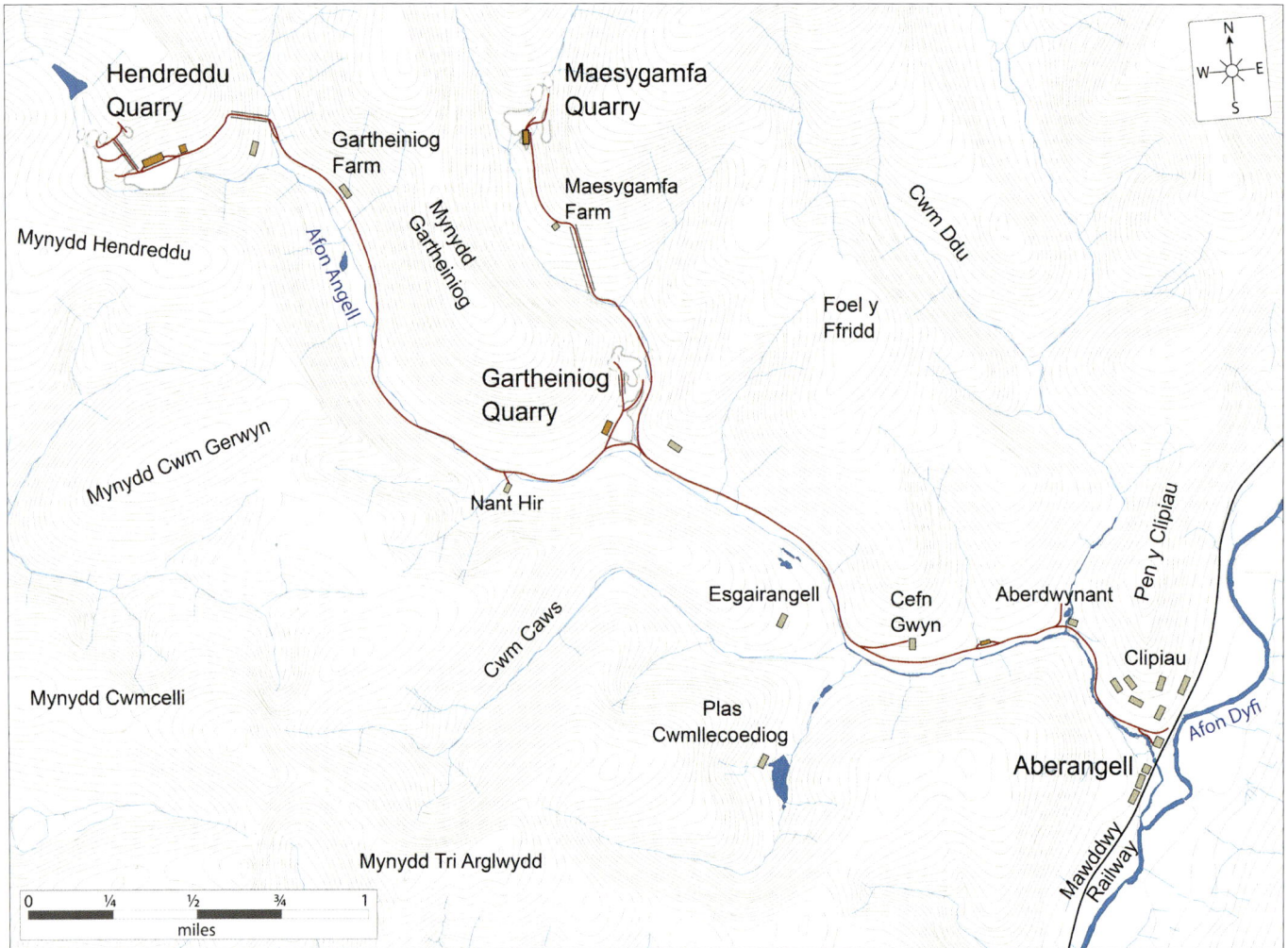

The tramway in 1901, at its greatest extent as a slate carrier. The tramways to Gartheiniog and Maesygamfa quarries are working and short branches serve Cefn Gwyn, Nant Hir and the brickworks at Aberdwynant.

Hendreddu produced just 186 tons of finished slate that year, a tiny amount for such a large quarry.[62]

Edward Hurst Davies bought Hendreddu in December 1908.[63]

The Mawddwy Railway's Third Closure and Revival 1908-1914

On 8th April 1908, the Mawddwy Railway closed for the third time.[64] The Cambrian Railways refused to take any more traffic at Cemmaes Road because 'our Boiler makers have reported both the Engines unsafe and dangerous to work'.[65] In truth the entire railway was dilapidated beyond practical use.

The slate quarries turned to road transport. Edward Hurst Davies contracted the Davies Brothers of Barmouth to carry Maesygamfa slab to Cemmaes Road. Between June and September 1909, they carried 29 tons and 15 hundredweight in twelve journeys.[66] The roughly surfaced roads of the district were unsuitable for heavy transport. The traction engines used weighed 7½ tons and hauled one or two trailers, each carrying up to 2½ tons of slab. In the three years up to June 1907 the Council spent £30 per mile per year on road maintenance; in the eight months after the

railway closed they spent £405 5s 1d on repairs.[66]

On 25th August 1909, David Davies, the Liberal MP for Montgomeryshire, paid Edmund Buckley £4,300 for the Mawddwy Railway Company.[67] He then persuaded the Cambrian to rebuild the line and run trains with their own rolling stock.[68] The Cambrian also purchased the crane on Aberangell Wharf for £10 from Bradwell's executors. It cost them another £15 to put it into working order.[69]

Imports of French and Belgian slate were on the rise and new asbestos tiles were proving a popular alternative to slate. In 1909, Hendreddu employed three men to operate the tramway.[59] The quarry restarted in early 1910, only to stop again later in the year.[70]

The Mawddwy Railway reopened on Saturday 29th July 1911, with David Davies leading the ceremony. As part of the celebrations, he received a 'massive inkstand made of slate quarried by three local quarries, Gartheiniog, Hendreddu and Maes-gamdda (sic) and subscribed for by a larger number of quarrymen and others who benefitted from the re-opening of the railway. The inkstand was enamelled in black with marginal decoration in gold and the fittings were of solid silver'.

John Parry's Attempted Takeover of Hendreddu, 1911

E.H. Davies put Hendreddu up for sale in early 1911. John Parry of Gartheiniog attempted to lead a takeover; he wrote to W.J. Evans, private secretary to David Davies,[71] on 17th June 1911: '*Re. my conversation with you last Wednesday at Aberangell in regard to Hendreddu Quarry - I am in communication with Estate Agent and hope to receive full particulars in the course of a few days.*'[65]

Parry did not receive the particulars, so he wrote his own report, which he sent to Evans on 5th July. The report is worth quoting in full, as it gives great insight into Hendreddu before the First World War, and illustrates Parry's charms as a salesman.

'Situation

The above quarry is situated in the Parish of Mallwyd in the county of Merioneth, within 4½ miles of Aberangell Station, on the Mawddwy Rly, which Rly has direct communication with the Cambrian Rlys at Cemmes Rd., thus affording easy and rapid access to all the interior markets, and also to all the ports of Gt. Britain and Ireland.

Facilities

A tramway is laid from Abermynach Farm up to the Quarry of a gauge of 2 feet (this is part of the Property on Sale with 2 feet outside each outer rail, making total breadth 6 feet) for a distance of 4 miles. Special provision is made for carriage of materials from other Quarries in the district along this Tramway, charge exacted being 6d per ton. Rail from Abermynach Farm to Aberangell Station - a distance of ¾ ml - is part of the Walton Estate and the rate is 6d per ton. The Tramways are extensive, well-laid and conveniently placed for Quarry development including an incline in good condition.

The Vein

Under the late management only one vein was wrought upon, 25 to 30 yards thick. The excellent results that have been secured in connection with this vein, which is identical with the Aberllefenni, Ratgoed & Gartheiniog Quarries's vein speak well of its unexcelled quality, and promise highly satisfactory produce. It has excellent longitudinal direction and dip, and is practically inexhaustible. Within my personal knowledge 80 to 100 tons per month have been produced by 25 to 30 men, but with efficient and correct opening there is ample vein capacity to yield 300 to 400 tons of raw material per month. The vein is well defined and separated from the surrounding uncleavable country rock, free from stripes and other objectionable discolourations, with foot and back joints so placed that slabs of any commercial size can be secured. It runs to meet the Ratgoed and Aberllefenni Quarries, and is part of the permeating vein. It is a noteworthy point that the waste in working would be exceedingly small for bearing and underlay is similar to those of above mentioned Quarries. Further, I have no hesitation in stating, following my wide experience in Quarry management that the deeper this vein is worked, the cleavages would become more parallel, and consequently more adapted for the Production of Slates as well as Slabs.

Method of Working

There are two or three Galleries at least, already driven from the surface to meet the vein. One Chamber is in fair condition to produce blocks at the shortest notice, but in order to render justice to the Quarry it is imperative to open new Chambers for future use. All these must be underground, and would vary in their opening from 20 to 25 yards by the thickness of the vein. The Machine House which contains the Machineries or Plant for manufacturing new materials, covers a considerable area. The Plant consists of 14 sawing and 6 planing tables, connected with a main shafting driven by a powerful turbine worked by water which gives a motive power of c. 60 to 80 H.P. Two reservoirs in splendid position are connected with the turbine by cast iron pipes. The importance of an ample supply of water as motive power cannot be overestimated as it reduces cost of manufacture to a minimum, and enables the fortunate possessors of this natural force to compete at great advantage with those who have to use steam as a necessity.

A Rough Inventory of Working Materials on Quarry

Tilling machine, grinding stones, cranes to shift blocks in machine house.
Good rolling stock of iron waste-waggons
18 slab trucks to transport slabs from Quarry to station
Powder magazine. Weighing machine (5 ton limit)
Turn-tables and cranes inside chamber
Timber sawing machines and other miscellaneous instruments indispensable to the working of this concern.

General Remarks

In Quarry Environments are the Six Cottages (rented at 10/- per month). One barracks that has lodged 15 to 20 men and a well-erected Manager's Office
The Past history of this Quarry, the productive possibilities of the vein, the fact that slab can be manufactured immediately, I conclude to be favourable and ample inducement for introduction of capital and a more extensive and energetic development. If this Quarry were worked in a practical, systematic and economical manner by a person of approved ability in the Trade, everything tends to substantiate my firm belief that highly remunerative results would accrue from the undertaking.'

Parry had plenty of enthusiasm but did not have the capital to purchase and work Hendreddu. Evans passed the report to David Davies. On 18th July, Evans wrote to Parry to say that '*Mr. David Davies yesterday … directed me to inform you that he regrets that he cannot see his way to take any financial interest in this quarry*'. Not easily deterred, Parry attended the grand reopening of the Mawddwy Railway on 29th July where he collared Davies and extracted a promise to take a closer look at Hendreddu. Hearing nothing more from the MP, Parry wrote a rather peevish letter at the end of September :

'*The agent of the Hendreddu Estate has asked me to communicate to him any new developments in regard to purchase of the above. In all probability you have forgotten the promise you made at the opening of the Mawddwy Railway to come and inspect the Quarry at your earliest convenience. I should be pleased to hear whether you intend to adhere to your promise or no. Awaiting the*

The inkstand presented by the Aberangell quarrymen to David Davies to celebrate the reopening of the Mawddwy Railway. The elaborately carved slab shows the exquisite craftsmanship of the workers.

very kind favour of your reply.'

The reply he received from Evans made the MP's position clear:

'I have not forgotten your wish that I should have a look at the Hendreddu Quarry, but I spoke to Mr. Davies again on this question, and, as he had definitely decided that he would not interest himself in the Quarry, I thought that no good purpose could be served by a visit to Aberangell. I am quite sure that he will not alter his decision and, therefore, that you must consider the matter closed.'[65]

The End of the Buckley Baronets 1883-1919

Despite his bankruptcy in 1876, Sir Edmund Buckley continued to live at the grand Plas yn Dinas. In 1883, his first wife, Sarah, died aged 45.[72] In 1885, he married Sara Mysie Burton, the widow of a Chicago businessman.[73] 1885 also saw his son, Edmund, marry Harriet Olivia Louise, daughter of the Reverend Maurice Lloyd;[74] the following year the newlyweds had a son, Edmund Maurice Buckley.

By 1893, Edmund's health was declining, and his youngest son William took over as acting agent for the Aberhirnant Estate.[75] In 1900, ill-health meant Edmund Buckley had to move out of Plas yn Dinas and relocate to Aberhirnant Hall, near Bala.[76] William died in 1909.[51]

On 21st March 1910, Sir Edmund Buckley died at Aberhirnant.[77] Thus ended an extraordinary life, during which he transformed Dinas Mawddwy, spent over a decade as an MP, lost a great fortune and to a small extent recovered

The notice of sale of Hendreddu quarry that appeared in the *Cambrian News* of 13th September 1912.

his local influence. What is clear is that the 1st Baronet loved Wales. He married a Welsh woman and despite his connection to the north of England, chose to live almost all his life in Mid Wales. He is buried at Rhosygwalia Church, less than a mile from Aberhirnant Hall.

Sir Edmund Buckley's eldest son, also called Edmund Buckley, survived him. Unfortunately, he had inherited his father's profligate ways, spending recklessly while at Oxford, and after graduating. In late 1902, he left Wales for British Columbia, to escape his debtors, leaving his wife and young son behind. He was declared bankrupt in January 1903 owing £5,789. He returned to Wales in 1911 shortly after his father's death, to settle the estate and his debts. By arrangement with the courts, he paid 7s 6d for every pound of debt.[78] He also assumed the Baronetcy from his father, becoming Sir Edmund Buckley, 2nd Baronet. He died at Aberhirnant Hall in 1919 and was the last Baronet of Mawddwy.[74]

The Years Before the War

The slate industry fell into a deep depression in the decade before the First World War. Eight quarries at Blaenau Ffestiniog closed and Oakeley laid off 350 workers in 1909 alone. Many workers left the slate districts now haunted by unemployment and low wages.[14]

After 1908, E.H. Davies kept the Hendre Ddu Tramway running, though he had no capital to invest and the track gradually deteriorated. Between 1910 and 1914 trains mostly served Gartheiniog and Maesygamfa, though goods and passengers went further up the valley.

The Walton family continued to expand their empire in the pre-war years. In the 1890s, Frederick Walton had founded the United Flexible Tubing Company in London to exploit his oil-based sheeting patents. Around 1910, F.J. Walton became a director of the company. Amongst his fellow directors were Lord Berkeley Paget and William Kaznow Bowley.[79] Paget was the nephew of Lord Alfred Paget, a director of the North Staffordshire Railway and a principal investor in the Cambrian Wynne quarry[80] at Esgairgeiliog. William Kaznow Bowley's family came from Melton Mowbray, and he was a cousin of William Bowley who would be a key player after the First World War.

E.H. Davies's attempts to sell Hendreddu came to nothing, and in early 1914, he reopened the quarry on a limited scale. By this time many quarrymen in the district had moved away[81] and Davies struggled to find enough men willing to work in the quarry.

War was now imminent, and the conflict was about to change life in Dyffryn Angell forever.

John Parry at Bethania Chapel, just before the First World War. The minister, R.W. Jones stands at the back. From the left in the front row are Thomas Breese, Edward Jones, Parry, D. Owen and Robert Davies.
[Gwyndaf Breese collection]

References

1   Martin Doyle, *A Cyclopædia of Practical Husbandry and Rural Affairs in General*, William Curry Jun. and Company, 1839.
2   Gwyndaf Breese, The deviation, unpublished manuscript.
3   Gwyndaf Breese, The Angell Valley Tramway. Unpublished manuscript.
4   Bill Breese, Notes on local quarrying and quarrymen, *Dolgellau Archive*, vol. ref ZM/6541/9, 1982.
5   Bill Breese, Bygone industrial activities in the Angell valley, *Cambrian News*, Jul. 9th 1976.
6   Gwyndaf Breese, Hard times on the tramway, unpublished manuscript.
7   Bill Breese, Notebook on tramroad and local quarrying, *Dolgellau Archive*, no. ref ZM/6541/5, c. 1970.
8   Alun John Richards, *Slate Quarrying at Corris*, Carreg Gwalch, 1994.
9   Miscellaneous, *Manchester Courier*, p.2, May 4th, 1891.
10   A Welsh railway stopped, *Cambrian News*, p.5, Apr. 15th, 1892.
11   Cambrian Railways company. Half-yearly meeting, *Montgomeryshire Express*, p.6, Aug. 16th, 1892.
12   Mawddwy Railway, *Cambrian News*, p.8, Feb. 10th, 1893.
13   Bullocks and Bradwells Records, ref GB 0220 Z/M/1090. Meirionnydd Records Office, Dolgellau Archive.
14   R. Merfyn Jones, *The North Wales Quarrymen, 1874-1922*, University of Wales Press, 1982.
15   Penrhyn Quarries, *North Wales Times*, p.3, Dec. 5th, 1896.
16   Henry Hall, Mines and Quarries report. Her Majesty's Secretary of State for the Home Department, 1897.
17   List of Mines in Great Britain and the Isle of Man, 1897. H.M. Stationery Office, 1898.
18   Census of England, Wales and Scotland 1901, piece 5060, folio 113, p.23.
19   Fatal accident at Hendreddu Quarry, *Montgomery County Times*, p.3, Aug. 27th, 1898.
20   Aberangell: damwain, *Y Negesydd*, p.1, Apr. 23rd, 1897.
21   Fatal accident at Hendreddu Quarry, *Towyn-on-Sea Times*, p.6, Sep. 1st, 1898.
22   Aberangell adjourned inquest, *Cambrian News*, p.6, Sep. 2nd, 1898.
23   Terrible death of a quarryman, *South Wales Daily News*, p.4, Sep. 8th, 1899.
24   Underground: falls of ground, in Reports from Commissioners, Inspectors and others: Mines, vol. 5, Her Majesty's Stationery Office, 1900.
25   1881 England, Wales & Scotland Census, piece 5544, folio 4, page 1, 1881.
26   Bill Breese, A Welsh Village at War: 1939-1945, unpublished manuscript, c 1970.
27   Upper Montgomeryshire Monthly Meeting, *Montgomeryshire Echo*, p.8, Oct. 5th, 1901.
28   Am Dro I Gwm Gartheiniog, *Y Negesydd*, Apr. 27th, 1900.
29   W. Gwenlyn Evans, Y geninen: cylchgrawn cenedlaethol. 1900.
30   Trefaldwyn Uchaf, *Y Goleuad*, p.11, Jul. 4th, 1904
31   The C.M. Presbytery, *Montgomeryshire Echo*, p.8, Jun. 25th, 1904.
32   National School Admission Registers & Log-Books, Aberangell School, 1910.
33   Bill Breese, A village of bridges, unpublished manuscript.
34   Marriages, *London Daily News*, p.1, Jul. 7th, 1903.
35   The Financial Review of Reviews, Investment Registry Ltd, 1908.
36   Welsh railway closed, *Welsh Gazette*, p.6, Jun. 6th, 1901.
37   Dinas Mawddwy: The Mawddwy Railway, *Welsh Gazette*, p.5, May 16th, 1901.
38   The Mawddwy Railway, *Welsh Gazette*, p.4, Jul. 4th, 1901.
39   The Mawddwy Railway: purchase proposal declined, *Towyn-on-Sea Times*, p.6, Jun. 20th, 1901.
40   Solomon's latest, *Rhyl Journal*, p.8, Oct. 26th, 1901.
41   Aberangell: off to the war, *Cambrian News*, p.7, Feb 16th, 1900.
42   Aberangell: dychweld o'r rhyfel, Y *Negesydd*, p.3, Jun. 21st, 1901.
43   Return of Lieutenant F.J. Walton, *Cambrian News*, p.2, Jul. 19th, 1901.
44   Gossip and Rumour. From various sources, *Welsh Gazette*, p.8, Mar. 12th, 1903.

45   Marriage of Mr. F.J. Walton, Cwmllecoediog, *Towyn-on-Sea Times*, p.6, Feb. 11th, 1904.

46   The fastest gun in the East, *Newcastle Evening Chronicle*, p.7, Oct. 14th, 1975.

47   Yn eisiau, *Y Negesydd*, p.2, Jan. 30th, 1902.

48   Local patents, *Western Daily Press*, p.5, Oct. 31st, 1902.

49   Aberangell, *Y Negesydd*, p.1, Dec. 4th, 1902.

50   1901 England, Wales & Scotland Census, piece 5252, folio 15, p.12, 1901.

51   Lewis Cozens, R.W. Kidner, Brian Poole, *The Mawddwy, Van and Kerry Branches*, Oakwood Press, 2004.

52   Engand and Wales Deaths 1837-2007, Dolgelly, p.486, vol. 11B.

53   The slate trade, *Cambrian News*, p.6, Jan 8th, 1904.

54   Aberystwyth Town Council, *Cambrian News*, p.6, Jan. 8th, 1904.

55   Machynlley: the drought, *Welsh Gazette*, p.5, Aug. 18th, 1904.

56   Petty Sessions: non-payment, *Cambrian News*, p.3, Oct 5th, 1906.

57   Petty Sessions: breach of Factory Act, *Cambrian News*, p.8, Dec. 20th, 1907.

58   Unfenced machinery, *Aberystwith Observer*, p.2, Dec. 26th, 1907.

59   Bill Breese, Tro ar fyd, *Cambrian News*, Jul. 17th, 1908.

60   Dolgelly: County Court, *Cambrian News*, Jul. 17th, 1908.

61   Peter Johnson, *An Illustrated History of the Great Western Narrow Gauge*, Oxford Publishing Co., 2011.

62   List of Mines in Great Britain and the Isle of Man, 1908. H.M. Stationery Office, 1909.

63   Rhosllanerchrugog a'r cylchoedd, *Baner ac Amserau Cymru*, p.12, Dec. 16th, 1908.

64   National Archives, Report of Mawddwy Railway meeting with the Board of Trade, Dec. 7th, 1909.

65   Letter, reference RAIL 1057/580/C, National Archives.

66   Claim for extraordinary road: the Mallwyd road, *Cambrian News*, p.3, Sep. 10th, 1909.

67   Records of Negotiations with Sir Edmund Buckley, National Archives, reference RAIL 1057/580/C.

68   Dinas Mawddwy Railway, *Cambrian News*, p.8, Sep. 17th, 1909.

69   Glyn Williams, The Mawddwy Branch, Part Two — Goods Only, *Great Western Railway Journal*, no. 60, Autumn 2006.

70   Prospectus of the National Welsh Slate Quarries Ltd, *Sheffield Daily Telegraph*, p.10, Mar. 17th, 1920.

71   Montgomery County Council and the Mawddwy Railway, *Montgomeryshire Echo*, p.5, May 22nd, 1909.

72   Sarah, Lady Buckley, *Illustrated London News*, p.22, May 12, 1883.

73   Marriages: Buckely-Burton, *Morning Post*, p.1, Jan. 2nd, 1886.

74   *Debrett's Peerage, Baronetage, Knightage & Companionage,* Debrett's, 1923.

75   Saturday, *Cambrian News*, p.7, Oct. 13th, 1893.

76   Bill Breese, A Glimpse of the Past, *Cambrian News*, Mar. 18th, 1977.

77   Death of Edmund Buckley, *Northern Daily Telegraph*, p.10, Mar. 22nd, 1910.

78   A Baronet's debts: Sir E. Buckley's admissions in court, *Liverpool Echo*, p.4, Jul. 11th, 1914.

79   United Flexible Tubing Company, *Gas World*, vol. 58, 1913.

80   Money market and City news, *Morning Post*, p.8, Aug. 15th, 1870.

81   Gwyndaf Breese, Timber Tycoons, unpublished manuscript.

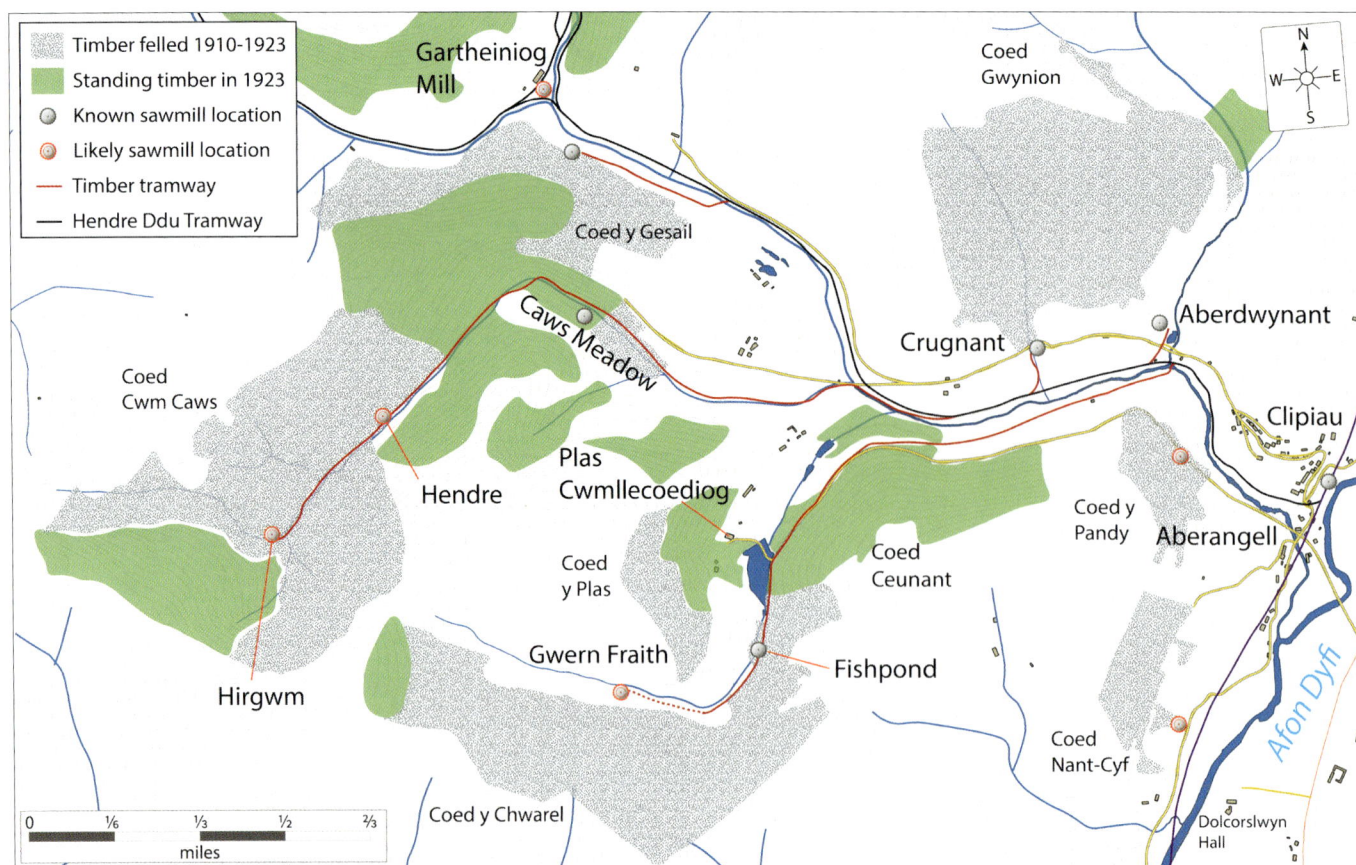

The woodlands west of Aberangell and the timber tramways built to serve them during the First World War. The woodlands in grey were felled between 1914 and 1922; the green woods were standing in 1923. The known tramways and sawmills are shown, along with likely sawmill locations. The names 'Fishpond', 'Gwern Fraith', 'Caws Meadow', 'Hendre' and 'Hirgwm' are modern, based on local landmarks.

9: The Tramway During the First World War

The First World War accelerated the decline of the slate industry. Germany had been a significant export market, and the war depressed private home construction: the 1915 Rent Act capped rent rises and only 17,000 new homes were built in 1916.[1] Quarries across Wales reduced production, and many closed outright. But demand for timber rose sharply, providing new opportunities in Dyffryn Angell.

The Fall of Slate

In August 1914, the remaining slate quarries were in a precarious state. Edward Hurst Davies had reopened Hendreddu a few months earlier, but the mill machinery was worn out and only a handful of men were willing to work in the hard conditions underground. On 11th November 1914, Davies bought land from James and Richard Pugh, the owners of Nanthir farm[2] and he attempted to work the slate there, but nothing came of it. Hendreddu operated from 1914 to 1916, but was on short hours in 1917 and closed completely in early 1918.[3]

Gartheiniog lost the Inigo Jones contract in 1914. Longtime owner Henry Mallory was in poor health and had retired to Bath, leaving John Parry in charge of the quarry, but it closed in 1916. The only glimmer of hope was the tiny Talymeirin quarry, which Inigo Jones leased in late 1913 and developed as a source of slab to replace the Gartheiniog contract. Talymeirin was the only quarry that worked throughout the war.

The Hendre Ddu Tramway

In 1914, the Hendre Ddu Tramway was in a decrepit state, particularly the track on Aberangell Wharf. On 17th July 1914, three weeks before Britain entered the war, John Parry wrote to Henry Warwick, the Superintendent of the Cambrian Railways, about the 'great want of repairs to the station tramway and turntable… I am given to understand that the Tramway Co's property only extends to the double-gate at the entrance to the enclosed quarters of the Station. During my experience of 25 years it has always been the practice for the Rly. Co. to make repairs in the enclosure and there are clear evidences of their work e.g. the rails are of a different size and type'.[4]

On 17th July, Warwick wrote to his Chief Engineer George McDonald: 'the tram line is in need of repairs; only 2 of our wagons [can be loaded] at the same time instead of 4 or 5, turntable requires repairs'. On 14th October, McDonald replied: 'I do not think the Company should be liable for the tramway … In no other case that I know of, however, are we responsible for narrow gauge tramways laid into our Station Yards.'[5]

With Parry's approach not showing any results, Edward

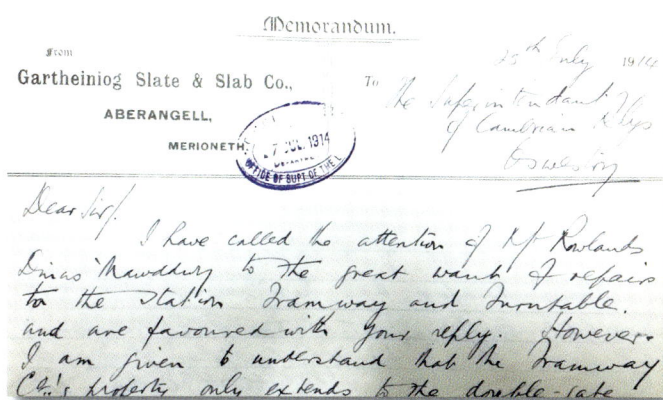

The start of John Parry's letter to the Cambrian Railways about the state of the trackwork at Aberangell Wharf. [National Archives]

Hurst Davies wrote to the Cambrian on 5th February 1915 complaining that one of the rails was loose on the turntable, causing them 'very great trouble'. The Cambrian once again tried to resolve who was responsible for the repair of the turntable and track. They asked Charles Williams, the former manager of the Mawddwy Railway, who responded on 23rd February:

'I was under the impression at first that the Turntable and the Tram Lines on the Aberangell Station Yard belonged to the Quarry Companies but on thinking the matter well out I think I am right now in saying that they belong to the Mawddwy Railway Company because I have an impression that this matter was set right by me by acquiring to purchase the Turntable and the Rails, and I think I bought them from Mr. Jacob Bradwell of the Hendreddu

Track on Aberangell Wharf shortly after the Second World War. These heavy, flat-bottomed rails are unlike the lighter rails used elsewhere on the tramway. The rails on the Wharf were not removed in 1939 because they were owned by the Great Western Railway. [Bill Breese collection]

Quarry. I have also an impression that the Railway Company bought a new Turntable from Messrs Turner Bros of Newtown, or at any rate if we did not buy a new one we had some repairs done by them to the Turntable. I am giving you this from memory as I have no Books to refer to but I would suggest that an inspection be made of the old Mawddwy Company's Books when probably the transaction will appear therein.'

This refers to the transaction of around 1894 when the Mawddwy Railway took over the Aberangell Wharf. The Cambrian tried to find the Mawddwy Railway's accounts, but after two months of effort, they concluded the books had been lost. They wrote to E.H. Davies acknowledging they owned the land and would repair the tramway and turntable. However, they expected the Hendreddu company in return to pay rent to use their facilities. Davies said that given the poor state of the slate industry, the best he could do was pay a nominal £1 annual rent.

On 2nd June 1915, E.H. Davies wrote to Samuel Williamson, the Cambrian General Manager, in a rather desperate tone: '*We cannot get through with our slates. The rails are absolutely loose so our trams are off continuously - the men in my employ who bring down these trams are so disgusted at having to lift weights of from 2 to 3 tons on to the rails that they have given me notice to leave at end of present week owing only to this.'*

Williamson promised that the repairs would happen the next week, and Davies agreed to pay the £1 rent for use of the Wharf. There was one more twist in this tale. On 16th

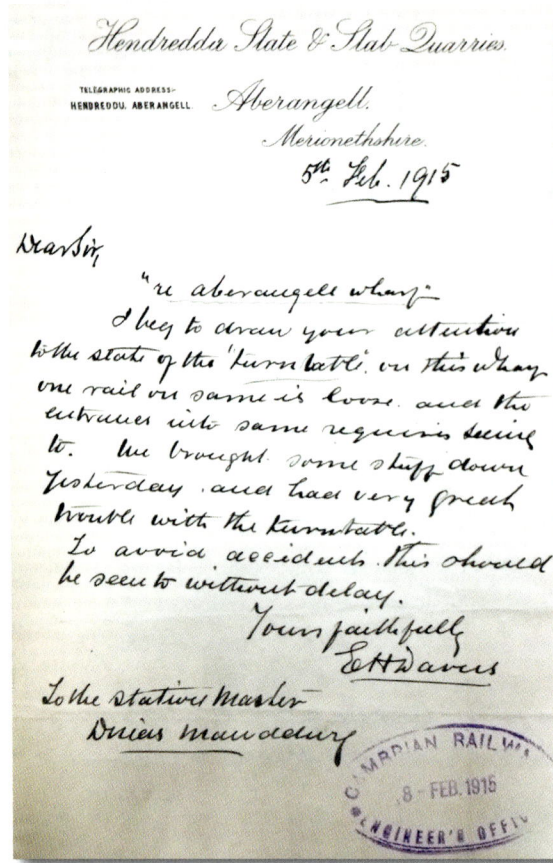

Edward Hurst Davies' letter of 5th February 1915 to the Cambrian Railways, complaining about the state of the trackwork and turntable on Aberangell Wharf.

June, Williamson wrote with bad news: '*I have had this place opened out and examined, I find it is a very much heavier job than at first appeared. The sleepers are actually rotted entirely away, and a smith will have to be sent down to fix the rails on the turntable. I have purchased timber for the new sleepers at a cost of £9 12s 4d and will have them laid as soon as possible, but I daresay it will be another week or so, before the Tramway is in working order.'*

This estimate proved ambitious; the work was not completed until the middle of October. Meanwhile, the quarries muddled through, with the Cambrian making it clear that the Wharf was used entirely at their own risk during this period. The final cost of the relaying work on the Wharf was £20 2s 4d.[6]

The Rise of Timber

Early in the war the government identified timber as a vital strategic resource for both the armed forces and industry. Coal mining alone used 3.5 million tons of pit props in 1914, and as the war escalated the munitions industry consumed ever-larger quantities of wood. Much of Britain's woodlands had been felled during the Napoleonic Wars for shipbuilding and charcoal making and there were then fewer than three million acres of woodland left, much of it unsuitable for commercial use and almost all in private hands.[7] In the years before the war Britain's timber industry was disorganised, producing just one million tons a year, while 11.6 million tons[8] were imported, mostly from Russia and Northern Europe.[9]

There was a substantial stockpile of timber at the start of the war, but the meagre home production was a significant problem. German submarines successfully impeded the inward flow of timber, with 5.1 million tons imported in 1915, dropping to 4.5 million tons in 1916, and just 1.9 million tons by 1917.[10]

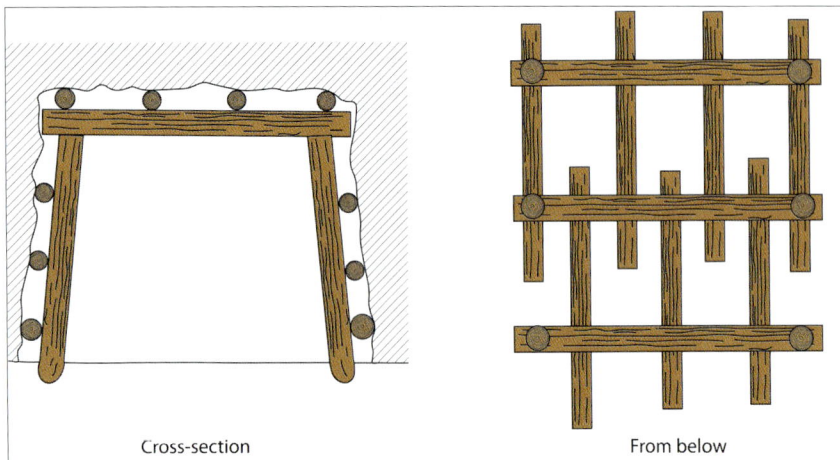

Cross-section   From below

A typical arrangement of pit props in a British coal mine. Nearly two tons of props were used for every 100 tons of coal extracted. Softwoods like larch and pine were preferred because they gradually buckled under pressure, thus warning of potential roof failures.

By October 1914, timber was in such short supply that the Army was struggling to build new training camps.[11] In early 1915, the government began a program to purchase timber for the War Office,[8] and on 24th November 1915, the Home Grown Timber Committee was established to oversee timber production, chaired by F.D. Acland. The Defence of the Realm Act of 1916 empowered the Army to requisition any timber for the war effort.

The government preferred to leave pitwood production in private hands: '*The provision of home grown pitwood is infinitely simpler than the provision of home grown sawn timber. There is an abundance of standing pitwood; its felling requires no special skill… [timber workers] would be paid by the Mine Owners, not by Government, and the Mine Owners would take and share the produce. A private undertaking such as this, is likely to give better results than operations that are managed by the State.*'[12] In March 1917, the Home Grown Timber Committee became the Directorate of Timber Supplies, part of the Board of Trade, led by the gloriously named Sir Bampfylde Fuller. British and Canadian troops began working in British forests to increase production. In Wales most of the hillsides stood bare, with only a few valleys still containing substantial stands of good timber; one of those was Dyffryn Angell.

Felling at Dinas Mawddwy 1914-1915

Sir Edmund Buckley started planting trees on his Dinas Mawddwy and Aberhirnant estates in 1859, a rare act of foresight on his part. At their peak, his forests contained more than a million trees, mainly Larch and Douglas Pine. In 1895, the Commissioner of the Woods and Forest Department examined Buckley's plantations and considered them a model of silviculture.[13] Larch and pine are particularly suitable for use as pit props — which are typically three to six inches in diameter and three to six feet long. They were supplied stripped of bark and needed to be seasoned before use. The props were usually cut to size at sawmills in the forests before shipping to collieries in railway coal wagons.[14]

Buckley's plantations above Dinas Mawddwy were the first to be felled, starting in the early days of the war.

Felling Starts in Dyffryn Angell 1915

At the outbreak of the First World War, Major F. J. Walton was sent to Blickling Hall near Aylsham in Norfolk.[15] He was particularly keen to begin timber production on his Cwmllecoediog Estate; as a serving officer, he understood the strategic need for timber. In 1871, his father had planted 100 acres with softwoods with an eye to commercial production, and by 1915, they were ready for harvesting. In 1916, he joined the council of the Royal English Arboricultural Society, considering the national impact of timber production.[16]

On 9th March 1915, Walton wrote to the Cambrian Railways asking them to provide timber wagons at Aberangell Station:

'*Mr. J. Evans of Hope Village Station […] has bought a good deal of timber from me and Mr. Frost and has asked me if I can do anything to get him trucks to get his timber away. I know he has been very much delayed. There are, I hear, plenty of trucks going up to Dinas but he says he has great difficulty in getting them at Aberangell. No doubt the Merchants at Dinas are a larger way of business but he has been a good customer to the Railway for the last three years and has a large quantity now waiting to come down.*'[17]

Evans is almost certainly John Evans, a timber merchant based at Bridge End, Hope, Flintshire, who was responsible for many early timber operations in the area, probably felling Buckely's plantations at Dinas Mawddwy. Frost is John Meadows Frost, the owner of Dolcorsllwyn Hall on the east bank of the Dyfi. He owned a large estate around Aberangell, including woodlands adjacent to Cwmllecoediog Estate and often worked with the Waltons on local projects.

Walton's letter caused some consternation at the Cambrian Railways. Samuel Williamson pointed out: '*I do not … recommend you to incur outlay in extending the present facilities at Aberangell inasmuch as the Government alone would benefit by the expenditure. As a matter of fact, it would be to the interests of the Mawddwy Company if this traffic passed after and not during the period of Government control.*'[18]

On 9th April 1915, Walton wrote to the Cambrian again. He wanted to ship timber from his estate using the Hendre Ddu Tramway, but:

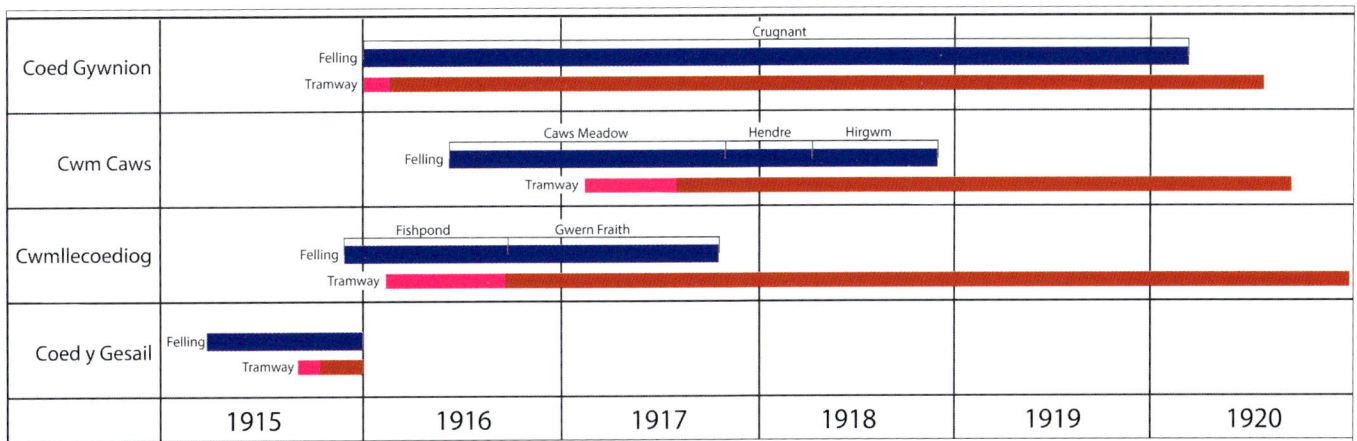

Felling operations in Dyffryn Angell that used the Hendre Ddu Tramway. The lighter section of the bars shows when tramways were constructed, the darker sections show when the track was in situ. The dates are approximate.

'The timber merchants are unwilling to buy at Aberangell on account of the congested state of the station yard. I am offering now some 16,000 trees of a good size - but the merchant's complaint is that on account of the blockage they do not feel inclined to buy. The lot I mention will come into the station yard by a tramline and their suggestion is to make a new piece of line from the old one to carry on to the far end of the station yard which is now I believe not in use. At the same time the poles could if practicable be heaped on my field adjoining the station yard as long as the road to Gwastadgoed farm was not made impassable. Would the company assist in the making of this extra piece of tramline? I have no spare metals. They are light tramway metals that are required. I should have to get consent of the local council to make a second line across the road - but this should be easy enough. The length of new line would be about 50 to 60 yards long I should say and would be easily laid. I take it the company would have no objection. While this sale is delayed it is keeping back a much larger amount of timber which I have ready for sale. Is there any means of reorganising or relaying the yard to get better results?'[19]

The tiny wharf could barely handle the slate traffic from Hendreddu, Gartheiniog and Talymeirin, let alone a huge

Major Frederick James Walton during his service at Bickling Hall, 1915. [Gwyndaf Breese collection]

amount of new timber traffic. The Cambrian were unable to help with surplus rail, but on 20th May they wrote:

'... there will be no objection to your putting in a connection with your tramway lines at a point about 20 to 25 yards north of the public roadway ... and removing the fence between the field and the railway Company's yard to the top side of the roadway to the farm. The tramway siding could then be used in the direction of Mallwyd as referred to by you, alongside the present position of the fence.'

Walton was posted to Egypt early in 1916; the hot conditions did not agree with him and he was posted home in 1917 to join the Denbigh Yeomanry at Aldeburgh. He moved to Oswestry later that year and in July was struck down with appendicitis.[20]

Henry Sharrock Higginbottom

In 1915, colliery owner Henry Sharrock Higginbottom came to Aberangell in search of a reliable supply of pit props.

Higginbottom was born in 1880,[21] the son of Samuel Wasse Higginbottom the Conservative MP for West Derby, Liverpool and a major colliery owner. Henry qualified as a chartered accountant[22] and in 1904 was elected to Liverpool

Higginbottom's Coed Talon colliery, on the left, just before the First World War. [Dan Quine collection]

The Coed y Gesail tramway where it joined the Hendre Ddu Tramway, looking towards Gartheiniog. Though the image is of poor quality, it is of great interest. It is the only known photograph of a horse-hauled train on the Hendre Ddu Tramway. Second from left is Edward Williams of Ivy Bush cottage, in the centre is Mr Smith, Higginbottom's timber agent. Thomas 'Tomi' Rees stands next to the horse, with Lewis Rees behind him. The dog on the top of the load was Togo. The horse is an ex-Army animal called Twinkle, who was so nervous after active service, that the slightest sudden noise would send him into a panic.[40]

The photograph shows a train of four timber bogies loaded with pit props. In front of the lead bogie and behind Rees is a car gwyllt that provided braking for the train. Some of the bogies would have had brakes that could be pinned down for the descent to Aberangell, with the car gwyllt providing fine control of the speed. The track is extremely light. Behind the horse is a rake of empty timber bogies, ready to be hauled to the sawmill after the loaded train has left. The width of the Hendre Ddu formation is obvious – showing how it was originally intended to be standard gauge. [Bill Breese collection]

City Council.[23] He owned at least nine collieries in the North West of England including Coed Talon, Phoenix[24] and Broughton near Wrexham;[25] New Moss Colliery near Audenshaw;[26] New Haden Colliery at Cheadle;[27] the Central Silkstone Collieries at Barnsley;[28] and the Lostock Colliery between Bolton and Wigan.[29] New Moss once boasted the deepest mine shaft in the world.[30] Some of these he inherited from his father, others he purchased before the war. By 1916, he was 'one of the largest individual colliery proprietors in the United Kingdom controlling an annual output of coal of over half a million tons'.[31]

In 1903, he married Martha Hartley, the daughter of Sir William Hartley the founder of Hartley's Jams. Higginbottom was something of a dilettante, owning a string of racehorses.[32] He was also an early aviation enthusiast. As vice-chairman of the Lancashire Aero Club,[33] he purchased his first aeroplane in 1909 from Monsieur

Ribeyrolles of Paris,[34] just six years after the first flight at Kitty Hawk. He offered a £1,000 prize for the first flight between Liverpool and Manchester. Ribeyrolles was the designer of the first successful car produced by A. Darracq & Co., a major Anglo-French automobile manufacturer. In 1916, Higginbottom purchased a large number of shares in Darracq[35] and he was appointed as a director, becoming chairman in 1917.[36]

Coed y Gesail 1915

Higginbottom lived at Gwasted Hall, north of Wrexham, within two miles of John Evans's timber yard at Hope. Evans likely supplied pit props to Higginbottom's Coed Talon Colliery before the war.

Higginbottom saw the potential of the woods of Dyffryn Angell, with fine stands of mature trees and a transportation system ready to be used. In early 1915, he leased the timber rights at Coed y Gesail from Evans, a large stand of trees opposite Gartheiniog Mill. The central section was planted with hardwoods, mainly oak and ash, while the northern section was larch and pine, suitable for pit prop production. Felling began in May 1915,[37] supervised by Higginbottom's timber agent, Mr Smith.[38]

A temporary sawmill produced the pit props, which were stored nearby to season. A short tramway was built from the Hendre Ddu Tramway to the storage area. Higginbottom had an agreement to use the Hendre Ddu to take the pit props down to the Wharf. Slate was still coming down from the three operating quarries, so the lower section of the tramway would have been busy. No doubt Davies was grateful for the extra income from Higginbottom's timber traffic, as Hendreddu quarry was struggling.

The Coed y Gesail Tramway was built by William Rees and David Williams, along with Elias, Thomas and David Davies of Nanthir.[39] It crossed the Angell on a wooden bridge —which was completed on 17th October 1915[37] — then ran along the northern edge of Coed y Gesail. This tramway was taken up in December 1915, but the tramway bridge continued in use as a footbridge to access Esgair Angell Farm. It appears on maps in the 1920s and was demolished shortly before the Second World War.

Coed Gwynion 1916-1920

After Coed y Gesail was felled, Higginbottom turned to Coed Gwynion, a large plantation north of Cefngwyn. It had been part of Buckley's estate before 1876 and was laid out for commercial use, with a grid of roadways to make planting and extraction easier. The tramway and sawmill from Coed y Gesail were moved to Cwm Crugnant, on the south edge of Coed Gwynion, in January 1916. The tramway ran along an old path from the sawmill down to the Hendre Ddu Tramway near Sied Ddu.

'Large trees were dragged down from Coed Gwynion, to be sawed

into various lengths as needed. The sawmill was built on a small bluff on the edge of the road to Cefngwyn Hall. David Richard Jones, the wagon builder for the main Hendre Ddu Tramway, hauled wagons up to the loading point near the sawmill. He was heard complaining that his horse was old and short of breath: "I will tell them you have fallen dead between the rails". One day he was sitting behind the horse, on his row of black wagons, when the horse did indeed lay down between the rails and die. All David could say was "There you have it, it's gone".'[41]

Higginbottom continued to work Coed Gwynion into the early 1920s. Meanwhile, Walton was looking for another timber merchant to continue felling on his estate.

J.H. & F.W. Green 1915-1916

In the early summer of 1915, Major Walton leased the timber rights at Cwmllecoediog to J.H. & F.W. Green, timber merchants of Whittington, Chesterfield. They had been felling in the Dyfi valley for several years — on 13th May 1897, the Mawddwy Railway extended the siding at Dolyfonddu for 'Messrs Green'[42] to load timber felled in Cwm Llwydo and between Cemmaes and Cwm Llinau. On 3rd July 1915, Messrs Green wrote to Samuel Williamson at the Cambrian:

'We have just purchased a large fall of timber at Aberangell, and we understand you are willing to divert the little Light Railway, which now runs into that Station-yard, or rather to put another Branch into it, so that timber may be carried to the far end of the Station-yard. We shall be pleased to hear if this is so, and when you think you could arrange to have this work done. There will be a big lot of this timber, and it will be important that every facility should be given to enable us to get this timber away as quickly as possible.'

They attached a sketch of the proposed tramway, diverging from the Hendre Ddu at the lower end of the Brynderwen cutting and crossing the road to run parallel to the Gwastadgoed Farm track.

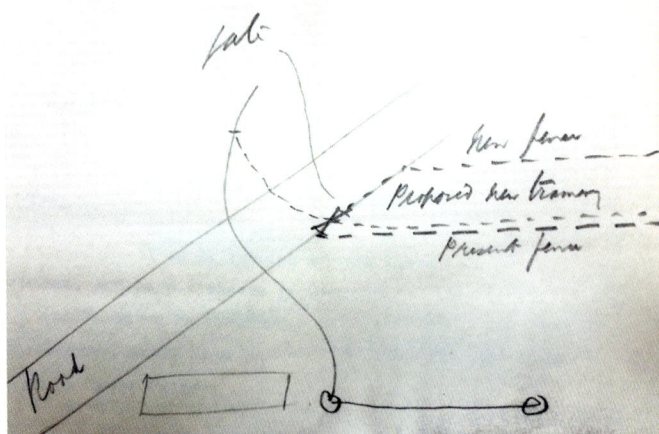

The proposed 'Green's Tramway' at Aberangell. It would diverge from the main line on the north side of the road, run through a new gate and into the yard. The fence between Walton's land and the Wharf is moved northwards to allow the tramway to run parallel to the Gwastadgoed Farm track. The existing tramway layout with two turntables and no sidings is not accurate.

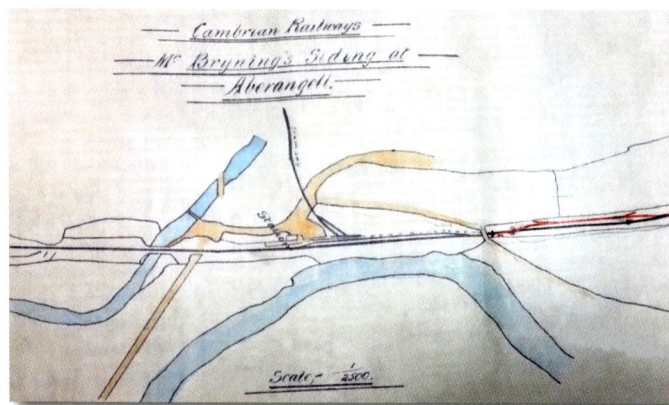

Plan produced by the Cambrian Railways in July 1916, showing the proposed new loop at Aberangell to accommodate Higginbottom's timber traffic. 'Mr Bryning's Siding', was named after Higginbottom's business partner, Andrew Bryning who managed several of Higginbottom's collieries.[45] The map does not show Green's Tramway that already ran along the west edge of the yard at Aberangell, and would have been extended under the bridge to Gwastagoed Farm, to the new standard gauge loop.

On the 15th July, J.H. Green met with Evans of the Cambrian Railways at Aberangell to discuss arrangements. He also talked with the district council and received permission for a second level crossing of the village road. On 12th August, Williamson wrote: '*I have now seen Mr. Green who will enter into an agreement for the extension of the tramway on our land, the removal of the fence to the new site, the gate at entrance to our property, indemnity as to protecting the Company owing to the gate being fixed, [and] restoration of the fence at completion of the traffic passing. With regard to the filling up of the space to enable them to load direct into trucks, Messrs Green agree to supply the necessary poles for the retaining wall…*'[18]

'Filling up of the space' refers to building a loading dock at the north end of the station yard. The tramway branch would run along the west side of the yard, then onto the dock. Pit props were to be stored on the dock ready to be loaded into Cambrian Railways wagons.

The final agreement was signed in August 1916, but the loading dock and Green's Tramway had been completed by February 1916.[43] The Greens did not feel the need to wait for officialdom to catch up with their plans. Despite obtaining permission for a level crossing, the points were put in on the wharf side of the road.

Higginbottom Takes Over 1916

As 1916 wore on, Higginbottom was looking for further sources of timber. On 6th June 1916, Williamson noted: '*I visited Aberangell together with the Engineer's assistant, and met [Higginbottom's] foreman there, who pointed out that it was proposed to run the present tramway, laid down by Messrs Green of Chesterfield, further on and to put in a loop… and load the timber, which will be cut into props, direct from the bank into trucks. The loops should be made to hold ten wagons as this would be the number which would require to be loaded daily.*'[44]

Negotiations continued, with the Cambrian producing a plan for the proposed new loop north of Gwastadgoed Bridge. On July 6th the Cambrian's engineer wrote: '*Mr. Bryning suggested… [we] should meet him at Aberangell on Friday last… but on Thursday evening he wired that he could not possibly meet us until Saturday. We went to Aberangell on Friday and found that there was only one site available, and explained this to Messrs Higginbottom's representative, Mr. Maskerry, who is in charge, and asked him to point it out to Mr. Bryning the following day… We heard eventually that Messrs. Higginbottom are in negotiation with Messrs Greens of Chesterfield to take over this timber, and the accommodation in our Aberangell yard and this possibly is the reason of their not writing us.*'

Higginbottom moved quickly and on 19th July, Williamson reported: '*Mr. Higginbottom informed me that he has bought the whole of Messrs Greens' timber*'; he was now the largest timber operator in Dyffryn Angell.

Higginbottom was unhappy at the lack of Cambrian wagons at Aberangell to take his pit props away, threatening to resort to road transport if his demands were not met. An internal Cambrian memo notes the following traffic loaded for Higginbottom during July 1916:

Week ending July 8th   37 box wagons*
Week ending July 15th   37 box wagons
Week ending July 22th   29 box wagons

Higginbottom continued to expand his timber operations in the area. He purchased several plantations around Dinas Mawddwy and took over Bullock's slate warehouse there (now Meirion Mill) in 1918 and converted it into a sawmill. In April, Higginbottom asked the Cambrian to add a siding into the sawmill, but by May had changed his mind and instead had them build '*a wooden staging, similar to Aberangell*' with a crane for moving logs into the mill.

Cwmllecoediog 1916-1920

J.H. & F.W. Green began felling on Walton's estate in 1916, working just south of Plas Cwmllecoediog on the east side of the valley, where a temporary sawmill was built in May. Higginbottom took over from Greens in July. The sawmill operated until November of that year before moving to a new location,[37] probably at the west end of the valley, near Cwmllecoediog Quarry. A tramway was laid into Cwmllecoediog,[46] starting in early 1916. Cozens and Boyd claim this was laid on the trackbed of an earlier Hendre Ddu branch from Aberdwynant to Plas Cwmllecoediog, but this was a completely new line.[47]

The tramway was mostly laid along existing roadways with relatively little earthwork, though some slate waste from the Cwmllecoediog Quarry tips was used to build up the trackbed in places. It was around two miles long. It was described by the men who worked it as a '*switchback fairground railway*'[39] because it made little attempt at a steady

---

* This type of wagon is usually referred to as an 'open wagon' but the Cambrian preferred the term 'box wagon', presumably to distinguish them from flat open wagons.

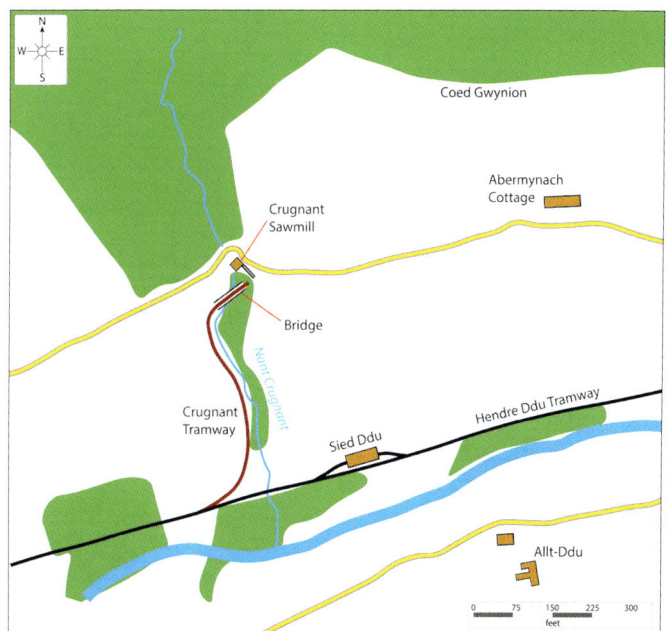

The steeply graded Crugnant Tramway, climbing to cross the Nant Crugnant on a wooden bridge just below the sawmill.

The gate on the south side of the bridge across the Afon Angell at Aberdwynant. The Cwmllecoediog timber tramway crossed the river on a wooden bridge here. The tramway trackbed curves gently to the right as it climbs towards Allt Ddu. Aberdwynant and the Hendre Ddu Tramway are behind the photographer. This bridge was built in the 1950s to replace the wooden bridge from the First World War.[40]
[Dan Quine]

wild and dangerous progress as they rushed along. They pulled on the brakes hardest as they ran past Allt Ddu cottage, hoping to skillfully stop on the embankment before the bridge. There the hauliers would replace the riders and re-attach the horses to pull the wagons to the junction with the Hendreddu Tramway over the new bridge near Allt Ddu.' [41]

The tramway began at Aberdwynant, where the old road to Allt Ddu and Cwmllecoediog forded the Angell. A wooden bridge carried the tramway across the river, where it turned to the west and ran south of and parallel to the Angell on a rising gradient. It passed Allt Ddu cottage, where there was a short, steep uphill section, then continued straight across the fields, rising steadily until it was due south of Cefngwyn Hall.[37]

The tramway then turned to the southwest and climbed uphill to meet Cwmllecoediog Drive. This section was extremely steep, about 1 in 7, and accidents were common as heavy timber bogies roared down towards Allt Ddu.

downhill gradient, instead rising and falling along its length. The line was likely laid in light flat-bottomed rail spiked to roughly cut timber sleepers.

The first load of timber was sent down the tramway on 14th October 1916.[39] Operations in the valley continued into 1917, and the tramway appears to have survived into the 1920s, but the exact date at which it was removed is not known. Bill Breese recorded the following vivid account of the timber tramway's operation:

'*On the far side of the river, a tramroad ran along the road from Allt-Ddu to Nyrs-y-Chwarel [Coed y Chwarel]. It ran past the lake and front lawn of Plas Cwmllecoediog and transported timber to the village station. The hauliers pulled the loaded wagons along Cwmllecoediog Drive to the top of the hill opposite Cefngwyn Hall (where George Hawkins, the manager of the forestry workers, lived). Here they detached the horses, and the riders climbed aboard the loaded wagons. The train was pushed over the crest of the hill and they descended the iron rails, in the direction of Allt Ddu. They pulled on the wagon brakes to slow their*

Aberangell from late 1916 onwards. The yard has been extended onto Walton's land and Green's Tramway has been laid along its western side, curving round onto the timber dock. The northern loop on the Wharf has been removed, with the two points probably reused on Green's Tramway and the balloon loop on the loading dock. By the entrance to the yard, Higginbottom built a temporary barracks to house forestry workers. The fence dividing the yard from Walton's land ran between Green's Tramway and the Gwastagoed Farm track.

Capel Horeb

Green's tramway

Capel Bethania

Loading dock

Higginbottom's barracks

Crane

Wharf

Brynderwen Cutting

Yard

Brynderwen

0 30 60 90 120
feet

The Crugnant sawmill in operation. The lightly laid tramway is just visible on the right on a wooden bridge across the Nant Crugant. The hillside behind has been cleared. The men on the right of the sawmill are standing in front of the wooden feed on which the logs were moved to the circular saw to be cut to length. Large stocks of pit props are seasoning before being sent down to Aberangell. The original caption notes the 'large number of Higginbottom's men used to operate the sawmill, and horses used to haul down timber'. At least seven horses are visible. The man standing at the front of the group just to the left of the sawmill may be Higginbottom. [Bill Breese collection]

by Green between May and July 1916 and taken over by Higginbottom. The tramway then followed the stream, climbing gently towards Cwmllecoediog Quarry.

About 450 yards south of the lake, the tramway turned to the west crossing the site of the quarry waste tips which were breached to allow the tramway to reach timber stands to the west, and to provide material for the tramway construction. Part of the earlier Cwmllecoediog Tramroad may have been relaid to access Coed y Plas on the western side of the valley, which was felled between 1916 and 1923. The main timber tramway was probably extended to the west of the quarry site when the Fishpond sawmill was relocated to the Gwern Fraith site.

Cwm Caws 1916-1920

Cwm Caws is a steep-sided valley that runs west and south from Pont yr Hirgwm. For many years oak forests along the valley were cultivated to provide timber for shipbuilding at Derwenlas on the mouth of the Dyfi.[49] There was a large stand of oak in the valley at the start of the war, with larch and pine plantations at the southern end.

Operations in the narrow confines of the valley were challenging: there were no roads along most of its length,

and the steep slopes made felling difficult. Easier access in other locations meant that Cwm Caws was not brought into production until mid-1916. There were probably three temporary sawmill locations along Cwm Caws. The first trees felled were softwoods at the confluence of Nant Caws Bach and Nant Caws, and a temporary sawmill was established in Caws Meadow on the south bank of the stream in the summer of 1916.

Caws Meadow was the furthest point along the valley with road access. Pit props were hauled to Cemmes Road station by horse and cart or using a pair of traction engines.[47] This proved unsatisfactory as the road was so poor, so a tramway was laid from Pont yr Hirgwm starting in October 1916. It reached Caws Meadow on 30th July 1917 and stored logs were then taken out to Aberangell.[39] The sawmill was relocated ½ mile south to Hendre and the larch and pine plantations there were felled. The tramway was extended to there in November, with the sawmill moving south to Hirgwm, probably in early 1918. The tramway was eventually extended a further ½ mile south to this final sawmill.

Felling continued in Cwm Caws after the war and the tramway was not removed until 1920.[40] The majority of the trees along the valley had been felled, though the large

This appears to be the temporary timber bridge over the Afon Angell at Aberdwynant, but it is not. The plate-framed Motor Rail locomotive dates this picture to after 1933, and this is most likely a timber tramway in Scotland during the Second World War. However, it gives a good idea of what the Cwmllecoediog Timber Tramway looked like as it crossed the Afon Angell. The Afon Angell bridge has substantial slate abutments similar to those seen here, the timber A-frame bridge is much like the one that spanned the river, and the timber bogies that make up the train are almost identical to those used by Higginbottom and his men, though they did not enjoy the assistance of a locomotive.[48]

The route of the Cwmllecoediog Tramway as it runs along the south bank of the Afon Angell, just west of Allt Ddu farmhouse, looking towards Cwmllecoediog. This section was laid on the main road to Cwmllecoediog built in the 1850s. Where the tramway enters the woodlands in the distance, it swings left to the southwest and climbs steeply up to Cwmllecoediog Drive.
[Dan Quine]

The course of the tramway south of the fishing lake, looking towards Cwmllecoediog Quarry. The trackbed has been built up with waste taken from the quarry tips. This is close to the site of the Fishpond sawmill.
[Dan Quine]

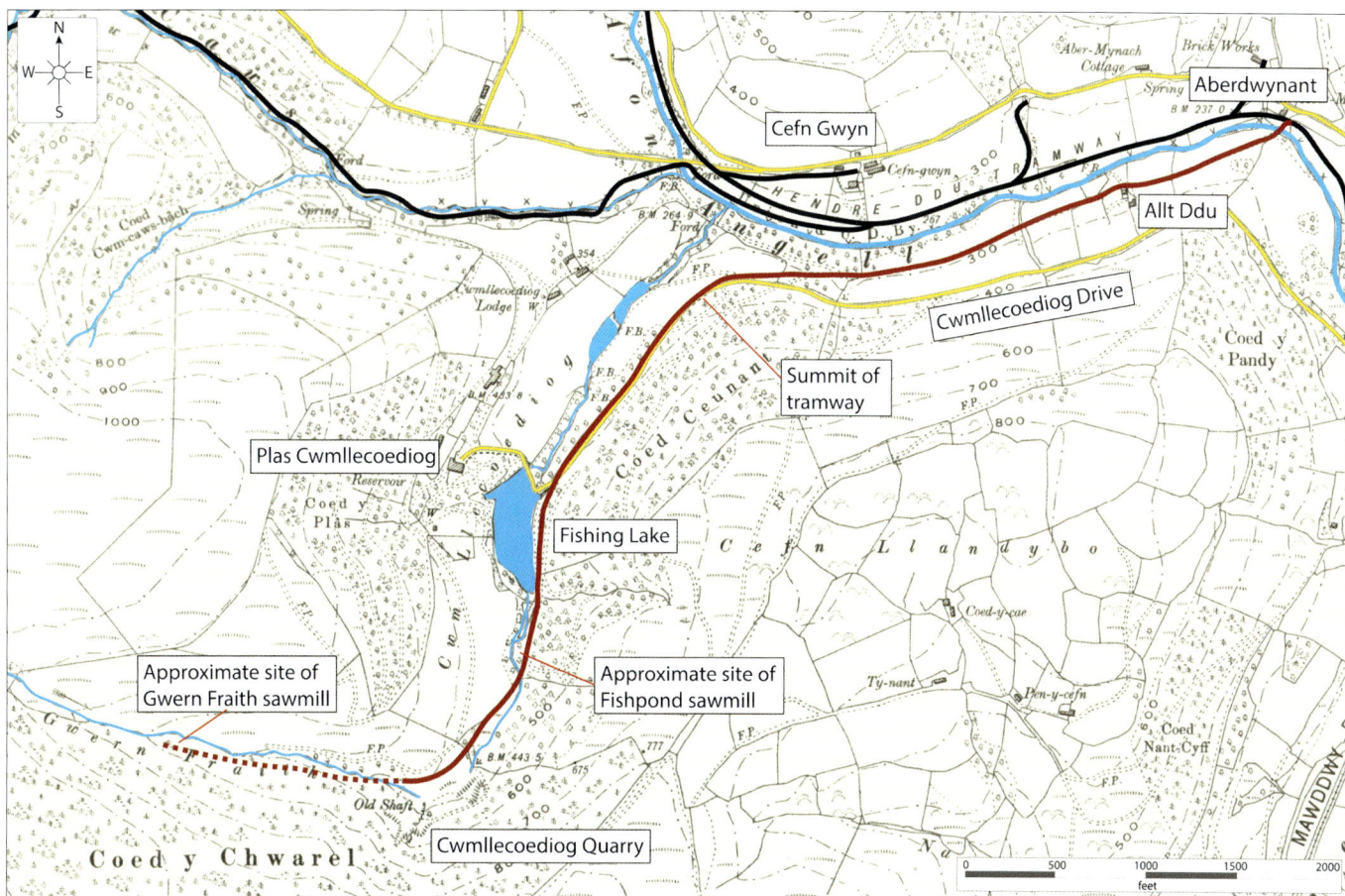

The route of the Cwmllecoediog Timber Tramway, shown in red. The exact extent of the tramway west of Cwmllecoediog Quarry is unknown.

section of oak and ash adjoining Coed y Gesail were left since they were not suitable for pit prop production. Most of the tramway was relaid in the Second World War, as detailed in Chapter 14.

The Cwm Caws Tramway was built to a high standard – it was not a 'rollercoaster' like the Cwmllecoediog Tramway. It required significant material to construct the trackbed and high-quality stonemasonry to build the bridges and embankments along its route. Some of the fill material for the trackbed was taken from the Gartheiniog waste tips.[39]

The stonemason working on the bridges and embankment was David Jones, an employee of Hendreddu Quarry. The Military Service Act of January 1916 introduced conscription for all single men aged 18 to 41, with the rules tightening over the subsequent months. Tribunals were held where men could appeal their call-up. Initially, most appeals were granted, but as the war dragged on and the need for men became more desperate, the tribunals became stricter. David Jones appealed in November 1917:

'Mr. R. Guthrie Jones [solicitor] appeared in support of the appeal of Mr. E. H. Davies, Hendreddu Quarry, Aberangell, for further exemption for David Jones, single, 37, High Street, Dinas Mawddwy, stone mason, employed on the construction of a tramway for the conveyance of pit props, etc. Mr. Davies said that about 1¼ miles of line had been constructed out of the two miles. The work had been delayed through lack of labour. He had three

men only of his own on the work. Exemption to May 13th.'[50]

The tramway left the Hendre Ddu at a junction directly south of Cefngwyn Hall. It ran on a low embankment which allowed it to remain level as it headed west towards Pont yr Hirgwm. The tramway crossed the Afon Angell on a well-built timber bridge on slate abutments. In 2016, a length of flat-bottomed rail, presumably from the tramway, held a wire fence across the river just west of Pont yr Hirgwm.

After crossing the Afon Angell, the line ran on another low embankment on the north side of the Afon Caws, heading into the valley. It crossed the Caws southeast of Esgairangell farmhouse and ran along the south bank before returning to the north side as the river turned to the northwest.

West of the confluence of the Afon Caws and Nant Cawsbach, the tramway passed Caws Meadow, the site of the first sawmill, before it crossed the stream once more, as the Caws turned sharply to head southwest. Here the mountains closed in, forming a narrow, steep-sided valley. The tramway crossed the stream once more, and for about a mile it held the west bank as it climbed steadily towards the head of the valley. The tramway crossed the Afon Caws for a final time before climbing steeply to site of Hirgwm sawmill, below the col of Mynydd Tri Arglwydd. Here, deep in the forest, it terminated.

Cwm Caws contained a large amount of timber, and traffic along the tramway must have been significant. The tramway workers struggled to keep up with demand for timber

Aberangell Wharf during or shortly after the First World War looking south. Pit-props sit on the timber loading dock built by Messrs Green. The north end of the loop of Green's Tramway curves round to run parallel to the standard gauge where a rake of 7-plank Great Central Railway box wagons are being loaded with pit props. The railways were under government control and rolling stock was often found outside its 'home' area. It may not be a coincidence that Higginbottom's New Moss Colliery was located next to the Great Central's Guide Bridge station. In the distance the stiffleg derrick is loading larger timbers onto what appear to be Cambrian Railways timber bolster wagons. The Hendre Ddu Wharf is beyond the derrick. The man on the left is Henry Sharrock Higginbottom, next to him is Lewis Davies, then John Jones, the Mallwyd postman.[41] The two men on the right are unidentified. [Mark Waites collection]

bogies, and on 2nd September 1918, several 2ft 2in. gauge slate wagons were transferred from the nearby Cae'r Abbaty quarry. These were quickly converted to 1ft 11in. gauge and put into use.[51]

Other Timber Felling

Other timber operations in the forests west of Aberangell probably did not use the tramway as they produced larger timber that was sent to permanent sawmills along the Dyfi valley. Bill Breese describes the work of the timber operations in Cwm Du and Coed Blaen-y-Cwm, north of Coed Gwynion:

'Hauliers urging their teams of sprightly horses that drew timber wagons overburdened with round timber through Clipiau continually managed to keep the Yard men occupied during the First World War. Railway wagon loads of pit props, sawn timber and cut firewood were dispatched regularly to consignees from all parts of Britain. Religiously inclined villagers, including womenfolk, crept into the yard after dark, so as to fill their sacks (and even skirts) with the already sawn firewood, which as implied in the song, would keep "their home fires burning".'[38]

There is circumstantial evidence of a temporary sawmill at Gartheiniog Mill during the war. Certainly, there was timber production there in the 1920s. Timber was felled along Dyffryn Angell above Gartheiniog and Nanthir farms, and some trees around Talymeirin were taken. This timber may have been taken down to a Gartheiniog sawmill, or perhaps it went further along the Hendre Ddu Tramway to the Aberdwynant or Wharf mills.

Sawmills and Timber Operations

The timber operations followed a common pattern. When a new area was to be felled, a temporary sawmill was installed at the bottom of the hill on which the trees stood. Long uphill paths were cut through the forest and the trunks were dragged or skidded down them, often along slides and skid roads formed of felled trunks. Timber was cut into pit props of uniform size at the sawmill and stacked on-site to season, before being transported out of the forest.

Pit props were typically untreated before use. Before the war, the major suppliers to Britain were the Scandinavian countries, where the trees were felled during the winter months when they were not producing sap.[52] Pit props containing sap were unsuitable for use underground, and

Timber operations in Cwm Caws early in the First World War, before the tramway came into operation in mid-1917. The only area in Cwm Caws where the valley floor was this wide was Caws Meadow. A team of horses stands ready to haul the cut timber out of the forest on large carts. There is a derrick just behind them used for loading the carts and the jib of a second crane is seen on the right. In the distance is a traction engine, which was probably powering the temporary sawmill. [Mark Waites collection]

seasoned props were preferred as they showed '*a distinct advantage in strength and durability*'.[53] The need for seasoning explains why the sawmills often operated for months before the tramways were laid, and had moved to the next location before the first pit props were taken away.

Accommodating the Workers

The forestry work attracted men from the local area and beyond. Wages were set by the Government and were relatively good, and overtime was plentiful. Timber work was initially a protected occupation when conscription was introduced; as a result, men flocked to the hills to avoid

being sent to the fronts. By April 1916, exemptions from military service were being sought because '*all the spare men in the district were engaged in timber work*'.[54]

Accommodating these workers in the village was a challenge, and barracks and messes were built for them. Any empty local houses were pressed into service; one of these was Allt Ddu, which provided a fairly high standard of accommodation, other workers ended up in temporary huts and converted farm outbuildings.[37] Cefngwyn Hall, once the residence of Jacob Bradwell, was used by the foresters. It became the headquarters of operations, occupied by George Hawkins, a well-known timber merchant from Newtown[55] and one of Higginbottom's two timber agents in the valley.[38] Hawkins gained a reputation as a hard taskmaster. His voice would echo along the valleys as he shouted "blow up" at the end of break time. His son, also called George, was a foreman and was known to all as 'Little George'.[37]

Tramway Operations

The operations used large numbers of horses as well as men. They hauled trains along the tramways, timber wagons on the roads

Pont yr Hirgwm in August 2013, looking downstream from the modern road bridge across the Afon Angell. There is a pair of older bridge abutments here, which were probably built by stonemason David Jones in 1917 to carry the timber tramway across the river and into Cwm Caws. [Dan Quine]

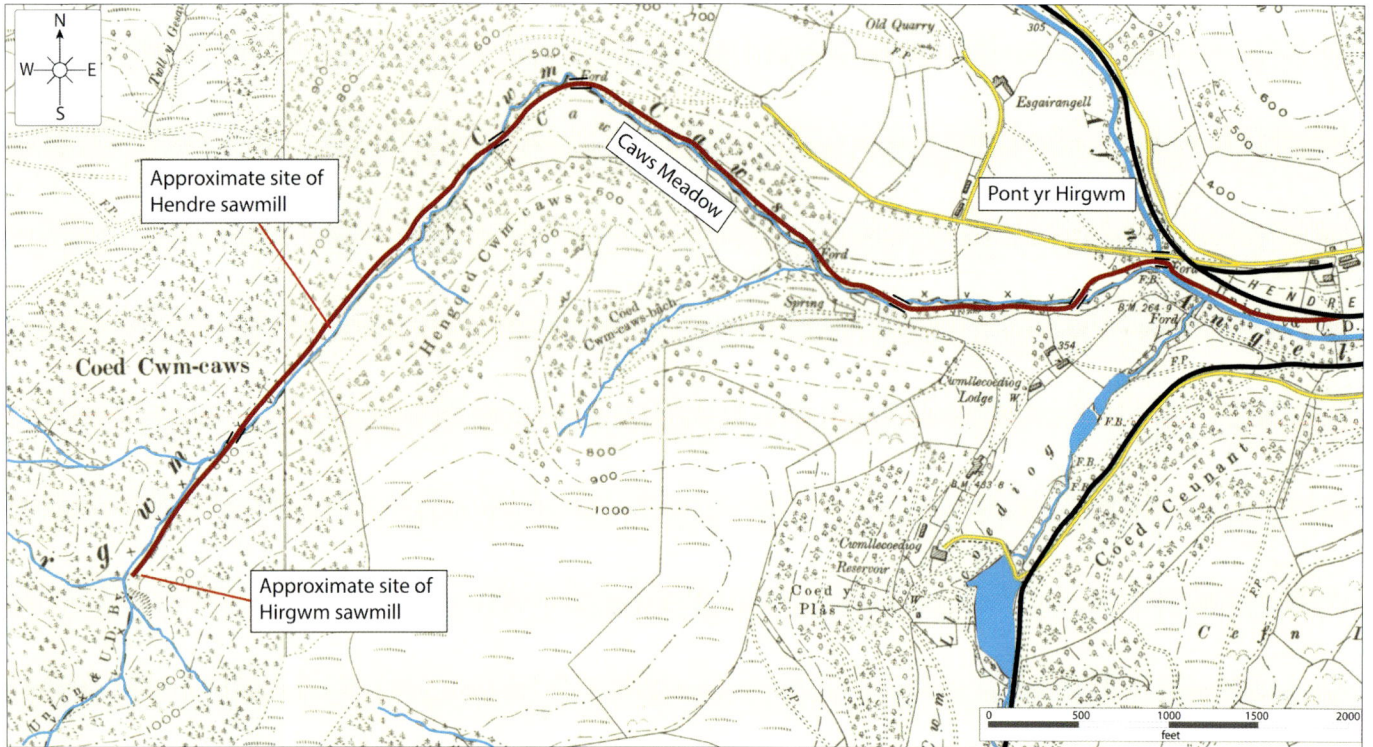

The route of the Cwm Caws Timber Tramway, running from Cefngwyn deep into the forest of Coed Cwm-caws. The map shows the extent of the woodland before felling started.

and sleds down the slopes to the sawmills. A chaff cutter was installed by the sawmill at Aberdwynant to cut down hay into easily stored horse feed. At the height of operations, ten horses were stabled at Cefngwyn, twelve at Esgairangell and another dozen or so in Aberangell. Further horses were hired from local farmers as needed.[37]

With such intensive operations, accidents were inevitable. Many were injured in the felling and sawing of timber. On 5th October 1917, Rhys Jones of Walton Terrace was killed in an accident on the tramway.[56]

Sied Ddu became the centre of tramway operations, building and maintaining the timber 'bogies' used to transport pit props out of the woods and down to the Wharf.[51] The main section of the shed was used for carpentry, while the east end was converted into a smithy.[41] Local carpenters Richard Francis, James Morris and John Ifans were employed on woodworking duties, while blacksmith Sam Francis made the metalwork, shod the horses and forged tools for the forest workers.[57] There was little that Sam was unable to turn his hand to when required. He was particularly skilled at making harpoons for the local poachers who would spear fish in the Angell and Dyfi, much to the annoyance of the local gamekeepers.[41]

Permanent Sawmills

As well as temporary sawmills in the woods, three permanent sawmills were installed to support Higginbottom's operations. The first of these was at Crugnant, the main sawmill processing timber from Coed Gwynion.

This was in place for at least two years from early 1916.

The second permanent sawmill was at Aberdwynant, built on the site of Bradwell's brickworks. The mill was installed here before the summer of 1918 and it may have reused the equipment from the Crugnant mill. Likely, the short branch to the brickworks was still in place when war broke out, and the large flat area beside the Afon Mynach made a good site for the sawmill and storage yards.

The mill was at first powered by the brickworks waterwheel. Sometime in 1918, a stationary steam engine was installed to provide power; it proved problematic and had to have its boiler replaced twice in a year, once after bursting in the severe frosts of February 1919.[37] The mill employed about a dozen men and was the heart of Higginbottom's business, surviving until near the end of his operations in early 1921, when the building was sold to Cefngwyn farm for use as an outbuilding.[57] Shortly afterwards the waterwheel was demolished; the quarrymen overestimated the amount of explosives needed for the job and bits of waterwheel rained down on a wide area.

The Davies Family During the War

Edward Hurst Davies's two sons were early volunteers for service in the war. His eldest, John Davies, joined the Welsh Guards in 1914. After taking part in the Battle of Neuve Chapelle he was promoted to Lieutenant in April 1915.[58] He was severely wounded at Loos-en-Gohelle in July 1915, during the run-up to the Battle of Loos. He eventually recovered from his injuries, though it took more

The Aberdwynant sawmill, with the workers lined up for a portrait. In the middle of the shed is the Pendulum Cut-Off Saw – the large Y-shaped frame swung out towards the camera, with the hangers at the top of the 'Y' pivoting on the drive shaft. Logs were fed in on the track at the left and the circular saw swung down to effect the cut. A flat belt (missing on this day) drove from the pulley at the top onto the pulley on the right end of the circular saw's mandrel. H.S. Higginbottom is on the far left. [Mark Waite collection]

than two years of recuperation.

Davies's youngest son, Iorwerth Gwilym Davies, joined the Royal Welsh Fusiliers in August 1914 as a private. Like his brother, he also fought in the Battle of Neuve Chapelle, where he received a commission. In 1915, he transferred to the Royal Flying Corps, initially in France. In November 1916, he was mentioned in dispatches for his distinguished services in Egypt during the battle for Gaza.[59] By September 1917, Iorwerth had been promoted to Flight Commander and was a Flight Instructor in Salonica where he was again mentioned in dispatches.[60] In 1918, he was promoted to Captain.

In August 1918, 26-year-old Iowerth returned from service and was assigned to the 54th Training Squadron at RAF Fairlop, in Ilford, Essex. He was planning a trip back to Aberangell and intended to fly there, landing his plane in the river meadows belonging to Blaen-plwyf-isaf farm.[3] But tragedy struck on the afternoon of Monday 2nd September.[61] Iowerth was performing aerobatics at Fairlop in Avro 504k No. D2110 when he crashed his plane and was killed.[62]

A large funeral was held at Cemmaes, with many of his fellow soldiers in attendance. Clearly, Iorwerth's death had a huge impact on his family and the broader community.

'*The body was brought to Cemmaes Road on Saturday and placed on a gun carriage provided by the King's Liverpool Regiment, Oswestry. Eight officers and a large number of soldiers were present. A firing party with reversed arms headed the cortege, under the command of Sergeant Lowe, and the officers followed under the command of Capt. Haslam, Oswestry.*

The officers acted as bearers from the gun carriage to the church. A service was held in the Church when the Rev. J. C. Evans read a portion of the Scriptures and the Rev. R. W. Jones, Aberangell, took part. The hymns "Dwy Aden Colomen Pe Cawn" and "Lead, Kindly Light," were sung, and the Dead March played by the Organist (Mr. J. E. Parry, M.A., Aberangell). The coffin, which was draped with the Union Jack, was borne to the graveside by Messrs. Lewis Rees, Thomas Rees, David Lewis Jones, and John Jones. At the graveside the Rev. David Harris, Bridgend, officiated. Three volleys were fired and the Last Post sounded, with roll of drums. The chief mourners were Mr. Davies, father; Mr. John Davies, brother (invalided out of the army); Mrs. Denton, sister; Mr. and Mrs John Howells, Bridgend, sister and brother-in-law; the Rev. David Howells, Bridgend; the Rev J. C. Evans and Mr. J. D. Evans, Borth, uncle and cousin, Lieut. Reynolds (who was in deceased's flight section); and Lieut. Horlick. The grave was lined with flowers and numerous wreaths were sent.'[63]

Iorwerth's name was later placed on the war memorial at Dinas Mawddwy, where he is remembered alongside Edmund Maurice Buckley, on a slab of Hendreddu rock. These two families who dominate the story of the Hendre Ddu Tramway, are connected once more, though in the most terrible of circumstances.

A variety of methods were used to bring the timber down to the mills. On the left is a typical timber slide, this one photographed in Idaho in the United States in 1913. Large logs were sent down the slide by gravity. Below is a skid road, from Washington State. Teams of horses hauled logs across trunks embedded in the ground. [Ralph Clement Bryant]

Dinas Mawddwy war memorial [Iwan Llwyd Foulkes]

References

1   Alan G.V. Simmons, *Britain and World War One*, Routledge, 2012.

2   Legal papers of Messrs. Howell, Evans, Gillart & Humphreys, reference M/D/HPA/3.

3   Bill Breese, Notes on local quarrying and quarrymen, *Dolgellau Archive*, vol. ref ZM/6541/9, 1982.

4   Letter from John Parry to Henry Warwick. RAIL 1057/580/C. Kew: National Archives.

5   Letter from Henry Warwick to George McDonald. RAIL 1057/580/C. Kew: National Archives.

6   Letter, reference RAIL 1057/580/C. National Archives.

7   Dennis Healey, British Forestry Commission 1919-69, *Unasylva - An International Review of Forestry and Forest Products, vol. 23 (I), no. 92*, 1969.

8   National Archives, History of the Timber Supply Department, reference BT 71/2/24119. 1918.

9   Michael Winter, *Rural Politics: Policies for Agriculture, Forestry and the Environment*, Routledge, 1996.

10   Encyclopedia Britannica, vol. 31. 1922.

11   The Problem of Timber, Board of Trade Journal, vol. 100, Mar. 1918.

12   National Archives, Timber Supply Department: labour requirements (1917-1918), NATS 1/1323.

13   Re-afforestation in Wales, *North Wales Times*, p.3, Jun. 29th, 1895.

14   Methods of timbering, *Sheffield Daily Telegraph*, p.24, Dec. 31st, 1914.

15   Letter from F. J. Walton to Cambrian Railways, reference RAIL 1057/581. Kew: National Archives, 1915.

16   Quarterly Journal of Forestry, vol. X, 1916.

17   Letter from F. J. Walton to Cambrian Railways, reference Rail 1057/1976. Kew: National Archives, 1915.

18   Letter from Samuel Williamson, reference Rail 1057/1976. Kew: National Archives, 1915.

19   Letter from F. J. Walton, reference Rail 1037/586. Kew: National Archives, 1915.

20   National Archives, War office record of Frederick James Walton, reference WO374/71635.

21   England & Wales Births 1837-2006, Ormskirk, vol. 8B, p. 843, 1880.

22   The Liverpool Chartered Accountants Students Association, *The Accountant*, p.680, Jun. 8th, 1901.

23   Proposed new freemen, *Liverpool Daily Post*, p.3, Jan. 21st, 1904.

24   Union and non-union miners: strike in Flintshire, *Yorkshire Post*, p.7, Oct. 16th, 1906.

25   Twenty Eighth Annual Report of His Majesty's Inspector of Explosives. HM Stationery Office, 1903.

26   Big coal deal. Famous Manchester colliery changes hands, *Manchester Courier*, p.6, Oct. 6th, 1915.

27   Notes, *Iron & Steel Trades Journal*, vol. 98, Mar. 13th, 1916.

28   Coal salesman's salary: Central Silkstone Colliery sued, *Sheffield Daily Telegraph*, p.12, Feb. 7th, 1912.

29   Lancashire colliery purchase, *Liverpool Echo*, p.5, Feb. 3rd, 1916.

30   Mike Nevell, *Tameside 1700–1930*, University of Manchester Archaeological Unit, 1993.

31   Lancashire colliery purchase, *Wigan Observer and District Advertiser*, p.2, Feb. 3rd, 1916.

32   Clifton Park, Blackpool, *Sheffield Daily Telegraph*, p.12, Jun. 16th, 1914.

33   Aviation meetings for Lancashire, *Wigan Observer and District Advertiser*, p.9, May 7th, 1910.

34   Flying machines ordered by Lancashire men, *Stamford Mercury*, p.2, Sep. 10th, 1909.

35   A. Darracq and Co (1905) Limited, *The Economist*, vol. 83, 1916.

36   Stock Exchange Official Intelligence, vol. 35. Spottiswoode, Ballantyne, 1917.

37   Gwyndaf Breese, Timber Tycoons, npublished manuscript.

38   Bill Breese, A Welsh Village at War: 1939-1945, unpublished manuscript, c 1970.

39   Bill Breese, Bygone activities of the Angell valley, *Cambrian News*, Jan. 7th, 1977.

40   Gwyndaf Breese, Hard times on the tramway, unpublished manuscript.

41   Bill Breese, unpublished research notes.

42   Glyn Williams, The Mawddwy Branch, Part Two - Goods Only, *Great Western Railway Journal*, no.60, Autumn 2006.

43   Letter from Cambrian Railways to the Mawddwy Railway Company. Kew: National Archives, 1916.

44   Letter from Samuel Williamson, reference Rail 1057/1951. Kew: National Archives, 1916.

45   Coed Talon Brick and Tile Co. Ltd, *The British Clay Worker, vol. 20*, p.75, Jun. 1920.

46   Bill Breese, Bygone activities within Angell valley, *Cambrian News*, Aug. 6th, 1976.

47   Lewis Cozens, R. W. Kidner, Brian Poole, *The Mawddwy, Van and Kerry Branches*, Oakwood Press, 2004.

48   Russell Meiggs, *Home Timber Production (1939-1945)*, Crosby, Lockwood and Son, 1949.

49   Timber to be sold by auction, *Chester Chronicle*, p.1, Feb. 12th, 1776.

50   Merioneth appeal tribunal, *Cambrian News*, p.7, Nov. 9th, 1917.

51   Bill Breese, The old quarrying days in the Angell valley, *Cambrian News*, 25th June 1976.

52   Arthur Johnson Bolling, Just Up and Down and 'Round About, *Lumber World Review*, Jun. 1915.

53   Supplies of pit timber, Journal of the Board of Agriculture, Dec. 1914.

54   Merioneth appeals. Farmers and their difficulties, *Cambrian News*, p.5, Apr. 7th, 1916.

55   Timber hauliers at variance, *Montgomery County Times*, p.2, Mar. 24th, 1900.

56   Bill Breese, Damweiniau Llenol, *Cambrian News*, Sept. 19th, 1975.

57   Bill Breese, Bygone industrial activities in the Angell valley, Cambrian News, Jul. 9th, 1976.

58   Aberangel: promotion, *Cambrian News*, p.2, Apr. 9th, 1915.

59   Cemmaes: distinction, *Cambrian News*, p.5, Nov. 10th, 1916.

60   Aberangell, *Cambrian News*, p.7, Sep. 7th, 1917.

61   Deaths, *Western Mail*, p.1, Sep. 5th, 1918.

62   Chris Hobson, *Airmen Died in the Great War*, J.B.Hayward & Son, 1995.

63   With full military honours: funeral at Cemmaes, *Cambrian News*, p.6, Sep. 13th, 1918.

NATIONAL WELSH SLATE QUARRIES
LIMITED.
(INCORPORATED UNDER THE COMPANIES ACTS, 1908-1917.)

CAPITAL - - - £280,000.
DIVIDED INTO

120,000 SEVEN-AND-A-HALF PER CENT. (Free of Income-tax) CUMULATIVE AND PARTICIPATING PREFERENCE SHARES OF £1 EACH

AND

2,000,000 ORDINARY SHARES OF 1/- EACH.

100,000 of the above Cumulative and Participating Preference Shares are now offered for Subscription at Par, Payable as to :

2/6 on Application.
2/6 on Allotment.
5/- Three months after Allotment.
5/- One month after Allotment.
5/ Two months after Allotment.

These Shares confer the right to a Cumulative Preferential Dividend at such a rate as shall, after deduction of the Income Tax payable, yield a clear return of 7½ per cent. per annum on the Capital paid up thereon. They are also entitled to participate as to 25 per cent. of the profits that remain after payment of the said Dividend. Dividends will be payable half-yearly.

Arrangements have been made to enable applicants for Preference Shares to purchase two 1/- Ordinary Shares at Par for each Preference Share subscribed. No Ordinary Shares will otherwise be available, as the whole amount has been allotted, as fully paid, to the Vendors, in part consideration for properties transferred.

No Debentures can be created without the consent of the majority of the Preference Shareholders.

£55,000 of the above issue have been subscribed for and taken firm by the Directors and their friends.

DIRECTORS.
MAJOR CHARLES FITZHERBERT BILL, Farley Hall, Oakamoor, Staffs., Chairman.
FREDERICK GEORGE HOUGHTON, Beech House, Harwood, Bolton.
GEORGE WILLIAM BRACE, Chaceley, Belgrave-road, Gloucester.
JACOB COHEN, 277, Pershore-road, Birmingham.
WILLIAM HENRY RHODES, "Watcombe," Kings Norton, Birmingham.

GEOLOGICAL ADVISER.
PROFESSOR O. T. JONES, M.A., D.Sc., F.G.S., "Fenton," Caradoc-road, Aberystwyth, and University of Manchester.

QUARRY MANAGER.
E. H. DAVIS, Brynderwen, Aberangell.

BANKERS.
THE NATIONAL PROVINCIAL AND UNION BANK OF ENGLAND, LTD., Horsefair, Birmingham, & all Branches.

SOLICITOR.
HAROLD ROBERTS, Carlton House, High-street, Birmingham.

BROKER.
F. E. SIMPSON, 6, Great Winchester-street, and Stock Exchange, London, E.C. 2.

AUDITORS.
WILLIAM J. JENNINGS AND CO., Chartered Accountants, 75, New-street, Birmingham.

SECRETARY AND REGISTERED OFFICES.
GEORGE ARTHUR MURRAY, Wheeley's Road, Birmingham.

The title page of the National Welsh Slate Quarries Ltd share prospectus, issued in 1920.

10: Questionable Dealings 1918-1922

'The Great War was a calamity to the whole civilized world. Not only was it full of indescribable horror while it lasted, but it can now clearly be seen to have brought all of Europe within imminent danger of ruin. From those who won, almost as much as those who finally lost, prosperity has gone, progress has been checked, and it is difficult to see how the complicated machine of modern industry and commerce can again be got to run with the smooth regularity which is necessary not merely to the well-being but to the actual existence of the people of Europe.'

John W. McConnel, Chairman of the Fine Spinners and Doublers Association and former Director of the Talyllyn Railway[1]

The war had an enormous impact on Dyffryn Angell. Many young men did not return from the conflict. Those who did return from the war wanted their world to be different. Strikes for higher wages and better working conditions swept through many industries, particularly mining and railways. There was resentment between those who had stayed behind to work in protected occupations and those returning from the war. The armed forces paid 1s 6d a day; those who worked in the forests at home had received considerably more.[2]

Personal tragedies were common. The death of his son Iowerth left E.H. Davies a broken man. He owned Hendreddu Quarry and the tramway, but it was clear his heart was no longer in the enterprise. Many families in Aberangell suffered similar heart-breaking losses.

As Britain recovered, David Lloyd George's government set about rebuilding the country. The 1919 'Addison Act'* allowed local councils to build large-scale housing estates for the first time. The Act called for the construction of 500,000 new homes by the end of 1922, and although only 213,000 were built, it triggered a post-war building boom and many new companies were established to build houses.[3] Many quarries in Merionethshire and Caernarvonshire reopened in 1919.[4]

The resurgence of the slate industry attracted capital and entrepreneurs who saw an opportunity for large profits. It created opportunities for the less than scrupulous to make fortunes at the expense of their fellow citizens. Shady dealings swept through the valley.

Key Players
William Clayton Russon

One of the most significant entrepreneurs involved with the quarries after the war was William Clayton Russon. Between 1919 and 1937, he helped revive both Hendreddu and Gartheiniog. He made his fortune in Mid Wales, though some of his dealings, and at least one of his close associates, were highly dubious.

Russon was born in 1872 in Birmingham, to Frederick and Sarah Ann Russon.[5] His father had run a brass foundry, and later began manufacturing bicycles; William trained in his father's cycle business. On 15th August 1894, he married Gertrude James[6] whose family ran the James Cycles Co., a well-known bicycle and motorcycle manufacturer, whose factory was on Gough Road, Edgbaston.[7] Their first son, also called William Clayton Russon, was born on 30th June 1895[8] at Kings Norton.

In 1892, Russon partnered with William Clayton Lloyd[9] to form Lloyd and Sons in Grove Lane, Smethwick. Lloyd was the lightweight amateur boxing champion of Birmingham and excelled in many sports, including ice skating, roller skating, tandem carriage driving and swimming.[10]

In 1896, Lloyd and Sons changed their name to the Claremont Cycle Manufacturing Company and were floated as a public company. Russon was Works Manager on a £500 a year salary. He also received £3,000 in cash, £2,500 in debentures and £9,000 in shares after the successful flotation.

In 1900, Claremont Cycle failed. Russon and Lloyd

Advertisement for Russon's Main Wheeleries company that appeared in the *Western Gazette,* on 19th June 1903.

---

* Formally the Housing, Town Planning, &c. Act 1919.

immediately started the Colossal Cycle Company, with Russon as the sole shareholder. Russon also created the United Trader's Syndicate trading from the same address.[11]

By 1902, Russon had created a third bicycle company, Main Wheeleries at Soho Road, Birmingham.[12] The relationship between Colossal Cycle and Main Wheeleries and United Traders is unclear. Russon's three companies failed in late 1904 and he was declared bankrupt.[11]

Following his bankruptcy, Russon disappeared from the business world for several years. In 1911 he was still living in Edgbaston with his family and gave his occupation as 'cycle manufacturer';[13] it is likely he had returned to work at his father's business while he paid off his debts.

Roland Morgan

The other major force behind the revival of the quarries was Roland Morgan. He was born in 1877 in Birmingham.[14] In the 1890s, he promoted a series of companies, mostly with unfortunate results. In July 1900, he made his first appearance in a bankruptcy court, though the order was rescinded.[15]

In 1905, Morgan was running a 'bucket shop' scam in London – an unauthorised company speculating in stocks and shares. Using the alias J.B. Mackenzie, he sold a business to his employee A.E. Weiss, which resulted in Weiss's bankruptcy a year later. Despite this, Morgan continued to operate bucket shops until at least 1908, and his multiple companies were described as: 'cover-system gambles on the good old principle of 'heads I win, tails you lose'.'[16]

By April 1911, Morgan was living in Brighton and gave his occupation to the census taker as stockbroker.[14] However, he was in financial difficulties and in August 1911 he appeared at Brighton bankruptcy court, with debts of more than £12,000.[15] He was declared bankrupt on 22nd December.[17]

Around 1913, Morgan moved back to Birmingham. In 1914, he bought shares in Mathias Ltd in Liverpool. By 1917 he had made £8,000 profit from these shares, half of which he used to pay off debts from his 1911 bankruptcy. He attempted to remove the bankruptcy, but the Official Receiver refused, stating that he had not paid off all sixty-nine debts.[15]

In 1915 or 1916, Morgan took an office at 27 Temple Row,

Birmingham and started promoting a series of companies. One was the Sedgley Hall Colliery Company,[18] though it appears it never operated and was struck off the register in October 1922.[19]

A business that Morgan took particular interest in was the Ryland Manufacturing Co. in Birmingham. Founded in 1912 it had quickly become a significant business, making chairs, motor car bodies, cabinets and other wooden goods. In 1914, Ryland took over two factories: the Sun Works in Wheeley's Road, Edgbaston and the Edgbaston Works in Gough Road.[20]

Morgan and Russon Join Forces

Ryland Manufacturing was owned by Sarah Ann Russon, and her son, William Clayton Russon, worked there.[21] By 1916, Russon appears to have paid off his debts, though it is doubtful that he had discharged his bankruptcy.

Morgan offered to invest £2,000, provided they created a new private company structure.[15] The Russons agreed, and in November 1916 a new company, Ryland (Joinery) Ltd was born.[21] Sarah retired, leaving William to run the new company. The new capital allowed Ryland to expand. Morgan and Russon were keen to secure timber supplies for their factories, and they leased woodlands near Aberystwyth. Russon moved to Wales to oversee the plantations and sawmill in Cwm Rheidol.

British Timber Plantations

After the war, Russon and Morgan sought to expand Ryland and their timber operations in Wales. They promoted a new company: British Timber Plantations . This ambitious venture would take over Ryland and lease further woodlands and a sawmill near Llanfyllin.

In July 1919, shares in British Timber Plantations worth £110,000 were offered to the public. Russon was a director of the company. Morgan does not appear in the official documents; he was an undischarged bankrupt and shunned the limelight. A great deal of the capital raised was paid directly to Morgan and Russon. The company's accountant was William James Jennings of New Street, Birmingham and the secretary was George Arthur Murray.[22]

British Timber Plantations continued the 'vertical integration' approach of Ryland — owning the whole production chain from growing trees to making the finished products.[22] The company acquired Ryland's existing woods at Twllwyd and Pant Mawr in the Rheidol valley and added Allt, Dingle, Woodcock and Bodyddon at Llanfyllin, Cwm Rhosfawr at Meifod and Giverni Gleision (sic) at Llanwyddyn. The company's sawmill next to Llanfyllin station had '*light railways… for the transport of timber from the plantations to the road*'.[22]

As well as timber for their factories, the new company supplied pitwood, with the Rheidol sawmill dedicated to producing props.[22] Meanwhile, Russon and Morgan had their eyes on an even bigger opportunity, in slate mines and housing construction.

Aberangell Quarries

Russon and Morgan wanted to capitalise on the booming home construction industry, where demand for slate was rapidly outstripping supply. Russon was aware of the quarries at Aberangell – their mills were still equipped, and the tramway had been maintained for wartime timber traffic, so they could be easily reopened.

Edward Hurst Davies restarted Hendreddu after the end of the war, but he was 64 and coming to the end of his career. By 1919, he was actively trying to sell the quarry, and in August, John Stanley Horrex of Birmingham produced a survey, valuing the tramway and machinery at £38,000 and the land and buildings at £48,500.[23] Russon purchased the quarry from Davies shortly afterwards.[24]

Aberangell was not the only slate area that Russon was interested in. He also purchased the quarries at Llangynog. The capital for these purchases came from the large payments he received from the floatation of British Timber Plantations.

The Sale of Cwmllecoediog 1919

After the war, F.J. Walton returned to Wales, but his health was failing. On 11th June 1919, he resigned his commission; his poor health was judged to have been caused by his war service. In October 1919, he put Cwmllecoediog Estate up for auction,[25] but on 27th December he died, aged 43. The auction split the estate into 7 lots totalling more than 1,000 acres. Lot 5 was Abermynach Farm, including:

'*The Tramway … a valuable adjunct to the Farm, is included in the sale of this lot; subject to the right of the owners or occupiers of Cwmllecoedig [sic] House, and the woods retained therein to use the said tramway for all purposes and subject to the running facilities at present enjoyed by Messrs. Higginbottom for the carrying of timber and Messrs. Vigar and Davies for the carrying of Silica stone.*'[26]

'Silica stone' is an inaccurate description of slate. 'Davies' is Edward Hurst Davies, while 'Vigar' is probably A.W.Vigar of Aberystwyth, a dealer in quarries and quarry machinery, who appears to have purchased Gartheiniog from Mrs Mallory just after the end of the War.

Russon, now the owner of the Hendreddu, failed to understand the significance of the auction. E.H. Davies, ever the shrewd businessman, realised that Lot 5 included control of the tramway from Abermynach to the wharf, and he purchased it for £800. He had Russon over a barrel, for trains could not get through to Wharf without his permission.

Davies sold the right to use the tramway to Russon for £400 – who had thought he already had them. In exchange, Davies was appointed as manager at Hendreddu. This was a smart deal by the canny Davies, and Russon had no choice but to accept.[27]

The Timber Industry After World War One
The End of the Timber Supply Department

There was continued demand for timber after the end of the First World War, though at a lower level than during the war years. British industry was recovering, and overseas supplies were unreliable. The Directorate of Timber Supplies was now renamed the Timber Supply Department (TSD). By the end of 1918, the TSD was hoping to cease operations but the War Cabinet decided to keep it running for at least the next year. In September 1919, the civilian Forestry Commission was established, replacing the military TSD.[28]

Higginbottom and the National Timber Company

Higginbottom continued felling in Dyffryn Angell after the war. Early in 1919, his workforce went on strike, though Higginbottom stood firm, and after two days the men reluctantly returned to work.[2] This discontent rumbled on into 1920 when Higginbottom closed down operations for a week to head off another strike.

In 1918, Higginbottom was charged by the Board of Trade with selling coal from New Moss Colliery for more than the statutory limit. The judge concluded that '*much of the evidence given by Mr. Higginbottom was untrue*'[29] and that he had '*systematically and deliberately paid no attention to the provisions of the limitations of the Coal Prices Order*';[30] he was found guilty and fined £1,097 plus £500 costs.[31]

In 1920 the Cwm Caws tramway was lifted, leaving just a short siding at Pont yr Hirgwm, which was retained for a few more years.[32]

On 20th April 1920, Higginbottom's partner Andrew Bryning formed the National Timber Company. The company's stated objectives were to:

'*Buy, acquire, sell, grow, fell, cut up, saw, prepare for use, handle, import, export, distribute, supply and deal with pit wood and timber and wood of all kinds… pit props and other materials… capable of being used in mines, quarries and collieries and work and buildings connected therewith… To carry on business as Timber Growers, Sawmill Proprietors [and] Timber Merchants.*' The directors of the company were Bryning, Higginbottom and Thomas Wain of Christleton, near Chester. Wain was the coal wholesaler for Higginbottom's New Haden Colliery[33] and held 22,000 of National Timber's 25,000 shares. In January

Bungalow Stores, a converted First World War hut, that operated from 1922 until the 1950s. It was initially run by Lewis Dawes.[34] In front of the fence, the rails of the cut back Green's Tramway are just visible. A modern cottage now stands on this site. [Lilywhite Postcards]

1921, the company added R.L. Percival of Cemmaes Road as the manager of timber operations.

From January 1920 until October 1921, National Timber rented Sied Ddu from the National Welsh Slate Quarries Ltd and paid wayleave to use the Hendre Ddu Tramway, sending 850 tons of timber over the tramway during 1921.

It is not known which woods were felled by National Timber; one possibility is they were continuing to work in Cwmllecoediog. The tramway there was used to move waste from the Cwmllecoediog quarry tips to resurface Cwmllecoediog Drive in the early 1920s and was removed shortly afterwards. If it did survive beyond 1920, it was likely because National Timber were using it.[32]

Rail from the tramway may have been reused in the early 1920s to relay the lower section of the Ratgoed Tramway. After Inigo Jones gave up working at Talymeirin in 1919, they got their supply of slab from Braichgoch. In 1921 they leased Cymerau quarry, north of Aberllefenni.

Cymerau was connected to the Ratgoed Tramway, and shortly after Inigo Jones took over, the section of the tramway between Cymerau and Aberllenni was relaid using light flat-bottomed rail which came from a 'local timber tramway'. Perhaps Cwmllecoediog was the source of the rail that Inigo Jones used? There is only circumstantial evidence to support this theory, but perhaps a part of Higginbottom's timber empire lived on until the Ratgoed Tramway closed in 1952.

Early in 1921, National Timber dismantled the sawmill at Aberdwynant the building being reused as a store at Cefngwyn Farm. By the end of the year, relations with the workforce deteriorated further and the company stopped work. Higginbottom removed the barracks opposite Aberangell Wharf. This was later replaced by an ex-Army hut that served as the village store until the 1950s.[2]

Higginbottom was replaced as a director of National Timber by timber merchant Frank Pinfold on 30th December 1922.[35] The company was officially dissolved on 19th February 1926.

Higginbottom's Disgrace 1921-1929

In 1921, Higginbottom's extensive colliery business was in serious financial trouble, as the coal industry was suffering a significant recession. In December he was forced into bankruptcy[36] with debts of £112,000.[37] He spent much of 1922 in bankruptcy court. He also owed his father-in-law, Sir William Hartley, at least £34,000. His ownership in the National Timber Company was discussed in court, and Higginbottom testified that Thomas Wain had no connection to any of his colliery businesses. This was untrue, and it is unclear what Higginbottom's motive was for perjuring himself. Further appearances followed, and Higginbottom was repeatedly unable to produce the required documents. On October 17th the court gave up and adjourned the enquiry indefinitely.

In June 1923, Higginbottom was charged with fraud. The case was that in 1918[38] he had paid his workmen a special war supplement in response to their demand for higher wages. While this extra money could be claimed for miners working underground, in reality, many of them had been set to repair Gwasted Hall, Higginbottom's private house.[39]

At trial, Higginbottom claimed he was drinking heavily at the time. His defence counsel pleaded his case as best he could: '*This is the tragedy of a young man who had too much money early in life without a father's restraining hand... he is a man of reckless energy and boundless ambition, who looked after the big things and neglected the small matter of accounts. He fell into the clutches of a school of sharks calling themselves friends and*

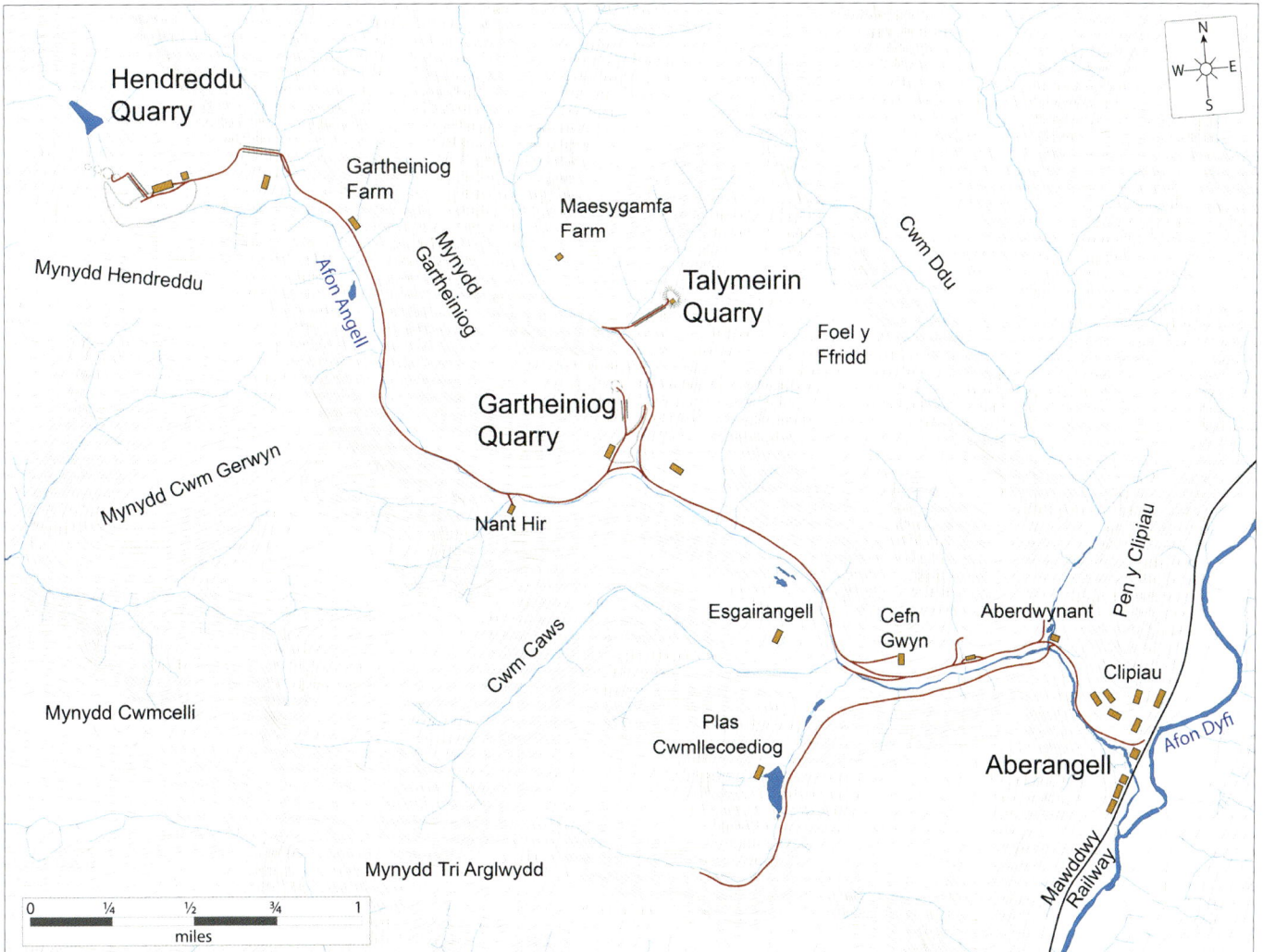

The Hendre Ddu Tramway in 1921. The Maesygamfa Tramway was cut back during World War One, with the lower section left to serve the revived Talymeirin quarry. The branches to the brickworks, Cefn Gwyn and Nant Hir were still in place. The timber tramway along Cwm Caws was removed in 1920, but the Cwmllecoediog Tramway is thought to have lasted until around 1922.

who were always wanting money. Later he got into the Bankruptcy Court, and his friends shunned him and tried to gain favour with the authorities by giving information.'[40]

Higginbottom was found guilty and sentenced to nine months in prison.[40] After serving his sentence, he was discharged from bankruptcy in 1926.[41] He died in 1929, aged 49, in London.[42]

National Welsh Slate Quarries 1919-1922
Company Formation 1919

In late 1919, a new company called National Welsh Slate Quarries Ltd (NWSQ) was formed to take over Hendreddu. On 1st October 1919, the company purchased the quarry from Russon for £50,000* in cash, and £130,000 of shares.[24] The NWSQ company was led by Major Charles Fitzherbert Bill from Staffordshire. Bill was born in 1873, the son of Lieutenant Colonel Charles Bill, the owner of Farley Hall in Alton. Charles Bill was the MP for Leek between 1892 and 1906, and the Chairman of the Leek and Manifold Light Railway.[43]

Charles Fitzherbert Bill graduated from Oxford University then became a partner in the engineering companies F.H. Smith & Co. and the London Scottish Engineering Company. In August 1914, he joined the North Staffordshire Regiment as a Captain.[44] In December 1915, while Captain Bill was on active service, his father died, leaving him the Farley Hall estate and £49,500.[45]

During the war, Captain Bill was promoted to Major and seconded to the Ministry of Labour, responsible for demobbing soldiers from the front lines in France and assigning them to civilian industry. Bill officially served with the North Staffordshires until 1920, though he was working on Hendreddu in 1919. The NWSQ Co. was registered on 14th January 1920, with its office at Wheely's Road, Birmingham, just around the corner from Gough Road.[24] The directors were Chairman Bill, Frederick George Houghton of Bolton and William Henry Rhodes[46] a glass merchant from Kings Norton.[47]

★ £2.5 million in 2020.

By March 1920, George William Brace of Gloucester and Jacob Cohen of Birmingham[46] had been added as directors. Cohen owned theatres across the north of England[48] and was the co-owner of the White Hall Cinema in Derby with J. Levy who lived at 66 Gough Road, Edgbaston.[49] They also added company secretary George Arthur Murray, who lived on Wheeley's Road in Birmingham, and who had been the secretary of British Timber Plantations.

NWSQ had more than 150 shareholders, including William Bowley of Melton Mowbray, who would play a significant part in the history of Hendreddu. Bowley knew John Heawood, a commercial photographer who had moved to Melton in 1906[50] and was the official photographer of the Melton Mowbray district council.

In 1919, Heawood moved to Gough Road in Birmingham where he met William Clayton Russon. Heawood would become a director of Russon's other enterprise, the Standard Housing Company. Excited by the prospects of NWSQ, Heawood invited fellow Meltonian Joseph Morris to join the Standard Housing Company board. Morris sat on the Melton Mowbray Board of Guardians in the decade before the First World War, along with William Bowley.[51] Bowley was introduced to Russon by Morris and Heawood and decided to invest in the NWSQ.

Other interesting investors include William and Gertrude Russon, William Herbert Bullock, brother of the owner of Minllyn Quarry, Richard Lewis the former manager at Maesygamfa and William Frank Pearce of 101 Gough Road.[46]

The company was covered in *The Economist* in 1920. After reporting the basic facts of the offering, they stated:

'*It is difficult to understand why the promoters should expect the public to pay £180,000 for assets valued at under £90,000, and the omission of the past financial record is also another unfavourable feature. The slate industry is in a remarkable state of development, but this proposition fails to attract us.*'[52]

In June 1920, one F.J. Nettlinghame was writing from the company's registered address promoting the company's stock to the public.[53] Between July and October, an additional director was appointed, William Rhodes Speller. 'Speller' was Roland Morgan using a false name – one very similar to William Henry Rhodes.[46]

The company offered the public stock worth £280,000,*of which about £90,000 was subscribed.[53] The money raised was used to purchase the quarry and to modernise operations. Captain Nathaniel Edwards Twitchen was mine agent and engineer,[54] A.J. Pilsbury the company secretary,[46] and E.H. Davies the quarry manager.

Nathaniel Twitchen (also written Twitchin) was born in 1883 in Leeds[55] and grew up there. From 1900 onwards, he was a member of the Territorial Army. He signed up at the outbreak of the First World War with the Royal Field Artillery.[56] He quickly rose to the rank of acting Major. In 1918, he volunteered for the White Russian Army under Generals Anton Denikin and Pyotr Wrangel, who were fighting against the Bolsheviks in the Civil War that followed the Revolution.

The Russians awarded him the St. George Medal, and on his return to Britain in 1919 he received an OBE. He led a quieter life during the 1920s, focusing on amateur dramatics and religious work with the 'Toc H' group, in Gloucester. He died in 1927 and was buried in Leeds.

The prospectus of the company makes for interesting reading. The quarry was described:

'*The superficial area available is 630 acres, with exclusive right to work the whole or any part thereof …The slate vein being worked is one mile in length, about 30 yards wide and 400 to 500 yards deep, and is estimated to contain approximately 18,000,000 tons of slate, all above the level of free drainage…*

The buildings consist of a very substantial stone built and slated machine house (236ft x 62ft), smith's shop, manager's house, engineering shop, offices and minor buildings, weighbridge, six cottages, workmen's barracks, two sheds at terminus of tramway, all in good order and condition.

Plant and machinery (fixed): sawing, planing, drilling, filing, punching and other machines, engineering lathes with pulleys, shafting, belting, overhead cranes, the whole being driven by a 60 h.p. turbine, which derives its power from specially constructed reservoirs owned by the Company… which it is proposed to utilise for driving dynamos to supply the quarries, machine shops, offices, etc. with electric light.

Plant (loose). Slab-wagons and trams, ropes, belts, tools, chains etc. Powerful winches and cranes, underground chain blocks, saws and planing tools, rock drills, passenger trams, etc.

Tramway: Specially constructed 2-foot gauge, about four miles in length, from the quarries to Aberangell Station (Cambrian Railway). Drumhead with tram line from quarry to loading-up wharf (about 200 yards). The trams at present are worked by horse-power and return to Aberangell loaded, by gravitation.'

The 'two sheds at the terminus of tramway' were Sied Ddu and Sied Wen. The 'passenger trams' are the car gwyllt and other quarrymen's conveyances.

The company had been working Hendreddu since mid-1919. In 1920, they began to diversify into new products. Two Griffin Mill pulverising machines were purchased from the Bradley Pulveriser Company in March and May 1920.[57] These mills were giant pestle-and-mortars that reduced slate waste to fine dust. The prospectus claimed:

'*At each quarry there is a tip… where waste slate is shot… These cast-off slabs have hitherto had no value, but science has now evolved a method of utilising them and giving them a high commercial value. The "waste" is pulverised and ground into eight grades of powder, the last being so fine as to approximate to vapour. From these dusts and powders are now manufactured… bricks of great density and strength… tiles, pottery, glassware of self-coloured green and amber… and the tyre and rubber, bootmaking and chemical trades will also consume great quantities… The most important commercial use… lies in the manufacture of Portland cement.*'

Even while the company was being formed, concerns were expressed about the large amount of capital it was spending

---

*£14 million in 2020.

to acquire the quarries. The *Western Morning News* devoted an editorial to the company's prospects:

'*The statement of affairs by the promoters of the National Welsh Slate Quarries Ltd. make poor reading. An independent valuation is given [of] £87,141 and the purchase price is fixed at £150,000…We would not object so much to the difference… but unfortunately the prospectus… informs us that they were opened in 1870, and then proceeds with refreshing candour to chronicle a record which at best can only be described as "unfulfilled hopes! But the sun may shine on the morrow".The statement that £250,000 has been spent on the quarries does not impress us. It would be interesting to know if the slate quarries have ever been run at a profit…The slate industry is booming, but then today the demand for most commodities is greater than the supply.The investor should look ahead - to when a period of trade depression may arrive.*'[58]

These concerns were to prove well-founded. The NWSQ company also invested in the tramway in late 1919 and early 1920, relaying large sections of the track, for the first time in decades. The quarry machinery too was overhauled after its hiatus during the war.

On 4th November 1920, E.H. Davies was replaced by Captain Twitchen as the manager of Hendreddu.[59]

John Breese

In 1920, John Breese started work for NWSQ. He was born on 3rd. July 1878[60] in Llanerfyl, about 20 miles northeast of Aberangell. His father was killed in the Anglo-Zulu War of 1879, and the family moved to the Rhondda Valley when he was young.[61] He joined the Welsh Regiment during the Second Boer War but did not serve in South Africa after being struck by lightning while waiting to embark.

After being invalided out of the Army, John found work in the coal mines,[62] first at Ocean Colliery in Treharris,[61] and then at Parc Colliery in Cwmparc where he installed and maintained the tramway inclines underground.[59] He rejoined the Army at the outbreak of the war, serving in the 15th Battalion of the Welsh Regiment. He was amongst the first men to serve in France and received the 1914 Mons Star.[63]

John married Elizabeth in Pontypridd in early 1919; John

Advertisement for the Griffin Mill, 1919.

was 41 and Elizabeth was 27.[64] The Breese family tended to use 'Breese' and 'Breeze' interchangeably. They moved to Aberangell in 1920. Between 1922 and 1934 John was the driver of the Motor Rail locomotive and maintained the track. On 20th. September 1921, Bill Breese was born in Machynlleth.[65]

John's brother 'Yede' Breese was also a quarryman. He lived in Era Terrace, Esgairgeiliog, was for some time the foreman of Cymerau quarry, and later worked at Llwyngwern.[66] Bill spent his childhood holidays with Yede and fondly recalled watching trains on the Corris Railway.[67] The Breese family lived at Penybanc in Clipiau. John Breese died in 1959, aged eighty-one.[68]

Developments in Aberangell 1920

In 1920, Edward Hurst Davies was flush with cash from the sale of Hendreddu to Russon. As well as being a quarry manager, he was a farmer and in 1892 wrote a booklet on livestock and butchery. He supplied meat to the village for many years. He built a stable below Brynderwen, with builder William Roberts starting work on 1st September 1920. It was floored with slabs from Hendreddu and it was known locally as 'Bilding Davies'.[59]

The main road into Aberangell in 2019, looking west. Bilding Davies in on the left. On the right above the caravan is Brynderwen. [Steve Culverhouse]

Incidents on the Tramway 1920-1921

In 1920, an accident occurred on the tramway at Rock Cutting between Nant Hir and Gartheiniog, where the tramway runs on a ledge above the Afon Angell. Winds from the west funnel through this narrow section of the valley and often created significant problems for trains heading to Hendreddu. On the morning in question, a single car gwyllt, loaded with quarrymen was being hauled by the Cloister, a horse from Abermynach Farm.

As they came into Rock Cutting the strong westerly wind made it impossible to continue. Richard Williams unhitched Cloister and headed back down the line, leaving the men to continue on foot. The wind became so strong that Cloister was picked up and hurled into the Gartheiniog Mill Race. The car gwyllt was sent flying and its wooden body was destroyed.

The workers were forced to retreat; one lost his oilskins, while the shortest member of the party was picked up and blown into a nearby tree. The remaining men sheltered behind the wreck of the overturned car until the wind died down. They were then able to walk to Hendreddu.[69]

On 22nd December 1920, Dafydd Jones and Twm Ifans were unloading slabs from a trestle wagon on Aberangell Wharf. They unloaded one side of the wagon, then pushed it onto the turntable to turn it and unload the other side. The wagon overbalanced and the remaining load landed on Dafydd. Twm managed to lift the slabs off Jones, but one of the slates had cut his neck, and he lost a great deal of blood. The local doctor sewed up the wound and saved his life. He was taken home to his wife Maggie, who had to keep him awake during the night to stop him from reopening the wound. Eventually, Dafydd recovered from his injuries and returned to work on the tramway.[27]

On 12th September 1921, Mrs D. Williams of Esgairangell Farm was travelling down the tramway in her family's car gwyllt when she collided with a Hendreddu train.

John Breese, father of Bill, seen shovelling coal behind Penybanc, Aberangell, the Breese family home. This photograph was taken after the Second World War. [Bill Breese collection]

Quarryman Richard Williams caught his arm in the collision and was seriously injured,[70] while Mrs Williams dislocated her shoulder.[71]

Introduction of Locomotive Working 1921

For more than fifty years, horses had hauled wagons from Aberangell to Hendreddu. In 1920, NWSQ decided to introduce locomotive haulage. Several of the directors had been impressed by the War Department light railways they saw operating during the First World War.[54] Captain Twitchen ordered a Motor Rail 'Simplex' locomotive to work the trains. This was a 20hp model, works number 2059 ordered from new. It was a standard 'bent frame' Motor Rail product but was fitted with special dumb buffers, essential for working with the wide variety of loose coupled Hendre Ddu wagons.

The locomotive was ordered in November 1920, with delivery anticipated in December that year, though problems at Motor Rail meant it did not arrive until 7th January 1921. A large crowd turned up to watch the new machine being lifted from a Cambrian Railways wagon at the Wharf.[54] The locomotive's first driver was John Roberts, the grandson of Thomas Pugh who was killed in Cwmllecoediog Quarry in 1868. John lived at

The clearest known photograph of the locomotive shed at the top of the Brynderwen Cutting. The shed was a simple corrugated iron structure on a concrete foundation with a wooden access door on the east side and probably wooden double doors on the west. The building in the top-right corner is Capel Bethania.

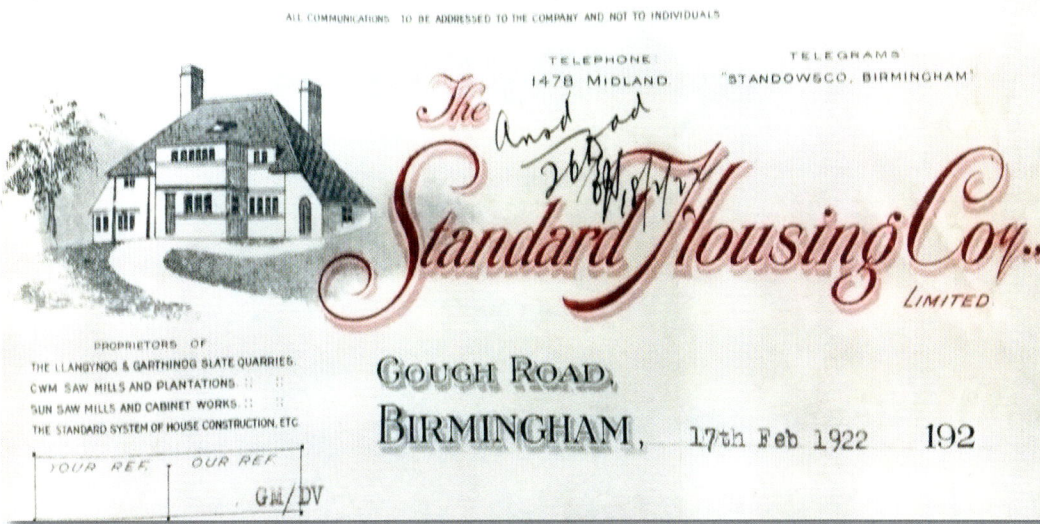

The attractive letterhead used by the Standard Housing Company Limited.

Ty Newydd, a house overlooking the tramway at Clipiau; having survived service in Egypt in the First World War, he sadly died unexpectedly in his sleep on February 28th 1922.[72] John Breese took over as driver.

The introduction of the locomotive meant a change in operations on the tramway. Loaded trains worked downhill by gravity, but the Motor Rail hauled empties back uphill. Gravity trains now ran straight through to the Wharf, and a corrugated iron shed was built over the siding at the top of Brynderwen Cutting to house the locomotive.

The Standard Housing Company 1920-1922

While NWSQ was reviving Hendreddu, another ambitious enterprise, the Standard Housing Company, sought to reopen Gartheiniog. On the surface, these two companies were independent, though behind the scenes, they were deeply connected.

Company Formation 1920

The Standard Housing Company (SHC) was formed in 1920 to take advantage of the housing boom. Its stated purpose was to mass-produce a new type of house, with a foundation of slate waste topped with low walls built from blocks made from ground slate. The main walls were slate slabs cemented into a timber frame. The inside walls were finished using a 'special fibrous material' which could be 'given the effect of oak panelling' by overlaying oak veneers. All this was finished with a slate roof.

SHC was incorporated on 14th July 1920. It was an ambitious undertaking, aiming to create a vertically integrated company controlling everything from quarrying through to house construction. The company aimed to raise £450,000 in a public share offering and took a full-page advertisement in *The Times* to persuade investors to subscribe. Their share prospectus described Gartheiniog:

'*The Gartheiniog quarries are two miles from Aberangell Station, on the Cambrian Railway. The quarry is connected by light railway… in quality, cleavage and other essentials the slate is excellent, and [the surveyor] estimates the slate contents at*

24,000,000 tons… blocks and slabs of any desired size and thickness can be got out without damage. The property comprises full plant and machinery, machine house, manager's dwelling, tram incline and drum-house, water course and reservoir, with 12in pipe laid to turbine engine, weighing machine and house, turntable, cranes etc. The whole is in good condition and the machinery ready for immediate use. There is abundant water power and ample tipping ground… with the present machinery 400 tons could be produced each month, but there is no reason why output should not reach 2,000 to 2,500 tons monthly. The total cost of production would be about £5 10s 0d per ton.'[73]

Standard Housing acquired Gartheiniog from Sidney Victor Wallis for £50,000 in cash and £100,000 in shares.[74] They also bought a brickworks and a wharf on the Medway from Wallis, and Llangynog quarry from William Clayton Russon for £25,000 in cash and £65,000 in shares.[75]

Sidney Wallis married Gertrude Irene Russon at Kings Norton in 1921.[76] Gertrude Irene was the daughter of William Clayton and Gertrude Emma Russon. Wallis and Russon made significant profits selling their properties to the Standard Housing Company at inflated prices. Wallis used some of this money to buy shares in NWSQ.[46]

SHC also bought a timber plantation at Gartheiniog and the whole of British Timber Plantations from Roland Morgan and Russon; the latter cost £47,000.[*] The total capital expenditure of SHC was over £295,000.[**] William Clayton Russon received a total of £200,000 in cash from his various sales to SHC.[74]

SHC appointed Robert Crooks as quarry manager; he moved from Northern Ireland to Francis Road, Edgbaston to take the position. William Bowley's friends Heawood and Morris were directors,[74] as was Walter George Silcocks from Bristol, the chairman of Keynsham Housing Committee. The SHC chairman was Walter Baxter, a stockbroker from Surrey. W.J. Penny of Birmingham was the Gartheiniog mine agent.[77]

The quarry itself had not worked since 1916, and the lower adit had silted up leaving the underground chamber flooded. Trefor Wood from Pantperthog was contracted to drain the workings. He set up his portable Blackstone oil engine and pump, but could not clear the chamber, despite

---

★ £2.26 million in 2020

★★ £14 million in 2020

Aberangell from the southwest in the early 1920s. The tramway runs across the bottom of the meadows behind the trees. Capel Hebron and Capel Bethania dominate the right edge of the village, while Clipiau is above the meadow. [Francis Frith]

running it day and night for two weeks.

The chamber was finally drained by careful unblocking the lower adit. Miners from Cwmllinau undertook the perilous work, aware of the huge pressure of water behind the blockage. They dug in as far as they dared, then took out the last of the material with explosives. An enormous torrent of water came out, washing the adit and the cutting below it clean.[59]

Building New Homes 1920-1921

The new company equipped Gartheiniog with air compressors to drive rocks drills and new machinery in the mill. They hoped to increase capacity above 400 tons a month. They also made extensive investments in the derelict Llangynog Quarry.

An article in the *Liverpool Echo* provides insight into SHC's progress and plans in 1920:

'*In these days when there is a pessimistic feeling abroad as to the housing problem... it is interesting to come across a building concern the directors of which are imbued with optimism... The Standard Housing Company... claims that they are in a position to build cheaper and quicker than any of their rivals.*

They possess their own quarries, timber plantations, saw-mills and brickfield, they estimate that they save £200 per home... Furthermore they apply the massed production principle, they anticipate a further profit of from £300 to £500 per home on construction... The writer inspected dwellings in all stages of construction, from the planning of the site to the finished house. They were being erected in the residential suburbs of Moseley and Edgbaston for private purchasers, and were all of the bungalow

type... The price of each was £1,500... the house can be extended as desired at little inconvenience, and at comparatively moderate cost ... Fifty houses on the lines of the one described are now in the course of construction in Birmingham, and the company's programme embraces 1,000 houses in Birmingham alone.

The Standard Housing Company has just entered into a contract to erect 122 houses for the Worcester Council. Other negotiations are proceeding, and in addition to the activity at Birmingham, houses are being erected for private purchasers at Melton Mowbray, Bournemouth and Dundee.[78]

In September 1920 the Worcester Housing Committee inspected the homes built in Birmingham and expressed interest in building 100 of them in Worcester.[79] *In November, they claimed that 18 of their men had built 3 houses in 42 days, much faster than traditional methods, and that 30,000 homes were "either finished or under construction".*[80]

SHC only completed between fifteen and fifty houses. None of the major contracts mentioned in the Liverpool Echo article were fulfilled. In 2016, thirteen of the houses are still standing on Webb Lane, Birmingham and one at Belle Walk, Moseley.

The Relationship Between the National Welsh Slate Quarries and the Standard Housing Company

Although technically separate companies, there were strong connections between NWSQ and SHC, centred on Roland Morgan and William Clayton Russon.

When William Clayton Russon sold Hendreddu to NWSQ, the purchase agreement contained a clause barring him from '*either solely or jointly with or as manager or agent for*

The tramway passing below Cefngwyn Hall and Farm in the early 1920s. The hall is the building on the left, with the farm on the right. The path from the hall to the tramway is gated at its lower end. The tramway track, most visible on the curve to the left of the gate, is in good condition, having been relaid by the NWSQ company.
[TuckDB archive]

any other person or persons or company directly or indirectly carry on or be engaged or concerned or interested in the business of a quarry owner or permit to suffer his name to be used or employed in quarrying or in any connection with any such business within thirty miles of the said quarries [Hendreddu and Nanthir] save so far as the Vendor [Russon] shall as a member of the company be interested or as an officer or servant or agent of the company be employed in the business of the company'.[24]

This is a very specific non-competition clause. The exception allowing Russon to work for another quarry as long as it was part of his duties as a member of NWSQ may have been a deliberate 'get-out' that allowed him to also work with the SHC.

In the May 1920 issue of *The Quarry* magazine, Russon discussed the reworking of slate waste by NWSQ:

'The National Welsh Slate Quarries Ltd... under the management of Mr. W. Clayton Russon is to study the utilisation of the waste from the start, and is also to branch out in a totally new direction... viz., a system of building construction without bricks or mortar, slate slabs and steel to take the place of these.'[81]

This system of building construction sounds a lot like the SHC's. The SHC houses needed ground slate to make building blocks, but Gartheiniog had no equipment to pulverise slate waste. Hendreddu, however, had installed Griffin Mills for just this purpose. SHC could only build its houses if the two companies worked together.

In July 1920, three new SHC directors were appointed: Joseph Schofield, 'Speller' and Russon,[74] with Russon and Speller taking over as managing directors. Speller was also a director of NWSQ. Russon purchased £77,000 of SHC shares. William James Jennings, the British Timber Plantations accountant, was appointed as the SHC auditor; he was also the auditor of NWSQ.

The Quarry interviewed Russon again in January 1921:
'The most interesting application [of quarried slabs] is the building of a new type of house. A considerable number of houses of this type of construction have been, and are being, erected in the neighbourhood of Birmingham. I am indebted to Mr. Clayton Russon for some details of this method of building... All steps, hearthstones, and paths are of slate; the paths consist of broken and rough pieces forming what is known as a "crazy pavement". The roof, of course, is of slate, but the chief novelty in the construction is the slate wall. The slabs of slate are fitted into an oak frame, which is rebated to receive them. The slabs are secured in this position from behind, and with appropriate provision for securing waterproof joints form the outer walls. The inner walls are composed of concrete blocks made of an aggregate of slate chippings and clinker or slab.'[82]

NWSQ and SHC shared investors and directors, many from one small area of Birmingham. They were essentially operating as one concern.

Failure

Both companies raised huge sums of money and spent extravagantly. For either to become profitable would have required an unprecedented expansion of production in their quarries. This did not come close to happening.

In April 1921, the South Wales coal miners went on strike demanding higher wages.[83] By June the price of coal was rising dramatically, as stockpiles ran low. The Cambrian Railways stopped running on Sundays due to the coal shortage, and both Hendreddu and Gartheiniog stopped working entirely.[84] The strike ended at the beginning of July and the quarries reopened shortly afterwards, but the damage had been done, and NWSQ and SHC failed shortly afterwards.

The Standard Housing Company

On the 10th March 1921, SHC was sued in the High Court by shareholder Reginald Geles to have his name struck from the company's register. He alleged that J.N. Morgan was fraudulently passing himself off as an agent of the company. J.N. Morgan was another pseudonym of Roland Morgan. By May, Geles had succeeded in freeing himself from the obligation to pay for the shares he had applied for.[85] He knew something was seriously amiss.

SHC was on the brink of collapse, with its quarries shut down and its finances seriously compromised. On 26th May 1921, it was placed into receivership at the request of the Inland Revenue.[86] On 5th September 1921, the Companies House registrar wrote to SHC's receiver, requiring a complete audit of their contracts, related to a mortgage the company held. Gartheiniog was suspended for part of 1921 but Llangynog stayed open in 1921 and 1922 under mine agent Jonathan Morris.[87]

SHC was admonished by Companies House in February 1922 for not filing an annual return. Later that month, five of the company's creditors sued the company for non-payment of bills. This was the end. On 13th March 1922, the company was notified it would be struck off the register in June. A few days later the AGM appointed H.S. Burgess as liquidator, though he quit his position two months later.[74]

In July 1922, SHC's creditors met in London. The Official Receiver, J. Barwick Thompson, said the "*company's career appeared to have been a chapter of mismanagement from beginning to end*". Roland Morgan admitted "*that many of the statements made [in the prospectus] were somewhat flamboyant but asserted that the agents employed to create a market for the shares were dismissed when the facts were brought to his notice*". Shareholders were warned that they should expect no return from their investments.[88]

In early 1923. Morgan and Russon claimed in court that the company failed because "*the stringent financial position which existed in the years 1920 and 1921, the inability of the company to obtain ordinary banking facilities, the overbuying by the general manager on a falling market, and the embarkation upon a bigger building scheme than was commensurate with the company's capital*". The Official Receiver was highly critical: "*The failure of the company is attributable to the reckless mismanagement of the company's affairs by the managing directors, Morgan and Russon, and to the failure of the directors to exercise ordinary supervision over the staff employed.*"[89]

SHC was finally wound up on 16th June 1931.[74]

The logo of the National Welsh Slate Quarries company, from a sketch by Bill Breese.

The National Welsh Slate Quarries

Meanwhile, NWSQ was also struggling and the company called on its shareholders for additional capital. In late July 1921, Major Bill literally sold his family silver, auctioning '…*Very Valuable ANTIQUE FURNITURE, Old Silver, China, Glass, etc., for Major C. F. Bill*'.[90] He leased Farley Hall to the Overdale School for Girls, who occupied the house from 1921[91] until 1927.[92] The Hall had been in the hands of the Bill family since 1607, so matters must have been desperate to warrant such action.

Journalists began to note NWSQ's struggles. In June 1921, *Truth* magazine published a blistering critique of the company. They had reported on Morgan's bucket shop operations in 1908:

'*National Welsh Slate Quarries… is a very shady business… of the same disreputable parentage as the Standard Housing Company of Birmingham. The chief promoter was one William Russon, an undischarged bankrupt, and in each case his son W. C. Russon was put forward as the dummy vendor at preposterously inflated prices of properties which he never owned. Associated with W. Russon in both ventures is a financial sharp named Roland Morgan who nowadays calls himself William Rhodes Speller… According to the statutory report - which, as usually happens in connection with Russon-Speller companies, was filed long after the statutory date and failed in other respects to comply with the law… The first annual report and accounts are now due, and I am afraid that a rude awakening is in store for the shareholders.*'[93]

On 8th October, *The Economist* carried a highly unflattering report of the company:

'*The whole of the development expenditure has been charged against revenue, and in light of this fact, no amount has been specifically provided during the period under review for depreciation of capital outlay. A list of missing vouchers has been supplied to your secretary. The heavy cost of the Belle Walk property does not coincide with the independent architect's valuation, and the contractors have been asked to account for the apparent overcharges. The preliminary expenses are very much in excess of the estimate given in the prospectus. No sinking fund has been created.*'[94]

The Belle Walk property was the SHC's demonstration house at 10 Belle Walk, Moseley. The cost of building this house was charged against the NWSQ account, which speaks to the degree of co-mingling of the two companies.

On 15th October *The Nation* and *Atheneum* (now part of *The New Statesman*) was scathing about the NWSQ Co.'s annual report, stating it '*provides small investors with an excellent*

Workers at Llangynog Quarry, restoring the mill building for SHC in 1921. The main incline winding house is on the left. The gentleman at the right of the front row is management; this may be Sidney Victor Wallis.
[People's Collection Wales]

lesson in the dangers of participating in new speculative enterprises'.[95]

On 20th October, barely a year after they started working at Hendreddu, NWSQ held an Extraordinary General Meeting in Birmingham. Their annual report made for stark reading. They could not meet their liabilities and appointed their accountant William James Jennings to oversee a voluntary liquidation.[46]

In November, company secretary A.J. Pilsbury wrote to the Companies House registrar, noting that he could not comply with their request to supply the private address of William Rhodes Speller, because '*he has no private residence in this name, though I understand unofficially that he uses the name of "M.B. Langton". I have enquired from him as to his private*

address and he declines to give it'.[74] The evasive Roland Morgan was hiding from the authorities.

On 20th December 1921, Jennings set up a committee of inspection led by Henry Drew English and including George Gale of Motor Rail. William Henry Rhodes and Jacob Cohen were also on the committee.[96] English was the co-owner with his brother of Moody Brothers, an established Birmingham printer who specialised in theatrical posters;[97] he was likely recommended for the committee by Cohen.

The winding-up of NWSQ took several years to complete. The quarry stayed open, with wages being paid by the company as late as April 1923. In 1924, NWSQ sued Major Bill — this was settled by the liquidator on 3rd November.[46] In September 1926, the company received a dividend payment from SHC of £116.

In 1927, Gertrude Emma Russon sued the company for £1,675 and Roland Morgan sued for £522. Jennings settled these claims for £500 and £150 respectively on 31st July 1928.[46] This concluded the short but turbulent life of NWSQs.

Bankruptcies and Criminal Trials

Several civil and criminal proceedings took place following the collapse of NWSQ and SHC. The common thread in these cases were William Clayton Russon and Roland Morgan.

William Clayton Russon's Bankruptcy 1922

In March 1922, Russon appeared in bankruptcy court in Birmingham following the failure of SHC. Morgan's role was a subject of much interest, and another of Morgan's companies, the Midland Produce Company was discussed. Midland Produce was described as "*conceived at a meeting of the Standard Housing Company to dispose of furniture*".[98]

Russon claimed Midland Produce was a shell company "*and that Standard Housing really carried on that business*". He said he was just a "*clerk in the office, and the man Morgan told him to do certain things*" which is extraordinary as Russon and Morgan were the managing directors of SHC. Many of the

Gartheiniog slabs being placed within the wooden framework of a Standard Housing Company house under construction in Birmingham. [*The Quarry* magazine]

One of SHC's completed houses at Belle Walk in Birmingham. [*The Quarry* magazine]

No's 24, 26, 28 and 30 Webb Lane, in Hall Green, Birmingham in November 2016. Although somewhat altered, their SHC origins are clear. [Steve Godden]

cheques written by SHC and Midland Produce were signed by 'Mrs M. B. Langton' which was Morgan, or possibly his wife. Russon said he had not met Mrs Langton.[98]

Russon was declared bankrupt, which was to be a significant factor in the subsequent ownership of Gartheiniog quarry.

Midland Produce was linked to yet another company promoted by Russon and Morgan, the Victory Oil and Cake Mills Ltd floated in 1919.[99] Victory Oil purchased the Midland Produce company for a highly inflated price and installed Walter Scoles as Chairman. Scoles was also the chairman of British Timber Plantations. Victory Oil then declared bankruptcy and Russon and Morgan walked away with their shareholder's money.[100]

Morgan's Bankruptcy and Imprisonment 1921-1923

In November 1921, under the name William Speller, Morgan was sued by William Garner of Liverpool who had invested £2,500 in Speller's Sedgley Hall Colliery Company, receiving as security shares in Rylands Joinery. The colliery company was another of Morgan's frauds and Garner demanded his money back. Morgan did not appear and lost the action.[18]

Morgan did appear in a bankruptcy court on 26th April 1922 under his own name and declared the aliases William Rhodes Speller and M.B. Langton. He gave his address as Wivenhoe Hall, Wivenhoe, Essex, with additional residences on Somerset Road, Edgbaston and Berkswell, Birmingham.[101] He owed at least £11,474.* Further debts of nearly £40,000 were being investigated by the Official Receiver. Morgan was declared bankrupt and the Official Receiver gave this damning verdict:

'[Morgan] appears to have lived luxuriously, keeping up estates [in Birmingham and] Essex, and one comes to the conclusion that a great proportion of the money spent has been money subscribed to these worthless companies, of which he has been the promoter, or which he has been largely interested.'[15]

In September 1922, a criminal case was brought against Morgan in the Birmingham Police Court. He was charged with 'offences of fraudulent conversion of money entrusted to him or his associates, who were directors at the Standard Housing Company'. In March 1923, he was sentenced to twelve

*£1.5 million in 2020

months imprisonment for 'trading in a name other than that in which he had been adjudicated bankrupt without disclosing such name.'[102] Morgan's 1911 bankruptcy had caught up with him.

The Wivenhoe Case 1922-1923

In December 1922, Robert Crooks, the former SHC quarry manager, was charged with demanding money in a menacing letter. The letter, addressed to Frederick Thomas Nettleinghame of Wivenhoe Hall had been written by Crook's wife Eleanor, without her husband's knowledge. Nettleinghame was married to Roland Morgan's daughter Lillian,[103] and he admitted under oath that he was an undischarged bankrupt and was receiving £4 per week from Morgan 'for forming companies'.

The case against Robert Crooks was dismissed, but his wife Eleanor was charged with the same offence.[104] Nettleinghame described himself as a 'financial organiser' with connections to both NWSQ and SHC. Morgan was described as an undischarged bankrupt who had used the names Langton, Speller and J.B. Mackenzie.[15] William Clayton Russon was identified as Morgan's partner in Rylands Joinery, British Timber Plantations and SHC.

Robert Crooks had bought £5,000 of shares in SHC, on the promise of a directorship and 30-35 per cent returns, and lost it all when the business failed. Eleanor had written the letter in desperate hope of recovering some money from Nettleinghame and Morgan. The jury immediately cleared her of all charges.[104]

Morgan's Criminal Trial and Imprisonment 1930

In 1930 at Portsmouth Crown Court, James Powell was charged with obtaining money by false pretences, trading as an undisclosed bankrupt and making false statements on a passport application. Among the many bogus companies he had promoted were NWSQ and British Timber Plantations. James Powell was yet another pseudonym of Roland Morgan. As well as his two bankruptcies and twelve months imprisonment, Morgan had been arrested in London on suspicion of investment fraud in 1923. He was described in court as "an exceedingly clever bogus business promoter of old standing and a large number of complaints had been received by the police regarding his shady business dealings". Other companies that Morgan had promoted included West African Concession Trust, National Share Exchange, American

Aberangell between the wars, showing many of the houses named in this book. The village of Clipiau was between Llwyn Onn and Brynmynach, while Aberangell was originally centred on Bryn-ffynnon. The opening of Hendreddu Slate Quarry started an expansion that saw the two settlements merge.

Rails, Coal and Metal Review, Premier Cuban Oil Co., Electrical Mineral Produce Ltd, and Rustic Joinery Co.[102]

He was sentenced to eighteen months of hard labour.[105] Little is known of Morgan's life after he was released from prison. He continued to live in the Wivenhoe area and died at Colchester in 1948, aged 72.[106]

A Sorry Affair

NWSQ and SHC had vastly overpaid for the quarries they purchased, to the personal benefit of Russon and his son–in-law Wallis. Morgan was an outright fraudster. While Morgan's schemes landed him in prison, Russon escaped criminal judgement. His son William purchased Glanymawddach House near Barmouth in 1943[107] and William Clayton and Gertrude retired there. William Clayton Russon's granddaughter remembers her grandparents in later life:

'*William was a lovely old man who wore a velvet smoking jacket and cap, and used to like to perform small magic tricks to entertain us, Grandma Russon was an invalid for part of her life, but always was dressed very formally, on the times I met her she had on grey, or brown lace outfits.*'[108]

William and Gertrude's son, also called William Clayton Russon, became a well-known businessman. In 1932, he purchased the gardening company R. & G. Cuthbert's.[8] He built it into the largest supplier of packet seeds in Britain, and wrote the immensely popular 'Mr Cuthbert's Weekly Garden Talk' which appeared on the front page of *The Times* from 1935 to the mid–60s.[109]

He was the first chairman of the North Wales Industrial Society, twice the High Sheriff of Merionethshire, the first president of the Llangollen International Eisteddfod, chaired the Committee for National Savings in Merionethshire, was a member of the Empire and Commonwealth Games Committee and chaired the Council for Wales panel for the promotion of tourism. He was knighted in 1958 for his services to public life in Wales.[8]

Despite Morgan and Russon's fraudulent dealings, NWSQ and SHC were genuine companies. Significant investments were made in the quarries and the tramway, and without this it is doubtful they would have survived into the 1930s.

Brynawelon in Aberangell may have been built by SHC. It is similar to the homes built by the company in Birmingham, but definitive evidence has yet to emerge that this was one of their houses. [TuckDB archive]

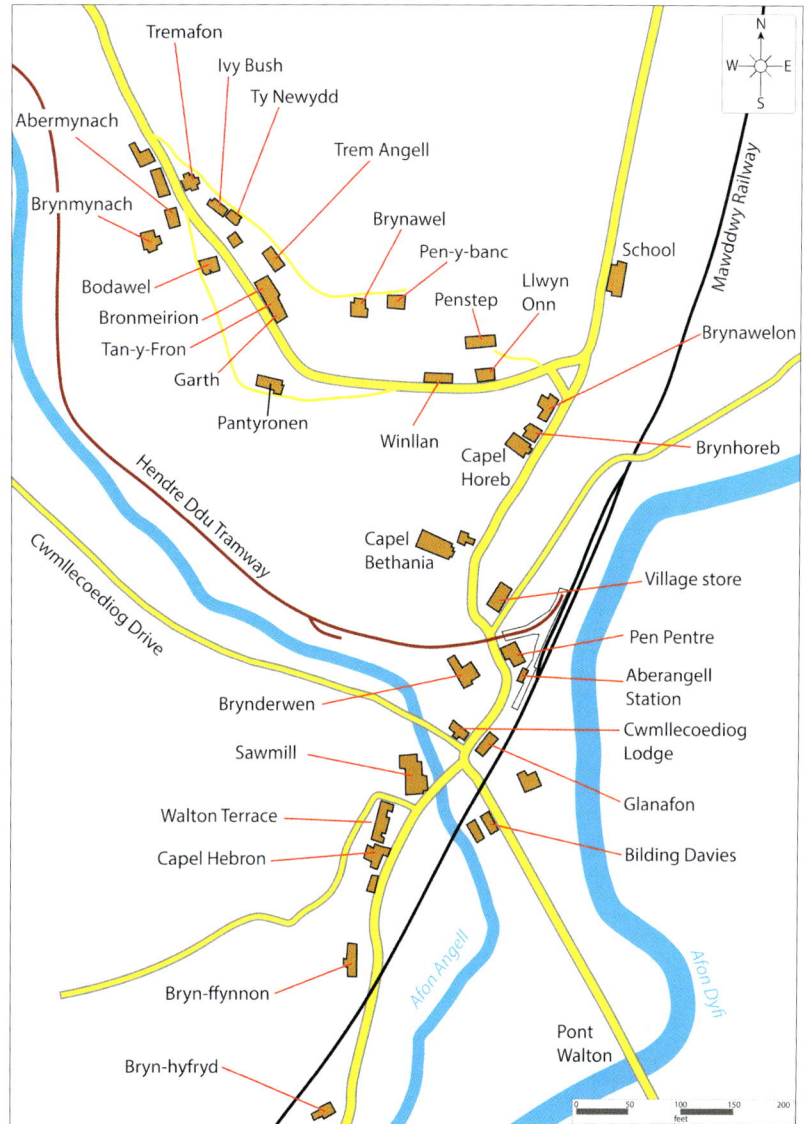

Edward Hurst Davies

Hendreddu Slate and Slab Quarry
Aberangell
(1870-1908)

Gartheiniog Slate Quarry
Aberangell
(1880-1920)

William Clayton Russon

William Clayton Lloyd

Maesygamfa Slab Quarry
Aberangell
(1892-1911)

Lloyd & Son
Smethwick
(1892-1896)

Main Wheeleries
Handsworth
(1902?-1904)

Claremont Cycle
Smethwick
(1896-1900)

United Trader's Syndicate
Smethwick
(1900-1904)

Roland Morgan

Hendreddu Slate and Slab Quarry
Aberangell
(1908-1918)

Ryland (Joinery) Ltd.
Edgbaston
(1912-1919)

Charles F. Bill

British Timber Plantations
Aberystwyth, Birmingham
(1919-1920)

Sidney Wallis

William Bowley

Son-in-law

Joseph Morris

Melton Mowbray

National Welsh Slate Quarries
Aberangell
(1919-1922)

Standard Housing Company
Aberangell, Llangynog
(1920-1922)

Hendre-ddu Slate Quarry
Aberangell
(1922-1926)

Gartheiniog Slate Quarries
Aberangell
(1921-1926)

Hendre-ddu Slate Quarry
Aberangell
(1927-1934)

G.E. Russon
Aberangell
(1927-1931)

Temple Hadrill

T. Glyn Williams

Gartheiniog Slate Quarry
Aberangell
(1932-1933)

Hendreddu Slate Quarry
Aberangell
(1937-1946)

Bowley's Quarries
Aberangell
(1935-1937)

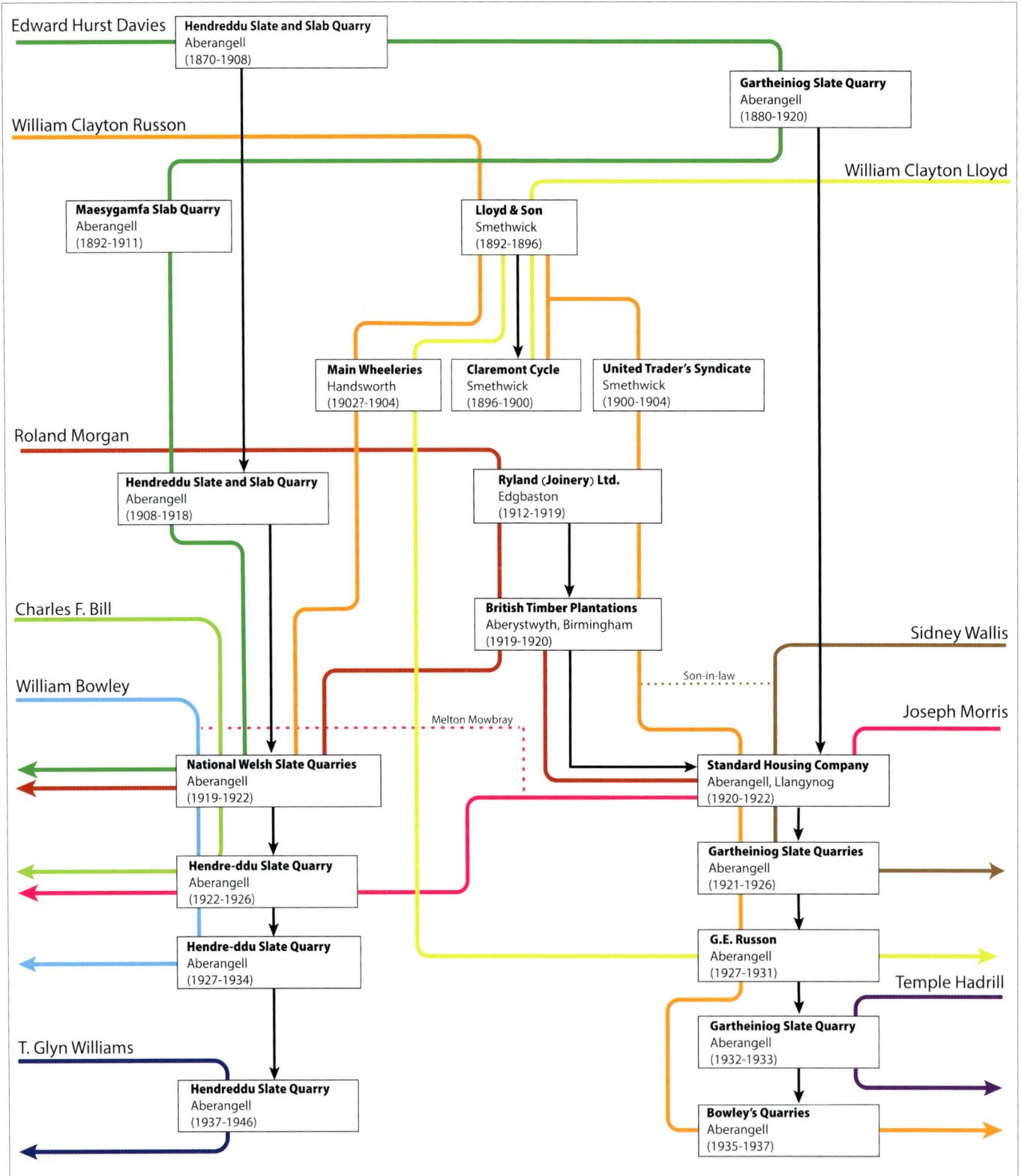

The major companies that preceded the formation of National Welsh Slate Quarries Ltd and the Standard Housing Company, and the Aberangell companies that followed them. The main people involved in this complex set of companies are shown. Edward Hurst Davies connects the pre-First World War owners with the post-war quarries.

William Bowley's shop in Melton Mowbray. When it was demolished in 1964 it still carried the name W. Bowley & Co. and was owned by the family. [Courtesy Kristi Dumais]

Right: William Bowley, with his fourth wife Elizabeth, shortly after the First World War. [Courtesy Kristi Dumais]

Birmingham was the centre of the tangled tale of NWSQ and SHC. Many of those who founded and ran the two companies came from the city, with Gough Road in Edgbaston as the epicentre.

William Bowley standing outside his house 'Corfe', shortly after it was built.
[Courtesy Kristi Dumais]

References

1   John W. McConnel, *Cotton growing within the British Empire*, Royal Colonial Institute, March 8th, 1921.

2   Gwyndaf Breese, Timber Tycoons, unpublished manuscript.

3   Sheila Marriner, *Cash and Concrete: Liquidity Problems in the Mass-Production of 'Homes for Heroes'*, in Business in the Age of Depression and War, R. P. T. Davenport-Hines, Ed. Routledge, 2013.

4   Notes, *Western Daily Press*, p.7, Dec. 17th, 1919.

5   England and Wales Census, 1891. Piece 2398, Folio 72, p.45, 1891.

6   William Russon and Gertrude Emma James, England & Wales Marriages 1837-2005 (West Bromwich), vol. 6B, p.1113.

7   James Bicycles, *Cycling*, p.47, Mar. 14th, 1912.

8   David Brinley Clay Jones, Russon, Sir William Clayton (1895 - 1968), industrialist, in Dictionary of Welsh Biography, 2001.

9   The Claremont Cycle Manufacturing Co. Limited, *St. James's Gazette*, p.16, Jun. 17th, 1896.

10   Died 30 years after 'month to live' sentence, *Birmingham Daily Gazette*, p.6, Jul. 10th, 1937.

11   Cycle trade finance: remarkable disclosures, *London Daily News*, p.8, Nov. 25th, 1904.

12   Cycles, cycles, cycles, *Peterborough Advertiser*, p.2, Jul. 2nd, 1902.

13   1911 Census For England & Wales, series RG14, piece 17912, schedule 199, 1911.

14   Rowland Morgan, series RG14, piece 5143, schedule 193, 1911 Census For England & Wales, 1911.

15   Financial tangle. Director's amazing career, *Birmingham Daily Gazette*, p. 3, Apr. 27th, 1922.

16   A bankrupt bucket-shop keeper, *Truth*, p. 34, Aug. 12th, 1908.

17   Wivenhoe Hall purchase, *Chelmsford Chronicle*, p. 6, May 5th, 1922.

18   Investor's claim: City company promoter to pay £2,884, *Birmingham Daily Gazette*, p.3, Nov. 10th, 1921.

19   Joint stock companies, *London Gazette*, no. 32754, p.7139, Oct. 10th, 1922.

20   British Timber Plantations Ltd, *Belfast News*-Letter, p.3, Jul. 28th, 1919.

21   Tale of a company: City promoter's deficiency of £1,714, *Birmingham Daily Gazette*, p.3, Mar. 9th, 1922.

22   British Timber Plantations Ltd. prospectus, *The Globe*, p.6, Jul. 28th, 1919.

23   National Welsh Slate Quarries prospectus, *The Scotsman*, p.4, Mar. 17th, 1920.

24   Hendreddu purchase agreement, in National Welsh Slate Quarries Ltd winding-up procedures, J 13/11472, National Archives, 1927.

25   Machynlleth. Sales of valuable freehold properties, *Cambrian News*, p. 1, Oct. 3rd, 1919.

26   Cwmllecoediog Estate Auction description, 1919.

27   Bill Breese, Notebook on tramroad and local quarrying, *Dolgellau Archive*, no. ref ZM/6541/5 , c. 1970.

28   Brains wanted in forestry, *West Sussex Gazette*, p.6, Aug. 7th, 1919.

29   To pay £2,800. Remarkable story told in coal case, *Liverpool Echo*, p.3, Sep. 17th, 1918.

30   Selling coal at illegitimate prices. Heavy penalties, *The Scotsman*, p.7, Sep. 18th, 1918.

31   Coal sales. Liverpool prosecution, *Exeter and Plymouth Gazette*, p.4, Sep. 18th, 1918.

32   Gwyndaf Breese, Hard times on the tramway, unpublished manuscript.

33   Obituary, *The Colliery Guardian and Journal of the Coal and Iron Trades*, vol. 146, p.689, Apr. 7th, 1933.

34   Poison-license application, *Chemist and Druggist: The Newsweekly for Pharmacy,* vol. 97, Aug. 5th, 1922.

35   Register of Members of National Timber Company Limited, BT 31/25856/166880, in Files of dissolved companies: No: 166880; National Timber Company, Ltd, National Archives, 1920-1932.

36   The Bankruptcy Act 1914, *Edinburgh Gazette*, no. 13768, p.2178, Dec. 13th, 1921.

37   At the Liverpool bankruptcy court, *The Iron and Coal Trades Review*, p.436, Mar. 24th, 1922.

38   Colliery Director in the dock, *Dundee Evening Telegraph*, p.7, Jun. 20th, 1923.

39   Ex-Councillor goes to prison for fraud, *Western Daily Press*, p.4, Jul. 21st, 1923.

40   Too much money: colliery director sent to gaol for fraud, *Northampton Chronicle*, p. 6, Jul. 21st, 1923.

41   Order made on application for discharge, *London Gazette*, no. 33211, p.6677, Oct. 15th, 1926.

42   Death of Henry Sharrock Higginbottom, England & Wales

Deaths 1837-2007, vol. 1B, p.61, 1929.

43 Armistead Cay, The Leek and Manifold Light Railway, *Page's Engineering Weekly*, vol. 5, p.123, 1904.

44 Captain Charles FitzHerbert Bill. Long service papers. WO 339/60615, National Archives.

45 Derby and Derbyshire and elsewhere, *Derbyshire Advertiser and Journal*, p.6, Feb. 18th, 1916.

46 Files of dissolved companies. Company number: 162816; National Welsh Slate Quarries, Ltd BT 34/4498/162816, National Archives, 1920-1932.

47 Mr. William Henry Rhodes, *The Pottery Gazette*, vol. 42, p.770, Aug. 1st, 1917.

48 White Hall (Derby) Ltd prospectus, *Derby Daily Telegraph*, p.2, Aug. 24th, 1920.

49 New companies, *Birmingham Daily Gazette*, p.7, Aug. 19th, 1920.

50 Two year holiday in America and Canada of well known Oakham and Melton Figure, *Grantham Journal*, p.16, May 14th, 1938.

51 Melton Urban Council and Guardians elections, *Grantham Journal*, p.8, Mar. 12th, 1904.

52 National Welsh Slate Quarries, Limited, *The Economist*, p.656, Mar. 20th, 1920.

53 Low tricks and high finance, *John Bull*, p.12, Dec. 8th, 1923.

54 Gwyndaf Breese, The Simplex Locomotive, unpublished manuscript.

55 Birth of Nathaniel Twitchen, England, Wales and Scotland Census 1891, Leeds, piece 3696, folio 35, p.4, 1891.

56 Captain Nathaniel Edwards Twitchin. Royal Field Artillery. WO 339/50434, National Archives, 1914-1922.

57 Letter from the Bradley Pulverizer Company to Jon Knowles. 1989.

58 Slate quarries, *Western Morning News*, p.6, Mar. 22nd, 1920.

59 Bill Breese, Notes on local quarrying and quarrymen, Dolgellau Archive, vol. ref ZM/6541/9, 1982.

60 John Breese entry, 1939 Register, Dolgelley, vol. RG101/7642C/003/20, 1939.

61 Cyril Evans, grandson of Bill Breese, Nov. 2018.

62 John Breese, son of Bill Breese, Jul. 2016.

63 Bill Breese, 18503 Pte. John Breese - 15th. Battalion (Carm) Welsh Regiment, unpublished manuscript.

64 Marriage of John Breese, England & Wales Marriages 1837-2005, vol. 11A, p.1723, 1919.

65 Death certificate of William Breese. Machynlleth, England & Wales Deaths 1837-2007, vol. 26, p.157, 1986.

66 Bill Breese, Unpublished research notes. .

67 Bill Breese, 8th May 1976.

68 Death certificate of John Breese; Merioneth South, England & Wales Deaths 1837-2007, vol. 8C, p.20, 1959.

69 Gwyndaf Breese, Travelling on the tramway, unpublished manuscript.

70 Bill Breese, Damweiniau Llenol, *Cambrian News*, September 19th, 1975.

71 Bill Breese, Bygone activities within Angell valley, *Cambrian News*, Aug. 6th, 1976.

72 Bill Breese, Atgofion: Twmplen Mam, *Cambrian News*, Jan. 7th, 1977.

73 Standard Housing Company prospectus, *The Times*, Nov. 20th, 1920.

74 Board of Trade, Companies Registration Office. Files of Dissolved Companies, Standard Housing Company. BT 31/26072/169031. National Archives.

75 Speller's Standard Housing, *Truth*, pp.21–22, Apr. 13th, 1921.

76 Marriage of Sidney Victor Wallis, England & Wales marriages 1837-2005, vol. 6D, p.34, 1921.

77 List of Mines in Great Britain and the Isle of Man, 1921. H.M. Stationery Office, 1922.

78 Critics of the housing subsidy. Building company's big profits claim and its investigation by the 'Echo,' *Liverpool Echo*, p.4, Oct. 8th, 1920.

79 Worcester housing, *Birmingham Daily Gazette*, p.3, Sep. 21st, 1920.

80 Rapid building. Standard Housing Company's fine achievement, *Nottingham Journal*, p.5, Nov. 13, 1920.

81 The Boom in Slate Quarrying, *The Quarry*, p.126, May 1920.

82 O.T. Jones, Slate and its Modern Uses, *The Quarry*, p.8, Jan. 1921.

83 The End of the Miners' Strike, *The Spectator*, July 1st, 1921.

84 Wales badly hit, *Pall Mall Gazette*, p.2, Jun. 11th, 1921.

85 Conclusion of proceedings of the Standard Housing Company, National Archives, June 24th, 1932.

86 In the matter of the Companies (Consolidation) Act of 1908, and in the matter of the Standard Housing Company Limited, *London Gazette*, no. 32336, p.4217, May 27th, 1921.

87 List of Mines in Great Britain and the Isle of Man, 1922. H.M. Stationery Office, 1923.

88 A puff and a burst. Shareholders must expect nothing, *Pall Mall Gazette*, p.2, Jul. 26th, 1922.

89 Mismanagement and supervision lack. Official Receiver on Standard Housing Company's affairs, *Birmingham Daily Gazette*, p.3, Jan. 23rd, 1923.

90 Preliminary announcement, *Derbyshire Advertiser and Journal*, p.1, Jun. 25th, 1921.

91 Overdale School for Girls, *Yorkshire Post and Leeds Intelligencer*, p.9, Jun. 18th, 1921.

92 Overdale School for Girls, *Staffordshire Advertiser*, p.6, Jan. 8th, 1927.

93 National Welsh Slate Quarries, *Truth*, p.26, Jun. 1st, 1921.

94 National Welsh Slate Quarries, Limited, *The Economist*, pp.540-541, Oct. 8th, 1921.

95 The week in the City, *The Nation and the Atheneum*, vol. 30, p.112, Oct. 15th, 1921.

96 In the matter of the National Welsh Slate Quarries Ltd, *London Gazette*, no. 32635, pp.2100-2101, Mar. 10th, 1922.

97 Breach of agreement. Injunction obtained against a printer, *Birmingham Daily Gazette*, p.2, Nov. 21st, 1907.

98 The mystery woman. Debtor's strange story, *Birmingham Daily Gazette*, p.3, Mar. 4th, 1922.

99 The Victory Oil and Cake Mills Ltd prospectus, *Yorkshire Post*, p.10, Apr. 9th, 1919.

100 Speller's promotions, *Truth*, p.26, Oct. 26th, 1921.

101 First meetings and public examinations, *London Gazette*, no. 32672, p.3076, Apr. 14th, 1922.

102 Bogus business promoter. Sentenced at Portsmouth, *Portsmouth Evening News*, p.5, Jan. 10th, 1930.

103 Marriage of Thomas Nettlinghame, England & Wales Marriages 1837-2005, Marylebone, vol. 1A, p.1191.

104 The Essex Assize: Wivenhoe case stopped, *Chelmsford Chronicle*, p.2, Feb. 9th, 1923.

105 Bogus companies. Horley man sent to prison, *Surrey Mirror*, p.2, Jan. 17th, 1930.

106 Death of Roland Morgan, England & Wales Deaths 1837-2007, Colchester, vol. 4A, p.443.

107 North Wales properties, *Liverpool Daily Post*, p.2, Jun. 12th, 1943.

108 Ancestry. co. uk message board posting, 19th September 2003.

109 Michael Leapman, Seeds: a packet history, *The Independent*, May 3rd, 1997.

The north chamber at Gartheiniog in 1932 or 1933. Temple Hadrill sits with two young visitors amidst the architectural grandeur of the quarry. The iron-bodied rubbish wagon survived into the 1970s. [Hadrill-McGuire family]

11: Mixed Fortunes 1922-1937

Hendreddu 1922-1935

Hendreddu and the tramway continued to operate after NWSQ failed, with the liquidator paying wages in the hope of selling it as a going concern. Charles Bill and shareholder William Bowley assembled a group of businessmen from Melton Mowbray to take it over. Negotiations took place with the liquidator in 1922 for the purchase of the quarry and tramway.

William Bowley

Bowley was born at Ab Kettleby, just north of Melton Mowbray, on 12th January 1846, the son of a carpenter.[1] He was a man of ambition, and by 1871 he was living in Melton Mowbray with his wife Mary and had established himself as a watchmaker and jeweller.[2] Bowley's business was extremely successful and left him a rich man. By 1900, he had moved with his family to Thorpe Arnold,[3] a mile northeast of Melton, and shortly afterwards he built a magnificent house there, called Corfe.

Bowley was a member of the Board of Guardians and Urban District Council of Melton Mowbray[4] and became the longest-serving member of the council. He was also known for being the first owner of a bicycle in Melton Mowbray, and he rode daily until late 1937.[5]

A New Company 1922

In 1921, 75-year-old William Bowley had invested in NWSQ. When that collapsed, Bowley and Bill got together to form the successor company, Hendre-ddu Slate Quarries Ltd. Bowley became chairman of the new company, and he was joined by two directors from Melton Mowbray: John Henry Harris the managing director,[6] and Joseph Morris. Morris had been a director of SHC and was an old friend of Bowley's, while Harris was a well-known Melton businessman. Major Bill was appointed a director, as was the somewhat mysterious Mr Stevens[7] whose identity is not confirmed – he may have been Lieutenant R.T. Stevens, another member of the Melton Mowbray Board of Guardians in the 1920s.[8]

The new company had a much more modest capitalisation of £1,000.[9] The mine agent was John C. Hargreaves, and the first quarry manager was Richard Lewis, who had been the mine agent at Maesygamfa immediately before the war.[10] By September 1922, members of the new company were working at Aberangell. On the 8th September, Hargreaves was driving the Motor Rail locomotive, most likely on a test trip up to the quarry. The locomotive derailed and fell into the Afon Angell, and Hargreaves ended up hanging from the branches of a tree.[11]

Bowley leased Hendreddu from the liquidator for a year, starting on 6th December 1922. On 4th October 1923, just before the lease was up, he paid a £350 deposit to purchase the quarry and tramway, and on December 5th he paid the remaining £3,159 to complete the transaction.[*12] Quarrymen were hired late in 1922, with six working by the end of the year.[13]

Rise and Collapse 1922-1926

Hendre-ddu Slate Quarries Ltd. specialised in supplying slab for electrical installations, but also produced a wide range of slate products, including: '*Billiard tables, for which there was a large market, laboratory tables, dust storage cells for the crematoria of Birmingham and Manchester, curing boards, tombstones (for humans and animals), dairy stones, bath surround panels, panels for electrical powerhouses, false bibles** and hundreds and thousands of different items, according to need and demand.*'[14]

At first, the quarry employed relatively few men: in 1923 there were three underground and eight above.[15] The overground workers included tramway driver John Breese, and brakesman Dafydd Jones, who were also responsible for maintaining the track.[16] John was the father of Bill Breese, and he continued as tramway driver for many years. Dafydd is probably the mason who helped build the Cwm Caws tramway during the First World War. The year 1924 saw the workforce expand to twenty-five, with ten underground and fifteen overground.[17] On 18th June, Huw Owen was injured while working on the tramway, though the details of the accident are not recorded. He died two days later in Aberystwyth Hospital.[11]

The 1925 Collapse

In early 1925, there was a major collapse at the quarry. The entire centre section fell, with rock coming down through Levels 1, 2 and 3, and *Tyllau**** 3 and 4 collapsing into the Level 3 chambers below. Bill Breese briefly describes this event: '*The roof of this chamber (where quarrying started) fell in the early morning. Some men walking over to Ratgoed Quarry heard its fall.*'[18]

At least four chambers completely collapsed, three more suffered partial falls, and the main twll lost its floor and was

---

★ Total equivalent to £500,000 in 2020

★★The 'false bibles' were either bookends or the carved bibles that sometimes adorn graves

★★★*Twll* is Welsh for 'open pit', '*tyllau*' means 'open pits'

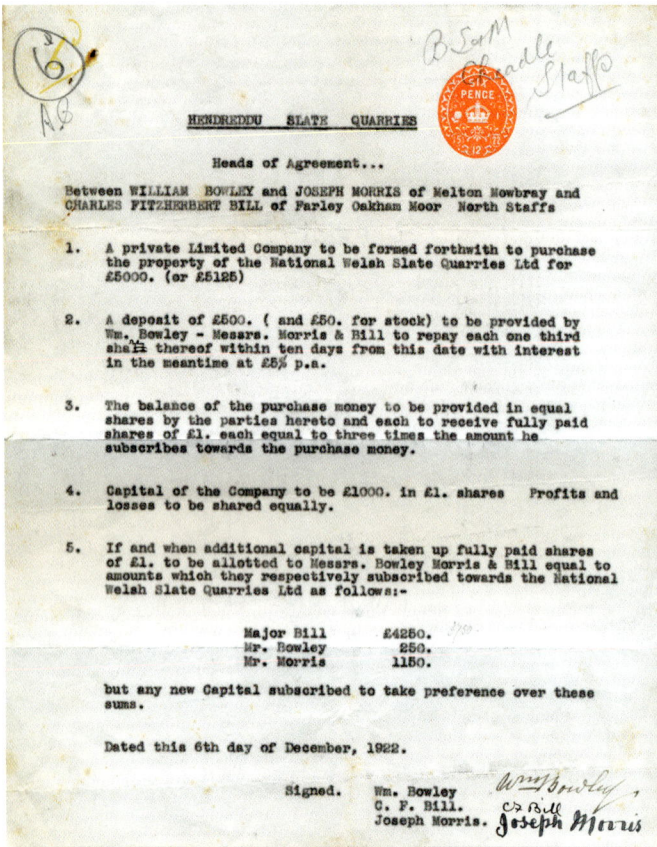

significantly enlarged. Around 140,000 tons, or 1.85 million cubic feet, of rock are estimated to have fallen. The cause is unknown, but suspicion falls on the fault running along the edge of chamber 1.5. A collapse of this magnitude could have been disastrous for Hendreddu. The working chambers on Level 3 were cut off and two of the largest chambers on Levels 1 and 2 were lost. Thankfully, no one was killed as the collapse happened before the workmen went underground for the day. Fortunately, the fall in Twll 4 exposed good rock, which could be easily accessed and supplied the mill while the Level 3 tunnels were repaired. Despite the collapse, 1925 was an optimistic year for Hendreddu. The mill received its first, rather crude, electrical system, powered by a new turbine in the machine shop, supplied from the reservoir through new pipes laid across the site.

Gillart's Incline was put back into working order so that rock lifted from Twll 4 could be taken to the mill. The task of relaying the incline was given to Twm Ifans, who was not experienced in track laying. He struggled, especially in creating the incline crimp which involves accurately bending the rails in the vertical plane. When Twm, working in the forge, failed to complete the work, the director Mr Stevens fired him. Richard Lewis, the underground foreman, was passing the caban when he heard Twm being ordered to collect his cards. Lewis admonished Stevens: "*Never, ever sack a workman for what he is unable to do, but put him to do a job that he can do*". He called for John Breese, who had installed and repaired tramways at the Parc Colliery, and asked him to make the crimp. Twm was saved from unemployment and the incline was brought into service.[19]

The agreement between William Bowley, Joseph Morris and Major Bill to acquire the quarry and tramway after the collapse of NWSQ.

Left: Aberangell Wharf in 1925. Richard Lewis was the Quarry Manager and Bob Richards worked with Bill Breese at Hendreddu in 1938. Other men in the photograph, but not individually identified, are D. Roberts, Williams Evan Jones, Mr Wells, Dafydd Foulkes, W. Hughes, John Roberts and Lewis Davies. The corrugated iron building on the right is the flour store.

Opposite Page Bottom: Aberangell Wharf layout around 1925. Green's Tramway, which ran along the west edge of the yard, has been cut back to a siding and the derrick has been removed. On the site of the slate weighhouse is the corrugated iron flour store. The weighhouse was likely removed during the First World War to allow large timber loads to enter the Wharf.

Inside the Hendreddu mill. In the foreground is the edge of a flat wagon. The machinery is driven from the overhead shaft powered by the turbines. The quarry has installed electrical lighting by this time. On the left is William Bowley wrapped up heavily against the cold. William Evan Jones is in the centre, standing next to a slab planing machine, with Lewis Jones beside him. On the right is Dafydd Roberts.
[Courtesy Mike Cowley]

Sales Brochure

Demand for slate grew in the mid-1920s, driven by post-war reconstruction. In late 1925, the company released a well-produced brochure, which included several photographs taken at the wharf and quarry.

The company added a two-storey building west of the mill. This was intended to house a stationary engine supplied by Davey, Paxman & Co. of Colchester. Paxman supplied its first commercial diesel engines in 1927, so this would have been one of their first sales, probably of a prototype. These first-generation diesels were four-stroke 'Cold-Starting Vertical Heavy-Fuel-Oil Engines'.[20] The engine was intended to power the Griffin mills, installed in 1920 to crush slate waste, and was accompanied by an engineer called Catchpole to teach the Hendreddu engineer how to operate it.

The installation of the engine was overseen by Mr Stevens. It was delivered to Aberangell station, then moved up the tramway to the foot of the exit incline. Here they hit a snag – they did not have a heavy enough load to counterbalance the weight of the Paxman on the incline. Stevens had a crane built next to the incline winding house, so the engine could be hauled up the hillside. The men knew he needed to turn the engine before lifting it, but he was not interested in their opinions, so they kept their counsel and followed his orders. After hours of work, Stevens said: "*That is it, all set and ready!*" A worker asked: "*And how can you insert the handles to turn it, Mr. Stevens?*"[7] They got the huge flywheel up to the mill, where it lay in pieces in the shed for some years, but not the engine. The fate of the engine is unknown, though it may have been returned to Paxman.

The sales brochure is a fascinating document, both optimistic about the quarry's future, and startlingly honest

Another view inside the mill. The week's production of slabs was stored in the mill until the weekend when they were weighed and stored outside for at least six weeks to mature before they were shipped out on the tramway. The unusual wagon on the right has a suspension system holding the deck above the axleboxes, which allows the deck to tilt to make loading and unloading easier. The axleboxes are open at the bottom, allowing the deck to be lifted off. [Mark Waite collection]

about the challenges faced:

'Welsh slate is the best in the world, and is exported to all countries, despite high freight costs and tariff walls. We cannot hope to compete with the foreign slate in first-cost - our wages bill per ton being higher than their selling price: but where quality and time for delivery are important we can hold our own against all comers... The working conditions are probably more primitive than any other place in the British Isles... From a sight-seeing standpoint there is much to recommend a visit: mountains, rivers, woodlands, waterfalls, are at their best between May and September. The salmon fishing is not to be overlooked, though the shooting is second rate.

Our Tramway connects the Quarry with the G.W.R. running 3½ miles up-hill, climbing all the way up the mountain side: our loaded trucks come down by gravity and our empties, with stores, workmen, and visitors are taken up by petrol Loco. For the last few hundred feet the gradient is nearly 1 in 1* and this is taken care of by wire rope haulage.'

The company's registered offices were at Batten Street, Aylestone Park, Leicester, close to Melton Mowbray, and they made clear that the quarry 'is concerned solely with production and does not touch the commercial side of the business'.[22]

The branch to Cefngwyn was lifted in 1925. The rails were used by local mason William Roberts to reinforce the concrete dam of the lower fishpond at Cwmllecoediog.[23]

In 1925, the company employed twenty-eight men,

A WORD ABOUT HENDREDDU SLATE QUARRIES LIMITED

The mill in 1925; the waste tip dominates the foreground. The main building is typical of the mills of the area, and is of similar design to the surviving shed at Aberllefenni, though Hendreddu has two gables. The two-storey building on the left is Sied Packsman (the Paxman Shed), then newly built to house the heavy oil engine which was never installed.[21] A telephone line runs across the hillside behind the mill. The small detached building in front of the mill is a weighhouse. The roof to the right of the mill is the quarry manager's house. [Mike Cowley collection]

* The exit incline was nowhere near as steep as 1 in 1

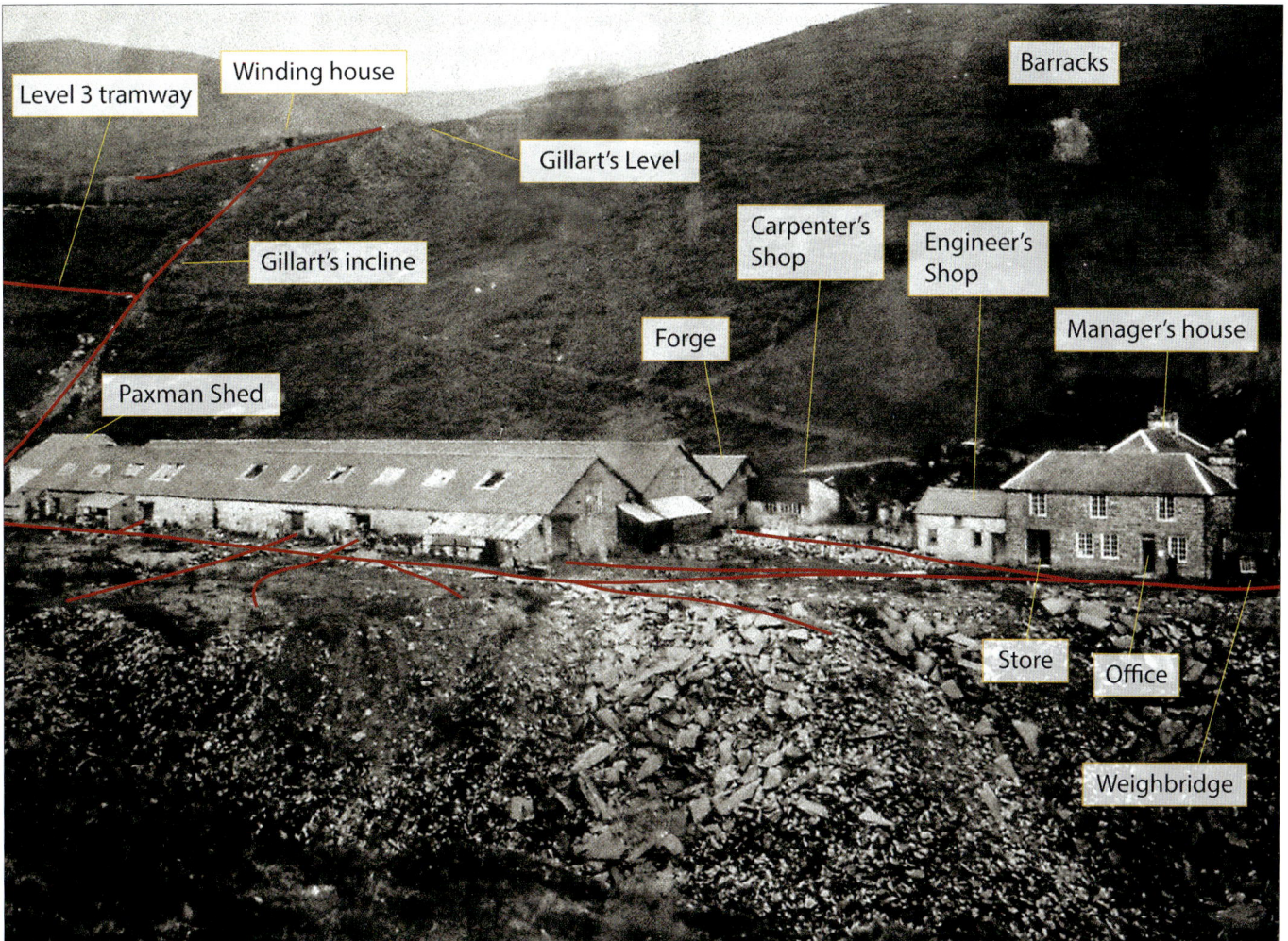

The mill from the southeast. The manager's house is on the right with the upper tramway running in front of it. The double-gabled mill was a vast building, erected at great expense by Sir Edmund Buckley. The Level 1 adit was about 150 yards to the left of the mill. The tramway to the open pits ran left from the Gillart's Level winding house. [Mike Cowley collection]

fourteen underground and the rest in the mill and on the tramway.[24] This total was maintained in 1926;[25] but trouble was brewing.

Last Years of Edward Hurst Davies 1920-1927

Edward Hurst Davies cut his ties with the quarries in the NWSQ days, but he still lived in Aberangell with his wife Margaret. The death of his son Iowerth left him heartbroken. A lifelong teetotaller, he turned to drink and increasingly relied on his servant David 'Defi' Thomas to help him. In February 1926, Edward and Margaret moved to live near their daughter Tilly Howells in Bridgend. They sold Brynderwen to Richard Pugh of Cefngwyn,[19] and Abermynach Farm and the Aberangell Meadows to farm tenant Richard Williams.[26]

On 26th June 1927, their eldest son John died, aged forty. Just twenty-two days later, having outlived both sons and a daughter, Edward Hurst Davies died. He was buried in the Calvinistic Methodist Chapel at Cemmaes, alongside Iowerth and John. Margaret survived until March 1940 and is also buried in the family grave.[27]

E.H. Davies's father had been instrumental in developing Hendreddu into a large and successful quarry. Edward Hurst worked at Hendreddu, Gartheiniog and then founded and owned Maesygamfa. He purchased Hendreddu and ran it after the death of Jacob Bradwell. He was a man of ambition and strong moral character and he treated the workers at his quarries well. He was a devoted chapel goer and, for much of his life, a member of the Independent Order of Rechabites temperance society.[28] When he became successful, he dedicated his spare time to social and political causes, not least to making education available to all local children. Davies was highly regarded as a quarryman, a manager and a leader. He raised his family in Aberangell within sight and sound of the Hendre Ddu Tramway. Bill Breese wrote of him:

'[He was] regarded by all as a brilliant scholar, an authority on quarrying operations, and [he was] assessed by London auditors as the wizard of accountancy… Possessor of a fertile mind… he [was not] a person deemed to follow the pattern already set by others.

Underground at Hendreddu, showing workers in one of the Level 1 chambers. Though posed, the photograph is full of fascinating detail. On the right are Mr Lewis and Norman Williams holding *jwmpahs* (jumpers), used to drill holes into the slate before blasting. Kneeling in the middle holding splitting tools are (left-to-right) Lewis Hughes, Ianto Gruff and Dafydd Roberts. Standing behind them is Henry Davies, the clerk of the quarry. The workmen are using candles though electricity had already been installed underground. [Mark Waite collection]

He acted on impulse and personal proficient inclinations.'[29] Edward Hurst Davies truly was the thread that binds together the story of the Hendre Ddu Tramway.

Reorganisation 1926-1929

In late 1926, the company was reorganized. Charles Bill and John Hargreaves left; both had sunk considerable personal wealth into the venture which they never recovered.[30] Major Bill emigrated to South Africa in July 1928. William Bowley continued as chairman and Joseph Morris remained a director.[19] Bowley appointed Herbert Harold Disley as quarry manager, replacing Richard Lewis.[10]

Herbert Harold Disley (1900-1972) came from a distinguished family of quarrymen. His grandfather, John W. Disley (1845-1925), was the clerk of Aberllefenni quarry from 1880 to 1911,[31] and Herbert's father, Henry Herbert Disley (1873-1954) was the manager there before and after the war.[32] Herbert Harold was the father of John Ivor Disley (1928-2016) who won the bronze medal in the 3,000m steeplechase in the 1952 Olympic Games and founded the London Marathon.[33]

In January 1927, John Henry Harris became a director and he replaced Hargreaves as the mine agent.[34] Harris lived in Melton Mowbray and was a successful sanitary engineer[35] – a civil engineer who specialised in constructing sewer systems. The company's commercial address moved to Harris's office at 3 Thorpe End, Melton Mowbray. Harris purchased £2,500[6] of shares in the new company. It is likely, though not certain, that Bowley invested further money. At least two other men invested, Powell and Smith.[19] Nothing further is known about them.

Chairman Bowley was now 81, and it was no doubt useful to have an agent who lived in Melton Mowbray rather than Leicester. Bowley was described as having '*a vigour that was unusual for one of his age and mentally he continued to show that alertness and individuality of thought which had marked the whole character of his life*';[36] nevertheless, the distance to Aylestone Park was considerable for an octogenarian who used a bicycle as his primary mode of transport.

The staff of the company dropped considerably in 1927, with eight men underground and seven working the mill and tramway.[34] The reorganisation gave the new management enough capital to upgrade the electrical system in the mill and underground[10] and update the tramway layout on the Wharf. The workforce had increased to twenty by 1929,[37] when Bill Milns, an English engineer, was appointed as the chief engineer of the quarry.[7] One of his first actions was to build a second locomotive for the tramway. This was constructed using parts from a lorry, probably a 1913/14 Willys-Overland Utility truck left behind by Higginbottom. In 1928, the nearby Shropshire and Montgomeryshire Railway was running a very similar locomotive converted from a Ford lorry, and this may have inspired Milns. The Willys-Overland locomotive was kept in Sied Ddu, the only shed on the line high enough to accommodate its cab. The radiator burst one particularly cold night and the locomotive was withdrawn.[16]

Two Serious Accidents 1929

The Hendreddu Incident Book recorded an accident on the exit incline in 1929. The brake failed while lowering loaded wagons and the brakesman, John Breese, was hit in the head by the long brake handle.[7] He was thrown from the brakesman's platform by the force of the blow, breaking his jaw and many of his teeth. His co-workers feared he had been killed. Breese survived, though he was seriously injured.

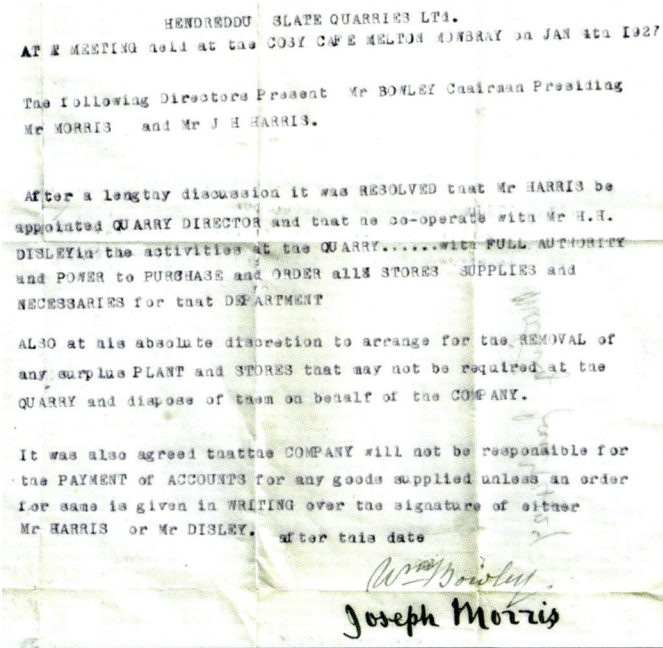

The minutes of the 1927 meeting in Melton Mowbray at which John Henry Harris was appointed Quarry Director. [Courtesy Stewart Katz]

He was rushed to Aberangell on a tramway wagon and taken to the surgery for treatment. He spent six weeks only able to take liquids and being fed potato mashed in milk and it was twelve weeks before he could return to work.[11]

In August 1929, Dafydd Jones and John Breese were working a single loaded wagon down from Hendreddu with the Motor Rail locomotive. Arriving at the top of Brynderwen cutting, Breese ran the locomotive into the shed and started preparing it for the night. Meanwhile, Jones opened the gates down to the Wharf and started the wagon downhill. He lost control on the steep descent through the cutting and was thrown from the wagon. Breese heard Jones's warning shouts and ran to the road, hoping to warn any traffic, though fortunately there were no cars. The wagon crossed the road at speed and ran into Aberangell Wharf.[38] The story is taken up by this account from the *Gloucester Citizen*:

'*A passenger train which had just arrived from Dinas Mawddwy was standing at the halt when a loaded slate quarry truck dashed, out of control, down the mountain incline, across the platform into the side of the waiting passenger train. There were two occupants of the compartment with which the truck collided, Mr. and Mrs. Leonard Jones of Woodford, Essex, were on an excursion from Barmouth, where they are on holiday.*

Seeing the truck approaching, they managed to reach the opposite end of the compartment before the collision occurred. Broken glass and splinters were scattered about the carriage, but Mr. and Mrs. Jones were unhurt. Suffering from shock, they were soon released from the compartment. It was some time before the loaded truck could be freed from the carriage into which it had buried itself. The coach was so badly damaged that it had to be detached from the train.'[39]

Henry Davies, the Aberangell postmaster who had served as a medical orderly in the war, aided the couple. Dafydd Jones was lucky to escape serious injury, but he took the blame for the accident, as he had in 1920. This time it was found that the wagon brake had locked the wheels during the descent, and instead of letting it off and reapplying it, Jones had pressed down so hard on the brake that the lever snapped, sending him flying.[38]

The company installed a sturdy oak barrier across the bottom of the cutting to stop runaways from crossing the road or entering the Wharf. A granite stop-block at the end of the southern siding on the Wharf prevented wagons from reaching the standard gauge line. A new rule was instituted that the points on the Wharf had to be left set so that runaways were steered into the stop-block; John Parry was in charge of enforcement.[38] Finally, all downhill trains had to have a locomotive on the Aberangell end to brake the trains.[16]

Depression and Decline 1930-1934

Production at Hendreddu rose steadily in the second half of the 1920s, but this was not to last. Following the Wall Street Crash of 1929 demand for slate began to fall, especially in overseas markets. In Britain, the building trade began to slump in 1930. The Welsh slate industry went into a recession that accelerated through 1931.[40]

December 1930 saw repairs needed to Aberangell Wharf. The Great Western Railway Engineer authorised £100 to be spent and the repairs started in November 1931 and were completed by January 1932.[41]

Directors' Specials

William Bowley was a well-liked figure in the valley. He always maintained an optimistic outlook and would urge the workers on with his favourite refrain: "*Come on my boys or the horse will die whilst the grass gets greener.*" Regular 'Directors' Specials' were run on the tramway to take Bowley and the other directors up to Hendreddu to inspect their business. These appear to have been as much

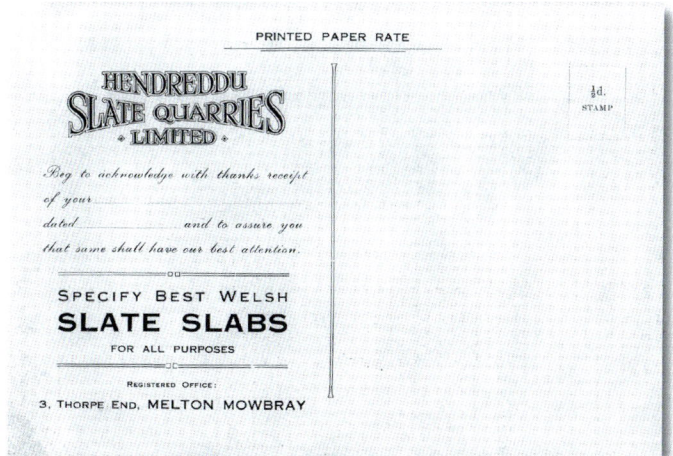

A Hendreddu reply card from the 1927-34 period. The registered office was 3 Thorpe End, the business address of John Henry Harris. [Courtesy Jon Knowles]

Aberangell Wharf in 1929. The loop from the turntable has been cut back into a siding and the points reused to connect the northern siding to the wharf line. After the 1929 accident, a large granite stop-block was added at the end of the south siding, and an oak log was placed across the bottom of Brynderwen Cutting.

works outings as formal inspections. On one of these trips Bill Breese recalls walking up to Sied Wen on a summer evening with his mother Elizabeth and his sister Ella, to deliver a packed dinner for his father. The train, driven by John Breese, arrived from Aberangell with Mrs Mary Harris in the special Directors' Car. Mary invited the Breese family to join her while John ate his dinner. Bill wanted to ride up on the train and made a whispered request to his mother in Welsh; she replied, also in Welsh, "*no, stop your moaning boy*". Mary guessed the nature of the conversation and asked "*does he want to join his dad on the loco? Let him go on the loco and you and your daughter can ride up the valley with me*". Bill was given the task of opening the many gates across the tramway – he

rode on the front of the locomotive, which would slow as it approached a gate. Bill jumped off and ran ahead to open the gate before the train arrived.[7] Bill regularly performed gate duties for the Directors' Specials after that and the directors always gave him a gift for his work.

On one of these journeys the train was approaching Gartheiniog Farm, and the farm horse Jack stood behind the tramway gate, refusing to move. William Bowley jumped off the train and hit Jack on the nose; Jack quickly moved out of the way.[19] Bowley admitted later that he was afraid he would be kicked by the horse for his troubles.[7]

On another occasion, John Breese was working a late train downhill after dark, returning the empty Directors' Special

Dolbadau Quarry in 1907, showing the steam crane that was sold to Hendreddu Quarry in 1931. [Tom Mathias]

to Aberangell. Just below Cefngwyn, the handbrake on the locomotive failed, leaving the train heading downhill out of control. Breese tried to lock the locomotive into low gear, then tried to derail it by throwing blocks under the wheels. Both attempts were unsuccessful. At Aberdwynant, he leapt from the accelerating train and watched it smash through the gates at the west end of Aberangell meadows, and head downhill towards Brynderwen Cutting. Fortunately, it was stopped at the bottom of the steep descent to the Wharf by the oak barrier installed after the 1929 accident. Hearing the sound of the crash, several local men rushed to the scene to find the oak barrier broken, and the locomotive surrounded by the debris of the gates it had smashed through. Bill Milns, the Hendreddu engineer was called for; on seeing the damage he proclaimed "*Leave the damn thing there until morning, I'll fix it then*", which he indeed did.[7] The brake failure was caused by a worn thread on the brake spindle. The brake was replaced by a hand-brake lever similar to those found on cars, supplied by Motor Rail.

Dolbadau Steam Crane

The company continued to expand in the early 1930s, despite the slowdown in the industry, as demand for its slab products held up. The workforce jumped to 34 in 1930 and 38 in 1931.[42] In 1931, the company purchased a steam crane secondhand from Dolbadau Quarry in Pembrokeshire to lift rock from the pits to the tramway level. The crane had a hugely long jib and to get it through Aberangell a length of iron fencing had to be removed from Cambrian Railways land.[43] The jib was wrecked on the journey up to the quarry and the crane was never installed at the quarry.[44]

The failure to install the crane meant rock could no longer be lifted from Twll 4, and the tramway from there to the top of Gillart's Incline was removed in early 1932. The loss of the pit meant that the company started to struggle. As the price of slate continued to fall, it could no longer pay its bills and went into liquidation later in 1932. J.H. Harris was appointed as the official receiver and the workforce was slashed to 12, all but one working underground[45] – the other was tramway driver John Breese. In 1933, the company came out of liquidation, but there was no money available to work the quarry. Bowley was genuinely concerned for his workforce and he offered them the quarry rent-free. This was a similar arrangement to the one at Maesygamfa in 1911. Richard Lewis, who had led the Maesygamfa experiment, stepped up to work Hendreddu with nine

An imperfect photograph, but of great interest, this is thought to be outside Chamber 1.5. The gentleman on the right, carrying a small torch, may be Henry Davies. The man next to him appears to be a visitor, though his identity is unknown. The track is laid with relatively heavy flat-bottomed rail. The conduit towards the top of the tunnel carries the electrical supply from the mill. The large pipes at ground level carried out water that entered the mine following the 1925 collapse. [Bill Breese collection]

The north chamber at Gartheiniog, showing two quarry flat wagons in use, and a third lying upturned next to them. The tramways converge on the adit leading to the mill. [Hadrill-McGuire family]

other quarrymen. They worked for six weeks but their attempt failed.[19]

Hendreddu remained in the ownership of Bowley's company. Herbert Harold Disley moved back to Corris, but his brother, John W. 'Jack' Disley stayed in Aberangell. From May 1936, he was the station agent at Aberangell. This was the role that John Parry had held until he died in the late 1920s.[10] Jack also served as ARP warden during World War Two.[30]

The company's generosity to the quarrymen was long remembered. At Christmas, each worker had received a large pork pie, provided by Joseph Morris who co-owned the Dickinson & Morris – the oldest pie shop in Melton Mowbray.[46] Bowley's offer of the quarry rent-free was appreciated, even though that venture did not succeed.[19]

In June 1935, John Henry Harris declared bankruptcy with debts of £6,594 and assets of just £999. He owned 2,188 ordinary shares and 400 preference shares in the Hendreddu Slate Quarry and had loaned the company £5,000 in 1933 to clear their debts. He had also bought 500 shares in Bullock and Co. slate enamellers, in the hope of generating more work for the quarry.[6] In September, Harris wrote to Bowley asking for the account book so he could defend a claim made against him by Barclays Bank who were trying to replace him as Receiver. Harris warned Bowley that the bank intended to scrap the machinery at the quarry to pay off debts: '*you can take it from me that if the Scrapping takes place, there will not be nearly enough realised… and the Debenture Holders will lose all their interest in the Quarry… we have always been candid with each other, I don't know who it is that is forcing the issue, but I do know that it will not do you any good if the Quarry had to face a forced sale at this time… there is nothing that I wish to keep from you or anyone else who are interested in the affairs which have proved so disastrous to us all.*'[47]

Gartheiniog 1922-1937
Gertrude Russon 1922-1931
After SHC failed in 1922, Gartheiniog was taken over by Gertrude Emma Russon, the wife of William Clayton Russon.[13] She was the owner and manager, an unusual position for a woman in those days. William Clayton Russon was bankrupt, so could not be a company director; it also appears that he transferred a lot of his money into his wife's name to shield it from his creditors – a manoeuvre he copied from his friend Roland Morgan. The quarry agent was B.B. Smith and three men were employed underground, with seven working in the mill.[13] The quarry specialised in producing slabs for electrical installations and also traded under the name The Electrical Mineral Product Ltd.[49]

In June 1924, 38-year-old Hugh Owen was killed by a rockfall. His death was ruled accidental at the inquiry.[48]

Smith remained the agent until 1925.[24] The quarry then went without a registered agent for the next decade. On 18th January 1926, the Russons began the process of creating a private company, Gartheiniog Slate Quarries Ltd capitalised with 4,000 shares at £1 each. This company listed its main business objectives as '*…Quarry masters and slate and stone merchants… to hew, split, carve, polish, crush and prepare for market or use slate or stone of all kinds. To carry on business as Timber merchants, sawmill proprietors and timber growers*'.[50] The listing of timber activities suggests the new company took over the local plantations that had been owned by SHC. Timber processing may well have continued at Gartheiniog until the late 1920s.

The new company was incorporated on 23rd January 1926, with Gertrude Russon as the principal shareholder, owning 1,500 of the shares. The three other directors were William Clayton Lloyd of Bournemouth, George Alfred Woodrow of Cefngwyn Hall and William Clayton Russon. Woodrow was from Kings Norton in Birmingham and William Clayton Lloyd was William Russon's business partner from before the war. The Russons were living in Bodawel in Clipiau, and this was the company's registered office. Other subscribers to the company's shares included George Butts of Smethwick and Thomas Cleaver of King's Heath, both suburbs of Birmingham.[25]

The new company struggled immediately and in May 1927, they halted operations, throwing thirty-five quarrymen out of work.[19] In July the company was sued by David Thomas Evans and thirty other workmen for £274 in back wages. They were granted an order for payment at the Dolgelly magistrates court.[51] The company ceased trading in September 1927; the official explanation was that a rockfall at the quarry had rendered further work unprofitable.[12] The Russons immediately formed a new company and restarted work, so it seems likely that they shut down Gartheiniog Slate Quarries to avoid their debts. The company was not officially wound up until 18th June 1929.[52] This manoeuvre left their shareholders nearly bankrupt, particularly Woodrow who lost £1,000,[*] and the local quarrymen outraged.[19] The Russons were not financially disadvantaged by the failure.

The new company was Gartheiniog Quarries Ltd and work at the quarry resumed almost immediately, with Mr Stevens of Cwmllinau and Tommy Rees of Aberangell as the managers;[19] Stevens may have been the ex-Hendreddu manager. Mrs Russon continued to operate the company until the end of 1931, employing eleven men that year.[42]

The Hadrill Era 1932-1933
In the winter of 1931/32 a new entrepreneur came to Dyffryn Angell. Lieutenant George Copland Temple Hadrill had served with distinction in the Royal Flying Corps during the First World War. Known to his family and friends as Temple, he cut an impressive figure. Hadrill was born in 1895, in Quebec, Canada, the son of the chairman of the Montreal Board of Trade.[53] He volunteered for the Royal Flying Corps early in the war and was shot down behind enemy lines in May 1917 by German ace Werner Voss.[54] He spent the remainder of the conflict as a prisoner.

[*] about £300,000 in 2020

Temple Hadrill with his second wife, photographed after the Second World War. [Hadrill McGuire family]

After the war, he settled in Sevenoaks, where he married his cousin Phyllis in 1920.[55] He qualified as a chartered accountant and by the end of the decade was a director of the battery company Accumulators of Woking (1928) Ltd.[56]

It is not clear why Hadrill decided to leave his accounting career, move to Aberangell and take up slate quarrying. His cousin Cedric Hadrill was married to Kathleen Oliver, the daughter of Edmund Lomas Oliver of Farchynys Hall, near Barmouth. Edmund owned the Waterhouse cotton mill at Bollington, and was a director of the Fine Spinners and Doublers Association, a trade group chaired by John W. McConnell, whose family owned Plas Hengwrt, just a few miles from Farchynys, and had built the Talyllyn Railway. Edmund Oliver was extremely wealthy. Temple and Phyllis likely visited their cousin at Farchynys. Perhaps one of these visits persuaded them to move to the area? Whatever the cause, Temple's arrival in the district was vividly described by Bill Milns:

'...[his] shabby suiting [came] from a good tailor a long time ago. Here were tough, heavy boots. Here was a tough, brown face with cold blue eyes. And here, so help me, was a Davey Crockett hat, albeit without a tail. Here was no city gent. This man had without a doubt been mining gold in the Yukon, and having decided to retire with his wealth in the Old Country, found that he could not leave mining alone.'[57]

Milns and Hadrill became firm friends after this rather remarkable first meeting, and they remained in touch until Hadrill's death in 1964. Temple was not the Yukon gold miner that Bill Milns humorously suggested him to be, but leased Gartheiniog from the Russons nevertheless. William Clayton Russon saw Hadrill as a source of capital that could revitalize the quarry and promised that he would leave the enterprise a wealthy man. Temple and Phyllis leased Cefngwyn Hall from Woodrow and moved to Aberangell. Russon was unhappy about this, as he preferred his partners to live far from the quarry while he syphoned off money from the operation.[7] As Bill Milns put it: 'From time to time, other gentlemen had come from London and... taken Gartheiniog

View from the reservoir, looking down onto Hadrill's mill. It is the only known photograph of the exterior of the working mill from after the First World War. The feed pipe runs down into the turbine house. To the right of the turbine is the smithy and beyond the mill building is the newly erected enamelling shed. [Hadrill-McGuire family]

slate quarry on a lease. [Temple Hadrill] was just another lamb en route to the Russon abattoir.'[57]

William Noel Milns was born in Stamford, Lincolnshire in 1903.[58] By 1911, his family had moved to Edgbaston.[59] In 1925, Milns married Margaret Irene Clarke in her home town of Melton Mowbray, where their daughter Doreen was born in 1927.[60] Margaret lived on the road to Thorpe Arnold, so they may have known William Bowley.

Bill's father was an electrical engineer and Bill also trained as an engineer. He moved with his family to Bryn Mynach in Aberangell in 1929[7] and took the job of chief engineer at Hendreddu. He is still remembered in the village for the motorcycle that he rode through the valley at great speed.[26]

On 1st April 1932, a new Gartheiniog Slate Quarries Ltd was registered, capitalised with 100 shares worth £1 each, with Temple and Phyllis as Directors.[61] They employed twenty-six men that first year, seven working underground and nineteen in the mill.[45]

Hadrill revived the quarry, bringing the mothballed equipment back into use and building an enamelling shed by the mill. This new business likely saved Gartheiniog, for the remaining slate was spotted and had numerous minor faults which could be hidden beneath the enamel.[19]

The shed was built on the waste tip, about 50ft east of the mill. It was built from slate blocks, with a corrugated iron roof laid over iron trusses. Its windows provided good natural light and at least one enamelling kiln was installed. Three men worked in the enamelling shed: Hugh Lloyd, who oversaw the work, Caradog Jones from Caernarfon and Mr Tamplin from Birmingham. They turned out a range of enamelled products including bath panels in Belgian blue, Merlin's green, Shell Saint Anne (a grey-green colour) and French Grey. Fire surrounds were available in light, medium and dark oak, light and dark walnut, rosewood and mahogany. They also produced electrical switchboards enamelled in black, with decorative veins applied to the surface.[19]

In the early 1930s, another Englishman, Thomas Edward Hayes, arrived at Aberangell and very likely worked for Temple at Gartheiniog. In 1935, Hayes married Muriel Williams[62] the daughter of Richard Williams of Abermynach Farm. The lower section of the Hendre Ddu Tramway crossed Abermynach land. Their daughter, Marieanne Williams (later Marieanne Mills), was born in 1937.[26]

Hadrill was a skilled engineer, good at installing and maintaining the machinery in the mill and enamelling shed, but he was not experienced at the business of running a slate quarry. By the early summer of 1933, Hadrill saw the writing on the wall, and the workforce was reduced to fifteen.[63] He asked Russon to let him out of his lease before he went bankrupt. Russon not only refused to let Hadrill off the hook but ordered him to stay off the quarry land.[19] Hadrill was stuck. He was losing money and could not even enter the quarry. In desperation, he hatched a plan with his friend Bill Milns. They decided to raid Gartheiniog and remove the key machinery to force Russon to negotiate.

John Breese was brought into the plan, and readily agreed to help; he remembered Russon's actions in 1927. Milns assembled a run of loaded wagons at the top of the Hendreddu exit incline. Breese ran a train of all the available empty wagons from Aberangell to the junction with the Gartheiniog Tramway. He charged up the steep branch into Gartheiniog yard, propelling the empties – the only recorded instance of a locomotive travelling up to Gartheiniog mill.

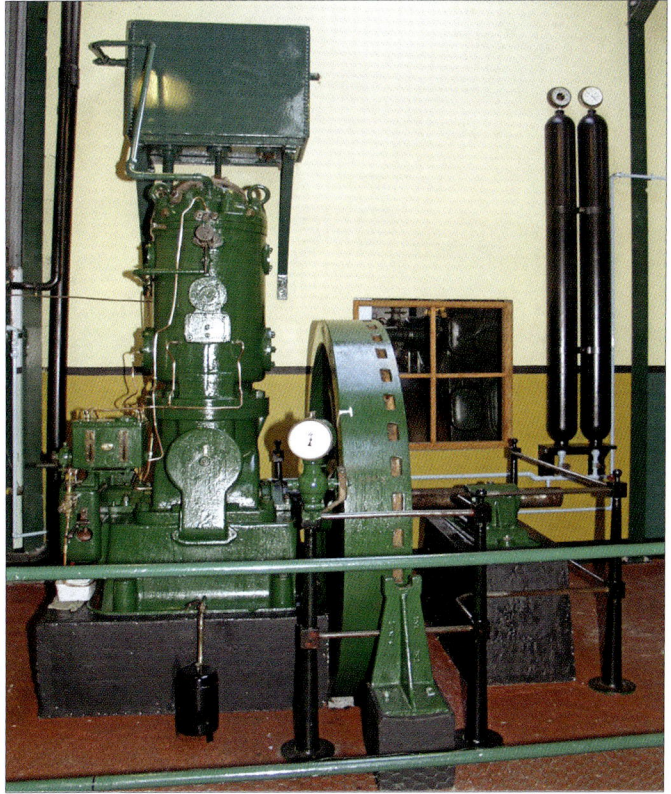

A 1912 Petter single-cylinder oil engine. Petter sold engines to this design through the war and into the late 1920s. The base arrangement is very similar to the concrete engine base that remains at Gartheiniog, so this is likely the type of engine used there. [Internal Fire Museum]

Hadrill and his workers were waiting and they quickly started loading machinery onto the train. A lookout on the Gartheiniog waste tips spotted James Russon approaching along the tramway below Ffridd. James Baron Russon, known to the locals as Barry, was the youngest son of William and Gertrude. The lookout alerted the men in the quarry and they ran the loaded train down to the main tramway and on to Hendreddu. Milns lifted it up the incline and ran the load into the mill. James Russon arrived at Gartheiniog to find the mill and enamelling shed ransacked. He followed the train up to Hendreddu, where Bill Milns walked out to greet him. Russon said: "*I insist on labelling every bit of machinery removed without my father's official permission*", to which Bill replied: "*Do so with pleasure, my friend, do what you wish now, for you will never have the opportunity again*".

James labelled the Gartheiniog machinery and retreated to Bodawel to confer with his father. Milns and Hadrill expected to receive a lawsuit but never did. William Clayton Russon was furious, but there was little he could do except meet with Hadrill and come to an agreement. Hadrill reinstalled the machinery, and in return, Russon reluctantly tore up his lease.[7] The brief Hadrill era was over. Milns's dawn raid on Gartheiniog had saved Hadrill from bankruptcy[19] and it cemented the life-long friendship between the two men. Hadrill's company was officially

The newly built enamelling shed. [Hadrill-McGuire family]

struck off the companies register in January 1935.[64]

In 1946, Hadrill co-founded the lamp makers Hadrill and Horstmann Ltd.[65] The company produced a range of iconic counterpoise lamps which are now much sought after. In 1955, the company merged with Simms Motor Units, and Hadrill became the general manager and a director of the consolidated Simms Group.[66]

Russon kept the quarry working for the early months of 1934, though it was probably mothballed in the late summer. Again, fifteen workers were reported with three underground and twelve overground that year.[67]

Bowley's Quarries Ltd 1935-1937

On 24th April 1935, a new company was formed to lease Gartheiniog from the Russons. Bowley's Quarries Ltd[68] issued 8,000 shares at £1 each, and had four directors: William Clayton Russon, father and son Archibald and Clement Shillan, and Robert Thursbee.[69] The company's headquarters were at the Wellington Works, Battersea

Bridge, London.[70] The new company was effectively a subsidiary of S. Bowley & Sons Ltd, also headquartered at the Wellington Works. S. Bowley & Sons had a long and distinguished history, it was founded by Joseph Bowley in 1744 in Westminster and moved in 1868 to Battersea.[71] Originally a manufacturer of soap and candles, it expanded into oil production at the turn of the century and was an early supplier of petrol to car owners; it also produced oil-based paints, enamels, shellac and similar chemical products.

Archibald William Shillan was born in Essex in 1873[72] and by 1927, he was a director of S. Bowley & Sons,[73] where Robert Thursbee was the managing director. Thursbee ran into trouble in 1935 when he was fined £150 for 'corruptly making gifts to John Henry Willden, a London County Council employee'. His fellow defendant was Archibald Shillan, by then the Chairman of S. Bowley & Sons.[74] Shillan, who lived in Hoddesdon, Hertfordshire, was found not guilty.[75]

William Bowley was 88 years old and had retired. Although he was not involved with Bowley's Quarries he

Inside the enamelling shed while the wooden floor was being installed. The tramway does not run into the shed though a line from the mill ended just outside the door in the east wall. The whole enamelling process can be seen. The barrel in the centre holds the vitreous powder which was mixed into a paste in the iron pail next to the barrel. The slabs were set on the wooden sawhorses and the paste was brushed on. The slabs were fired in the kiln at between 750C and 850C. One kiln is visible on the left. [Hadrill-McGuire family]

was a cousin of the owning family.

With the financial backing of S. Bowley & Sons, the business expertise of Shillan and the local knowledge of Russon, Bowley's Quarries was ready to revive Gartheiniog. By June 1935, they were advertising for a sales representative for the '*Building, Electrical and Sanitary Trades on a commission basis*'.[70] Unlike previous lessees of the quarry, the directors of Bowleys Quarries stood up to the Russons. William and Gertrude realised they could not bully the new owners and sold Gartheiniog outright to S. Bowley & Sons in 1936, and moved away from Aberangell.

By the time the Russons left, they were not well liked. The 1927 closure had left many local people angry, and the quick succession of English lessees who arrived and failed, while the Russons made money, did nothing to improve their reputation. William Clayton Russon was called the 'Little Man' behind his back, and many local people were glad to see him leave. Despite this, he had a consistent champion in Richard 'Dic Soar' Jones, an engineer who had worked at Gartheiniog for many years. Jones argued that the Russons had tried to keep men in work as much as possible, and noted that William was a devoted grandfather in his old age.[19]

Shillan appointed the tenacious Richard Lewis as his manager, with a Mr Jones from Llanberis as clerk of the quarry.[19] One of the first quarrymen taken on by Bowley's Quarries was Bill Breese. Bill finished school in 1935 and applied to work at Braich Goch, but there were too many Corris boys applying and he was not taken on.[76] Instead, he found work at Gartheiniog, initially as a saw sharpener, earning 10s 3d a week. Within a year he had been promoted and was earning 17s 7d.[14]

Quarry Operations

The incline and tramway through the upper access tunnel had been taken up before 1933, and quite possibly before 1931, leaving the 1886 adit as the access from the quarry to the mill. Gartheiniog had long suffered from water supply problems. The reservoir was too small and could only hold enough water for a few hours of work, so it was reliant on the inflow from the Afon Angell. Hendreddu controlled about half the water flowing into the Angell upstream, and they would often stop this entirely to fill their own reservoirs.[19]

To supplement the turbine, Ifor Thomas, the quarry engineer, purchased a Petter single-cylinder oil engine secondhand from Mold[19] and installed it behind the mill. The Petter allowed Gartheiniog to operate on days when there was not enough water to run the Pelton wheel. Unfortunately, shortly after the engine was installed, the con rod broke while Ifor was operating it. The rod hit his foot, breaking it badly and he had to be taken to hospital in Liverpool. Bill Breese remembered the kindness Archibald Shillan showed when he drove to Liverpool to bring Ifor back to his home in Dinas Mawddwy.[7]

Gartheiniog had two waste tipping grounds, one between

Richard Lewis, Jack Edwards and David Foulkes in the mid-1930s, probably standing outside Penybanc where Foulkes lodged with the Breese family. Lewis worked at the three main quarries in Dyffryn Angell. Edwards had been the chief engineer at Hendreddu and married John Parry's daughter in 1921.
[Bill Breese collection]

the head of the incline and the twll, the other to the east of the mill. The upper tips were not available as the tramway at that level had been lifted. The lower tips had filled the available land, so Bowleys decided to tip waste into the north chamber. A single-track incline was installed running across the chamber. Loaded rubbish wagons were winched up by the Overland engine recovered from the Hendre Ddu Tramway Willys-Overland locomotive. This was installed on the ledge on the north side of the pit and a series of pulleys took the cable to the head of the incline.

Transportation

Loaded wagons from Gartheiniog went down to Aberangell by gravity with the empties hauled back by horses hired from local farmers. The Motor Rail locomotive was the property of Hendreddu and remained locked away in its shed. In January 1936, in the grip of a particularly cold winter, contractor Evan Meredith refused to subject his animals to conditions he described as '*unfit for man nor beast*'.[77] The contract to provide horses went to Goronwy Williams of Abermynach Farm, son of Richard Williams.[26] Goronwy had taken over the farm following Richard's death in 1929.[78]

Later in 1936, Gartheiniog started to move over to road transportation. Enamelled products were packed in shipping crates and sent down the tramway to Aberdwynant where they were loaded into the lorries for onward shipment.[77] Aberdwynant was the nearest point to the quarry where a somewhat reasonable road met the tramway, and beyond here Bowley's would have had to pay fees to Goronwy to use his section of tramway. Eventually, Bowley's abandoned the tramway entirely and shipped their crates directly from the quarry using a secondhand furniture lorry[10] from S. Bowley & Sons; it had 'Bowley's of Battersea - Old English Paint' on its sides. The lorry was driven by Dai Rees of Walton Terrace, and it was just able to pass under the low Mawddwy Railway bridge across the only road out of Aberangell. The lorry lost its canopy in England when Dai misread a detour sign and collided with a low bridge. Dai had been travelling with Methodist deacon Lewis Jones of Capel Hebron and swore afterwards that he would not allow deacons in his lorry again, as they brought bad luck. Bill Breese remembers Dai delivering slabs '*all over Britain [with the lorry] in that pitiful condition… I had great pleasure in accompanying Dai Rees through the Mersey Tunnel, to deliver orders to Preston, Bradford, Manchester, Halifax, Blackburn and Hull*'.[43]

The company continued to suffer from the poor quality of the slate. The rock was brittle, and often cracked during transport. Customers complained, and the company added a disclaimer to their delivery notes against losses after the goods left the quarry, stating that complaints would only be addressed if customers paid for an inspector to come to the quarry. This was only of limited help and though no customers paid for an inspector, many demanded refunds anyway.[19]

The End of Bowley's Quarries

In late 1936, Gartheiniog temporarily halted work. It reopened by the beginning of 1937, when twenty-six men were employed,[68] but the end was in sight. Shillan met with the men and told them that operating costs continued to exceed revenue. The workers gathered in the enamelling shed to discuss the situation, while the young Bill Breese sat in the rafters listening.[19] Richard Lewis supported the management, praising their efforts to save the quarry. Jack Edwards from Dinas and Huw Lloyd of Aberangell made the case that the end was inevitable.[7] Their concerns were well-founded, for the quarry closed for good in February of that year.[79] After the quarry shut, the men sought work elsewhere. Many travelled over the mountains to the Ochor Draw (the 'other side') quarries along the Dulas Valley including Llwyngwern, Cymerau and Ratgoed.[19] Lewis was killed in an accident at Llwyngwern on 7th November 1939. Bill Breese, who had just turned 18, attended Lewis's funeral at St. Tydecho's Church in Cemmaes; it was the third such quarryman's funeral he had attended.[80]

Gartheiniog remained in the ownership of S. Bowley & Sons after closure.[30] Bill Breese had worked there for the entire period of Bowley's ownership and despite the poor end he remembered it as a '*…sunny spot, that was nicknamed the family quarry*'. After closure, he found work as a farmhand at Gartheiniog Farm, '*but the bluestone dust was in my blood, and even though they were always kind, I felt I was cut out for something quite different*'.[14]

References

1   Birth certificate of William Bowley, England & Wales Births 1837-2006, vol. 15, p.205, 1846.

2   Census record for William Bowley; piece 3295, folio 25, 1871. England, Wales & Scotland Census, Melton Mowbray, p.8, 1871.

3   Census record for William Bowley; piece 3013, folio 91, 1901. England, Wales & Scotland Census, Melton Mowbray, p.9, 1901.

4   Melton Urban Council and Guardians elections, *Grantham Journal*, p.8, Mar. 12th, 1904.

5   Melton's grand old people, *Grantham Journal*, p.6, Jan. 15th, 1938.

6   Heavy losses on shares, *Nottingham Evening Post*, p. 5, Jun. 8th, 1935.

7   Bill Breese, Notebook on tramroad and local quarrying, Dolgellau Archive, no. ref ZM/6541/5, c. 1970.

8   Oakham guardians, *Grantham Journal*, p.10, Mar. 13th, 1926.

9   Hendre-ddu Slate Quarries Limited, *The Quarry*, Apr. 1923.

10   Lewis Cozens, R.W. Kidner, Brian Poole, *The Mawddwy, Van and Kerry Branches*, Oakwood Press, 2004.

11   Bill Breese, Damweiniau Llenol, *Cambrian News*, Sept. 19th, 1975.

12   Files of dissolved companies. Company number: 162816; National Welsh Slate Quarries, Ltd BT 34/4498/162816, National Archives, 1920-1932.

13   List of Mines in Great Britain and the Isle of Man, 1922. H.M. Stationery Office, 1923.

14   Bill Breese, Tro ar fyd, *Cambrian News*, Jun. 1975.

15   List of Mines in Great Britain and the Isle of Man, 1923. H.M. Stationery Office, 1924.

16   Gwyndaf Breese, The Simplex Locomotive, unpublished manuscript.

17   List of Mines in Great Britain and the Isle of Man, 1924. H.M. Stationery Office, 1925.

18   Bill Breese, Notes on a sketch map of Hendreddu quarry, unpublished manuscript.

19   Bill Breese, Notes on local quarrying and quarrymen, Dolgellau Archive, vol. ref ZM/6541/9, 1982.

20   Richard Carr, Paxman's Seventy-Five Years of Diesel Engine Development (1925-2000). Paxman Archive Trust.

21   T. Glyn Williams, Hanes TGW y Hendreddu, private notes.

22   Sales catalogue of Hendreddu Slate Quarries Limited, private sales catalogue, 1925.

23   Gwyndaf Breese, Hard times on the tramway, unpublished manuscript.

24   List of Mines in Great Britain and the Isle of Man, 1925. H.M. Stationery Office, 1926.

25   List of Mines in Great Britain and the Isle of Man, 1926. H.M. Stationery Office, 1927.

26   Marieanne Mills, Jul. 2016.

27   Montgomeryshire Memorial Inscriptions, Cemmaes Calvinistic Methodist Chapel, grave reference M182.

28   Independent Order of Rechabites, Aberystwith Observer, p.5, Apr. 1st, 1909.

29   Bill Breese, Bygone activities within Angell valley, *Cambrian News*, Aug. 6th, 1976.

30   Bill Breese, A Welsh Village at War: 1939-1945, unpublished manuscript, c 1970.

31   John Disley, Disley family records.

32   Slate trade industry, *Liverpool Daily Post*, p.8, Apr. 2nd, 1917.

33   John Disley obituary, *The Guardian*, Feb. 17th, 2016.

34   List of Mines in Great Britain and the Isle of Man, 1927. H.M. Stationery Office, 1928.

35   P.C. hopes so too, *Grantham Journal*, p.12, May 28th, 1927.

36   William Bowley funeral invitation, Courtesy Hadrill McGuire family, 1940.

37   List of Mines in Great Britain and the Isle of Man, 1929. H.M. Stationery Office, 1930.

38   Gwyndaf Breese, Tramway accidents.

39   Truck crashes into train, *Gloucester Citizen*, p.9, Aug. 15th, 1929.

40   Jean Lindsay, *A History of the North Wales Slate Industry*, Newton Abbot: David and Charles, 1974.

41   Glyn Williams, The Mawddwy Branch, Part Two – Goods Only, *Great Western Railway Journal*, no. 60, Autumn 2006.

42   List of Mines in Great Britain and the Isle of Man, 1931. H.M. Stationery Office, 1932.

43   Bill Breese, A village of bridges, Unpublished manuscript.

44   Alun John Richards, *Gazetteer of Slate Quarrying in Wales*, Llygad Gwalch, 2007.

45   List of Mines in Great Britain and the Isle of Man, 1932. H.M. Stationery Office, 1933.

46   There's more to Melton Mowbray than meat and pastry, *The Telegraph*, May 5th, 2018.

47   Letter from John Henry Harris to William Bowley, Courtesy Stewart Katz, Sep. 16th, 1935.

48   Aberangell fatality, *Western Mail*, p.8, Jun. 24th, 1924.

49   The Electrical Mineral Product Ltd, *The Electrical Review*, vol. 91, no. 2338, Sep. 15th, 1922.

50   Files of dissolved companies. Company No: 211285; Gartheiniog Slate Quarries Ltd, National Archives, vol. BT 31/29385/211285, 1926-1932.

51   *31 plaintiffs in wages claim*, Flintshire County Herald, p.4, Jul. 22nd, 1927.

52   Joint stock companies, *London Gazette*, vol. 33507, p.4033, Jun. 18th, 1929.

53   Andrea McKenzie, *War-Torn Exchanges: The Lives and Letters of Nursing Sisters Laura Holland and Mildred Forbes*, UBC Press, 2016.

54   Barry Diggens, *September Evening: The Life and Final Combat of the German World War One Ace Werner Voss*, Grub Street, 2003.

55   Marriage of George C T Hadrill, Sevenoaks, England & Wales Marriages 1837-2005, vol. 2A, p. 2265, 1920.

56   Accumulators of Woking prospectus, *Garcke's Manual*, vol. 32, p.1116, 1928.

57   Bill Milns, Letter to Temple Hadrill, Courtesy Varel Hadrill-McGuire, 15th September 1961.

58   Dan Quine, Interview with Varel Hadrill McGuire, 2017.

59   Census record for William Noel Milns, Edgbaston. Piece 17918, schedule 272, 1911 Census For England & Wales, 1911.

60   Birth certificate of Doreen Milns, Melton Mowbray, England & Wales Births 1837-2006, vol. 7A, p. 476A, 1927.

61   Gartheiniog Slate Quarries Limited, *Roads and Road Construction* magazine, vol. 10, 1932.

62   Marriage certificate of Thomas E G Hayes, Dolgelly, England & Wales Marriages 1837-2005, vol. 11B, p.746, 1935.

63   List of Mines in Great Britain and the Isle of Man, 1933. H.M. Stationery Office, 1934.

64   Companies Act 1929, *London Gazette*, no. 34123, p.312, Jan. 11th, 1935.

65   Hadrill & Horstmann, *The Foundry Trade Journal*, vol. 78, p.308, Mar. 14th, 1946.

66   Brian Morgan, *Acceleration: the Simms story from 1891 to 1964*, Neame, 1965.

67   List of Mines in Great Britain and the Isle of Man, 1934. H.M. Stationery Office, 1935.

68   D. Dylan Pritchard, *The Slate Industry of North Wales: Statement of the Case for a Plan*, Gwasg Gee, 1946.

69   Bowley's Quarries Ltd, *Roads and Road Construction*, vol. 13, 1935.

70   Established slate quarry supplying slate slab products, *Hull Daily Mail*, p.2, Jun. 1st, 1935.

71   Sherwood Ramsey, *Historic Battersea*, G. Ravencroft & Co., 1913.

72   Census record for Archibald W. Shillan. Piece 484, folio 17, page 28, 1881 England, Wales & Scotland Census, 1881.

73   Mr. Archibald William Shillan, The Directory of Directors for 1927, 1927.

74   Pleaded guilty, *Hull Daily Mail*, p.7, Sep. 14th, 1935.

75   Gifts to L.C.C. clerk. Free supplies of petrol, *Daily Herald*, p.7, Sep. 14th, 1935.

76   Bill Breese, May 8th, 1976.

77   Gwyndaf Breese, Rolling Stock.

78   Mr. Richard Williams of Abermynach, *Western Mail*, p.6, Mar. 4th, 1929.

79   List of Mines in Great Britain and the Isle of Man, 1938. H.M. Stationery Office, 1939.

80   Welsh news in brief, *Liverpool Daily Post*, p.8, Nov. 9th, 1939.

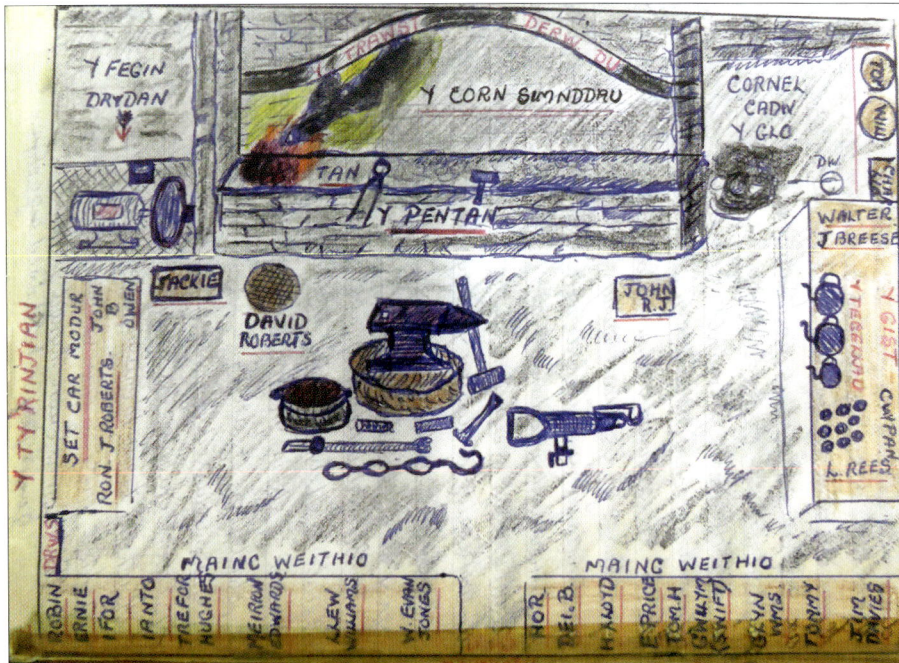

The seating arrangement in the forge at Hendreddu between 1938 and 1940, as sketched by Bill Breese. 'Y fegin drydan' are electric bellows, 'y trawst derw du' is the cracked black oak, 'y corn simnddau' is the chimney stacks, y gist y tegellau' is guests and kettles, 'cor'nel cadw y glow' is firekeeper's corner, 'mainc weithio' is workers' bench, 'set car modur' is lorry crew, 'y pentan' is the fireplace, and 'y Ty Rinjian' is the Engine House meaning the Mill.

The workers at Hendreddu in 1937, the first year of T. Glyn William's operation. T. Glyn, aged just 23, is on the left end of the second row from the top, with his hand on Bill's shoulder. Edwin Williams was T. Glyn's nephew and not an employee. Ernie Bach was the lorry driver. Charlie Roughsedge was Bill Breese's best friend. Ianto, whose last name is not known for certain but may be Griffiths, was the plane operator in the mill and Bob Richards was Marieanne Mills's uncle[13] – he had worked at Hendreddu since at least 1925. The remaining men are Thomas Hayes, Dafydd Williams of Abermynach,[14] James Ellis Pugh and John Roberts [Courtesy Tecwyn Williams]

126

12: The Last Go at Hendreddu 1937-1946

Before the Second World War
Thomas Glyn Williams

In the summer of 1937, Thomas Glyn Williams purchased Hendreddu from William Bowley. Williams came from a family with a long association with slate quarrying. Thomas Glyn's father T.O. Williams was a major figure in the Welsh slate industry, he owned Abercorris quarry from 1920 to 1928.[1] During this time he was the mining adviser to Amalgamated Housing Industries Ltd, an enterprise remarkably similar to SHC. Amalgamated Housing was set up to mass-produce houses and intended to purchase Abercorris, Braichgoch, Gaewern and Rhognant quarries, along with brickworks, concrete plants and timber production.[2] It failed in 1924.[3] After the failure of Amalgamated Housing, T.O. purchased Llangynog Quarries in 1925 with his partner B.H. Bevan[4] – Llangynog had been part of SHC just a few years before.

T.O. Williams went on to manage Braichgoch and Aberllefenni mines at Corris,[1] and Wrysgan quarry at Blaenau Ffestiniog in the 1930s.[5] His uncle, Robert Owen Williams, was the manager of Bryn Eglwys quarry from 1919 to 1946.

Thomas Glyn – almost always called T. Glyn – was born on 11th July 1913.[6] He went to school in Barmouth but left aged 14 to enter his father's business, working at Wrysgan and living by Llyn Cwmorthin. He then joined his uncle W.O. Williams, the well-known machinery merchant and scrap dealer in Harlech. W.O. would lift the Corris Railway two decades later.[7] T. Glyn returned to Wrysgan, and in 1933 moved on to run Braich Ddu slab quarry near Trawsfynydd, employing fifteen men including several from Beddgelert and Rhyd Ddu.[8]

T. Glyn had a great interest in modernising slate quarry operations. In the summer of 1936, he left Braich Ddu and moved to Cwm Pennant, about four miles north of Criccieth, where he took over the other Hendreddu quarry with several of his brothers.[9] While there he met and courted Lizzie Roberts of Moelfre Farm; they married in Pwllheli in 1939.[10]

Reopening Hendreddu 1937

T. Glyn's time in Cwm Pennant was short. Early in 1937, he purchased the moribund Hendreddu quarry at Aberangell, moving into the manager's house with his wife. His father, T.O. moved into Brynderwen the same year, thus continuing its connection with slate quarry owners.[9]

T. Glyn quickly assembled a team of local quarrymen to reopen Hendreddu. Bill Breese, fresh from his work at Gartheiniog, approached James Ellis Pugh for a job and got this rather alarming response: "*It is a place that destroys young lads, they become fractious old men, rough and foul-mouthed, and sometimes vain and aggressive, you know!*" Bill recalls: '*I defended the quarry, saying I remembered several of the men, deacons, the church secretary, the organist and the treasurer of the Sunday School, all quarry workers. I finished off by pointing out that our minister the Rev. R.W. Jones had started as a quarryman. In my opinion, far from leading anyone astray, the bluestone was a place that fostered high moral standing.*'[11] Bill got the job.

During 1937, Williams brought in Martyn Ivor Williams-Ellis, the General Manager of Llechwedd quarry, to advise on the reopening of Hendreddu. Williams-Ellis helped with technical work and approached his contacts in the slate trade to drum up business for Hendreddu.[12]

T. Glyn brought in new equipment including a Pelton Wheel fitted with an Austrian hydraulic governor and new pipework. This powered the generator supplying electricity to the mill and underground. He also installed a new diamond saw built by the Anderson-Grice Co. of Carnoustie, which could saw ten times the number of slabs as the old saws. Overall the mill had six slate planers and three saw tables per planer.[8] Williams appointed Bill Milns as his engineer. Milns was the engineer at Hendreddu in the early 1930s and had worked with Temple Hadrill at Gartheiniog. He was responsible for installing the new equipment and getting the older machines working again after the shutdown. He installed a new overhead crane in the mill.[14]

Williams laid a tramway from the middle of Gillart's Incline to the Level 3 adit, which gave underground access to the open pits. Chambers on Level 1 and 2b were also worked.[15] In 1937, when Bill Breese joined, the quarry employed fifteen men[16] and a year later seventeen were working.[5]

Working the Quarry 1937-1941

Work started underground in the existing chambers, but they had not been properly developed after the First World War, and the results were disappointing. Williams struggled to pay weekly wages to his men as losses mounted. Fortunately, a fall in Bargain 14 (Chamber 1.6) revealed a good new working face.[8] In 1938, Williams found a new market for insulators and electrical switchboards. Vickers, GEC, Allan West and others placed orders, and wages in the quarry were raised to £2 per week. One large order for £800 worth of slab was received and filled two GWR wagons at Aberangell. Bill Milns's father worked in Malaysia and put in an order for gravestones, which were taken from Chamber 1.6, known for producing particularly high-quality slabs.[17]

More men were taken on, rising to a total of twenty-five at the peak, with Walter Breese leading a team working in Twll 4, and several men joining from the recently closed Gartheiniog quarry. However, by early 1940, customers were reporting that their slabs were cracking and splitting and several refused to pay. Williams had to borrow money from his mother and his wife to keep the men employed.[8] With no capital to develop new chambers, Williams took the well-trodden path of robbing the pillars. Bill Breese described this practice in unhappy terms:

'... no cash was being invested so as to create fresh chambers for extracting good material from the vein. Prospecting, it seemed, had become a thing that belonged to the past. A dangerous mining practice had been forced upon miners and rockmen. Tons of top quality slate were removed from massive safety pillars left purposefully by those experts who realised that chamber roofs had to be strongly supported if serious mishaps were to be avoided. Those who toiled underground, felt that their lives were being put at stake. Very soon the quarry would be as unworkable as it would be inprofitable [sic] for its risky owner...'[18]

Two of the supporting walls between the main chambers on Level 1 were removed. All of these Level 1 chambers have suffered at least partial collapses after quarrying ended, showing that Breese was correct in his assessment.

Bill Breese wrote two articles later in his life recalling his time at Hendreddu, sitting in the forge where the quarrymen took their meals during winter. He is likely describing the winter of 1938/39 which was particularly cold and prolonged:

'I will mention one small incident involving John Roberts, who had a reputation for his fiery temper. One day at tea time, he spotted a particle of dirt floating in his tea. He became as angry as a nest of hornets, and threw his cup and its boiling contents past the ear of a fellow quarryman and through a window. Broken glass fell onto the lawn outside. After he calmed down, he apologised. It takes all sorts to make the world...

Mice lived in the walls of the Forge, drawn by the warmth. They would run round the feet of the diners, grabbing pieces of cheese dropped on the floor as if they were the most luxurious items. A white owl would sometimes visit to feed off the mice, and roost in the rafters. Some claimed the owl carried ancient wisdom. All I know is she turned her head towards each man as he spoke, as if listening to his words...

No sunshine reached the open pits between October and the end of March. The ground froze badly every night and frost lay over everything each day, covering every stone and tool. One Monday we found a robin, which usually kept warm in the roof of the Forge, frozen to death. Usually rubbish was thrown onto the waste tips, to be buried, but we dug into the frozen soil and carefully laid the robin to rest in Cae'r Fules behind the mill.

Sometimes we behaved childishly. But there was no shortage of poets, singers, narrators and accompanists. There were plenty of almost too-gentle rhymes and verses. We remembered the more complex arrangements for voices that the late Lewis Rees had once put together in the old Forge.'[19]

A mule was kept in the field behind the mill called Cae'r Fules ('Mule's Field'), under the care of Gruffydd Thomas. The mule hauled the wagons within the quarry and to the exit incline, and was renowned as a cantankerous beast who would only respond to Thomas.[20] Gruffydd was born in

A photo from just before the war; written on the back is: 'Bill Breese and his pal Charlie Roughsedge. Home from the quarry on a summer's evening.' Charlie had a reputation as a flirt and pursued several local girls. He was one of the first men in the village to sign up at the outbreak of the war, but not before he married his girlfriend Mary Barnett from Cemmaes on 16th March 1940.[23] Charlie was born in Kettering, on 16th January 1916.[24] Tragically, he contracted Black Fever while on duty in Haverfordwest, and died on January 10th 1941, just four days after his 25th birthday.[18]

A quarrymen's trip to Aberystwyth, just before the outbreak of the Second World War. In the background are part of the castle walls and the impressive Castle Theatre. T. Glyn Williams sits on the left of the group, with Bob Richards second from the right in the front row and Ifor Thomas on the right of the top row.
[Bill Breese collection]

1855 and lived at Penybanc in Aberangell, and was in his 80s when he worked for T. Glyn Williams and had worked as a mule handler for the Bradwells in the 1890s.[17]

For probably the first time in the quarry's history, roofing slates were produced. These were relatively crude and thick, but some of them still survived in 2016 on the roof of a cottage in Blaenau Ffestiniog.

One of the quarrymen working for T. Glyn Williams was Ifor Thomas, who later became the Aberangell coal man. He had a reputation in the village of being a 'character' and rather fancy with the ladies. The Hendreddu quarrymen took tea and sugar with them to put into the communal urn. One day, Ifor's mother mistakenly gave him Epsom Salts instead of sugar, which caused the whole quarry to suffer terribly. Ifor did not dare own up, in fear of what his colleagues would do.[13]

Accidents and Injuries

Hendreddu maintained a *Llyfryn Cofnodi Damweinia* (accident record book) in the quarry office and Bill Breese recorded several items from it. In 1937, Breese tore the tendon in his right ankle when rocks collapsed on it. William E. Jones suffered a head injury when he was hit by a train on the tramway near Rock Cutting. William Owen from Corris was caught in a collapse near the opening of his chamber and lost both legs. Dafydd Roberts suffered burns to his face while working in the mill. Lewis O. Jones slipped on ice and broke his ribs. Charles Roughsedge was hit on the head by a shovel while working in Chamber 2.3.[21]

Bill and his friend Charlie Roughsedge, who lived at Brynawel in Aberangell,[22] worked at Hendreddu from 1937 onwards, but some of these incidents may have been before then, as the book covered the mid-1920s onwards.

In 1938 there was a spectacular, though thankfully fairly minor, accident on the tramway. T. Glyn Williams, Ifor Thomas and Bill Breese were returning from the quarry on Car Melyn – a homebuilt gravity carriage. They were heading downhill and had just picked up speed on the steep section near Pont yr Hirgwm. As they rounded the curve below Cefngwyn, they derailed, and the three passengers were thrown off. All three ended up bloodied and sore, but no bones were broken.[21]

A much more serious accident happened on 9th June 1939, when quarryman Ernest Price of Nanthir fell to his death underground.[25] Bill Breese was working in the quarry at the time and witnessed the aftermath of the accident: '*A worker fell 99ft to his death from the upper chamber [Chamber 2.3]. I was a youth standing by his side in case assistance was required, while Evan Davies and Mrs. T. G Williams (Manager's wife) rendered first aid pending arrival of Dr. Ll. ap I. Davies. He died of severe multiple injuries.*'[26]

The End of the Tramway

While T. Glyn Williams concentrated his efforts on the quarry, he also looked into reviving the tramway. The Motor Rail locomotive had been locked in the shed at the top of Brynderwen Cutting since 1934.[27] Edwin Williams recalls that T. Glyn '… *modified a truck or carriage with wooden seats back to back and would use the engine to go to chapel on a Sunday morning, also picking some other people on the way.*'[28] Some trains were run during 1937 and 1938, mostly to take the men up to the quarry. The practice of running loaded trains to Aberangell by gravity was revived in 1937, but the tramway was abandoned in 1938; this brought to an end sixty-four years of slate trains on the Hendre Ddu Tramway.

T. Glyn Williams saw that the future lay in road transport and purchased a Morris Commercial lorry to take slate down to Aberangell, driven by Ernie Bach. Loaded wagons went down by gravity and were hauled back by the Morris straddling the rails. This damaged the track, and mud thrown up by the lorry blocked the drainage culverts. In 1938, they switched to running the Morris in both directions and no longer used the tramway. The exit incline was still used but wagons were loaded directly onto the lorry from the transhipment wharf at the foot of the incline.

The quarry also bought a charabanc with wooden wheels to transport the workers up from Aberangell, but it was never used.[9]

The tramway rails were lifted in late 1939 for the wartime scrap drives by George Cohen,[29] including the main line from the foot of the exit incline down to the Wharf and the remaining branches, notably the Maesygamfa and Gartheiniog tramways. Bill Breese recalls the operation: '*When Aberangell villagers first sighted the transference of hundreds of tons of scrap iron from Quarry tramroad drams to Mawddwy*

Bill Breese in uniform during the Second World War. His tunic looks new and does not have any regimental insignia, so this may have been taken when he first enlisted. [John Breese]

Railway waggons on the Transhipment Wharf at Station Freight Yard, they formed an opinion that it would probably be the only worthwhile contribution that such a tiny village as theirs could possibly provide towards the much heralded Armaments, and also Munitions Drive.'[18]

T. Glyn sold some quarry equipment to Aberllefenni quarry in 1939 and 1940, including winch parts, galvanised wire rope, hand cranes and new jackhammers. His father was running Aberllefenni at the time. Some of this equipment may have come from Gartheiniog, which T. Glyn purchased around this time. T. Glyn may also have been working the tiny Broad Vein quarry at Waun Llefenni, about two miles northwest of Aberllefenni. One Hendreddu wagon was purchased by Aberllefenni and is noted in the quarry Day Book as 'Iron Waggon from Waun for sinks' – it was presumably regauged to 2ft 3in.[30]

Most of the tramway rail was gone by the end of 1939, but many sleepers remained in situ into the 1980s.[31] A few short sections of track survived the scrap drives. The rails on Aberangell Wharf were not owned by the quarry and so were left in place until 1952. Sied Wen remained intact, but the wooden framing of the Black Shed had deteriorated and it was demolished during the war, with some parts being reused by local farmers.[32]

The Wharf tramway was used during the late 1940s and early 1950s by the Forestry Commission to move timber around the site and some lengths of rail survived into the 2010s. The short Nanthir branch was also not lifted in the war, presumably considered the property of the farm. It survived into the mid-1970s.[33]

War Again
The End of the Quarry

In September 1939, war broke out in Europe. Williams kept the quarry open, but several of his workers volunteered or were conscripted – slate mining was not a reserved

occupation. The quarry struggled on into 1941, but that was the last year of slate working at Hendreddu.[34] Bill Breese worked at the quarry until the outbreak of war when he took a job as a sawyer at Aberangell sawmill. This was a protected occupation, which meant he had trouble enlisting. In the meantime, he served as the youngest member of the Aberangell Home Guard. In 1941, Bill was finally able to join up. He served with the Royal Welsh Fusiliers, fighting in India, and was wounded in the shoulder while on active service in Burma.[18]

Hendreddu was down to just five men in 1940. The pillar robbing had turned the mine into a treacherous place to work. Early in 1941, the men complained that Chamber 2.1 was unstable and they feared it would collapse. Williams did not trust the local rockmen, so he brought in two experienced Blaenau Ffestiniog men, likely from Wrysgan. They inspected chambers 2.1 and 1.3, using a powerful searchlight to illuminate the roof. They were horrified and asked Williams: '*Dear little man, how can you tolerate seeing men work in such a dangerous place, I wonder?*'[17] They looked at the other underground workings and gave him a 'stern no' on the rest of the quarry too. This damning opinion forced Hendreddu to close.

Ammunition Storage

Dyffryn Angell was an attractive location for ammunition storage, miles from the nearest major settlement and German bombing routes. The Ministry of Supply leased both Hendreddu and Gartheiniog, and T. Glyn Williams accepted the position of manager in charge of the stores. A compulsory order from the Ministry required the mills to be cleared of machinery so up to 4,000 tons of munitions could be stored there.[8] The planes and saw tables were dragged out of the Hendreddu mill and left on the waste tips near the Level 1 adit. Some attempt to preserve them was made, Alford Jarvis covering them with an anti-rust solution, but inevitably they decayed as the war drew on.[18]

Starting on 22nd December 1941, explosives were delivered by the GWR to Aberangell. Purpose-built, sealed ammunition vans were left in the loop by the Wharf and from there, fleets of lorries carried the munitions to the quarries. T. Glyn provided his two quarry lorries, while the rest came from haulage contractor D. Williams of Machynlleth. The explosives were

The remains of the Ministry of Supply road bridge across the Angell below Hendreddu Cottages, on 12th May 1979. The Cutiau Bach sheds had been on the far bank. The bridge girders were still in place, though much overgrown, in 2016.
[Graham Fairhurst]

packed into containers: larger crates resembling tea chests carried TNT, while smaller metal boxes held cordite. The quarry had no proper road access until the Forestry Commission built their road in the 1960s, so the miner's track that ran from the mill down past Hendreddu Cottages was used as a crude road. This descended at 1 in eight and there was a deep ravine on the east side, so it was a dramatic journey for the lorry drivers.[8] The Angell was bridged at the foot of the new road, at the site of the Cutiau Bach.

The haulage contractor's lorries were driven by: brothers Griff 'Skin' and Dai 'Bach Skin'; Griff 'Cotton Wool'; Griff Evans; 'Big Bill' and Arthur. The two quarry lorries were driven by brothers Ronald and H. Meirion Thomas of Mallwyd. The younger brother, H. Meirion, was fortunate to escape injury when he lost control of his lorry and crashed into the Afon Angell near Pont yr Hirgwm.[18] He had been distracted by the sight of one of the local young ladies.[8] Most of the lorries drove along the road through Clipiau, but the two Hendreddu lorries were untaxed, so could not use the council roads. Instead, they followed the tramway route through Brynderwen Cutting and across the meadows to Aberdwynant.[18]

Edryd Price recalls the lorries passing through the village when he was a child. One day there was a loud explosion in the village. Edryd's older brother went to investigate and reported that a box of black gunpowder had fallen from a lorry and exploded opposite Brynderwen. As Edryd said, it was a good thing the box did not fall under the wheels of the lorry and set the whole load off.[35] On another occasion, one of the older D. Williams lorries was struggling and misfiring on the steep final climb to the quarry. Flames shot out from under the bonnet and everybody ran for their lives. T.

One of the Hendreddu slates used to roof a cottage in Blaenau Ffestiniog in 1946. The difficulty in splitting the Hendreddu slab into thin slates is evident, as is the characteristic blue shade of the rock. [Tecwyn Williams]

Glyn Williams managed to open the bonnet, take off his coat and extinguish the fire.[8] He was heard to exclaim afterwards that "*the consequences could have been catastrophic!*"[13]

Gartheiniog mill was also used to store ammunition. Thomas Hayes, who had worked for T. Glyn Williams at Hendreddu, was employed as overnight fire watcher ready to raise the alarm if fire broke out. He stayed in the red brick building just to the south of the mill.[13] All clerical duties related to ammunition storage were handled by Miss Jones who worked from an office in Brynderwen house.[18]

The munitions were mostly TNT and cordite, but phosphorus-based chemical weapons made by Albright & Wilson of Oldbury, known as AW Bombs, were also sent to the quarries. The men who handled the transshipments recall that their mouths would dry out completely and their skin was stained yellow while handling them.[18] The AW Bombs were extremely volatile and needed to be stored in the mills, away from the elements.

After the War

After the war, T. Glyn Williams hoped to resume quarrying. In 1945, he planned to modernise Gartheiniog, much to the bafflement of the locals who knew that the remaining slate was too expensive to reach. In the end, it did not reopen. Williams regained ownership of Hendreddu from the Ministry of Supply in 1946.[36] The quarry machinery was still out on the tips, and Williams

Aberangell wharf in 1952 during the demolition of the Mawddwy Railway. Some of the remaining rails of the Hendre Ddu Tramway can be seen just in front of the car, and the turntable can just be made out above the pile of standard gauge chairs in the bottom right. [R.W. Kidner]

asked the Ministry to restore the mill to the state it had been in when they requisitioned it. He was told that if he restored the machinery, he could then claim payment, but he lacked the necessary capital.[8] Williams gave up Hendreddu at the end of 1946;[9] the machinery was scrapped and Ernie Davies and Meirion Thomas assisted Williams in demolishing the mill. They stripped the slates from the roof and the vast timber trusses were sold to Evan Tudor & Sons timber merchants of Trawsfynydd.[18] David Tudor had purchased Braichgoch quarry around this time,[37] and was re-equipping it and the trusses may have been reused there. The Forestry Commission purchased the 22½ acre quarry site.[38] In 1948, Hendreddu Slate Quarries Ltd was removed from the Companies Register[39] and dissolved, and in 1950 the official returns ceased.

Williams moved to Blaenau Ffestiniog with his family in late 1946.[31] There he started his quarrying and road haulage company, beginning with Wrysgan. In 1971, he bought the massive Oakeley quarry; starting with just three men, he developed it into a profitable enterprise. He went on to buy Cwt-y-Bugail and Pen yr Orsedd quarries as well, and his quarrying company employed nearly 200 men at its peak. His road haulage company was still in business in 2018.

This concludes the story of slate quarrying in Dyffryn Angell. Much of the valley was planted with spruce and fir trees by the Forestry Commission, and the remains of most of the quarries disappeared beneath a blanket of green. The tramway trackbed, now a road, continues to be a lifeline to the remote farms and houses along the Angell. Occasionally the forests reverberate with the roar of engines as rally cars blast along the narrow lanes, but otherwise, Dyffryn Angell is once again a quiet and lonely place, more populated by sheep and ravens than by people.

References

1   Alun John Richards, *Slate Quarrying at Corris*, Carreg Gwalch, 1994.
2   Prospectus of Amalgamated Housing Industries Limited, *Pall Mall Gazette*, p.10, Jun. 21st, 1921.
3   Joint stock companies, *London Gazette*, no. 32987, p.7897, Oct. 31st, 1924.
4   New companies, *Western Mail*, p.12, Aug. 31st, 1925.
5   List of Mines in Great Britain and the Isle of Man, 1938. H.M. Stationery Office, 1939.
6   1939 record of Thomas G Williams; Hendreddu Quarry, National Archives, p. RG101/7642C/005/1, 1939.
7   Dan Quine, Not to be: The sad end of the Corris Railway, *Heritage Railway*, Oct. 2016.
8   T. Glyn Williams, Hanes TGW y Hendreddu, private notes.
9   Dan Quine, Private correspondence with Tecwyn Williams, Apr. 2017.
10   Marriage of Thomas G Williams, England & Wales Marriages 1837-2005; Pwllheli, vol. 11B, p.901.
11   Bill Breese, Tro ar fyd, *Cambrian News*, Jun. 1975.
12   Letter from Martyn Ivor Williams-Ellis to Commander P. Dean, Courtesy Jon Knowles, Oct. 18th, 1937.
13   Marieanne Mills, Jul. 2016.
14   Bill Breese, Snow in the Mill, unpublished manuscript.
15   Bill Breese, Notes on a sketch map of Hendreddu quarry, unpublished manuscript.
16   D. Dylan Pritchard, *The Slate Industry of North Wales: Statement of the Case for a Plan*, Gwasg Gee, 1946.
17   Bill Breese, Notebook on tramroad and local quarrying, Dolgellau Archive, no. ref ZM/6541/5, c. 1970.
18   Bill Breese, A Welsh Village at War: 1939-1945, unpublished manuscript, c 1970.
19   Bill Breese, Hen Efail y Chwarel: part I, *Cambrian News*, Jan. 14th, 1977.
20   Gwyndaf Breese, The Angell Valley Tramway, unpublished manuscript.
21   Bill Breese, Damweiniau Llenol, *Cambrian News*, Sept. 19th, 1975.
22   1939 record of Charles Roughsedge; Aberangell, National Archives, p. RG101/7642C/003/29, 1939.
23   Marriage record of Charles Roughsedge; Machynlleth, England & Wales Marriages 1837-2005, vol. 11B, p.361, 1940.
24   Charles Roughsedge, Birth certificate of Charles Roughsedge; Kettering, England & Wales Births 1837-2006, vol. 3B, p.248.
25   Quarryman Ernest Price, Edinburgh Evening News, p.18, Jun. 10th, 1939.
26   Bill Breese, Relics of the old quarrying days, *Cambrian News*, Jun. 15th, 1975.
27   Gwyndaf Breese, The Simplex Locomotive, unpublished manuscript.
28   Dan Quine, Private correspondence with Edwin Williams, 2016.
29   Gwyndaf Breese, End of the line, unpublished manuscript.
30   Dan Quine, Private correspondence with Jon Knowles, 2020.
31   Lewis Cozens, R. W. Kidner, Brian Poole, *The Mawddwy, Van and Kerry Branches*, Oakwood Press, 2004.
32   Gwyndaf Breese, Hard times on the tramway, unpublished manuscript.
33   Rob Pearman, Letter from Rob Pearman, *Narrow Gauge News*, vol. 227, p.24, Jul. 1998.
34   List of Mines in Great Britain and the Isle of Man, 1945. H.M. Stationery Office, 1946.
35   Dan Quine, Interview with Edryd Price, Sep. 2015.
36   Bill Breese, Notes on local quarrying and quarrymen, Dolgellau Archive, vol. ref ZM/6541/9, 1982.
37   Lewis Cozens, *The Corris Railway*, Cozens, 1949.
38   Minutes of the 11th Meeting of the Wales National Committee, Forestry Commission, Oct. 1st, 1946.
39   Companies Act 1909, *London Gazette*, no. 38268, p.2537, Apr. 23rd, 1948.

13: Rolling Stock, Operations and Permanent Way

Aberangell Wharf in 1925, in a posed photograph for the company catalogue. Loaded slab wagons would never have been taken uphill to the quarry. Motor Rail No. 2059 is at the head of the train. The locomotive's distinctive vertical buffers and multi-height coupling block were necessary to cope with the wide variety of rolling stock used on the tramway. Behind the locomotive is a box top carriage with four workmen on it, three ceir gwyllt, each seating four, and four trestle slab wagons. To the left of the train is a line of box wagons, carrying sawn timber. To the right of the locomotive is the corrugated iron weighhouse that replaced the earlier stone-built version. [R.T. Pugh]

For the first forty-five years of the tramway's life, the motive power was people, horses and gravity. Despite the successful introduction of steam locomotives on the Talyllyn and Corris railways in the 1860s and 1870s, there was no attempt to use steam on the Hendre Ddu. The track was too light, the profits from the quarries were meagre, and the existing system worked well enough. It was not until after the First World War that a locomotive was purchased.

The tramway used carriages and wagons of a variety of interesting designs. The most distinctive item of rolling stock was the 'car gwyllt', a type of gravity carriage that was peculiar enough to have been immortalised in poetry.

Locomotives

Boyd and Cozens claimed that Baguley No. 774 worked on one of the First World War timber tramways, but recent research shows that it was used on the Pennal Tramway.[1]

Motor Rail 2059

NWSQ introduced locomotive working on the tramway in 1921. Several company directors had experience of light railways in the war and were impressed with Motor Rail's rail tractors.[2] There were still many secondhand locomotives available as war surplus, but the company decided to order a new locomotive.

The 'bent frame' Simplex design was one of the first mass-

133

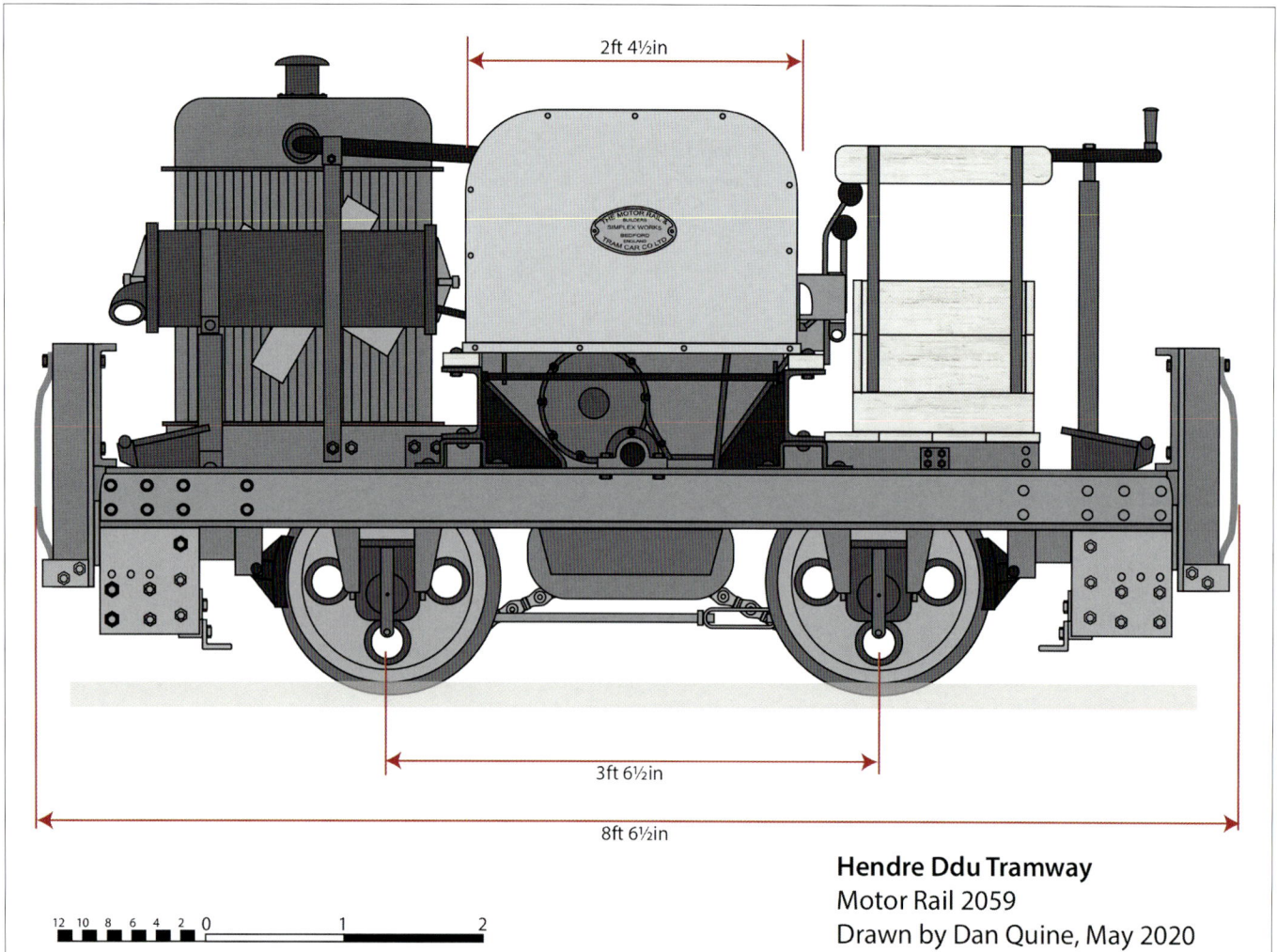

Side elevation of Motor Rail No. 2059, as delivered to the Hendre Ddu Tramway. The buffers with a sprung plate riveted on were specifically designed for the Hendre Ddu.

produced internal combustion locomotives. It used a W. H. Dorman & Co. 2JO petrol engine, coupled to a heavy flywheel and an inverted cone clutch which drove through a Dixon-Abbott patent spur wheel gearbox. Motor Rail claimed '*this combination ensures steady running and no jar when running and hauling various loads from 1 to 12 miles per hour. This makes for less wear and tear than is experienced with a steam engine of similar capacity*'.

The locomotive supplied to Hendre Ddu cost £697. The order specified a multi-height central coupling block at both ends, and large sprung buffers. It used a magneto from Thomson-Bennett Ltd for ignition.

Gwyndaf Breese described its arrival in 1921:

'*The new engine's arrival was an important episode in the history of the quarry, and a number of onlookers, ranging from the curious to the mildly interested, gathered to watch it being unloaded with the help of the huge station yard crane, and eased onto the tram rails. It was an impressive sight, freshly painted and displaying its works number, 2059, and the maker's name on the bonnet. The gleaming brass fittings on the throttle control and the brake hand grip were also much admired.*'[2]

Several modifications were made to the locomotive during its time on the tramway. In 1929, it ran away in Brynderwen cutting because the thread on the brake spindle was badly worn. The brake was replaced with a car-type hand-brake lever. There are records of spare parts being supplied to the Hendre-ddu Slate Quarries Ltd in Melton Mowbray for No. 2059 by Motor Rail through the 1920s.[3]

At some point, the radiator was replaced with a galvanised tank by the quarry engineers. The sanding gear proved a constant problem as it was impossible to keep a supply of fine sand dry. The sandboxes were removed by 1925, and sanding was done manually, often by a local youth who would sit on the buffer beam and drop sand through the holes where the sandboxes once sat.[2]

No. 2059 was usually housed in the shed at the upper end of Brynderwen cutting. From 1925, it was supplied with petrol from a pump serving 'Pratt's Perfection Spirit' outside Norman Jones's sawmill. Cans were used to carry a week's supply to the shed on Friday night. John Breese would run No. 2059 down to the Wharf on Sunday evening ready for the first departure to the quarry on Monday morning. He

Motor Rail No. 2059 at the Gillingham Pottery in 1970, being shunted by Ruston No. 189972. No. 2059's engine cover has already been removed, ready for transport. It has the National 'D' engine, with a rectangular fuel tank behind. The sandboxes and radiator had been refitted, probably by Fred Watkins. [Pete Nicholson]

was careful to avoid the evening service at Capel Bethania lest the more devout members berate him for working on the Sabbath.

Bill Breese recounts an attempt by his father John and quarry engineer Bill Milns to operate No. 2059 underground at Hendreddu. This must have been while the Willys-Overland locomotive was in operation between 1929 and 1931. They hauled the Motor Rail up the exit incline, then ran it into the Level 1 adit. The exhaust fumes produced a poisonous atmosphere underground and the experiment was quickly ended.[4]

The locomotive provided good service along the tramway until June 1935. No. 2059 was shut up in the shed at Brynderwen and did not work again until it was briefly used in 1937 and 1938. It was sold in 1939:

'*Its departure to unknown destinations saddened the villagers, particularly the children, [for its] crisp staccato bark had often woken them at 6.30 a.m. Scampering out of cozy beds they would flatten tiny noses against rain-lashed windows, searching for the penetrating gleam of its carbide lamps as it conveyed fathers and brothers on the four mile uphill journey to the quarry.*'[2]

The locomotive was purchased by railway dealer Fred Watkins of the Forest of Dean. He replaced the original J2O petrol engine with a National 'D' diesel unit[5] and advertised it for sale.[6] Watkins probably also refitted the sandboxes and a standard Motor Rail radiator in place of the galvanised tank. In 1940, the locomotive was purchased by the Gillingham Pottery Brick and Tile Company in Dorset, where it worked for several years.

The Pottery closed in 1968 and No. 2059 was abandoned. It was purchased in December 1970[7] by Robin Pearman and moved to his home in Potters Bar in April 1971.[8] In 2020, the locomotive is owned by Robin's son and remains largely unrestored.[9]

No. 2059 being dismantled for transport. This rear view shows the mounting for the multi-height coupler, the custom spring buffers and the replacement hand brake lever. [Pete Nicholson]

A 1913 Willys-Overland Utility ³/₄ ton Truck. The chain drive and solid tyres were common features of early lorries. The frame and chain drive appear identical to those in the 1929 Willys-Overland locomotive.

The left side of the remains of the locomotive. Further stakes hold the front of the chassis in place. To the left of the chassis is a concrete block with a short metal pillar embedded into it. This held the starter handle for the engine. The radiator is notable for its absence. Willys used trans-axles like this until 1918, confirming that the chassis predates the 1929 engine block. [Donald Sills]

The Willys-Overland Locomotive

The slate industry boom of the 1920s saw Hendreddu and Gartheiniog expand production. To cope with the extra traffic, Hendreddu Quarry built a new locomotive in 1929. While details of this locomotive are scarce, it has been possible to construct a plausible account of it.

Lorry Haulage

Cozens reports that a road lorry was used to haul wagons along the tramway immediately after the First World War.[10] While this has not been corroborated, Higginbottom could well have moved one of his colliery lorries to Aberangell to haul timber bogies along the tramway.

The 1929 Locomotive

If Higginbottom did use a lorry on the tramway, it may well have stayed in the district after he left. When the Hendreddu company built their new locomotive in 1929, they used the chassis and other parts from a 1913 vintage Willys-Overland truck, which could have been Higginbottom's lorry.

The Willys-Overland locomotive worked on the tramway for two years and was popular with the locomotive crew. It had a short working life. In early 1931, it was left outside of Sied Ddu overnight[4] and the radiator burst.[2] It was dismantled and parts were used to build the Gartheiniog winch in 1935. Other parts were used to build Car Melyn, one of the large gravity cars.[4]

The Gartheiniog Winch

There are no surviving photographs of the Willys-Overland locomotive. The remains of the winch survived at Gartheiniog until 1984, where Donald Sills photographed them, a vital resource in understanding what

the locomotive looked like. It is clear from the winch remains that the 1929 locomotive was indeed assembled from the chassis and transmission of a 1913 Willys-Overland Utility truck.

The chassis had a six-cylinder Overland side-valve petrol engine with a chrome-nickel molybdenum iron block. The gearbox had four gears R, 1, 2 and D. The differential came from the Willys-Overland lorry and drove a sprocket on the right side of the chassis, with a roller chain that presumably was connected to a similar sprocket on the outside of the driven wheelset. The chassis was 6ft 11¼ inches long and formed of pressed steel channel bolted together.[11]

The chassis at Gartheiniog was missing its radiator, which

The right side of the Gartheiniog winch in 1983, from the rear. The six-cylinder Overland engine block is on the right. The roller chain is attached to the transaxle. The gear gate and lever is set for left-hand drive; the gearbox and the axle from the engine block to the rear transaxle are missing. Two steel stakes bolted to the left end of the chassis are driven into the rock to hold it in place. The chassis has been shortened from its original configuration and the rear sub-chassis has been removed. A section of the nearside chassis next to the engine block is missing. [Donald Sills]

Artist's impression of the Willys-Overland locomotive. [Jonathan Clay]

into the locomotive. The glazed cab from the lorry was retained, a definite advantage for drivers compared to the open Simplex.[2]

The locomotive lacked adhesive weight, with the heavy engine block at the front sitting over the unpowered bogie. A large slab of slate was built into the rear of the chassis to add weight over the driving wheels. The size and arrangement of the rail wheels are not known for certain, so the artist's impression is necessarily speculative. It was developed from measurements of the chassis remains and photographs of 1913 Willys-Overland trucks. The top of the cab would have been about 8ft above the rails.

confirms cause of the locomotive's demise. The winch would have been used in short bursts, so could have operated without a radiator.

The Locomotive Described

The roller chain from the Willys-Overland lorry was used in the winch, so the rear wheels of the locomotive were probably chain-driven. Assuming the lorry sprocket was reused on the locomotive, the approximate size and location of the locomotive's rear wheels can be established. The long chassis meant a front bogie was necessary, and it is known that a Hudson wagon chassis was incorporated

Operation

The radiators on the Utility lorries were not fitted with a fan, so the locomotive would have faced uphill to generate airflow over the radiator when hauling wagons. Trips down to Aberangell were made with the locomotive in reverse, providing braking as the train gravitated back.

Motorised Wagons and Home-Made Locomotives

Both sides in the First World War made extensive use of narrow gauge railways. After 1918, war surplus material

During the 1920s, Robert Hudson of Leeds produced several simple locomotives using a 6hp Austro Daimler petrol engine mounted on a skip chassis. These were offered with a wooden box on the right side, to be filled with ballast to improve balance and adhesion. The Hendre Ddu motorised wagons may have looked like this. [Collection of Ron Fitzgerald via Stewart Liles]

A 15in. chassis at Gartheiniog Farm in 1971. Although the image is imperfect, it does show the construction of these chassis. This is the remains of a box wagon, as shown by the iron pockets. [Pete Briddon]

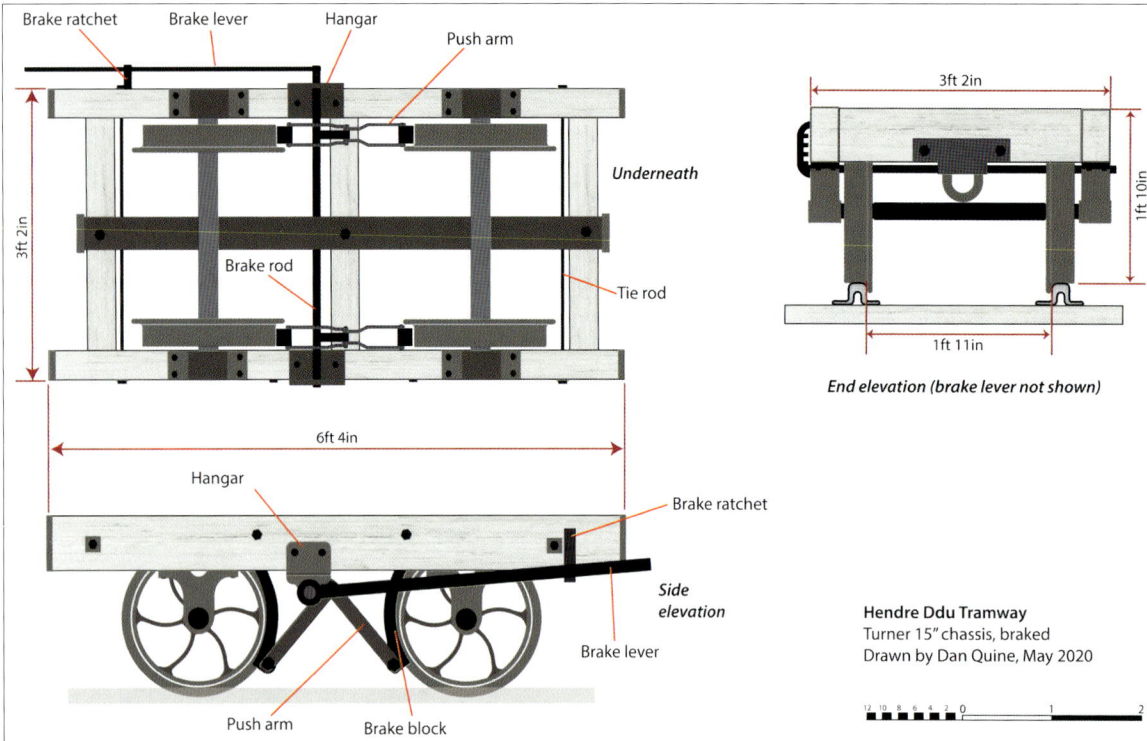

Brake ratchet   Brake lever   Hangar   Push arm

Underneath

3ft 2in

Brake rod

Tie rod

6ft 4in

Hangar

Brake ratchet

Side elevation

Brake lever

Push arm   Brake block

3ft 2in

1ft 10in

End elevation (brake lever not shown)

1ft 11in

Hendre Ddu Tramway
Turner 15" chassis, braked
Drawn by Dan Quine, May 2020

The 15in. chassis. The dumb buffers were extensions of the solebars bound with iron wrappers. The simple loop to which couplings were attached is shown. Surviving wheels show little coning to the tyre or taper on the flange; whether this is an original feature or a result of wear is unclear.

flooded the market. Petrol engines, transmissions and other components were relatively easy to come by. The quarry engineers and local farmers constructed simple locomotives to run on the tramway.[4]

Bill Breese recorded one of these, built for James Pugh of Gartheiniog Farm in the 1920s. Nathan Evans constructed it using an engine from a Morgan three-wheeler car and the chassis of a car gwyllt. Pugh installed a short siding into a garage south of his farmhouse. It was used into the 1930s.[12] Pugh was an accomplished amateur engineer and received a patent in 1930 for his bracken cutting machine.[13]

Breese also described a motorised 'Engineers wagon' which dated back to the NWSQ period and was used over the years by quarry personnel within Hendreddu quarry and on the main tramway.[4] There are also reports of a motorcycle being converted for use on the tramway in the late 1930s. Richard

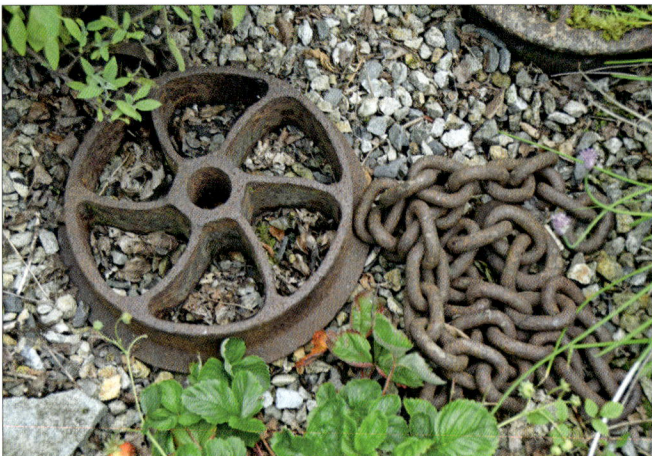

A surviving 15-inch diameter cast wheel. [Dan Quine]

Lewis was well known for riding his Coventry Eagle bike, and it may have been his machine that was used.[14]

Boyd describes two home-made locomotives in use on the tramway after the First World War:

'*Old Ford engines mounted in former wagon underframes… Perhaps the most unusual was a Hudson wagon frame with a petrol engine mounted on it; overall was fitted with a huge wooden box, with footboards and side sheeting which, when in motion, resembled some monstrosity by Leonardo da Vinci.*'[15]

Bill Breese called these the 'American Cars' and said one was painted green, the other chocolate brown.[14] Unfortunately, no photographs of these contraptions survive.

Later Use of Lorries

After T. Glyn Williams took over in 1937, he purchased a Morris lorry which was used to haul trains along the tramway. In late 1938, the Morris lorry broke down and was hauled up the incline so John Williams in the quarry workshop could repair it. The Gartheiniog Farm horse dragged it from Rock Cutting, where it had failed, to the foot of the incline. John Breese was the brakesman for this tricky operation while T. Glyn Williams steered the lorry as it ascended.[4]

Wagons and Carriages

There were three major wagon building periods for the tramway: the mid-1870s when Buckley first equipped the system; during the First World War when a large number of timber bogies were added; and in the 1920s when new wagons were purchased. The wagons were maintained by the companies that owned Hendreddu.

For couplings, each wagon had metal loops fixed to the

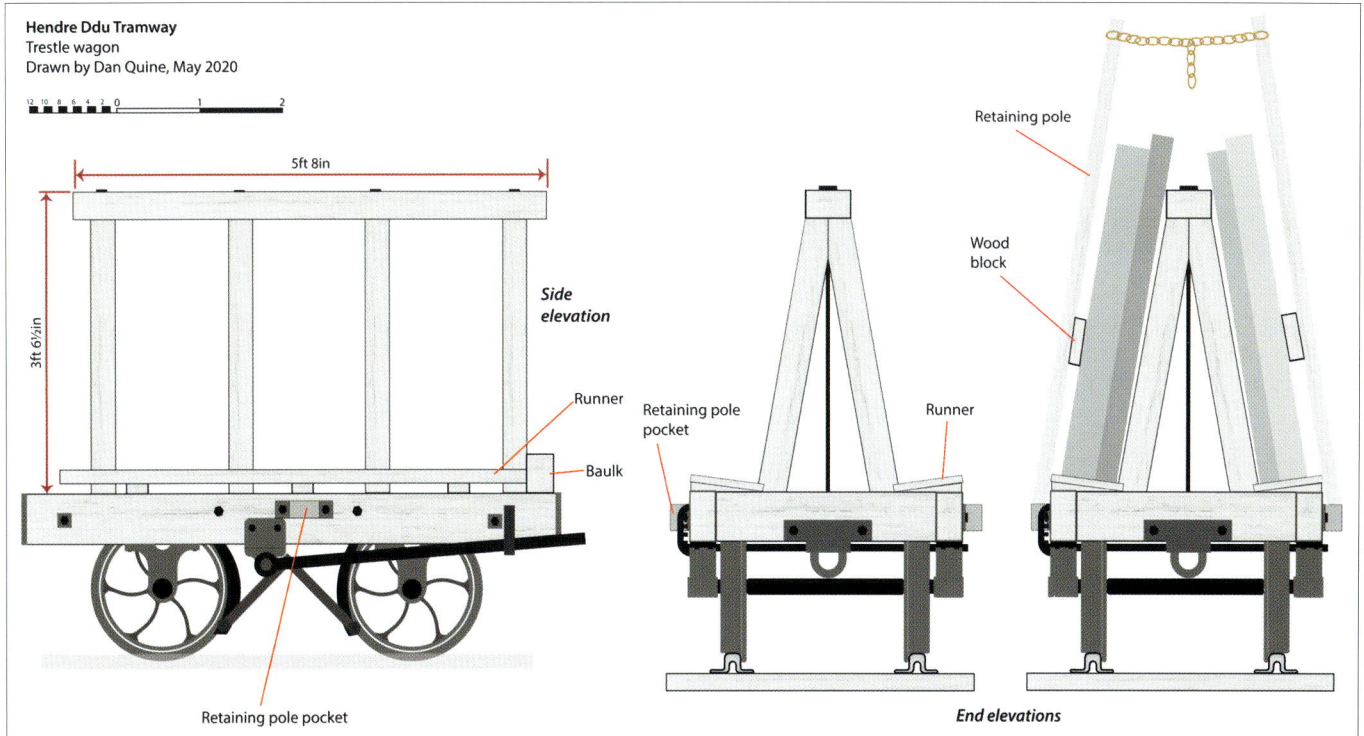

Hendre Ddu Tramway
Trestle wagon
Drawn by Dan Quine, May 2020

5ft 8in

3ft 6½in

Side elevation

Retaining pole

Wood block

Retaining pole pocket

Runner

Baulk

Retaining pole pocket

Runner

End elevations

A typical trestle wagon. The individual wagons varied slightly. On the right end of the wagon is the baulk that held slabs in place while descending the Hendreddu exit incline. The metal pocket in the centre of the solebar held a retaining pole when loaded.

drawbar that ran their length. A link and hook attached to the loops allowed adjacent wagons to be coupled. In later years, up to eight loaded wagons could be taken down to the Wharf using the locomotive.

Turner Brothers Wagons

The original wagons were built on site using ironwork supplied by Turner Bros of Newtown. They were probably assembled at Hendreddu Quarry, using the carpentry shop and forge. In later years, the quarry kept a supply of seasoned oak for wagon construction and had tools to brand 'HSQ' onto the solebars. From the late 1880s onwards, wagon building and maintenance was moved from the quarry to Sied Ddu.[12]

Several of the original Hendre Ddu wagons bear a remarkable similarity to wagons on the nearby Corris Railway. There were significant connections between Edmund Buckley and members of the Corris Railway.

Loaded trestle wagons showing the retaining poles in the pockets and chained together. [R.T. Pugh]

Two trestle wagons on Aberangell Wharf in 1925. The nearest wagon has been unloaded and its retaining poles are laid on the runners; it will be turned before it is returned to the quarry. The second still has a large slab waiting to be moved into the standard gauge wagon behind. The horseshoe-shaped loop attached to the drawbar has a link coupling hook. The nearside wheel shows the taller pedestal axlebox and also a brake block.

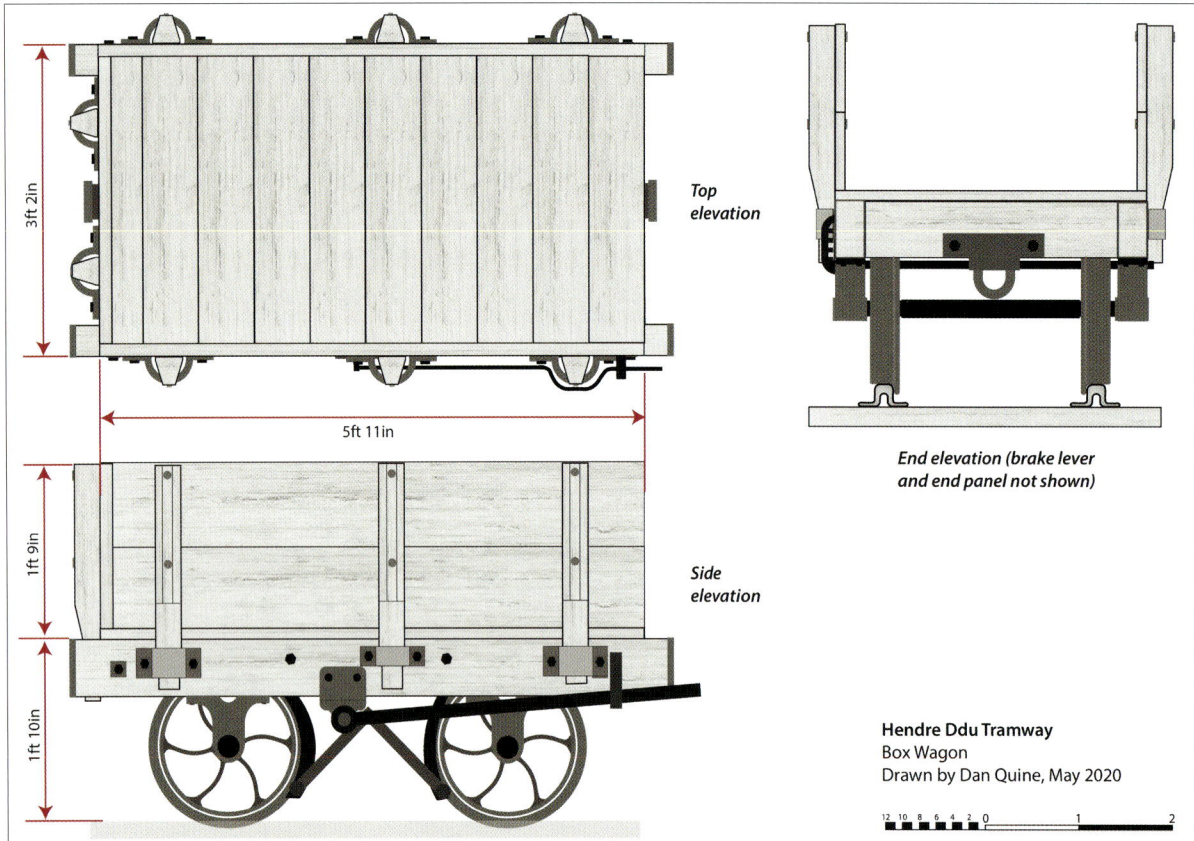

A three-sided box wagon for carrying slabs, timber, coal and general goods, built on the 15-inch chassis. The brake lever has a loop in it to pass around the iron pocket.

Top elevation

End elevation (brake lever and end panel not shown)

Side elevation

3ft 2in

5ft 11in

1ft 9in

1ft 10in

Hendre Ddu Tramway
Box Wagon
Drawn by Dan Quine, May 2020

Many early Corris wagons were also built using parts supplied by Turner Brothers. Corris practice certainly influenced the fledgling Hendre Ddu Tramway.[16]

Turners supplied two sizes of wheels to Hendre Ddu: 15 and 24 inches in diameter. All the vehicles were braked so they could be gravity-operated. The 15-inch wheels used conventional block brakes, while the 24-inch wheels used band brakes. The number of wagons over the years is not recorded, but in 1911, Hendreddu Quarry had eighteen slab wagons in working order while Gartheiniog Quarry had seven.[17]

15-inch Chassis

The standard Hendre Ddu chassis had 15-inch diameter wheels and a 3ft wheelbase. The wheels had six curved spokes and were cast as a single unit. They were press-fitted to the axles with shoulders to stop them moving inwards and outside pedestal axleboxes to stop them moving outwards. The chassis frame was a pair of oak solebars, held together by wooden cross-members and iron tie-rods. The underhung drawbar ran the length of the chassis; this

A tram drawn by Bill Breese. The caption reads: 'The 'lump stone' has been split ready for sawing and treatment'. The track is interesting: lightweight rails in chairs, probably representing T-rail, and a sleeper spacing of between 2ft and 3ft. The quarryman's tools are nicely illustrated, with a long crowbar for dislodging slabs and a mallet and wedges for splitting the slate.
[Courtesy of Mike Cowley]

Four box wagons at Aberangell, carrying large sawn timbers. They have the lower pedestal axleboxes and only three sides are fitted. Behind the box wagons are three more wagons. On the right is a trestle wagon carrying a large slab packed for shipping. On the left are two more rail vehicles, which may be the large gravity cars.

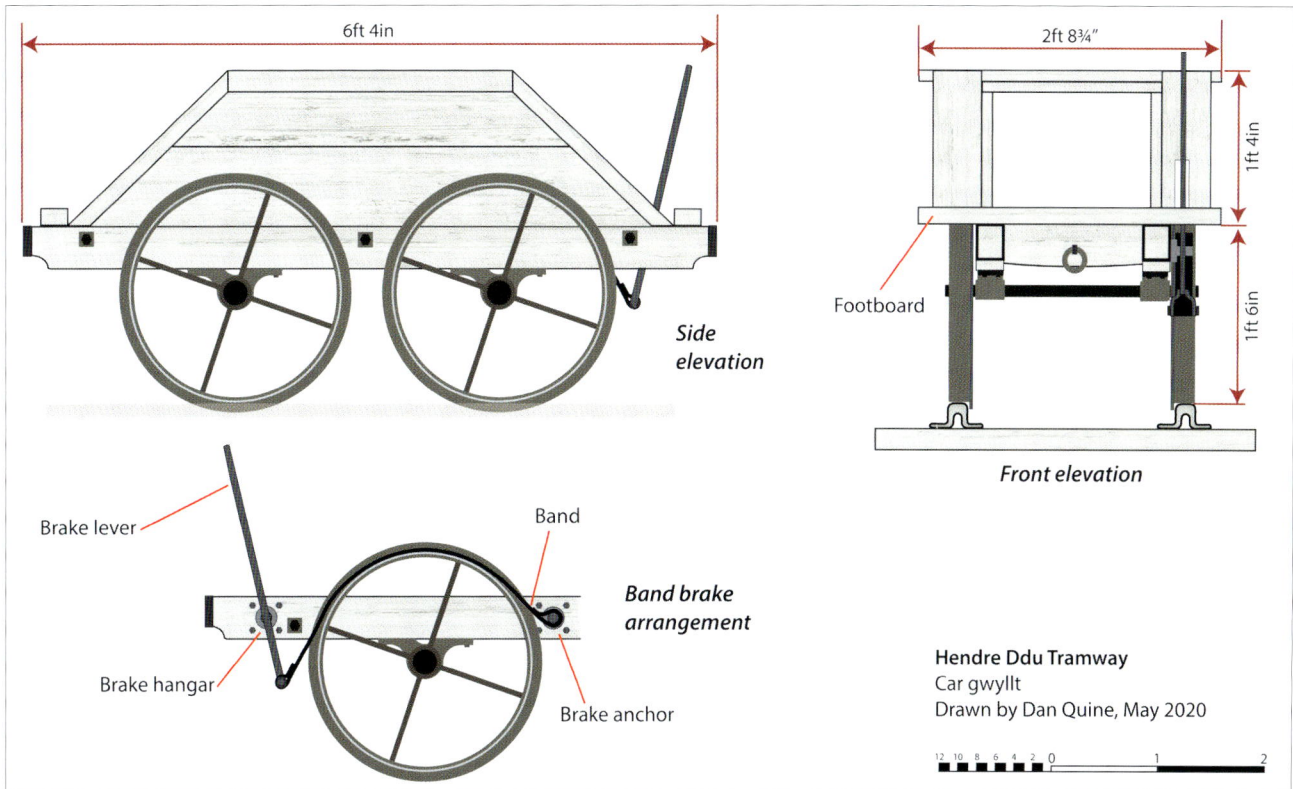

A typical car gwyllt. The band brake arrangement is speculative.

followed Corris practice and had the disadvantage that when the timber started to rot, the drawbar could drop and catch on pointwork and sleepers. At least two sizes of pedestal axlebox were used.

The 15-inch chassis had block brakes acting on the wheel treads. A long brake lever passed through a ratchet on the

Although of imperfect quality, this photograph is exceptionally interesting. It shows one of the car gwyllt in operation, shortly after the First World War. On the right is Edward Hurst Davies towards the end of his life. Bill Breese believed the other passenger was a relative of Davies's.[14] Davies has his feet on the footboards and his left hand on the brake lever. His passenger is sitting off-centre on the right side of the car. The location is just below Llidiart Dwbl with the car about to go downhill having just passed through one of the tramway's gates. [Bill Breese collection]

outside of the frame, so the brakes could be pinned down. The lever rotated a brake rod that ran across the wagon, held in place by hangars at both ends. A short extension arm acted on the push arms that applied the brake pads to the wheels.

Trestle Wagons

Specialised wagons were needed to carry the large slabs produced by the quarries. Trestle wagons were used which were almost identical to those on the Corris Railway. They were known locally as 'wagen cyfrwy', literally a saddle wagon.[4]

The trestle wagons used the 15-inch chassis, mounted with oak A-frames. The slabs sat on angled runners at the bottom of the A-frames and were secured against the uprights by two retaining poles fitted into iron pockets on the solebars. The poles were squared at the bottom to fit into the pockets, and were chained together at the top to hold the slabs in place, with wood blocks wedged between the pole and the load. When returning empty, the poles were taken out of their pockets and laid on the runners. A horizontal timber baulk ran across one end of the wagon to hold the slabs in place when descending the exit incline at Hendreddu.

15-inch Box Wagons

The Hendre Ddu used box wagons to carry smaller slate products, coal, timber and general goods. The first type was a 15-inch chassis with a two-plank body 71 inches long and 21 inches high. The wagons had removable sides to make loading and unloading easier. Vertical stakes bolted on the sides fitted into iron pockets on the solebars. Some

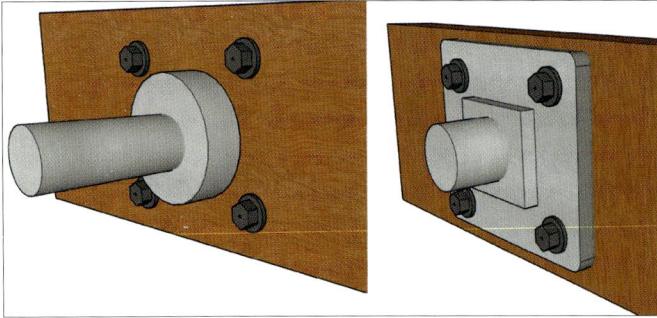

A Turner Brothers band brake anchor. No photographs survive of the braked side of a car gwyllt; this drawing is of the brake anchor on the surviving Corris Railway manrider, which was also a Turners product. Left is the anchor rod on the outside of the solebar; right is the retaining plate on the inside. The brake band wrapped around the anchor rod and was riveted together to hold it in place.

had end doors on one end only, others on both ends. The Corris Railway some similar box wagons, also built on a Turner chassis.

Slab Trams

Simple flat wagons, known locally as trams, were built on the 15-inch chassis. Planks mounted longitudinally carried the loads. Similar wagons were used by several of the quarries along the Dulas Valley, and a number remained in use at Aberllefenni into the 1960s.

All the Hendre Ddu quarries had similar trams. Both Maesygamdda and Gartheiniog used them to transport large slabs to Aberangell.[10]

24-inch Chassis

Turners also supplied 24-inch diameter wheels with wide tread. Some had six curved spokes and others four straight ones. They were used with inside axleboxes. A broken wheelset survived in the Afon Angell close to the location of the 1877 accident. It was recovered in the 1980s and is now in the Narrow Gauge Railway Museum collection in Tywyn.

Car Gwyllt

An almost unique form of transport on the tramway was the 'car gwyllt' ('wild car', plural: 'ceir gwyllt'), built on the 24-inch chassis. These were passenger vehicles that were light enough to be pushed uphill at the start of the day. Quarrymen gravitated back on them at high speed, and they could be coupled together in a train. Each car had a brake lever that operated a band brake acting on the wheel treads, to control downhill speed. The bands were steel, though they may have been faced with leather or wood to increase the friction on the wheels.[18] Band brakes were widely used in the slate industry, particularly for incline winding drums, but they were not common on railway vehicles.

The ceir gwyllt were about 6 feet long with a seat 2 feet 7 inches wide.[19] Cozens and Gwyndaf Breese claim these cars could carry ten quarrymen, but surviving photographs suggest that four workmen sitting back-to-back was usual.

The ceir gwyllt were painted in different colours to identify their ownership. They were kept in immaculate condition, which explains why many lasted until the end of the tramway's life. There was keen competition between the workers for the unofficial title of fastest car in the valley; in the 1930s this was held by Evan Rees of Cwmllinau, whose car had superior bearings, to which Evan liberally applied lubricant.[20] In later years as the cars were repaired in Sied Ddu, they were repainted a uniform slate grey.[12]

The basic shape of the cars was the same, but they varied in detail; the height of the bodies varied, as did the arrangement of the side panels.

Cranked Axle Car Gwyllt

At least two ceir gwyllt had a cranked axle so they could be pedalled uphill. They were likely fitted with a smaller two-person seat at the rear. They were unbraked so the pedaller had to slow the car using the pedals going downhill.[18] They had a lighter chassis, with 3in. high solebars instead of the 5in. ones on the non-pedalled type. The solebars were shorter and there were fewer cross-members. No photographs of a complete cranked axle car have survived, but Boyd captured the chassis of one on Aberangell Wharf in 1946, which shows the basic construction and allows approximate measurements to be determined.

A CAD model of a car gwyllt, based on surviving photographs. Riders placed their feet on the primitive wooden footboards above the buffers. Those facing backwards must have had a particularly unsettling ride.

Corris Manrider

The Corris Railway had a manrider vehicle similar to a car gwyllt. Its remains were recovered in the mid-1950s and are now in the Corris museum. It was 2ft 2½in. gauge and one of the wheelsets has a cranked axle. The manrider could have been a Hendre Ddu car gwyllt that was sold to the Corris and regauged, or it could have been built for the Corris to a similar design.

Car Gwyllt Operations

The Hendre Ddu ceir gwyllt could be easily lifted from the track by two or more men. The tramway had several 'run-outs': short sidings at right angles to the track where ceir gwyllt were stored during the day. One run-out was below the tips of Gartheiniog, one at Esgairangell, one at Ffridd and one at Ty Hen Dderwen – an old oak tree halfway between Aberangell and Gartheiniog. The run-outs were used until 1933-35, the last users being William Breese's father John and David Jones of Tynwydd.[12]

At least two ceir gwyllt survived the tramway's closure. The cranked axle version Boyd photographed, and one at Gartheiniog Farm. The fate of these cars is unknown, though two wheelsets and at least four single wheels survived in Bill Breese's collection.

Box Top Carriage

The tramway had at least one 'Box Top' carriage built with 24-inch wheels and a unique type of axlebox. Only one is known for certain to have existed. This vehicle accomodated four quarrymen and appears to be an alterntive design to the ceir gwyllt; it notably had outside frames and two separate seating units.

24-Inch Box Wagon

The second type of box wagon used the same chassis as the car gwyllt. No photograph has survived, but a speculative diagram has been drawn from meagre contemporary descriptions.

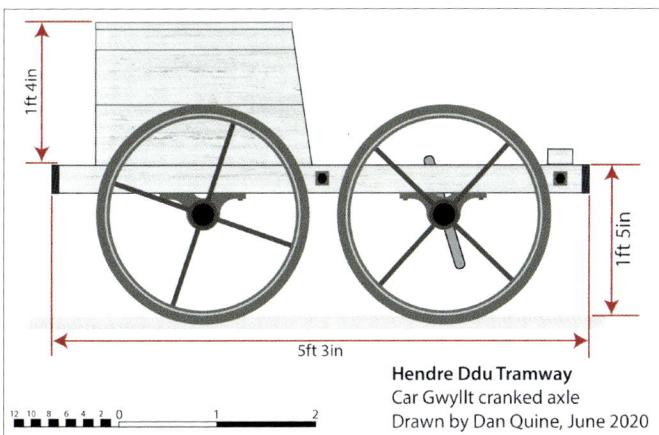

The surviving photograph of a Box Top carriage, taken in 1925 at Aberangell Wharf. It is a quite different design the the car gwyllt behind it. [R.T. Pugh]

Other Rolling Stock
The Private Carriage

Jacob Bradwell maintained a private carriage on the tramway. Little is known about it, beyond its name, the 'Old Lady' and that it was stored in Sied Ddu below Bradwell's Cefngwyn Hall.[20]

During the 1920s and 1930s, the tramway had a Directors' Car, which was probably the Old Lady. It was likely the tramway's only covered passenger vehicle. The Directors' Car was used on the regular Directors' Special trains run by William Bowley. It was also used on Friday mornings to carry the quarrymen's wages to the quarries.[4]

Timber Bogies

During the First World War a large number of 'timber bogies' brought pit props down to Aberangell Wharf. The exact quantity of timber carried is unknown, but in 1916, the Cambrian was loading thirty-seven open wagons a week from Aberangell. These wagons held about 1,000 6ft-long pit props, so the tramway was carrying around 37,000 props a week – 6,100 a day. The timber bogies carried 40-50 props each, so 120 loaded bogies arrived at the Wharf each day. Trains of four bogies would arrive every 15-20 minutes, assuming an average downhill journey time of thirty minutes and uphill journeys of sixty minutes, plus thirty minutes of loading/unloading time at both ends. To sustain this rate, the tramway would need at least 100

Hendre Ddu Tramway
Car Gwyllt cranked axle
Drawn by Dan Quine, June 2020

A possible configuration of the cranked axle ceir gwyllt. The body is speculative, based on the seat from the box top carriage. All measurements are approximate.

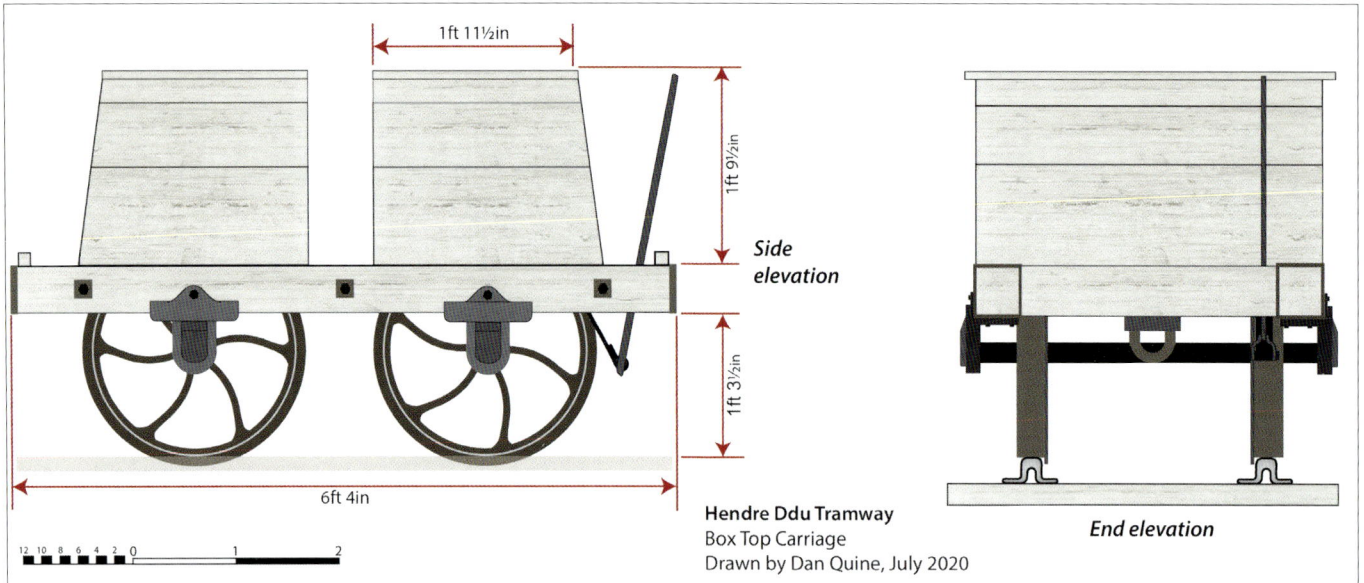

1ft 11½in
1ft 9½in
Side elevation
1ft 3½in
6ft 4in
12 10 8 6 4 2 0 1 2

Hendre Ddu Tramway
Box Top Carriage
Drawn by Dan Quine, July 2020

End elevation

The box top carriage. It probably had a band brake. The axleboxes are unlike others used on the tramway, though their details are hard to make out.

bogies. Given the high rate of damage and accidents, they would need a stock of 150 to maintain that many in working order. The men employed at Sied Ddu had their hands full building and repairing the bogies. The timber bogies appear to have followed a design used on many timber tramways: a simple frame chassis in metal or oak, with four vertical stakes to hold the props in place.

Large Gravity Cars

Gwyndaf Breese noted two 'large gravity cars',[19] which Cozens also described:

'*There were two large gravity cars built on Hudson chassis with all timber top and brake handle in centre. These cars, in common with all the other rolling stock, were springless. For the quarrymen's convenience, footboards encircled these cars, the seating capacity of which was 16 each. Principal dimensions were overall length: 10ft 6in; width of seat 3ft 3in; wheel base 3ft 10in.*'[10]

Bill Breese called these vehicles '*Car Mawr*' ('big car') and the '*Car Melyn*' ('yellow car'). Car Melyn incorporated the axles and some of the bodywork from the Willys-Overland locomotive and was noted for its weight and free running, so was used as the leading car in gravity trains.[4]

No clear photographs of these cars survive. In order to carry 16, the cars would have had back-to-back seats along the length of the car. This would allow 8 men per side, sat facing outwards and with their feet on the footboards. This would have given each man about 15 inches of seat. Breese describes Car Melyn derailing near Cefngwyn in 1938.

Internal Quarry Wagons
Flat Wagons

A variety of wagons were used in the quarries to move slate about. These were usually designed for hand working. They typically had no couplings or brakes, as

they moved short distances on relatively level track. Most common were flat wagons also called trams. These had a simple wooden chassis with slabs loaded directly on top. The only surviving photograph was taken at Gartheiniog in 1932/3.

Rubbish Wagons

The three major quarries used iron bodied rubbish wagons of various designs to move waste to the tips. The body of one of these wagons was found at Maesygamfa in 2017.

A Turner Brothers rubbish wagon was photographed at Gartheiniog during the Hadrill era. It had sheet iron sides, with one end open for tipping, and a very short wheelbase. The wagon had a wooden frame,[21] and single-flanged wheels. It was probably purchased after the First World War possibly by Hadrill.

The Hadrill rubbish wagon was photographed at Gartheiniog Mill in 1971 but had disappeared three years later. Its fate is unknown. Hendreddu had several similar wagons.

Tipper Wagons

At least one tipper wagon was used underground at Hendreddu quarry. Its body remains at the bottom of the vertical shaft down to Level 1. It appears to be a typical Hudson 'Rugga' design and was probably purchased by T. Glyn Williams.

Operations
Horse and Gravity Working

For many years, the tramway was the only practical way to get slate and timber out of Dyffryn Angell and goods and workers in. Quarrymen arrived at Aberangell by train, cart, bicycle or on foot, then travelled to work on the tramway.

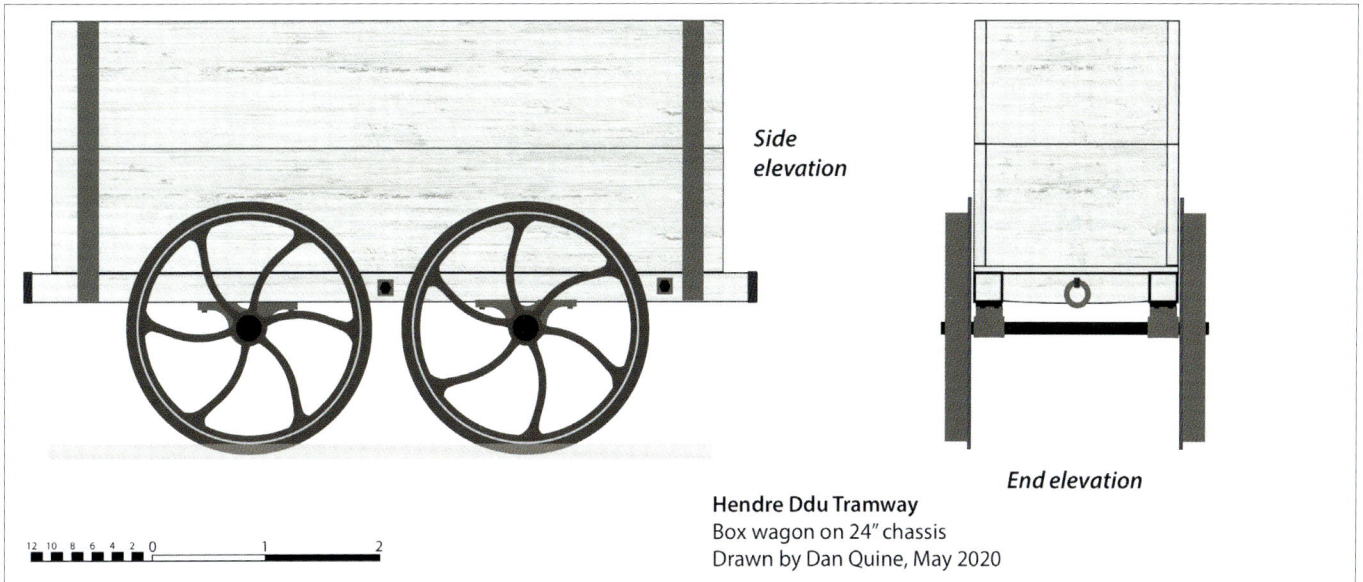

Side elevation

End elevation

Hendre Ddu Tramway
Box wagon on 24" chassis
Drawn by Dan Quine, May 2020

A possible arrangement of the box wagon with 24-inch wheels. Measurements are not given, as the size of the wagon body is speculative. It likely had band brakes similar to those on a car gwyllt.

Some men stayed at the quarries during the week. Hendreddu had a barracks and six quarry cottages. Local farms also rented rooms to the quarrymen; Hendre Meredydd Farm lodged Maesygamfa quarrymen for many years.[22]

The horses that hauled the trains uphill were owned by local farms that provided the animals and workers to lead them. These contracts provided valuable extra income for the farmers.[23]

Train Formations

Before the First World War all loaded trains gravitated downhill. At its peak in 1898, Hendreddu produced 1,400 tons a year. If all of the production had been billiard tables which weigh about 450 lbs, then forty slabs were shipped each day, two per trestle wagon. This would require five trains of four wagons. There were loops at the foot of the Hendreddu exit incline, at Aberdwynant up until 1894, and on Aberangell Wharf.

Hendreddu Quarry was the sole user of the tramway until 1887 and would have sent down a run of wagons when they were ready and brakesmen were available. The quarry was connected to Aberangell by telegraph from at least the 1880s, if not earlier. Most likely a bell system was used to coordinate up and down trains.

Turntables were vital equipment. The trestle wagons had to have the baulk on the downhill end when they descended the Hendreddu exit incline. When trains arrived at the Wharf, the slabs nearest the standard gauge railway were unloaded first, then the wagon was turned to unload the other side. The wagons were turned at Aberangell before returning to the quarry to ensure the baulk was on the downhill end – it also kept the retaining poles in place on the exit incline.

Sharing the Tramway

Once Gartheiniog started to use the tramway after 1887, and Maesygamfa around 1893/4, working must have changed to allow trains to share the tramway. The early morning was reserved for uphill traffic when the quarrymen travelled to work. Loaded trains came down later in the day. A possible form of working was to allot specific times for each quarry to send loaded trains down to Aberangell – the Corris used this system before the introduction of locomotives.[24] All three quarries were connected to the telegraph system, so they may have coordinated trains that way.

Careful control of downhill trains was essential so they could be stopped at the gates across the line, which had to be opened and closed by the brakesman. The details of gravity

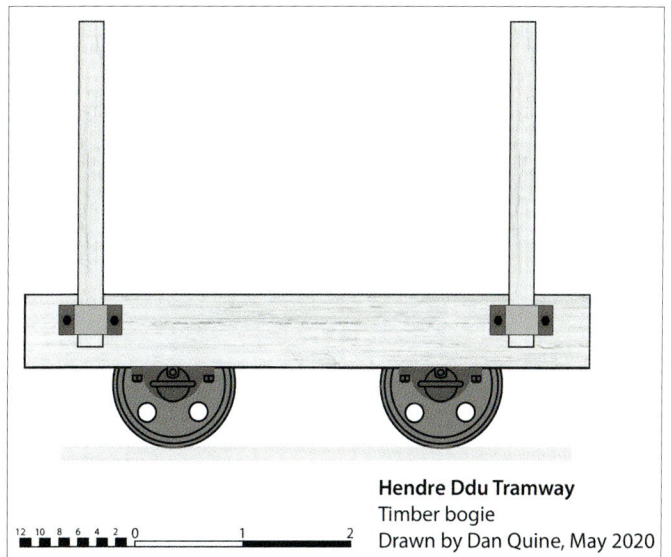

Hendre Ddu Tramway
Timber bogie
Drawn by Dan Quine, May 2020

A timber bogie of the type used by Higginbottom, based on the surviving 1915 photograph and similar bogies used elsewhere. This example uses metal components from Robert Hudson.

145

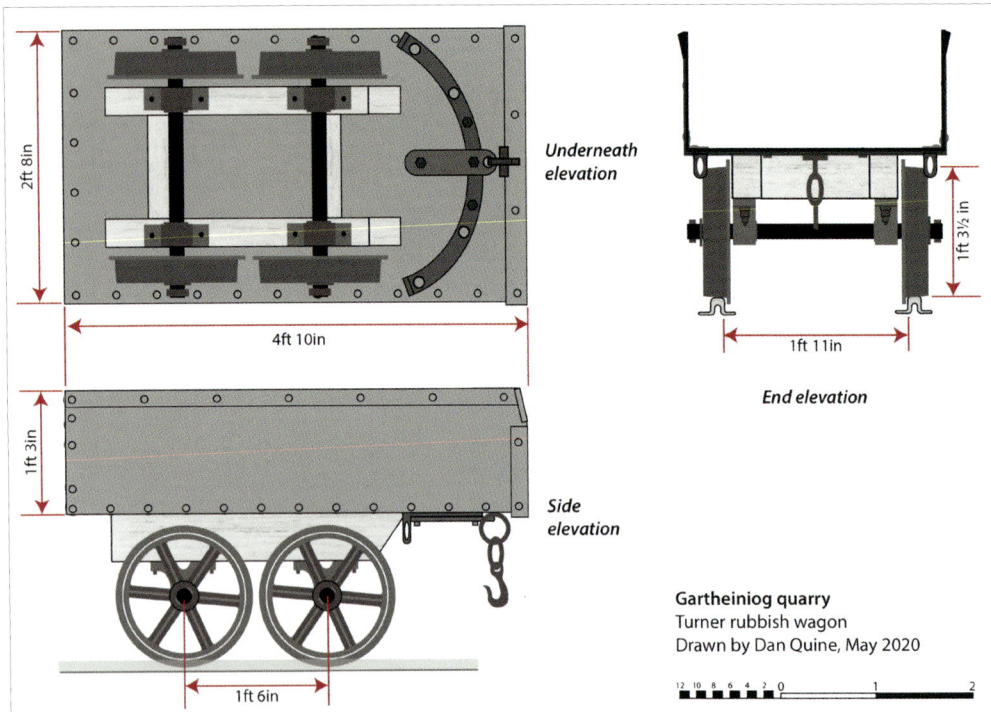

Underneath elevation

2ft 8in

4ft 10in

Side elevation

1ft 3in

1ft 6in

End elevation

1ft 11in

1ft 3½ in

The Gartheiniog rubbish wagon supplied by Turner Brothers. It has a coupling at one end to attach to an incline cable. The drawbar does not run the full length of the wagon, instead an arc iron running under the wagon floor spread the drawbar forces. It had downward-facing eyes to allow a hook-and-chain to be attached to prevent the wagon from going over the end of the waste tips when it was unloaded.

Gartheiniog quarry
Turner rubbish wagon
Drawn by Dan Quine, May 2020

trains operation are not recorded, but we have some hints. Bill Breese refers to trains having multiple brakesmen.[25]

The timber trains in the First World War used car gwyllt on the downhill end to provide braking control. The loaded bogies would have been hard for brakesmen to ride on, so likely their brakes were partly pinned down, and the brakesman travelled on the car gwyllt, using its brake for fine control. This use of a car gwyllt may indicate how pre–war gravity trains were braked.

Accidents

As the tramway had no signals, accidents were common.[23] The section below Cefngwyn was particularly prone to collisions, as loaded trains would accelerate down the gradient west of Pont yr Hirgwm and run at speed to Aberdwynant.

Operations were made more complex by the farms which also used the tramway. Gartheiniog, Nanthir, Maesygamfa, Esgairangell and Cefngwyn farms are known to have used the tramway, and several collisions between farm and quarry trains occurred over the years.

Quarrymen's Trains

Hendreddu ran morning quarrymen's trains from Aberdwynant to the foot of the exit incline, initially hauled by horses and later by locomotives. The journey took about an hour by horse.

Gartheiniog did not hire horses to run trains for its workers.

Two trams in the north chamber at Gartheiniog in 1932 or 1933. A simple wooden frame forms the chassis and the carrying surface. The nearer wagon has two wooden baulks across the chassis. To the left of the working wagons, another lies upside-down and broken; it is missing one axle entirely and the other has only one wheel. It has Turner pedestal axleboxes. [McGuire-Hadrill family]

The Turner Brothers rubbish wagon in the north chamber at Gartheiniog, in 1932 or 1933. It had an extremely short wheelbase to make tipping easier. Wagons of a similar design were used at Braichgoch and Aberllefenni quarries. [Hadrill-McGuire family]

Bill Breese built a model of the tramway for his museum, with three types of wagon. Although these models are crude, they are recognizable as Hendre Ddu wagons and are charming in their own right. Top left: a typical flat wagon carrying a slab. Top right: A loaded trestle wagon, showing the poles and chains used to hold the slabs in place. Bottom right: Trestle wagon side view, showing how the major features of the wagons are well represented, even if the scale is not accurate. Bottom left: A steel-bodied open wagon of otherwise unknown type. The chains at the near end suggest horse-haulage. [Dafydd Pughe]

Instead, the men had to push their ceir gwyllt up to the quarry. The first quarrymen to arrive at Aberdwynant would push their car to *Ty Hen Dderwen* ('The Old Oak Tree') at the halfway point to the quarry and leave the car on the run-out there. The next men walked up to Ty Hen Dderwen and pushed the car gwyllt to the run-out at Llidiart Dwbl. This process was repeated to move multiple cars up to the quarry.

Agricultural Traffic

The tramway carried agricultural produce, but this traffic was rarely recorded. Bill Breese describes an accident between the wars, involving a wagon carrying wool from Maesygamfa Farm. Simon Jones, the tenant farmer, was riding on the wagon. Edward Davies of Pengwern Farm was taking a train of wagons of stones uphill to Esgairangell where they were to be used for building work. He had been told to wait in the siding at Pont yr Hirgwm to allow the Maesygamfa wagon to pass. Jones arrived earlier than anticipated, and despite his best efforts was unable to brake in time and ran into Davies's train opposite Alltddu.[25]

Hendreddu Exit Incline

Operating the incline was a highly skilled job and apprentices spent some time learning how to 'drop the load'. The incline was prepared early in the morning each day. Two empty wagons were left overnight in the loop at the foot of the incline. These were rolled forwards and attached to the incline cable. Wagons always travelled the incline in pairs – a common practice in Welsh slate quarries. Loaded wagons were sent down from the mill along the Upper Tramway in disconnected pairs, with a brakesman on each. If the front wagon slowed, the following wagon would bump it along.

When the loaded wagons arrived at the head of the incline, they were coupled together and attached to the other top of the cable. The cable ended in a metal loop with a cotter pin, which had to be checked to make sure it was fully attached after coupling up. The loaded wagons were carefully rolled to the crimp and held with a chain placed under the leading wagon's wheel.

When the brakesman was ready, the chain was removed and the wagons descended. They were allowed to run over the top third of the incline, picking up speed. As they approached the passing loop, the brakesman slowed them, before letting them pick up speed again as they came out of the bottom of the loop. They were slowed once more as they crossed the bridge at the foot of the incline. As the empty wagons crested the crimp, the loaded wagons below had enough momentum to turn the sharp corner onto the embankment, if the brakesman had judged the speed correctly.

Occasionally the descending wagons would stop short, on the incline side of the curve. If this happened, it would leave the empty wagons hanging below the crimp. The only remedy was to hook the loaded wagons to the horse or locomotive waiting at the foot of the incline, and haul them around the curve, pulling the empties over the crimp.

The upside-down body of an iron rubbish wagon at Maesygamfa in April 2017, near the upper reservoir. It has a longitudinal drawbar with coupling eyes. This would have sat on a simple wooden chassis. Why this wagon was near the reservoir is unknown, and puzzled Bill Breese in the 1970s. He speculated it might have been used for the construction of the dam.[4]
[Dafydd Pughe]

This was a difficult operation because the sharp curve could derail the locomotive.

Loaded wagons could also get stuck on the crimp. In this case, the brakesman would bounce the cable between the drum and the wagons, which rocked them back and forwards a few inches and allowed them to start their descent. Bill recalls the trestle wagons descending easily, but the box wagons being harder to control.[4]

Ownership and Maintenance

The main tramway was initially owned entirely by Sir Edmund Buckley. After his bankruptcy in 1876, his estate was split up. Where the tramway crossed one of the lots, that property was sold '... *subject to a right of the owners for the time being of the Hendre-ddu Slate and Slab Quarries forever to maintain upon the said land on its present site, and to use a tramway for the purpose of conveying slates and slabs from their quarry to Aberangell, by itself*',[26] This established the ongoing legal basis of the tramway.

The owner of the tramway was responsible for maintaining the trackbed, which was six feet wide along its length. This included the repair of bridges, drainage ditches, culverts and retaining walls. The gates across the tramway were frequently damaged when trains failed to stop, which kept the tramway carpenters busy. The hedges that bordered the tramway were maintained by local farmers.[18]

Protecting Against a Public Right of Way

From the earliest days of the tramway, there was concern that local people would use it as a road. It was by far the easiest route along Dyffryn Angell and passed close to many of the farms. Buckley, and particularly Bradwell, were keen that the tramway did not become a public right-of-way.

A principle of law in England and Wales is 'presumed dedication' which creates a right of way if there is

unchallenged public use of land as a highway for four to six years.[27] To prevent a presumed dedication of the tramway, every Good Friday a toll of one penny was charged to any pedestrians wanting to walk along the tramway route. This met the legal requirement of a challenge. This practice was enshrined in 1894 in the agreement between Bradwell, Walton and Davies, but a similar arrangement may have been in place before then.

Between the wars, John Breese would wait at the bottom of the Brynderwen cutting, and Dafydd Jones at Aberdwynant, to collect the annual toll. The quarries were shut on Good Friday, so there were no trains and very few visitors. Whatever tolls were collected by midday were delivered to the quarry manager.[28]

In 1922, John Henry Harris, managing director of Hendre-ddu Slate Quarries placed a notice on the south wall of Aberdwynant House, next to the tramway. It read:

'*Hendre-Ddu Slate Quarries Ltd. will not be responsible for accidents on the Tramway, to anyone paying for the use of the same, or to the Public using the footpath. Horses, Carts and Motor Cars are strictly forbidden past this board. Application for permission and terms for the use of the Tramway must be obtained in every case.*

By order of the Board,

J.H. Harris, Governing Director.'

Despite the toll, and the stern warning notice, the tramway was used as the main road along the valley. As late as 1933, the *Gossiping Guide to Wales* was recommending: '*at Aberangell there is a beautiful walk (along a tramway leading to slate quarries) up the Angell river, which is broken into several falls near the station*'.[29]

Locomotive Operations

Captain Twitchen drove the first trial runs of the Motor Rail locomotive out of Aberangell. After he was satisfied that the track was good enough for regular use, he handed over the driving duties.[2] At first, the locomotive only hauled trains uphill, and downhill trains continued to run by gravity. The workmen's trains left from Aberangell Wharf instead of Aberdwynant, for the first time running the full length of the line.[23]

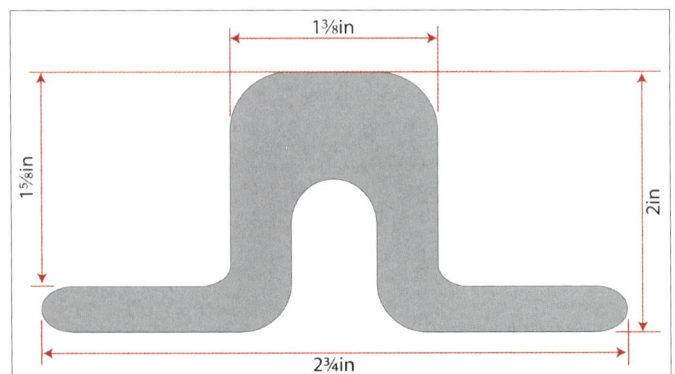

Typical Hendre Ddu 16 lbs/yard bridge rail, from field notes taken by Mike Cowley at Gartheiniog.

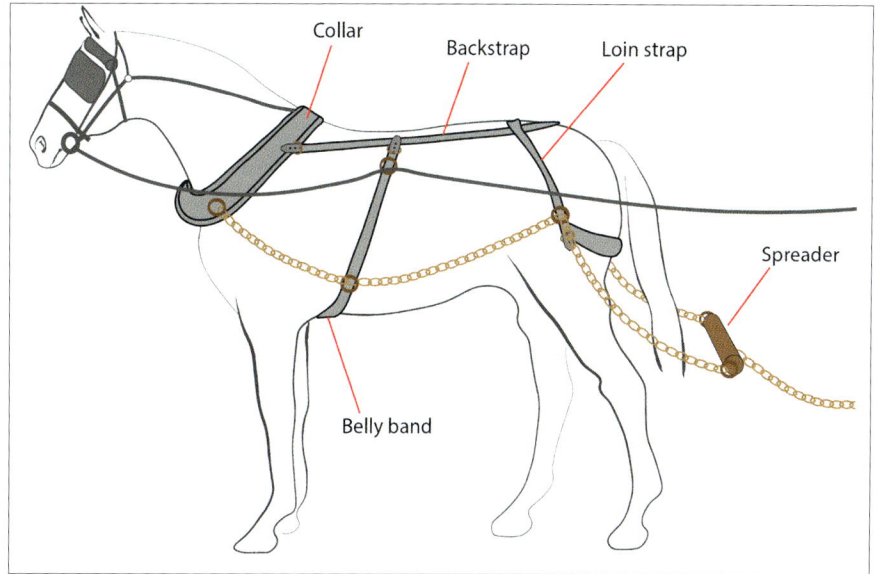

Typical harness arrangement for wagon haulage, based on the 1915 photograph of the Coed y Gesail train. Most of the weight is carried on the collar — the chains are pulled taut when under load.

Gravity working stopped after the August 1929 accident. The company was fortunate that no one was injured or killed, but it was obvious to J.H. Harris that gravity working could not continue. After that, all down trains were locomotive hauled. Cozens reports that typical downhill trains were made up of six to eight loaded wagons while returning uphill trains would leave Aberangell with as many empty wagons as were on hand.[10]

The Permanent Way
The Original 1874 Track

The original track was light bridge rail, weighing about 16 lbs/yard. Instead of conventional fishplates, adjacent rails were held in line with plates with a raised bar that sat within the bridge section of the rails to hold them in alignment. The sleepers were oak between 3ft 6in. and 3ft 9in. long, laid at two-foot intervals.[30] The Corris Machynlleth & Dovey River Tramroad was using 15 lb/yard bridge rail at the time the Hendre Ddu was constructed.[15]

The 1894 Deviation

The deviation from Aberdwynant to the wharf was laid in flat bottomed rail between 1891 and 1894. This was a substantial upgrade from the original bridge rail. It was spiked directly to oak sleepers and used fishplates at rail joints.

The 1921 Relay

When the Motor Rail locomotive arrived, Captain Twitchen decided to relay half a mile of track from Llidiart Dwbl to Esgairangell. This bridge rail on this section would have been heavily worn, as it carried trains from all the quarries and bore the brunt of the timber traffic during the war. Boyd describes the relaid rails as '... *the same material as was the Croesor Tramway - light T section rail with*

a projection on one lower side only. This entered a corresponding recess on a light chair, the rails being of wrought iron. Joints were made in a longer chair.'[15]

The relaying happened at about the same time that the lower section of the Croesor Tramway was relaid in flat bottomed rail ready to be used as part of the Welsh Highland Railway. It is tempting to suggest that the T-rail used on the Hendre Ddu was purchased secondhand from the Croesor, though there is only circumstantial evidence to support this.

Points and Turntables

Boyd reports that the tramway used stub points throughout, but single-bladed points were certainly used. The only surviving photographs of points are all of the single-bladed type. Bill Breese's model of the tramway has single-bladed points throughout, and while the model is not to scale, the technical details are generally accurate.

Single-bladed points (also known as 'vee and sword points') would be operated by manually moving the blade into position, often by kicking them over. They are generally unsuitable for locomotives, or for gravity working at speed, though both were used on the Hendre Ddu Tramway. The Wharf at Aberangell had a wagon turntable supplied by Turner Brothers, almost certainly installed in 1873/4. The turntable survives in the collection of Dafydd Pugh.

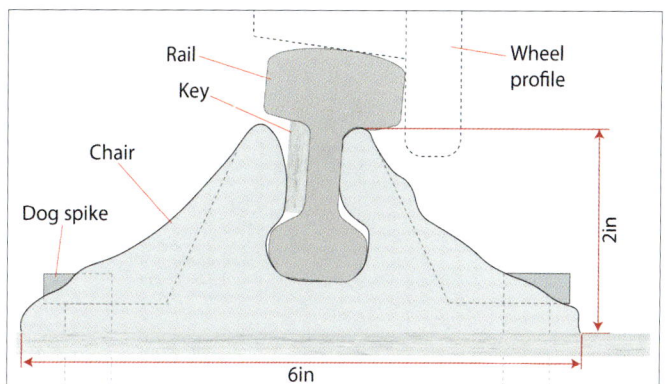

Maesygamfa chaired bullhead rail from a sketch by Bill Breese and a remaining example of a chair. The profile of the rail is speculative.

Left: Festoon, Motor Rail works number 4570. It was officially built in 1929 but is thought to be an earlier locomotive refurbished after service in the war. It is almost identical to Motor Rail No. 2059 which worked on the Hendre Ddu Tramway. The major differences are Festoon's awning and lack of dumb buffers. It gives a good sense of how No. 2059 would have looked while in service on the Hendre Ddu.
[Dan Quine]

Below right: The Turner Brothers turntable from Aberangell Wharf, discovered at a farm in Wales in July 2016. It still has its bridge rails intact.
[Simon Crow]

Below left: In March 2019, the Festiniog Railway Heritage Group laid a length of T-bulb track on slate sleepers in the wagon shed at Minffordd. The track will later be ballasted above the tops of the sleepers.
[Tim Elsby]

Right: Schematic of a single-bladed point. As no clear photographs of the Hendre Ddu pointwork survive, this diagram is based on other Welsh examples. The sword was connected to the cast vee using fishplates and was kicked over to the opposite stock rail to change the point.

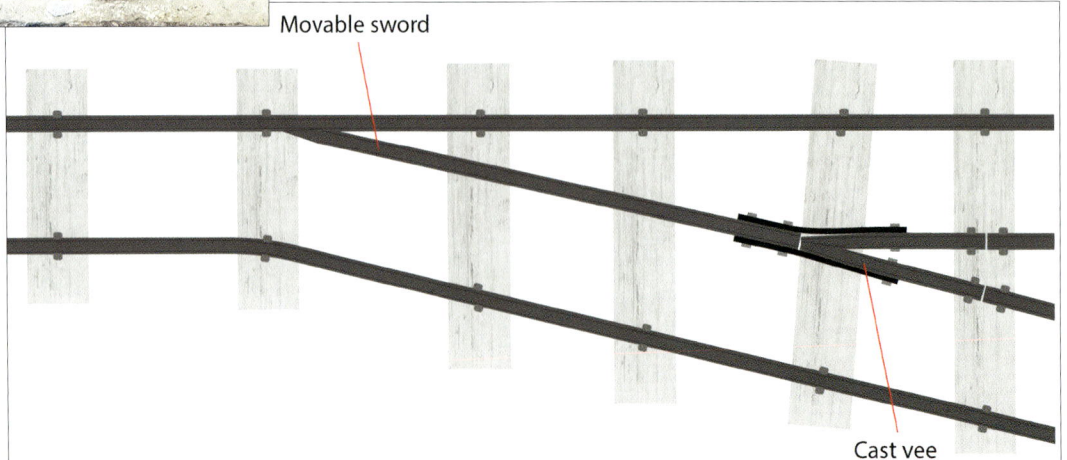

Movable sword

Cast vee

Left: Part of Bill Breese's collection of Hendre Ddu trackwork. The two chairs on the left are from Minllyn Quarry and held T-rail. The chair on the upper right is for Maesygamfa Tramway bullhead rail. The lower right chair held T-bulb rail in the relaid section between Llidiart Dwbl and Esgairangell.[4] It is identical to a Croesor Tramway chair in the collection of Francis Stapleton. At the bottom right is a length of flat-bottomed rail that would have been spiked directly to wooden sleepers. [Dafydd Pughe]

Below: Four surviving 24-inch diameter wheels, rescued by Bill Breese and now owned by Dafydd Pughe. These show the two spoke patterns used. The green and silver paint was applied by Breese in the 1970s. [Dafydd Pughe]

Below left: An oak sleeper from the tramway, complete with track spikes. This likely held flat-bottomed rail. Given its condition, it was probably a replacement from the 1920s. [Simon Crow]

Below right: The remains of a 24-inch wheelset, recovered from the Afon Angell in the late 1980s. It has the smaller pedestal axlebox. The upper end of the axle shows the shoulder that held the wheels to gauge. [Narrow Gauge Railway Museum]

Track Maintenance

The owners of the Hendreddu quarry maintained the track between the quarry and the Wharf. Other tramways were the responsibility of their owners. During the 1920s and 1930s, responsibility for maintaining the tramway fell to John Breese and Dafydd Jones.

There was a '*massive chest where all the equipment to repair the tramroad was kept*' in the Forge at Hendreddu Mill in 1937. It contained '*a pick and shovel … and dedicated hammers for the "dogs" [track spikes] as well as the "Jim Crow" used to maintain an effective gauge of 1' 10 ¹/₂ in, and other tools needed for the [track] work*'.[32]

References

1   Dan Quine, Baguley 774 and the Pennal Tramway, *Industrial Railway Record*, no. 228, Mar. 2017.

2   Gwyndaf Breese, The Simplex Locomotive, unpublished manuscript.

3   Vic Bradley, *Industrial Locomotives of North Wales*, Industrial Railway Society, 1992.

4   Bill Breese, Notebook on tramroad and local quarrying, Dolgellau Archive, no. ref ZM/6541/5, c. 1970.

5   Dan Quine, Personal correspondence with Andrew Neale, Apr. 2016.

6   Machinery, wagons &c, *Western Mail*, p.2, Jun. 21st, 1940.

7   Hendre Ddu Tramway locomotive, *Narrow Gauge News*, vol. 68, p.19, Dec. 1970.

8   Gillingham Pottery locomotives, *Narrow Gauge News*, vol. 70, p.10, Apr. 1971.

9   Private correspondence with Rob Pearman, 2016.

10 Lewis Cozens, R. W. Kidner, Brian Poole, *The Mawddwy, Van and Kerry Branches*, Oakwood Press, 2004.

11 Donald Sills, Field Notes, 1983.

12 Bill Breese, Bygone activities within Angell valley, *Cambrian News*, Aug. 6th, 1976.

13 Getting rid of bracken, *Aberdeen Press and Journal*, May 21st, 1935.

14 Bill Breese, Notes on local quarrying and quarrymen, Dolgellau Archive, vol. ref ZM/6541/9, 1982.

15 James I. C. Boyd, *Narrow Gauge Railways in Mid-Wales*, Oakwood Press, 1965.

16 Dan Quine, Over the hills: the Corris Railway and the Hendre Ddu Tramway. Part One, *Correspondent*, no. 212, Jun. 2020.

17 Offer of Quarry, subsequently refused, to David Davies, National Archives, p. RAIL 1057/583, 1911-1916.

18 Bill Breese, Bygone industrial activities in the Angell valley, *Cambrian News*, July 9th, 1976.

19 Gwyndaf Breese, Rolling Stock, unpublished manuscript.

20 Gwyndaf Breese, The Angell Valley Tramway, unpublished manuscript.

21 Dan Quine, Private correspondence with Francis Stapleton, 2018.

22 Dan Quine, Private correspondence with John Davison, 2017.

23 Gwyndaf Breese, Travelling on the tramway, unpublished manuscript.

24 Dan Quine, Private correspondence with Richard Greenough, 2018.

25 Bill Breese, Damweiniau Llenol, *Cambrian News*, Sept. 19th, 1975.

26 The Great Sale at Dinas Mawddwy of Sir Edmund Buckley's Property, *Cambrian News*, p.8, Oct. 20th, 1876.

27 John William Smith, *A Selection of Leading Cases on Various Branches of the Law: with notes*, C. H. Edson & Company, 1889.

28 Gwyndaf Breese, The deviation. Unpublished manuscript.

29 John Askew Roberts, Edward Woodall, *Gossiping Guide to Wales (North Wales and Aberystwyth)*. Simpkin, Marshall & Company, 1933.

30 Bill Breese, The old quarrying days in the Angell valley, *Cambrian News*, Jun. 25th 1976.

31 Charles Edward Lee, *Narrow-gauge Railways in North Wales*, Railway Publishing Company, 1945.

32 Bill Breese, Hen Efail y Chwarel: part II, *Cambrian News*, Jan. 21st, 1977.

The type of brass works plate used on Motor Rail locomotives between 1918 and 1931. It is likely the style of plate carried by Motor Rail 2059, though the surviving photograph of the locomotive at Aberangell is not clear enough to confirm this.

14: Forestry Commission Tramways After 1948

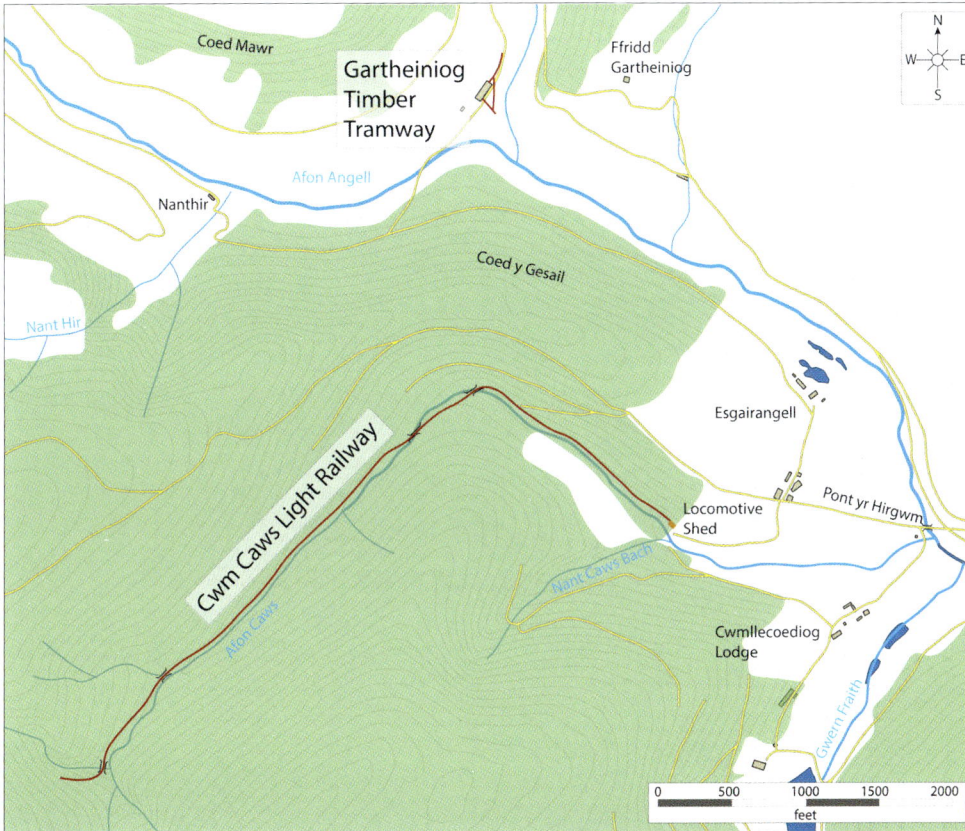

The Forestry Commission tramways shortly after the Second World War. The main forestry roads and plantations are shown. The section of the Hendre Ddu Tramway between Esgairangell and Nanthir was not converted into a road by the Forestry Commission until around 1965.

The Forestry Commission (FC) began buying land in Dyffryn Angell shortly after the First World War, starting with plantations in Cwmllecoediog. In the two decades after the Second World War they purchased much of the land between Aberangell and Aberllefenni. They used two narrow gauge railways for their operations, one along Cwm Caws and the second at the former Gartheiniog Mill.

Cwm Caws Light Railway

The first railway ran along Cwm Caws, south and west of Pont yr Hirgwm. This 2ft gauge light railway* was laid on part of the trackbed of the First World War timber tramway. It began at a small locomotive shed and loading dock at the point where the Nant Caws Bach joins the Afon Caws, about ½ mile from Pont yr Hirgwm. From there it ran about 1½ miles southwest along Cwm Caws, crossing rivers several times as it threaded its way along the narrow valley bottom. A forestry road was driven from Esgairangell

* The Forestry Commission consistently used the term 'light railway' for this line

to the loading dock and lorries were used to take the timber to Aberangell Wharf.

A Forestry Commission report from 10th April 1939 notes: '*The Cwm Caws Valley [sic] was walked up... It was noted that the previous... crop was extracted by a light railway along the valley bottom.*' This refers to trees felled in the First World War and taken out by the original timber tramway.

In 1941, the Ministry of Supply set up the Timber Production Department (TPD) to manage forests and timber production. They laid the light railway along the valley, probably just after the end of the war. The TPD was wound up in July 1947[1] and its responsibilities were taken back by the Forestry Commission. An FC report from 29th August 1948 notes: '*The light railway running up the Cwm Caws valley which will be used to extract the produce from above and other compartments was inspected. The light railway was taken over from T.P.D. and has been in use for over six months and serves a valley of plantations for over a mile in length, and the plantations are all at the thinning stage. It was thought that more use should be made of light railways in such places... It was considered that the first thinning would be a moderate one. The produce will now go out by the light railway.*'

Another FC report notes: '*This light railway was installed on the site of a former railway, so the cost of the formations was relatively small.*' A handwritten note adds: '*I have discussed the question with the directorate engineer, and have asked for a detailed comparative statement of costs for road and railway.*'[2] In January 1950, the Engineer Branch of the FC compared the costs of the light railway and an equivalent roadway. The capital costs of the railway were:

The estimated total cost for 1½ miles of roadway was £3,480.* The report noted that the cost of rails, locomotives and bogies were the disposal prices from the TPD and the

Formation	£700
Labour	£716
Rails	£792
Locomotives	£300
Bogies	£15
Total	£2,523

sleepers were constructed from timber thinnings priced at labour only. The annual running costs were less favourable for the railway:

The cost of maintaining forestry roadways was given as £50/mile, for a total of £75. The cost of running lorries was given as 2.5p per cubic foot of timber moved per mile. The

Fuel	£34
Wages	£306
Loco maintenance	£15
Track maintenance	£50
Bogies	£15
Total	£405

cost of transshipment from rail to road at the north end of the light railway was 0.75p per cubic foot. Assuming 15,000 cubic feet of timber extracted per year, and including interest at 3 per cent on the capital costs, the railway cost 8.43p per cubic foot, while a roadway would have cost 5.38p per cubic foot. The report concluded that the light railway was more expensive to operate and also 'suffers badly through not being able to work over steeper gradients than 1 in 25 and the need for double handling i.e. railside to bogie and bogie to railside to lorry'.

Cwm Caws was producing pit props, felling 4½ inch diameter spruce trees that were 10-12 years old. The forest was thinned rather than clear-felled. The majority of the props went to 'a coal mine near Chirk'[3] most likely Ifton Colliery.

By 1952, the FC had introduced a Fordson Major tractor to work in Cwm Caws. This was the last mention of the light railway in the commission's records. By 1957, a report records that 'an

The trackbed of the Cwm Caws Tramway in 2011 looking south, now used as a Forestry Commission road. The steep sides of the valley and gradients of the former tramway are evident. [Dan Quine]

inspection of the north east bank of Cwm Caws was made and it was agreed that another road was necessary. The only way to gain the height required was to double back for some 850 yards off the bottom road' – doubtless the 'bottom road' was built on the railway trackbed.

Rolling Stock

The light railway was supplied with equipment from the FC's Chirk Depot. It was laid with a mix of Jubilee track and light flat bottomed rail spiked to rough wooden sleepers. Hudson flat wagons were used for transporting felled logs. Boyd and Cozens visited the light railway in May 1953, and the photograph on page 5 of the Second Edition of Cozens's book shows them riding on a Hudson skip wagon chassis.** Boyd, writing in his obituary of Cozens, recalls this occasion:

'One weekend, Cyril Lockhart and I, having spent a day with [Cozens] at Rhydyronen burning much of the cut-down boscage which had accumulated on the [Talyllyn Railway] in those days, went over to Mawddwy to introduce him to a railway about which he had not then written - this involved a gravity run on a flat wagon (no brakes) down through the woodlands of Aberangell on a Forestry Tramway. There were many sharp curves and bridges; our speed increased and the garden rake, which we had taken to use as a brake lever, failed in its task. Cyril and I shouted to Cozens "Bale out" and left our vehicle to its fate. Cozens did not appreciate the need for haste - he was somewhat portly - and our last view of him was being shot over the edge of a timber bridge after the wagon derailed on the next sharp curve.'[4]

Two Motor Rail locomotives are known to have worked on the light railway. They were part of a batch of five 20/26hp petrol locomotives, no's 7093 to 7097, ordered by the Ministry of Supply from their offices in Bristol in 1940. In the autumn of 1933, Motor Rail redesigned their 20hp locomotives with a frame of riveted steel plate rather than the channel frame used in earlier locomotives. By then diesel was gaining in popularity over petrol, so the new design was offered with a choice of twin-cylinder engines, either the Dorman 2JOR petrol engine (known as the '20/26 H.P.' Class) or the Dorman 2HW engine (the '20/28 H.P.' Class).

The Ministry of Supply ordered a mix of petrol and diesel locomotives depending on the fuel that would be most readily available in the often remote locations.

---

* £200,000 in 2020

** The location is incorrectly identified as the Mawddwy Railway, which had been lifted by this date

A wagon built from a Hudson chassis, with a timber frame bolted on top in June 1975. The metal loops on the solebars held tall wooden poles to retain the timber — a similar arrangement to the timber bogies used during the First World War; this wagon may be a relic of that time. It is standing on a turning plate. Behind it are the two creosote tanks, covered with tarpaulins, with the central chimney between them. [Donald Sills]

Between 1940 and 1944 – with one exception – the whole of Motor Rail's production of petrol locomotives went to the forestry railways, either new builds or refurbished contractors' locomotives.

Motor Rail 7097 was ex-works on 18th February 1941 and probably sent new to the Cwm Caws Light Railway. Around 1949, it was transferred to the Forestry Commission depot at Chirk for storage, and replaced by a similar locomotive, almost certainly Motor Rail 7093. Ex-works on 4th July 1940, No. 7093 was dispatched with No. 7094 to Arthur Jones-Humphries at the depot at Vivod, Llangollen, and delivered to Whitehurst Halt on the GWR. Both locomotives were used on temporary timber tramways in the Llangollen area. In 1943, No. 7094 was transferred to a similar operation at Llanwyddyn Forest, Vyrnwy where it survived until about 1960. After the war No. 7093 was transferred to Chirk depot for storage and, after overhaul in

February 1948, was subsequently moved to Cwm Caws to replace No. 7097. It was returned to Chirk depot in June 1955 and subsequently resold for further use.[5] The principal driver of the second Motor Rail locomotive was Dafydd Hughes of Mallwyd.[6]

The Cwm Caws Light Railway probably stopped working in October 1954 and was certainly removed before 1956, when Edryd Price worked there for the FC. He recalls riding on the tramway when he was growing up in Aberangell in the late 1940s.[3]

Gartheiniog Timber Tramway

The second timber tramway was laid at the Gartheiniog mill sometime between 1949 and 1953. Gartheiniog, along with twelve acres of surrounding land, was purchased by the FC in 1947[7] and inspected by the chairman of the commission in April 1948. The mill was used as a sawmill and centre for local timber operations. It provided shelter to allow work to continue in poor weather conditions. They produced pit props and products including 'fire beaters, rustic furniture, gates, show material and home-grown roofing shingles'.[8]

A ¼ mile-long tramway was laid on the trackbed of the Gartheiniog Quarry Tramway north of the mill, with further lines to the east. It was purely hand-worked.

The tramway was mostly laid in 'Jubilee' track panels. Some rail may have been reused from the original Gartheiniog Quarry Tramway. The FC used a variety of wagons mainly built on Hudson chassis or using Hudson parts. Some wagons are likely to have been transferred from the Cwm Caws Light Railway.

The tramway was used to move logs from the stacking yard into the sawmill. Sawn timber was trammed from the mill to the creosote tanks. Two flues ran underneath the tanks, connected to a brick chimney between them. The flues heated the creosote to speed up the pickling process. Marieanne Mills distinctly remembers the strong smell of creosote drifting across Aberangell while pit props were being pickled shortly after the Second World War.[9] Treated timber was left to dry in the area north of the tanks, then finally returned to the mill to be made into 'rustic furniture' or other products. Logs for the stacking yard arrived from the forests on lorries, and finished products left by road.

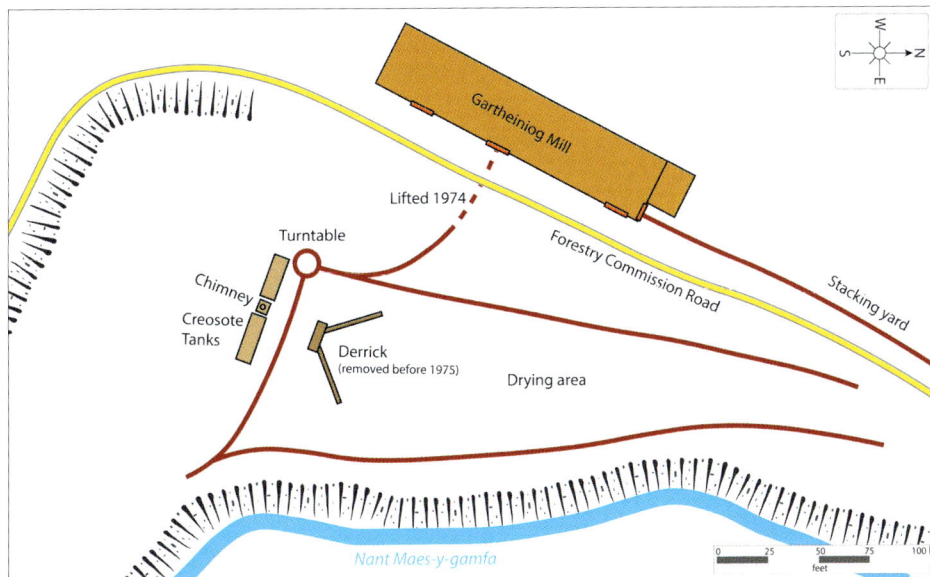

Sketch map of the Gartheiniog Timber Tramway in the early 1970s, based on a drawing by Donald Sills in June 1975.

Gartheiniog Mill on 20th August 1974 with the timber tramway disused, but largely intact. On the left are the creosote tanks. Piles of fence posts sit on the right, drying in the summer sun. The derrick crane was used for loading and unloading timber from the tramway wagons. [John Bonser, courtesy Alasdair Roberts]

In 1971, when Richard Kidner visited, the line from the stockyard to the mill was still in use, but the derrick was out of use. It was rebuilt on new concrete foundations, suggesting that creosoting resumed in 1972/3. On 12th April 1974, Andrew Neale visited and found the tramway out of use but largely intact.[5] Later that year the track connecting the mill to the drying yard was lifted, much of the remaining track was out of gauge and the creosote tanks had been removed from their bases. In early summer 1975, several wagons were purchased by Raymond Street, the operator of Meirion Mill in Dinas Mawddwy. Street had been running the mill as a tourist attraction since the 1960s and was adding a narrow gauge railway.[10]

Gartheiniog mill in 1971, with two items of particular interest. In the foreground is the distinctive iron-bodied rubbish wagon which was photographed in use underground in 1933. On the left is a remaining section of the east wall of the enamelling shed, also dating back to the Hadrill era. Both items had gone by 1974. [R.W. Kidner]

Looking south across the Gartheiniog waste tips in 1971. The derrick stands just in front of the chimney and creosote tanks. On the hillside beyond is a ledge just below the forestry road which may be the western end of the Coed y Gesail timber tramway. [Pete Briddon]

Donald Sills visited Gartheiniog that summer and recorded the wagon stock at both locations. He found eight wagon chassis, seven with steel frames and one discarded wooden frame. The steel wagons were a mixture of Hudson frames, and homemade frames using Hudson's wheelsets. They had a variety of bodies: two steel side-tipping skips, one steel end-tipping skip, two wooden bolsters and two wood frames with metal loops to hold poles for timber loads.

At Meirion Mill, Sills recorded another ten wagons, all believed to have come from Gartheiniog. Seven of these were built on steel Hudson chassis and three were timber-framed. All used Hudson wheels and axle boxes, except for one of the steel wagons which had axleboxes from Du Croo & Brauns of Amsterdam. The timber-framed wagons are particularly interesting and appear to have been built by the FC with metalwork supplied by Hudson. The substantial timber solebars were held together with metal tie rods and lighter timber bolsters; they were designed for hand working. The Meirion Mill Railway ran for two years until Easter 1977.[10] Much of the equipment was sold off, however several ex-Gartheiniog wagons remain on site.

The track and wagons at Gartheiniog were offered for sale in 1977 and remained there until at least May 1978 when they were seen by Andrew Neale.[5] The remains of one wooden framed wagon were photographed by Graham Fairhurst on 12th May 1979.[11] Most of the track and the wagons had been removed by the time Brian Clarke visited in 1981, although sleepers and lengths of rail could be found in the undergrowth as late as 2013. In 2016 the site around the mill was cleared for it to be converted into a house, though lengths of Jubilee track and much older bridge and flat-bottomed rail were to be found.

The DuCroo & Braun tipper chassis, being used for track laying, at Meirion Mill, June 1975. [Donald Sills]

Steel chassis with stanchions for an end-tipping body. Axleboxes and wheels as supplied by Hudsons. [Donald Sills]

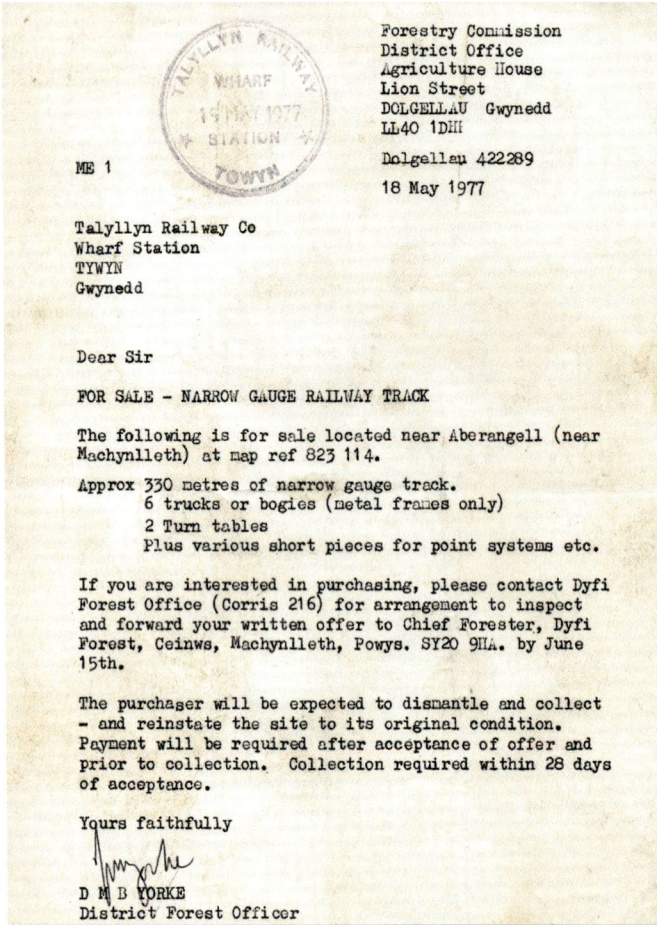

Above: A recovered steel sleeper from the Gartheiniog Timber Tramway. The distinctive 'spade' ends were designed to dig into the ground and reduce lateral movement of the track.
[Dan Quine]

Left: Forestry Commission letter sent to the Talyllyn Railway in 1977, offering the remains of the Gartheiniog Timber Tramway. The Talyllyn declined the offer.
[Letter courtesy of the Talyllyn Railway Archives]

Below: Wooden-framed wagons at Gartheiniog in 1974, both using Hudson axleboxes and wheelsets. The wagon on the right has distinctive iron tie-rods connecting the main frame timbers.
[Photo: John Bonser, courtesy Alasdair Roberts]

References

1   Sir S. Steel's New Post, *Aberdeen Press and Journal*, Jul. 12th, 1947.

2   FC April 1948, Forestry Commission report, Apr. 23rd, 1948.

3   Dan Quine, Interview with Edryd Price, Sep. 2015.

4   Talyllyn News, *Talyllyn News*, vol. 59, pp.34–35, Sep. 1968.

5   Dan Quine, Personal correspondence with Andrew Neale, 2016-2018.

6   Gwyndaf Breese, End of the line, Unpublished manuscript.

7   Minutes of the 17th Meeting, Wales National Committee of the Forestry Commission, May 6th, 1947.

8   Report of a visit by the Chairman of the Forestry Commission, Forestry Commission, Apr. 1963.

9   Marieanne Mills, Jul. 2016.

10 Dan Quine, Trixie and the Meirion Mill Railway, *Narrow Gauge World*, Nov. 2016.

11 Dan Quine, Personal correspondence with Graham Fairhurst, Apr. 2017.

15: The Main Tramways Described

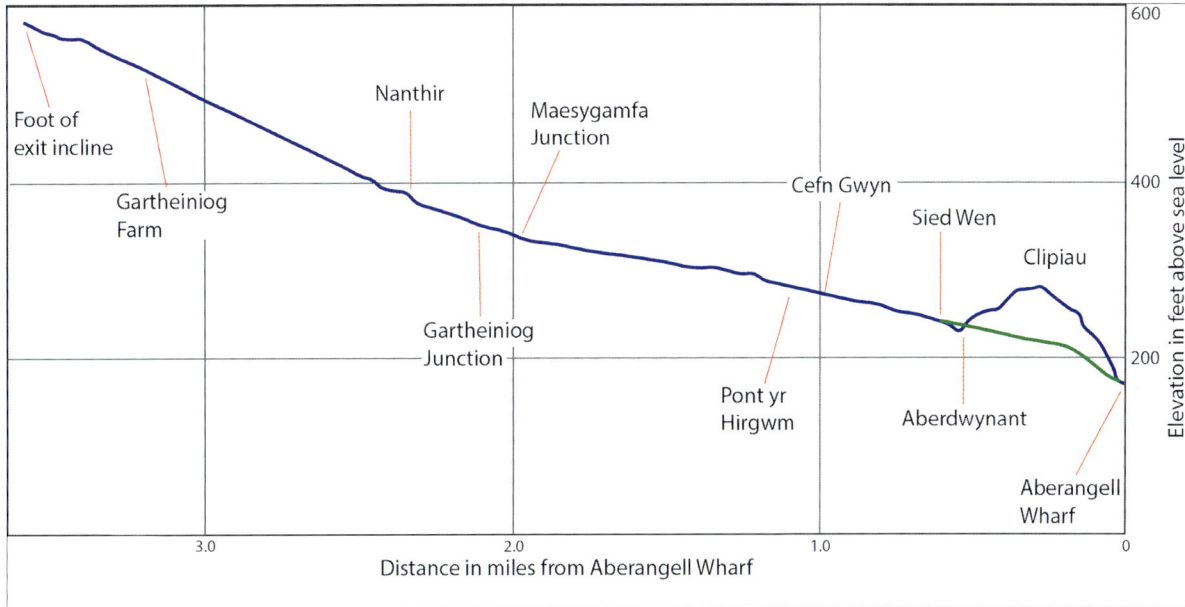

Gradient profile of the Hendre Ddu Tramway, showing the original line over Clipiau in blue and the 1894 deviation in green.

The Hendre Ddu Tramway dropped 400ft from the foot of the exit incline to Aberangell Wharf. It maintained a steady downhill gradient that supported gravity working, apart from the steep climb over Clipiau; the Clipiau section was later bypassed by the 1894 deviation across the Aberangell Meadows. This chapter describes the main tramway and its major branch to Maesygamfa Quarry.

Aberangell to Aberdwynant

The tramway started on the Wharf at the north end of the Mawddwy Railway's station. A substantial slate platform about three feet high, built from local materials, put the Hendre Ddu wagons at the same height as the floor of standard gauge wagons in the loop. The stiff leg derrick at the wharf was likely installed around 1870. It was removed in the mid-1920s. Just before the Second World War, the GWR installed a six-ton hand crane that was scrapped in the summer of 1949.

During GWR ownership, the standard gauge loop was operated as two independent sidings, rather than a full passing loop, which allowed two trains to be loaded at once. This mode of operation probably dates back to the First World War. The March 1943

operating instructions for Aberangell states:

'The siding is connected with the running line at both ends, the points being worked from a Ground Frame locked by Annett's Key attached to the Wooden Train Staff. The line is on a gradient of 1 in 103, falling towards Cemmaes, and care must be exercised by the Guard in performing the work at the siding. Before the engine is detached the train must be secured by the Van Brake

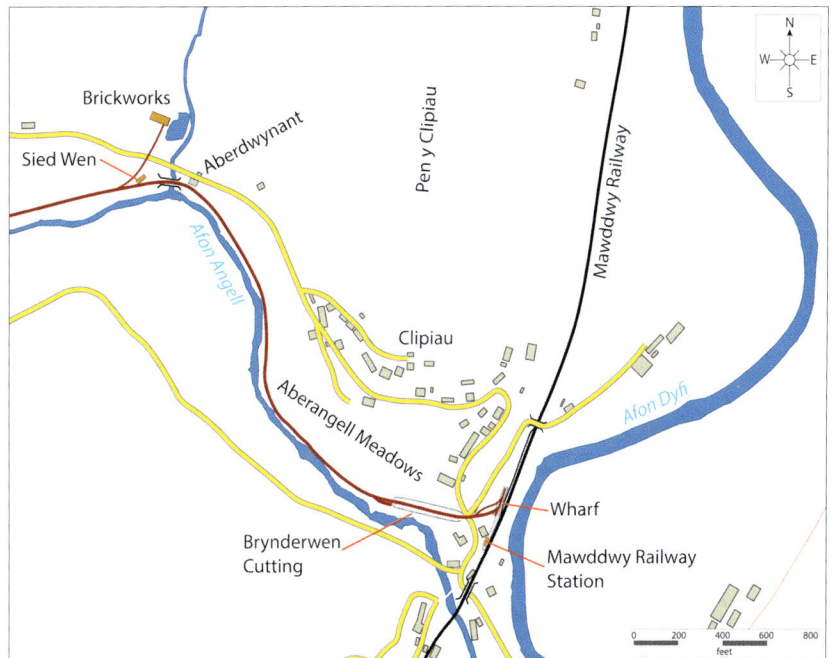

Right: The Mawddwy Railway's Aberangell Station building in September 2015, now part of a private garden. [Dan Quine]

Below: The Wharf at Aberangell in 1925 after being rebuilt by NWSQ. A train of trestle wagons is being unloaded, with a rake of box wagons in the loop, carrying timber. Standing in front of the Hendre Ddu train, from left to right, are Ianto Gruff, Norman Williams, quarry manager Richard Lewis, Dafydd Roberts, Robin Richards and William Hughes. On the right of the group is Herbert Disley, who would replace Lewis as quarry manager two years later. Between the two rakes of wagons is a large uncut slate block, and the bull wheel and lower section of the stiffleg derrick. There are rails in the mud in the foreground – the remains of the return loop of Greens Tramway. [R. T. Pugh]

Right: The entrance to Brynderwen Cutting with the gates of Brynderwen House on the left. The date 1897 is carved into the right-hand pillar, which is when the cemetery wall was constructed. The hinge pins remain for the oak barrier at the bottom of the cutting.
[Dan Quine]

Left: Looking east down the cutting in 1952, showing the curving descent to the Wharf.
[Richard Kinder]

Right: The top end of Brynderwen cutting, looking east, May 2016. The tramway ran through the gate and down to the Wharf. On the right is the site of the siding and locomotive shed. The 1895 construction tramway down to Brynderwen headed through the trees on the right of the gate. Capel Bethania can be seen on the left, across Aberangell Meadows.
[Dan Quine]

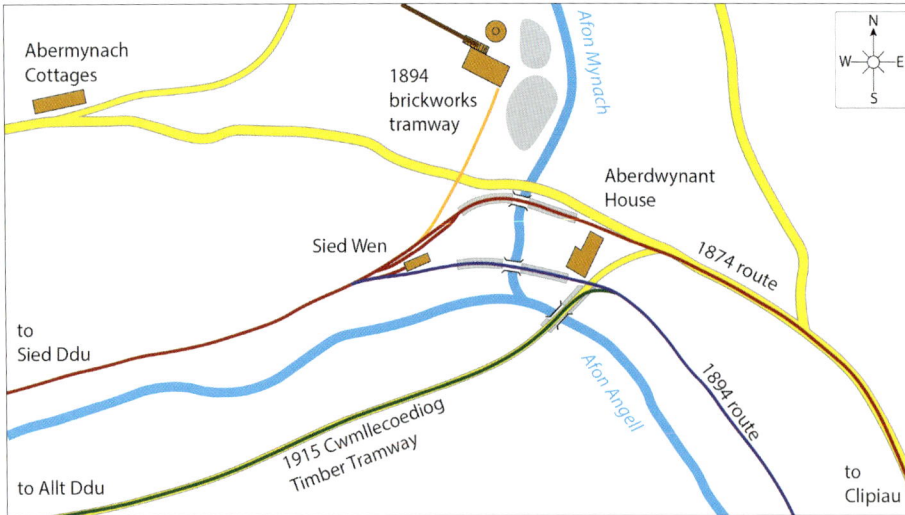

Left: The area around Aberdwynant. The original route, built in 1874, ran to the north of Sied Wen, where there was a storage loop. It ran along a slate embankment and across the bridge over the Afon Mynach, then passed Aberdwynant House and climbed to Clipiau. From 1894 onwards, the line ran south of Sied Wen and passed into Walton's meadows.

Below: The route of the tramway between Aberdwynant and Pont yr Hirgwm.

being tightly applied, also a sufficient number of Wagon Brakes and if necessary making use of sprags in accordance with Rule 151 to prevent the train, or any portion of it moving. The Siding will be worked by Up and Down trains. Coaching stock containing passengers must not be shunted into the siding alongside the loading wharf at the Cemmaes end. The Ground Frames will be worked by the Guard who will be responsible for seeing that the wagons left in the siding are secured by Wagon Brakes and also sprags applied on wagons placed alongside the loading dock at the Cemmaes end.'[1]

The entrance to the Wharf was gated during the life of the tramway, to prevent farm animals from straying through the Wharf and onto the Mawddwy Railway. The gates opened outwards across the road to protect the line from road traffic. The gates also established the private ownership of the Wharf. At the end of the tramway's life there was a sign attached to the gates which read: *'The penalty for leaving this gate open is forty shillings.'*[2]

For much of the lifetime of the Wharf, a weighbridge stood next to the road crossing. This was originally a stone building, replaced in corrugated iron around 1920 which in its later years was used as a flour store. The Wharf itself was fairly level, and the line began to climb on a curve as it crossed the main road through Aberangell

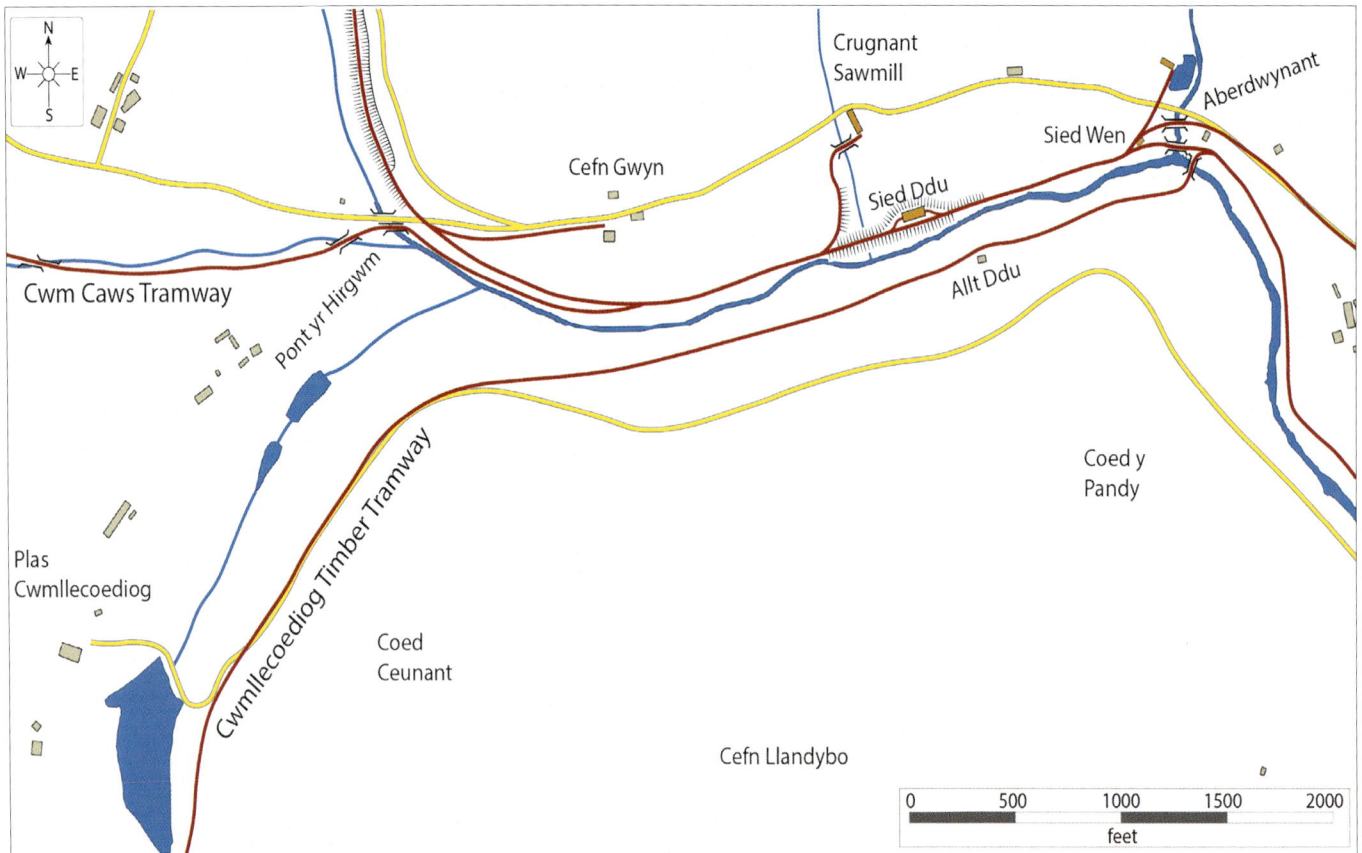

Right: Looking east from Aberdwynant towards Aberangell in September 2015. The 1894 route swings across the meadows heading towards the wharf. The houses on the horizon are Clipiau.
[Dan Quine]

Left: The 1894 tramway bridge across the Afon Mynach, seen on 12th May 1979. This view has since been lost to tree growth. The stone abutments built by the Maesygamfa quarrymen are clearly seen. The bridge deck may be a World War Two replacement to take the weight of the ammunition lorries, it is certainly not the original wooden tramway deck.
[Graham Fairhurst]

Right: The north side of Sied Wen in 2015. The substantial slate built building was likely originally roofed in slate. The 1874 route and storage loop ran on this side of the shed. The length of the building allowed it to store many ceir gwyllt overnight.
[Dan Quine]

Left: Sied Wen from the west. The 1894 deviation ran along the road on the right. The 1874 route and the later brickworks tramway both went through the gate on the left. There was a siding into the shed until 1894. The doors are believed to have come from Sied Ddu.
[Dan Quine]

Right: The site of Sied Ddu in 2013, looking east towards Aberdwynant. The Afon Angell is on the right. Sied Ddu sat where the road widens with the loop line on the left running through the shed. Nant Crugnant passes under the trackbed in the foreground. The short branch to the Crugnant Sawmill diverged from the main tramway just behind the photographer.
[Dan Quine]

Left: The trackbed of the Crugnant sawmill branch, looking towards the junction with the Hendre Ddu Tramway. The main tramway is shown in red, the route of the branch is outlined in white.
[Dan Quine]

village. The original route turned sharply to the north and climbed at 1 in 9 to Clipiau. The deviation crossed the road and entered Brynderwen cutting. Rising at 1 in 25, the line curved through the cutting and after about 100 yards entered the meadows west of Aberangell. There was another gate across the top of the cutting.

The south wall of the cutting is also the garden wall of Brynderwen House. About halfway along the cutting, the wall becomes noticeably higher, about 10ft above the trackbed. There are two openings, used to deliver coal for the house.

Immediately west of the gate, there was a siding on the south side of the main line. This was the start of the construction branch that Edward Hurst Davies built in the mid–1890s. After it was cut back, it was used to hold trains heading down to the wharf. It was on a slight uphill gradient, so descending gravity trains could be braked to a halt in the siding. The brakesman then walked down to the wharf, opening the gates as he went. After returning to the siding, he would allow the wagons to roll back onto the main line, switch the points, and run down to the wharf. After the Motor Rail locomotive was purchased in 1921, the locomotive shed was built over the siding. The shed appears to have been a simple construction with a wooden frame clad in corrugated iron, in a similar style to several local buildings. The locomotive shed survived the closure of the railway and was used as a farm shed for many years. It was finally demolished in the 1970s.

Brynderwen cutting was used for many years to pen sheep for away-wintering. The animals were held between the gates ready to be loaded onto standard gauge trains and taken away to lowland areas like Criccieth for the winter.[2]

East of the locomotive shed the tramway crosses Aberangell Meadows on a low, well-constructed embankment that maintains a steady gradient to Aberdwynant.

Half a mile from the Wharf, the tramway reaches Aberdwynant. The 1874 route passes to the north of

A pair of slate sleepers in April 2004, below the incline. [Keith Allen]

Aberdwynant house and the 1894 route passes to the south. There is a bridge to the south of the tramway where it leaves the meadow. This was built in the 1950s to replace the wooden bridge that had carried the Cwmllecoediog Timber Tramway. The main tramway heads west across a fine slate embankment and over the bridge over the Afon Mynach.

Aberdwynant to Pont yr Hirgwm

Sied Wen (the 'White Shed') was probably built in 1874, as a shelter for the ceir gwyllt. Loaded wagons coming down from the quarries were held in the storage loop ready to be hauled over Clipiau.

West of the Sied Wen, the deviation joins the original route and the main line heads southwest towards Cefngwyn, running on the north bank of the Afon Angell, and rising at a gentle 1 in 40 on an earth embankment. After ¼ mile is the site of 'Sied Ddu' (the 'Black Shed') built in the mid–1880s. This shed was about 60ft long and was built of slate and wood, the latter covered in the black felt which gave the shed its name. There was a loop here, with the north track passing through the shed. Sied Ddu was removed in the early 1940s.

West of Sied Ddu, the line crosses Nant Crugnant which runs in a culvert under the embankment. Just to the west was the short tramway to the sawmill at Nant Crugnant, built by Higginbottom during the First World War.

The Hendre Ddu Tramway continues southwest for about ¼ mile, on a gentle uphill gradient, and passes below Cefngwyn Farm. A gated road rose to Cefngwyn Hall to the north and the Cwm Caws Tramway branched off to the south and running parallel to the main tramway. Both tramways curve to the right and arrive at Pont yr Hirgwm, where

Looking east from Pont yr Hirgwm. The main tramway runs towards Sied Ddu along the road on the right. The left road leads up to Cefngwyn Farm and the branch to the Hall ran to the right of the road. Hauling coal wagons up the branch would have been a significant effort, but the downhill gravity ride would have been thrilling. [Dan Quine]

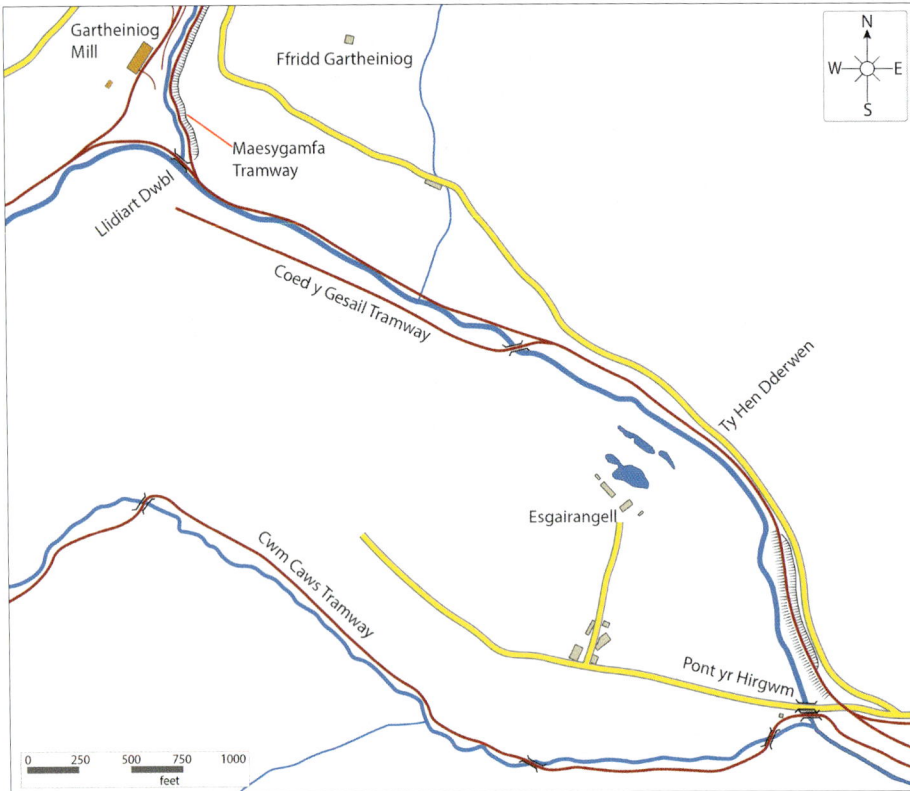

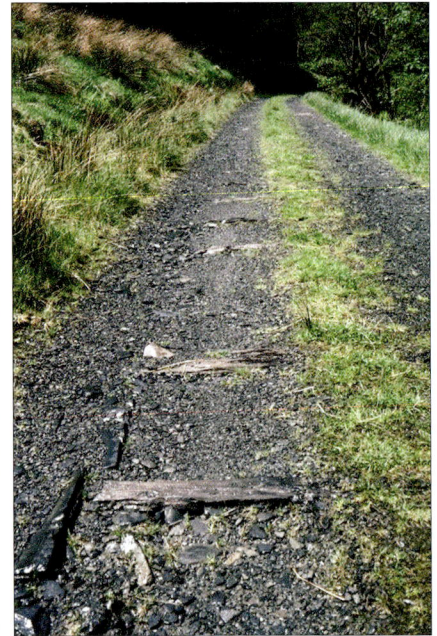

Above: Looking towards Aberangell near Ty Hen Derwen in 1981, before the trackbed was metalled. Oak sleepers remain in situ. [Brian Clarke]

The route of the Maesygamfa Tramway.

the Cwm Caws Tramway heads south and crosses the Afon Angell.

Cefnwgyn Farm is about 75ft above the main tramway and was connected to it by a short branch that rose at 1 in 5 over its lower section.

Above: The upper half of Maesygamfa Incline in August 1987, showing the trackbed on a low embankment, and the ruins of the winding house. [Dave Billmore]

Pont yr Hirgwm to Llidiart Dwbl

Beyond Pont yr Hirgwm, the main line curves to head northwest and climbs more steeply towards Gartheiniog, on a slate embankment. The Afon Angell runs through the narrow Esgairangell gorge, with steep walls on either side and the tramway is on a ledge cut into the hillside, about 50ft above the river. The tramway curves left and leaves the gorge, as the valley opens out again. Esgairangell farmhouse is on the far bank and Ty Hen Dderwen on the near bank, where there was a run out for storing ceir gwyllt. The tramway is level or even slightly descending in this section. The 1915 Coed y Gesail Tramway branches off to the left, crosses the Angell and runs along the south bank of the river.

On the hillside to the north is the ancient farmhouse of

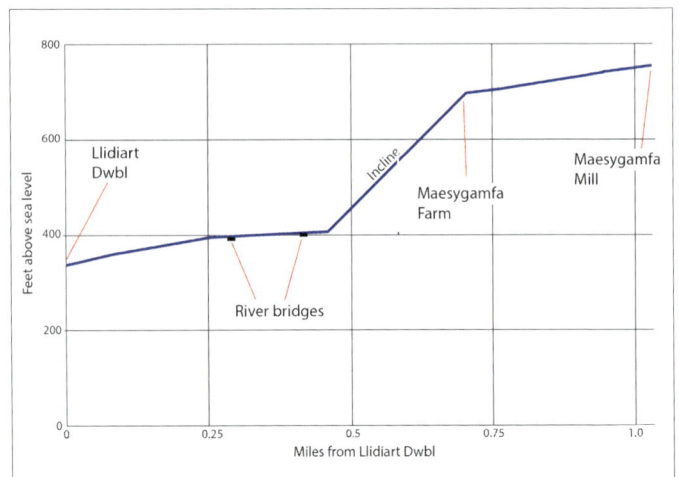

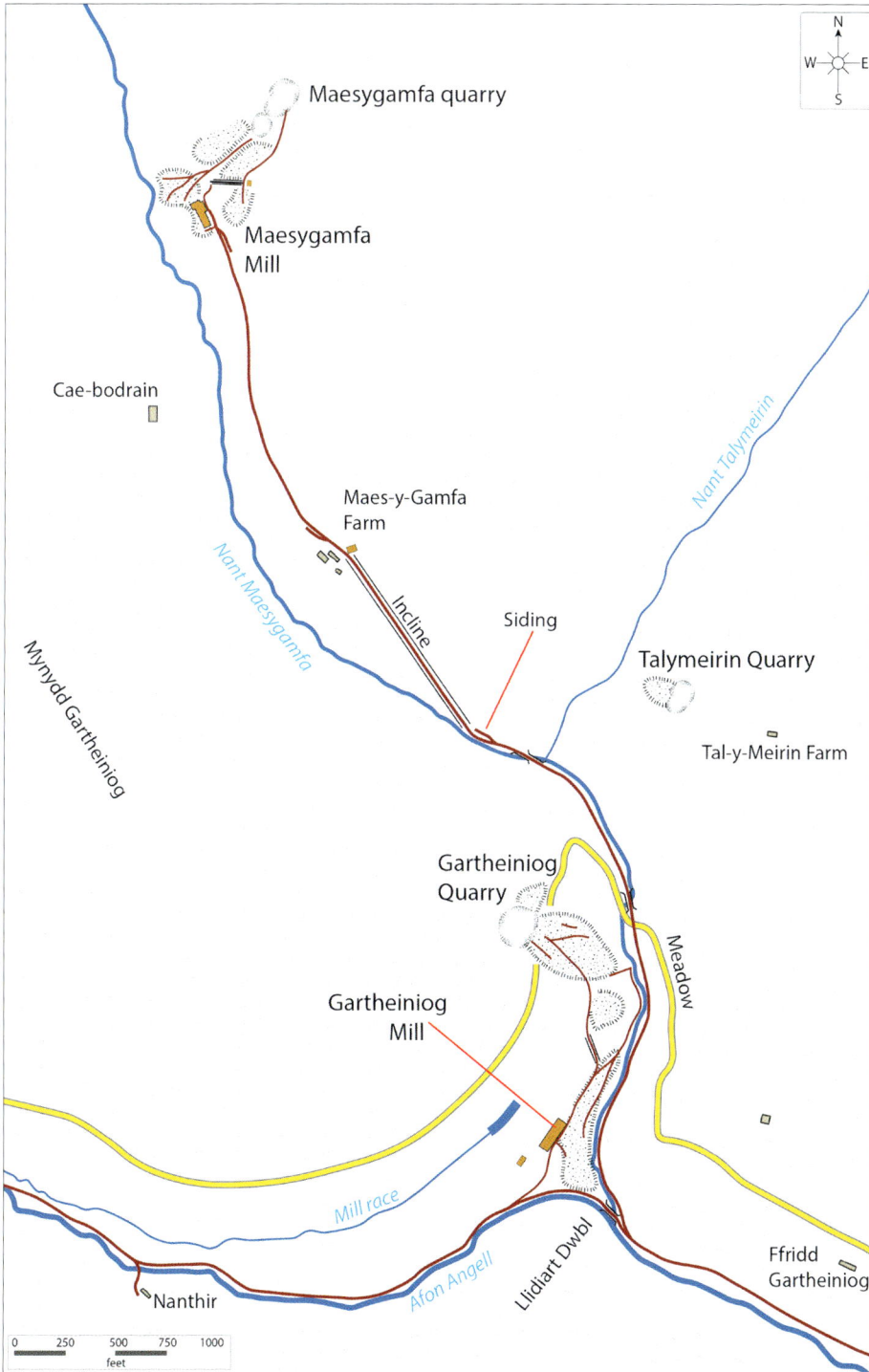

Above: Lengths of flat-bottomed and bridge rail found in April 2004 near the foot of the Maesygamfa incline. The tramway was laid in bullhead rail. The bridge rail comes from the incline, the flat-bottomed rail may have been from the Talymeirin incline.
[Keith Allen]

Right: The first tramway bridge across the Nant Maesygamfa, taken from the ford where the road crosses the river. This section is on a relatively gentle gradient and features some well-engineered embankments built from slate blocks, reflecting the substantial investment made in building the tramway.
[Keith Allen]

Left: The steep lower section of the Maesygamfa Tramway, looking north towards the quarry. Nant Maesygamfa is below to the left, and the waste tips of Gartheiniog Quarry are just visible through the trees.
[Dan Quine]

Right: Immediately north of the first bridge the tramway runs on a shallow embankment. This section is delightful but very boggy, and it is possible to sink waist-deep into the mire, as the author found to his cost.
[Dan Quine]

Left: The second of the two tramway bridges that cross the Nant Maes-y-gamfa, in September 2015. The steel deck was installed by a local farmer in late 2004. A length of bridge rail runs under it. The abutments of the tramway bridge are to the right of the modern deck.
[Dan Quine]

Left: The incline winding house, with the upper tramway running past on a slate embankment. The winding house walls were still remarkably intact in 2016.
[Dan Quine]

Right: Looking towards the incline winding house showing the slate embankment where it widens, which may have carried a short siding.
[Dan Quine]

Left: Looking north along the tramway into Maesygamfa Quarry. The mill sat on top of the lower tips to the left.
[Dan Quine]

The winding house in 1987, looking towards the quarry. The tramway passes to the left. [Dave Billmore]

The approach to Gartheiniog Farm in 1981. The farm buildings can just be seen in the centre. In the distance, Mynydd Dolgoed rises above the head of the valley. [Brian Clarke]

Ffridd Gartheiniog, often called Ffridd. It was immortalised in the poem that won the 1900 Eisteddfod at Capel Horeb. Two miles west of Aberangell, the tramway reaches Llidiart Dwbl. Here the Maesygamfa Tramway branches off to the north and the main line passes over the Nant Maesygamfa on a bridge. There were gates across the two tramways – hence the name Llidiart Dwbl meaning 'Double Gates'.

The Maesygamfa Tramway

The 1 mile 24 chain long Maesygamfa Tramway begins at Llidiart Dwbl, where it diverges north from the Hendre Ddu Tramway and follows the east bank of Nant Maesygamfa, climbing steeply as it parallels the river. The tramway is on a narrow ledge cut into the rock. On the far side of the river are the waste tips of Gartheiniog Mill.

Once past the Gartheiniog mill, the tramway climbs steadily, turning right, then swinging sharply to the left as it passes the Gartheiniog adit on the opposite bank. By now the tramway is at the level of the stream, and the valley opens out into a broad meadow. The tramway levels off and heads north.

As the tramway crosses the meadow, a road drops down from the southeast to meet it. This is the original road connecting Aberangell to Hendreddu. The road crosses the river at a shallow ford at the north end of the meadow. Here, the tramway crosses to the west bank of the river on a slate-built bridge. There are substantial embankments on both sides of the bridge and several lengths of original bridge rail can be found in the river, as well as supporting the modern bridge deck. North of the bridge, the tramway curves gently to the west, running close by the river. It is supported on a low slate embankment that crosses several tributary streams. The ground here is often waterlogged and boggy.

After 300 yards, the tramway crosses Nant Maes-y-gamfa once more to regain the east bank, over another bridge of similar design but slewed at a significant angle.

On the far side of the bridge the tramway heads northwest.

There was a trailing junction that crossed the Nant Talymeirin on a low bridge to the foot of the incline to Talymeirin Quarry. The main tramway continued for about 100 yards to the foot of the incline up to Maes-y-gamfa Farm. There was a short siding on the east side, where empty wagons waited to ascend the incline. Much of the tramway was laid on slate sleepers, some of which survived in situ as late as 2020.

The long double-track incline crosses the open hillside, rising from 425ft above sea level to 672ft, over a horizontal distance of 1,300ft, at an average gradient of 1 in 5. It is cut by a farm road just below the winding house, but is still clear for most of its course, running on a low slate embankment.

The winding house walls show the remarkable craftsmanship of the Maesygamfa stonemasons. The winding house is angled to face down the incline to give

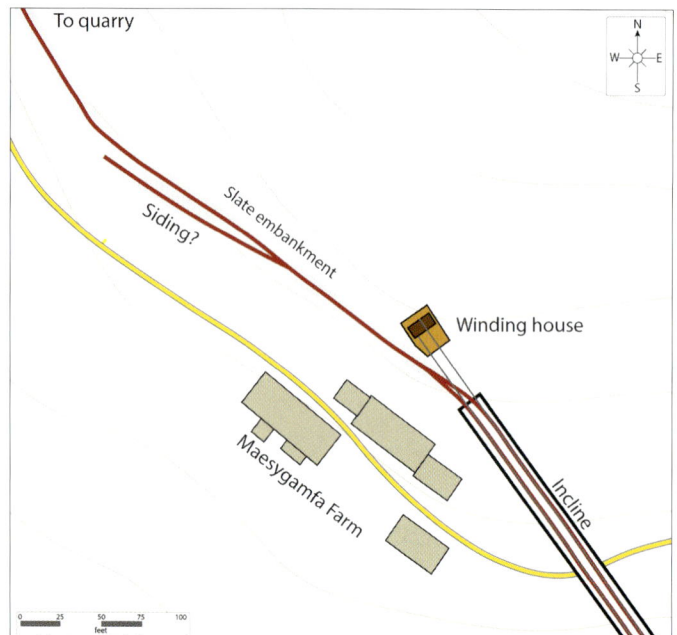

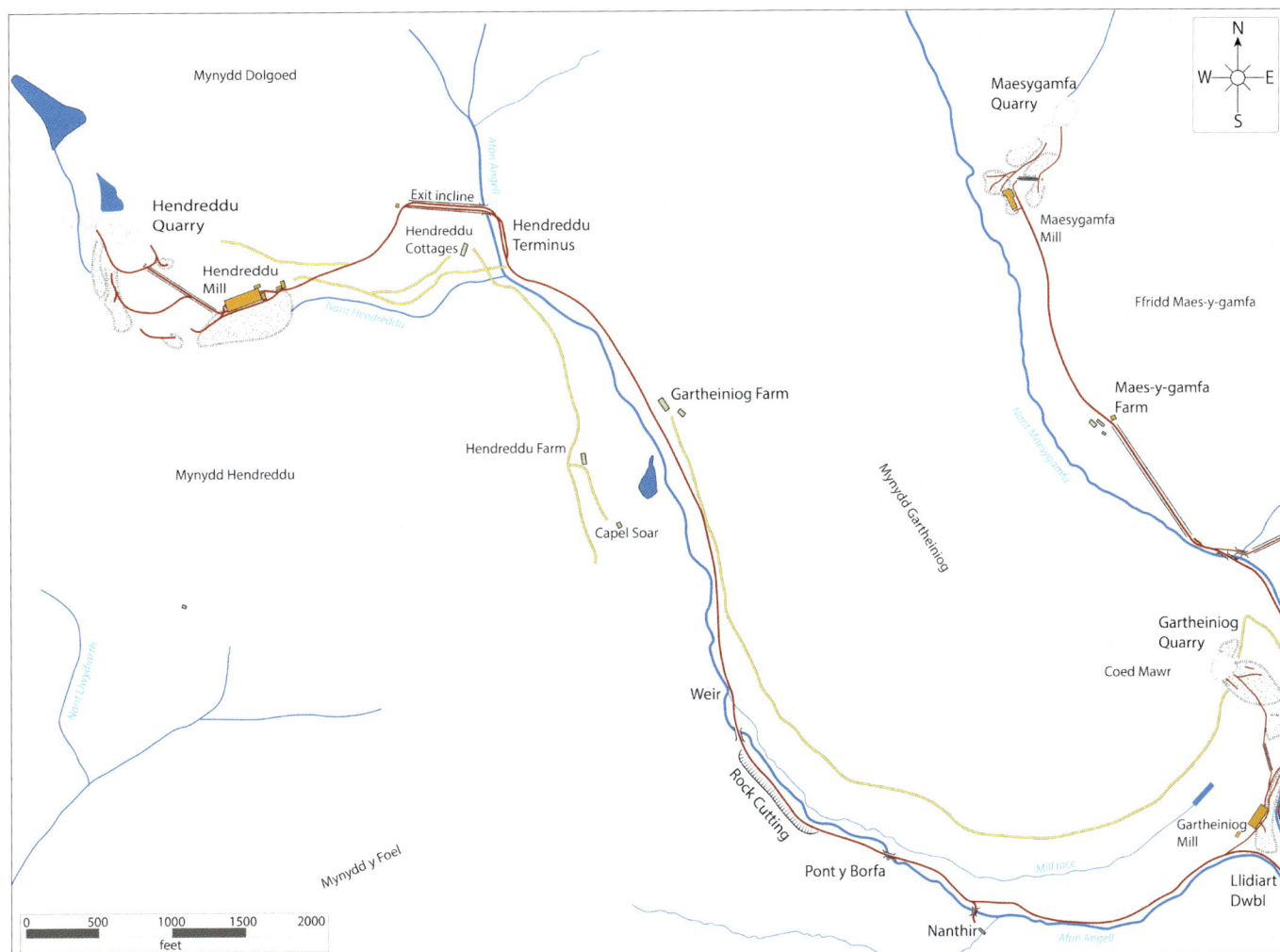

enough room for the tramway to pass to the south. After the tramway was lifted, the winding house was used by the local farmer for storing cut bracken up until the 1970s.[3]

From the head of the incline, the tramway ran above Maes-y-gamfa Farm on a low slate embankment. The embankment widens just past the winding house and there may have been a siding here to store loaded wagons waiting to descend. From here the tramway curved to the right, then headed nearly due north across low moorland to the quarry.

Llidiart Dwbl to Hendreddu

Returning to Llidiart Dwbl, the Hendre Ddu Tramway passes over Nant Maesygamfa on a low bridge then swings left on a long, steady curve. It runs below the Gartheiniog waste tips, where a path runs up to the Mill. After the Second World War, the Forestry Commission widened the path to allow timber lorries to get to the sawmill. This may originally have been intended as the exit tramway from Gartheiniog. If so, it was quickly replaced with the later exit tramway to allow more controlled descents of loaded slab wagons. There was a small building at the bottom of the path which may have been a shed over the car gwyllt run out.

The tramway curves southwest to the junction of the Gartheiniog exit tramway. It must have been quite a sight to see loaded wagons coming down from the mill at speed, head uphill on the main tramway, slow and come back downhill, while the single-bladed point was kicked over to allow them to head to Aberangell.

The tramway followed the Afon Angell round the shoulder of Mynydd Gartheiniog, through a reverse curve to head westwards. A junction took a short siding across the Afon Angell to Nanthir Farm. The Nanthir siding was used to deliver coal and store a car gwyllt for the family's use, stored in a small slate shed.[4] It also saw occasional use as a 'refuge' so that trains could pass on the tramway. The bridge was particularly weak and care had to be taken when running loaded wagons over it. In 1889, the Nanthir siding came off a facing junction, this was later replaced by a trailing junction, but the date and reason for this change is not recorded.

West of Nanthir, the tramway crosses the Afon Angell for the first time at Pont y Borfa. For about 300 yards the line continues along the south bank, following the course of the river as it swings north. The valley is narrow here and this is the section formerly known as the *Cytun Craig* ('Rock Cutting'). Westerly winds often came through at gale

Left: The overgrown embankment at the end of the Hendre Ddu Tramway. It is about 4ft high and was intended as a transhipment wharf for the standard gauge line to Aberangell. The exit incline is off to the right.
[Dan Quine]

Right: Looking west along the Hendre Ddu Tramway in May 2016. On the right is the road to Gartheiniog Mill. The ramp is built of sawn slate blocks and swings around the southern edge of the waste tips. It was widened by the Forestry Commission after the Second World War to provide access for timber lorries. The exit tramway from the mill is highlighted in white.
[Dan Quine]

Left: Hidden in the trees at the terminus of the Hendre Ddu Tramway are the remains of a building. Boyd describes this as a locomotive shed and it may have been used as one after 1920. It likely dates back to the construction of the embankment around 1870 and is thought to be intended for the standard gauge line that was never built.
[Dan Quine]

The abutments of the bridge that carried the Nant Hir branch; the main tramway is on the far side. The branch would have been no more than 50 yards long.
[Dan Quine]

The only known photograph of the Maesygamfa Tramway with track still in situ. It was taken in the 1930s, looking down from the waste tips north of Gartheiniog Mill, just before the tramway reaches the meadow. Although overgrown, the rails can just be seen and still saw occasional trains to and from the farm. The track is ballasted almost to the top of the rail level – to avoid the horses hitting their hooves on the chairs holding the bullhead rails.
[Bill Breese collection]

force.[5] After the trackbed was taken over by the Forestry Commission, Rock Cutting was removed so that logging trucks could pass.[6]

The tramway crosses back to the north bank of the Angell on a bridge by the weir feeding the Gartheiniog leat. The valley widens again, and the mountains are noticeably higher as the line approaches Gartheiniog Farm.

The tramway curves slightly to the left as it nears Gartheiniog Farm. There was a siding on the right in later years, certainly after 1923, which ran into a garage that housed the farm's car gwyllt fitted with the engine from a Morgan three-wheeler.[4] The tramway continues through the farmyard, makes a final left curve and comes alongside the river.

Hendreddu Terminus

The tramway ends 200 yards north of Gartheiniog Farm on a 4ft high slate embankment, with a loop for empty wagons waiting to ascend the incline and loaded runs

waiting to run to Aberangell. At the north end of the loop, the line turns sharply left to the foot of the incline; this is the end of the Hendre Ddu Tramway, at 586ft above sea level. The embankment was probably constructed in 1870 or 1871, as a transhipment wharf for the planned standard gauge branch from Aberangell. When narrow gauge was chosen instead, the tramway was simply extended to the south, past Gartheiniog Farm and on to Aberangell. A slate building at the east end and below the embankment was probably built as a weighhouse for the standard gauge line. Boyd claimed it was used as a locomotive shed after 1920.

The tramway ends at a lonely spot, just over three and a half miles from Aberangell. There are no houses higher up the valley. For seventy years the tramway was the major transport link, for quarrymen and farmers alike. Mynydd Gartheiniog and Mynydd Dolgoed loom high above the valley floor. Here ends the Hendre Ddu Tramway.

Looking east from the trackbed of the Upper Tramway from the head of the exit incline to the quarry. The roofs of Hendreddu Cottages are below. The cottages were built around 1875 for quarrymen with families; there were originally six in the terrace, but only the leftmost three survive. The trackbed of the tramway can be seen curving along the valley, above the cottage roof. The buildings of Gartheiniog Farm are just visible above the trees in the bottom of the valley. [Dan Quine]

References

1   Appendix to No. 16 Section of the Service Time Tables, *Great Western Railway*, Mar. 1943.

2   Lewis Cozens, R.W. Kidner, Brian Poole, *The Mawddwy, Van and Kerry Branches*, Oakwood Press, 2004.

3   Bill Breese, Notes on local quarrying and quarrymen, Dolgellau Archive, vol. ref ZM/6541/9, 1982.

4   Bill Breese, Bygone activities within Angell valley, *Cambrian News*, Aug. 6th, 1976.

5   Gwyndaf Breese, Travelling on the tramway, unpublished manuscript.

6   Gwyndaf Breese, End of the line, unpublished manuscript.

16: Maesygamfa Quarry Described

Maesygamfa is a remote location, and working practices there were determined by the local topology. Two deep pits were dug into the steep ravine of the Nant Cwm-rhedynog. The Broad Vein here is nearly vertical, more than ¼ mile wide and is made up of grey-blue mottled mudstones, interspersed with beds of true slate varying in width from a few inches to about 50ft. One bed of slate outcrops at the top of the ravine and initial workings in the 1860s dug directly into the hillside, forming a shallow, narrow pit next to the stream. Richard Jones, an overseer at Hendreddu in the 1880s and 1890s, believed that the slate was better on the west side of the valley at Cae-bodrain.[1] That land was part of the Gartheiniog estate, which is why Walton and Davies chose to dig on the east side of the valley at Maesygamfa.

Early Workings 1862-1870

Maesygamfa grew into a substantial working, though smaller than Hendreddu and Gartheiniog. The 1862 quarry though was only a small surface pit beside the Nant Cwm-rhedynog. A second attempt to work the site was made in 1868 or 1869. A trial adit is thought to have been driven next to the pit. Only a small amount of slab can have been produced. Testimony at the 1875 case of Edwards vs Buckley appears to confirm that there was not a mill on the site in the 1860s.

Early Development by Davies and Walton 1886-1890

In 1886 Edward Hurst Davies leased Maesygamfa and in partnership with Frederick Walton started working and extending the 1860s pit. By 1887, a tramway had been laid to the head of a short trwnc incline. The 1ft 11in. gauge wagons were carried on a wide-gauge transporter wagon under which ran a counterbalance-sled. Similar inclines were used in Corris, notably at Braichgoch and Aberllefenni. Like the main Aberllefenni incline on the Foel Grochan side, the Maesygamfa trwnc incline may have had a turntable mounted on the carrier platform.

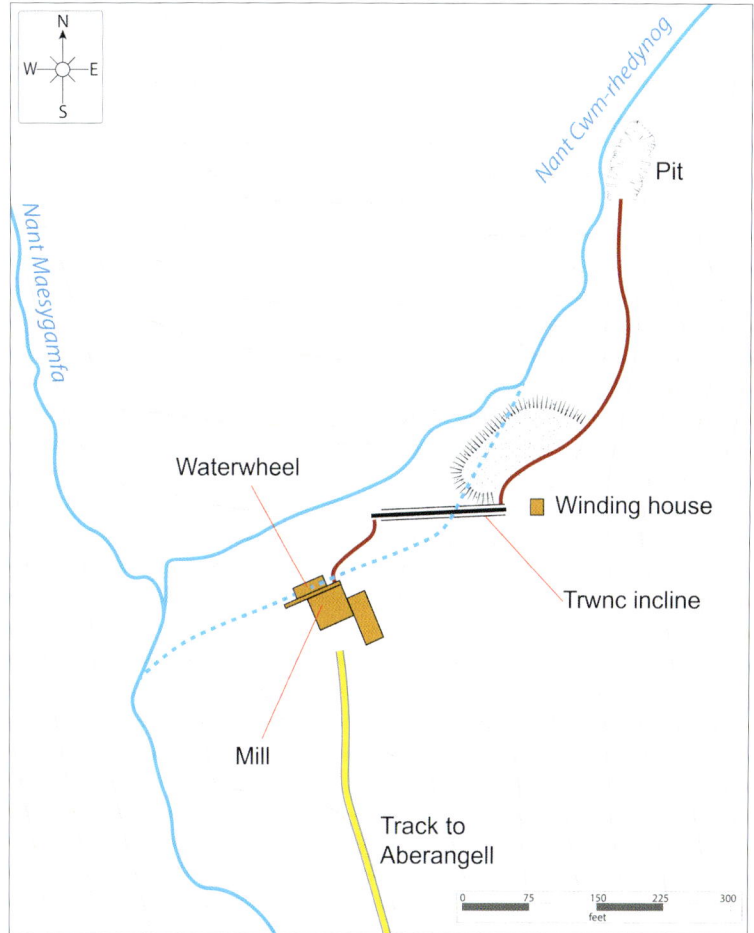

Above: Maesygamfa in 1887, with the original pit in production. A mill has been built near the foot of the trwnc incline, powered by a waterwheel fed from the Nant Cwm-rhedynog. The likely route of the water feed is shown.

Right: A trwnc incline on the tramway between Braichgoch and Gaewern quarries in Corris Uchaf. This incline was built before 1889, probably around the same time as the Maesygamfa trwnc. The large carrying wagon is still attached to the cable. The brakeman's platform is on the nearside of the winding house, and behind it is the counterbalance sled. [Malcolm Ravensdale]

Left: The tramway from the head of the trwnc incline into the upper pit. The ravine is extremely steep and a narrow ledge of slate blocks makes up the trackbed. The upper pit is just visible in the trees in the centre of the photograph. The lower pit is behind the trees on the left. [Dan Quine]

Right: The trwnc incline winding house made of rough stone, showing that it was built before the mill was operating. [Dan Quine]

Left: The head of the trwnc incline. The winding house is at the top right and the incline drops down to the left. The slate wall on the left of the crimp is the loading stage where slab wagons were pushed onto the carrying wagon. [Dan Quine]

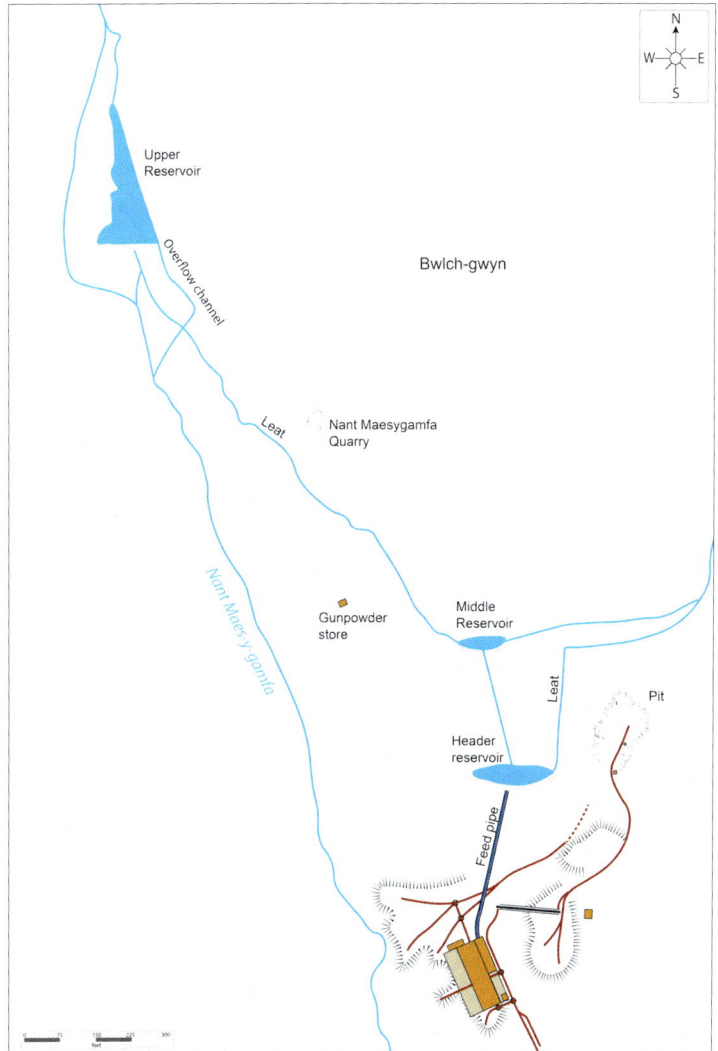

The Maesygamfa water system, built between 1890 and 1891. There was a short length of timber launder where the leat crossed a small stream between the Upper and Middle reservoirs. The small Nant Maesygamfa Quarry was the source of rock for the reservoir dams.

At the foot of the incline a small mill about 30ft x 30ft, was built, made of rough slate blocks. There was a waterwheel on the north side of the building driving the machinery. It was about 20ft in diameter, based on the size of the pit and markings on the remains of the north wall. On the east side of the mill was a smaller building, about 30ft x 15ft, that shared a common wall with the mill. This smaller building contained the smithy which was certainly in use in the 1880s. This smaller building was likely a 'beudy' (cowshed) used by Maesygamfa Farm before the mill was built.[2] It was converted for industrial use by Davies.

This first mill produced the sawn blocks used to expand it, much as the mill at Gartheiniog was expanded in 1884. This is one of several similarities between the two quarries which were connected by E.H. Davies. In the early 1880s slabs were taken out by packhorse or cart to Aberangell, a difficult journey over rough mountain tracks.

Expansion 1891-1894

Walton and Davies spent much of 1890 surveying the existing quarry and planning a major expansion. A page of the quarry ledger recorded by Bill Breese shows some of the payments for the expansion work:[3]

Expenditure	1892 cost	2018 cost
Ingersoll-Sergeant air compressor, drill and bar channelling machine	£125 17s 5d	£55,000
Item	1891 cost	2020 cost
Machinery for the mill	£236 14s 6d	£104,000
Building work	£221 5s 1d	£98,000
Clearing the new level to the chamber	£11 7s 3d	£5,000
Wages for the quarrymen	£81 8s 3d	£35,600
Total	£676 12s 6d	£300,000

The mill was expanded to the south, tripling its length to 100ft. The extension was built with mortared, snecked slate blocks, produced in the original mill. The beudy was extended north and south to nearly 60ft long, adding a storeroom, caban and turbine house along the east wall of the mill. The Maesygamfa Tramway was built around 1891. A siding was laid at the head of the tramway to store wagons.

The west wall of the mill contained a row of tall windows, an unusual feature for a slate mill, where skylights were more common. The north wall of the stockyard was substantially higher than the rest of the walls, perhaps built with an eye

to a further expansion of the mill to the west.

Though the upper pit remained in production, in early 1892 a tunnel was driven from the mill level and a chamber developed below and to the southwest of the pit. The Ingersoll-Sergeant air compressor and drill system were purchased for this work.[3] The 20ft waterwheel was not large enough to power the extended mill, which was equipped with multiple saws, as well as planing machines and shaping tools. Rather than install a larger wheel, Davies purchased a water turbine. This was likely a Pelton wheel, then a relatively new invention and the most efficient water-driven power plant available. An extensive system of reservoirs and leats were built to provided a head of water for the turbine.

The large upper reservoir dammed Nant Maes-y-gamfa about half a mile upstream of the quarry. The dam was about 10ft high and 100ft wide, made of rammed earth, with a stone inner face. The main outlet was in the middle of the dam with an overflow channel in the southeast corner.[4]

From the main outlet, a leat ran above the 1000ft contour to the Middle Reservoir directly to the north of the mill. The leat was lined by vertical slabs, held in place with steel rails. A pipe led down to the Header Reservoir, while an overflow

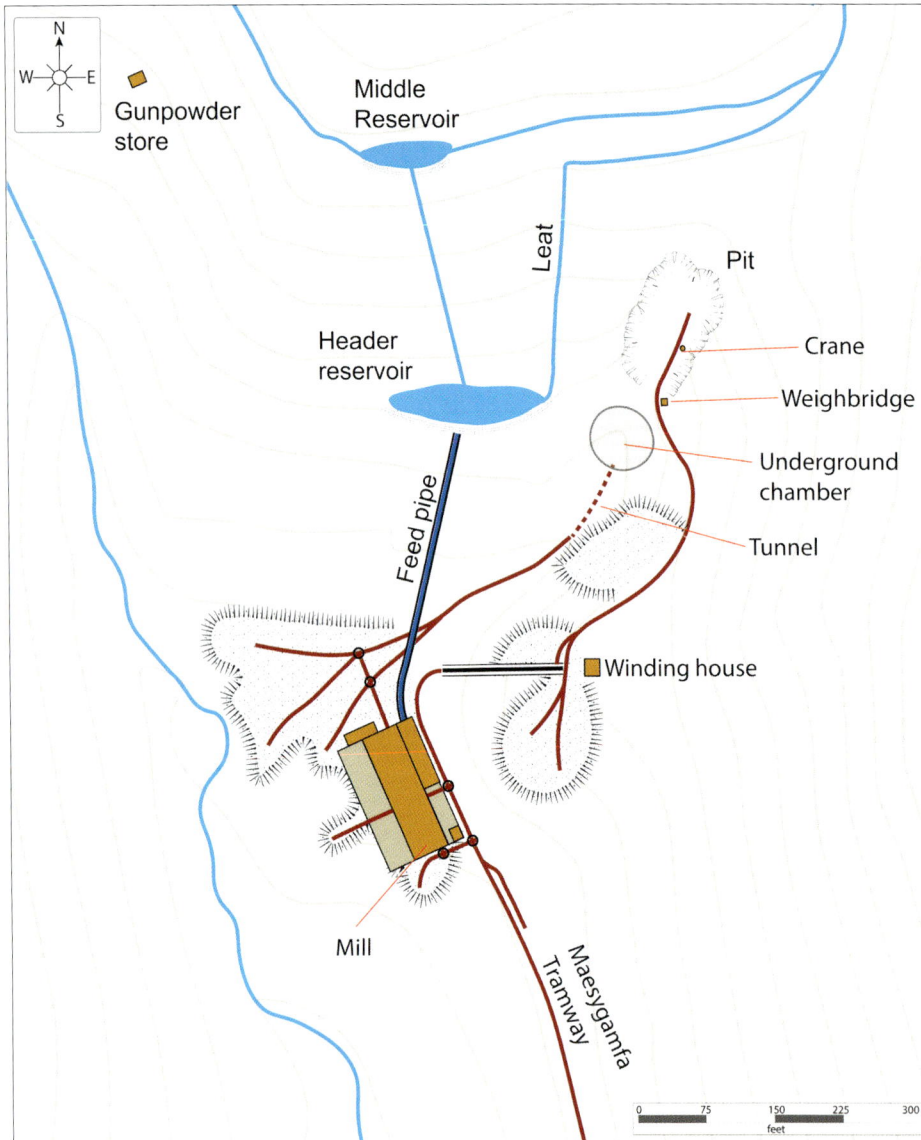

Maesygamfa around 1893. The pit has been significantly expanded and the Nant Cwm-rhedynog has been diverted to the west into the leat down to the Header Reservoir. The Maesygamfa Tramway is complete and a tunnel has been driven at mill level into the underground chamber.

leat ran east to join the Nant Cwm-rhedynog. The dam of the Header Reservoir has a rubble and earth core, faced with stone, and is about 130ft long, 16ft wide and five feet high. It has an overflow channel at the west end and the main outflow is in the centre of the reservoir at the foot of the dam wall. The water was likely carried from the dam to the turbine house in an iron pipe – some remains of broken cast iron pipes were still to be found at the mill in 2019.

The expanded mill allowed production to be greatly increased. The upper pit grew to the north and west. The turbine drove both the mill machinery and the air compressor for the rock drill; compressed air lines ran from the turbine house into the chamber. There is evidence that compressed air was briefly supplied to the upper pit: on the waste tips south of the head of the trwnc incline is a slab showing the characteristic perforations of a compressed-air drill. The drill was probably tested in the upper pit while the tunnel to the lower chamber was being driven.

The Second Pit 1896-1908

Sometime in the mid-1890s, production focused underground. An untopping pit was started above the chamber, with a tramway running through a shallow cutting to waste tips below the header reservoir. There is evidence that a crane was installed above the mill-level tramway where it exits the tunnel, to lower good rock from the untopping pit to be sent to the mill. The untopping pit eventually broke through into the chamber. By 1900, the upper pit was no longer in use, and the tramway to the head of the trwnc incline had been partly lifted.

Around 1905 a trial adit was driven into the vein on the west of the lower pit at the height of the tipping tramway. A tramway from the adit ran onto the waste tip where a weighbridge had been installed. Good rock was lowered by crane into the pit and taken out to the mill through the tunnel.

178

Right: The most complete remains on the mill level are the buildings that stood to the east of the mill. The nearest of these buildings has a prominent fireplace and chimney and was probably the mill office or caban. The walls on the left are built from rough country stone and are probably the original cowshed walls.
[Dan Quine]

Left: The Maesygamfa Tramway looking south from the mill, with slate sleepers in situ. The embankment widens here to accommodate the siding on the left.
[Dan Quine]

Right: In 2016, the north wall of the mill was still partly standing. The photograph is taken outside the footprint of the mill looking west. Nearest the camera is the waterwheel pit, with the footing of the wall that supported the wheel bearing on the right. The wheel was probably an overshot type of about 20ft diameter, fed by a wooden launder from the stream. It drove a line shaft that ran along the west side of the mill.
[Dan Quine]

The mill from the south east. The weighhouse in the near corner was used to weigh finished products before they were shipped over the Maesygamfa Tramway.

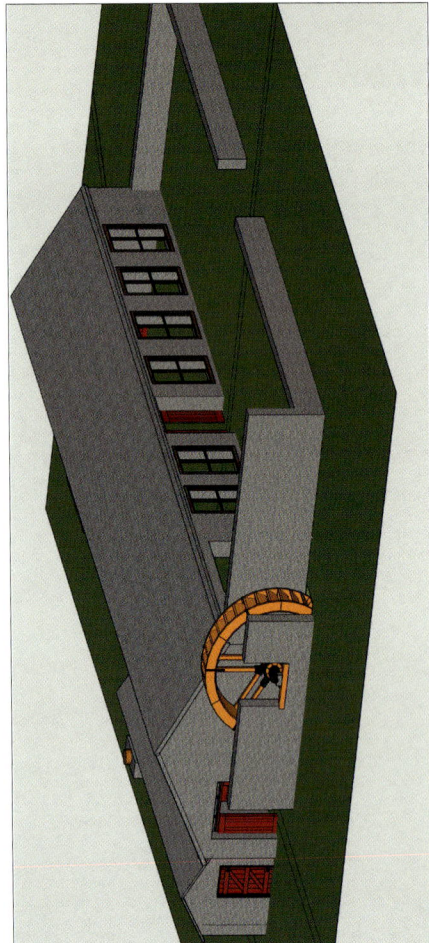

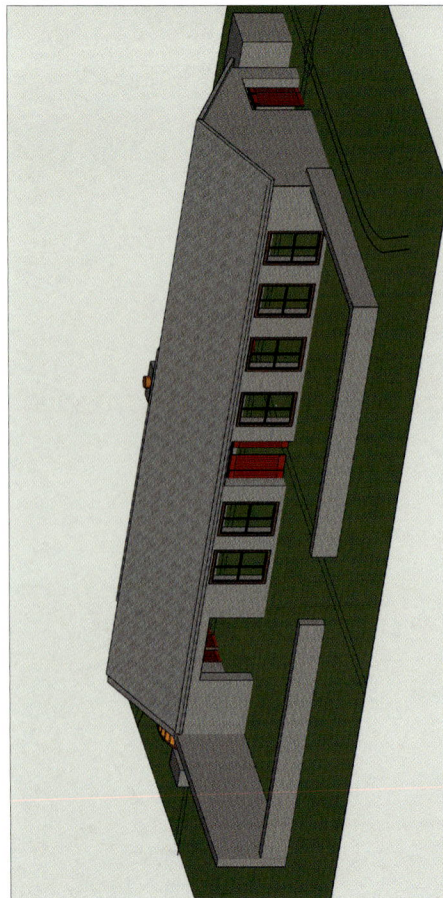

A computer model of the mill after expansion, seen from the north west. No photographs have survived from Maesygamfa's working period, so this is necessarily speculative, based on maps, ground surveys and interviews with people who recall the remains of the mill in the 1960s. The north wall of the stockyard was as high as the mill walls in anticipation of a further expansion of the mill to the west.

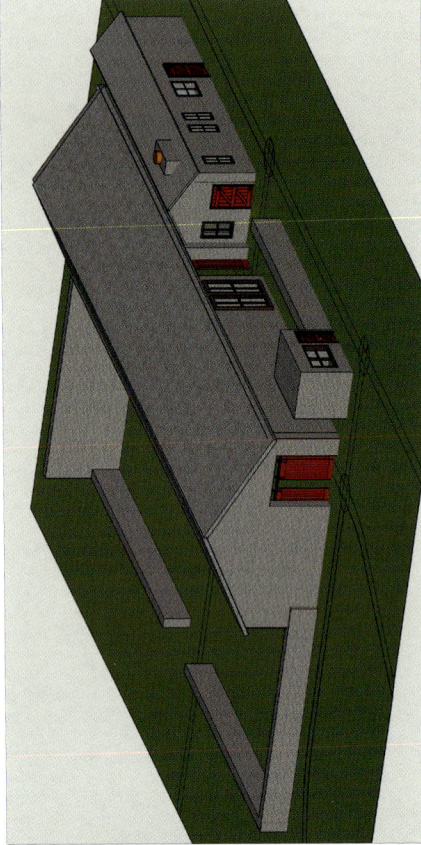

The mill from the north east — this is approximately the view from the top of the trwnc incline. The nearest building contains the smithy, stores and caban, probably converted from the cowshed. The windowless turbine house, added in 1892, is at the north end.

The mill from the south west. The striking row of tall windows would have given good light in the mill, particularly in the afternoon. The opening at the far (north) end was in the wall of the old mill and probably also had sliding doors.

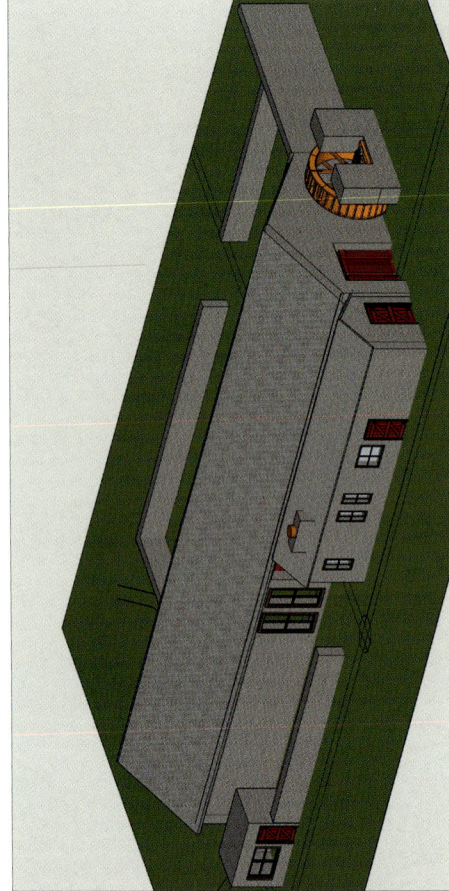

The remains of the mill from the north in 2019. The ruined buildings on the left are thought to be the smithy, caban and stores, with the turbine room nearest. One tramway ran inside the mill along the east wall; another crossed at right angles; and a third ran outside along the stockyard on the left. The telegraph pole allowed the mill to coordinate trains running down to the Hendre Ddu Tramway.
On this page the buildings on the east side of the mill are labelled: A the turbine and air compressor house, B the smithy, C the store, and D the caban/office. [Dan Quine]

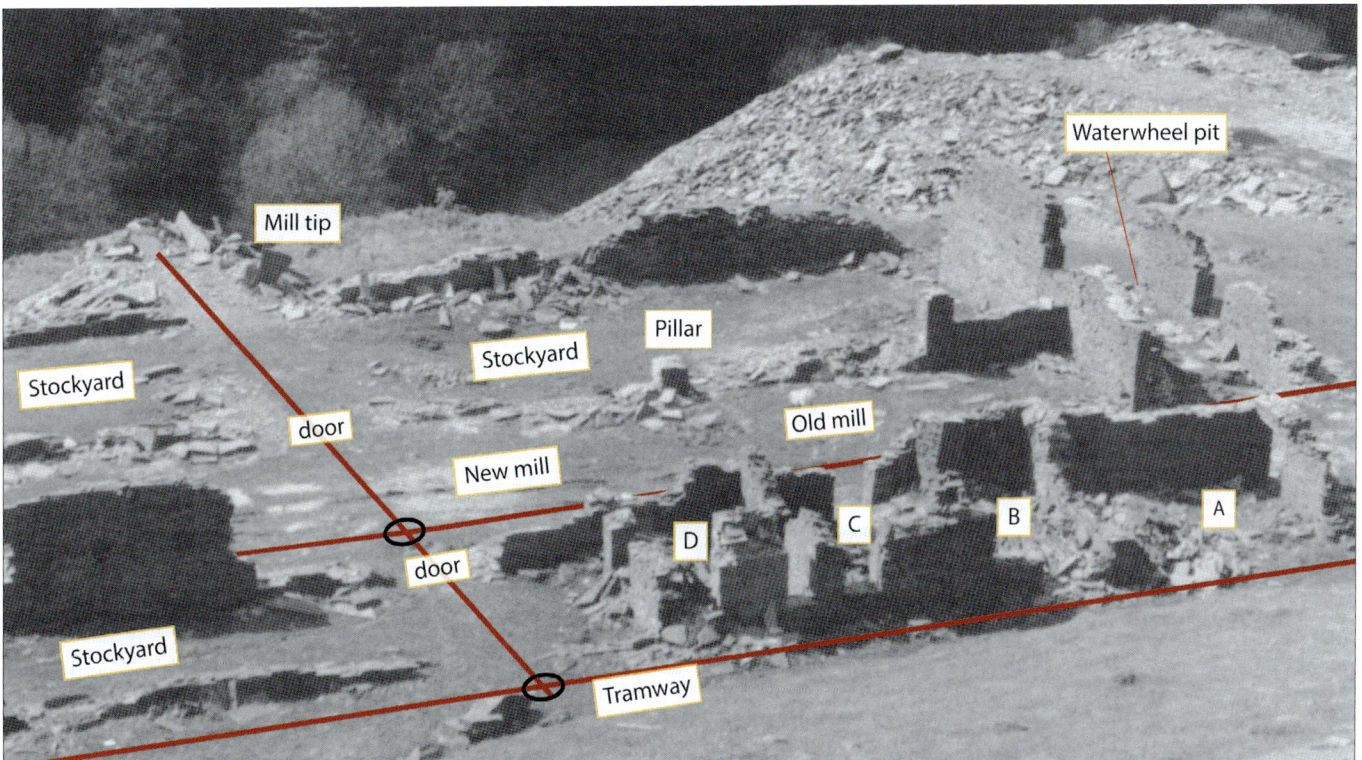

Annotated view of the mill site in August 1987, when many of the walles were higher. The pillar marked in both photographs is the southwest corner of the old mill; there is a large opening to its right. [Dave Billmore]

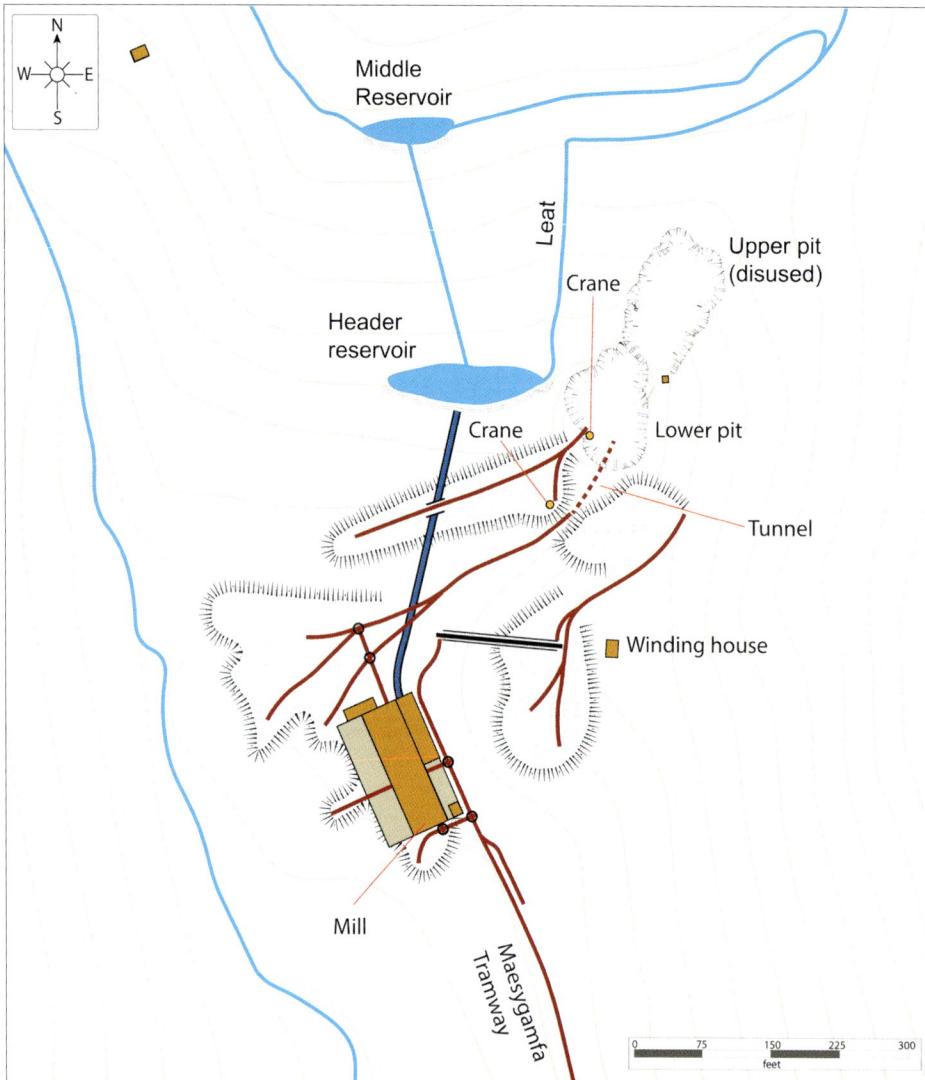

Left: The quarry in 1900 after the chamber was untopped. During untopping, slab was lifted using the crane on the edge of the pit, then lowered down to the tunnel tramway using the second crane which sat on a slate bastion. After the pit was untopped, slab from the lower pit was worked through the tunnel to the mill.

Below Left: The west wall of the deep lower pit showing the steep dip of the slate bed.
[Dan Quine]

Below right: Looking south to the mill from the header reservoir, along the route of the turbine feed pipe. The pipe dropped through the 'notch' in the waste tip below the dam wall. The lower waste tip to the right of the notch was probably created with a tramway that crossed the pipe on a low bridge. When the adit was driven in 1905, a lot more waste rock had to be tipped, and a retaining wall was built to the left of the pipe. The higher tip on the left was built up behind the wall.
[Dan Quine]

Right: The weighbridge pit, probably installed around 1905. Wagons were weighed here, then pushed back through the cutting where the rock was lowered by crane down to the mill-level tramway.
[Dan Quine]

Left: Looking south through the cutting leading to the waste tips below the header reservoir. Behind the photographer is a ledge 75ft above the pit floor. A large steel pin is embedded in the ledge where the crane was sited.
[Dan Quine]

Right: A slate sleeper on the Maesygamfa Tramway, with the outline of a chair still visible.
[Dan Quine]

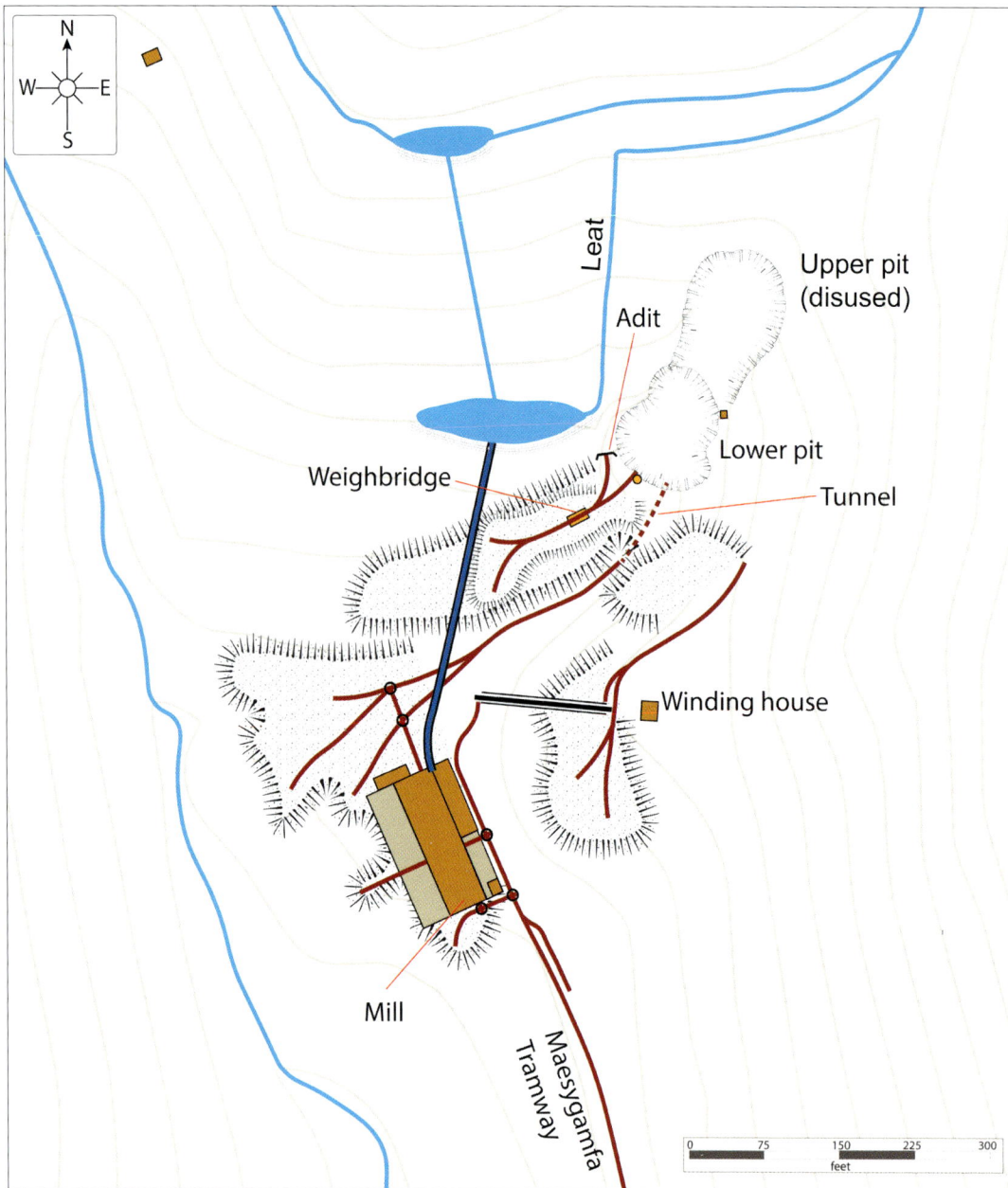

Maesygamfa in its final form in 1908. The adit and weighbridge are in place below the header reservoir.

Final Period 1911-1914

The last phase of operation was between 1911 and 1914 when Evan Jones worked the quarry with a small number of men. They appear to have worked the sout-west corner of the lower pit. The output must have been small. They had use of the mill, but it is unclear if they sent trains along the Maesygamfa Tramway.

References

1   Bill Breese, Notebook on tramroad and local quarrying, Dolgellau Archive, no. ref ZM/6541/5, c. 1970.

2   Celia Hancock, Maes y Gamfa Slate Quarry: Agricultural Building/Office/Caban, Report of the Plas Tan y Bwlch Study Group, 2018.

3   Bill Breese, Notes on local quarrying and quarrymen, Dolgellau Archive, vol. ref ZM/6541/9, 1982.

4   W. B. Horton, "RCAHMW Uplands Initiative Project," Royal Commission on the Ancient and Historical Monuments of Wales, Dec. 2012.

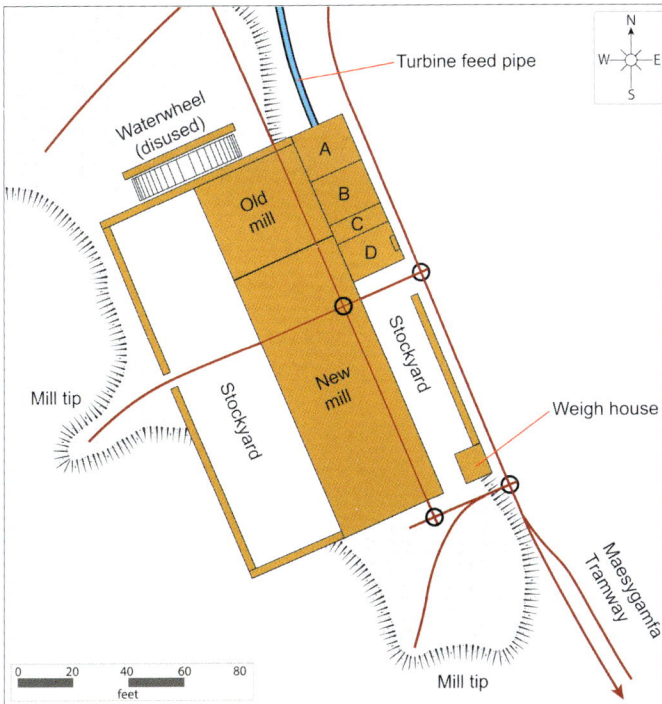

Inside the mill between 1889 and 1908; the exact layout of tramways is uncertain. The waterwheel was out of use, replaced by the turbine. The use of the buildings on the northeast side is speculative. Rock came into the north end of the mill. Processed slabs were likely first dried in the mill, then moved to the west stockyards to season. Seasoned slabs were brought into the southern section of the mill for final processing, before being stored in the east stockyard, ready for dispatch.

The wheel that controlled the outlet valve from the Maesygamfa middle reservoir. It was bolted to a vertical oak beam set in the middle of the dam wall and operated a steel sluice gate in the centre of the dam.
[Dafydd Pughe]

Looking north east from north of the mill. The upper pit is behind the grove of trees at the horizon. The trwnc incline dropped along the edge of the hillside on the right. The turbine feed pipe ran from the header reservoir, through the 'notch' in the untopping waste tip and across the site to the mill turbine house. Straight ahead, running at the foot of the left-hand waste tip is the tramway into the lower pit. [Dan Quine]

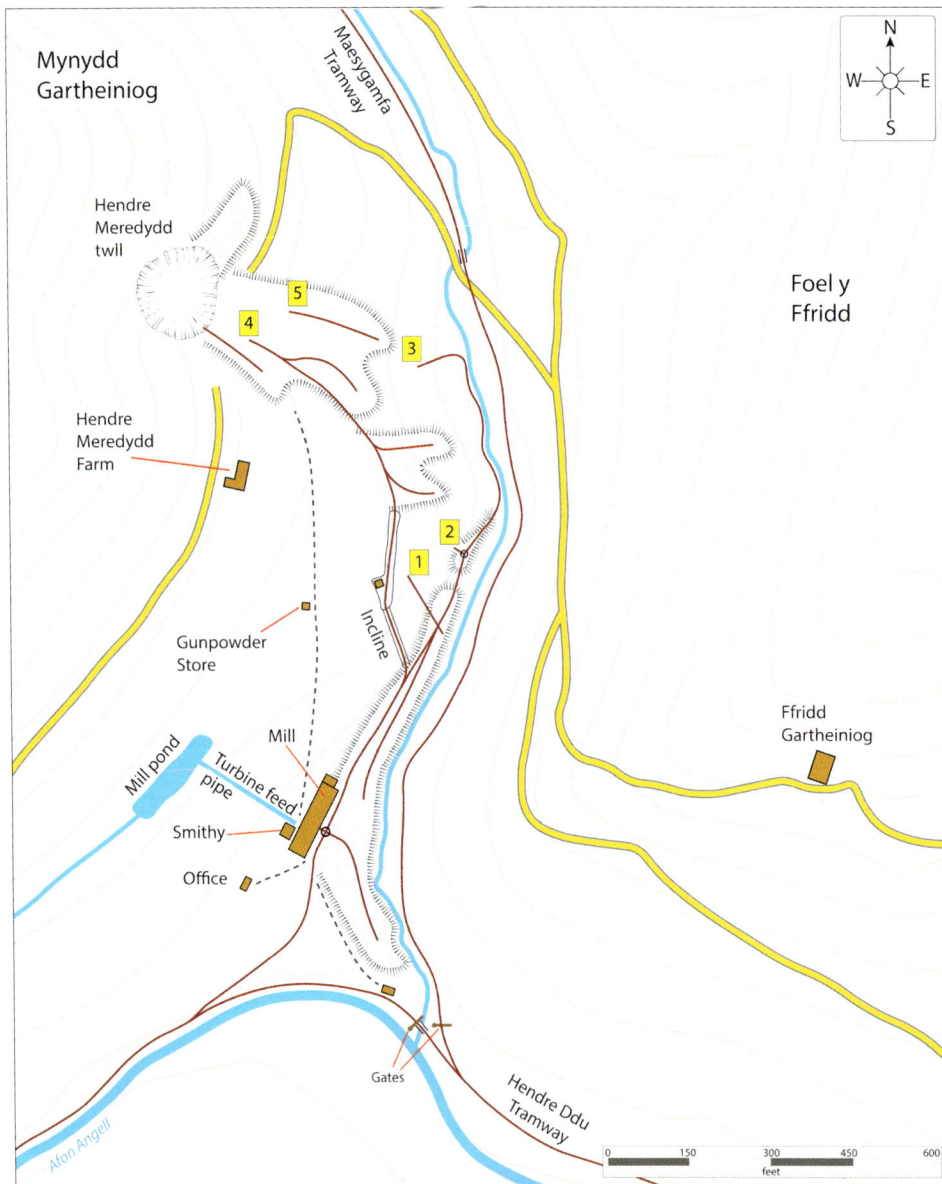

Left: The major surface features of Gartheiniog, with the tunnel portals numbered. The road past Hendre Meredydd Farm was cut in the 1890s as the pit and tips grew.

Below left: Tunnel 4 into Hendre Meredydd pit. Debris has raised the floor level, but it was never a large bore. The tunnel is about 50 feet long, with a short rock cutting at this end. The far end comes out on a small ledge about 30 feet above the present pit floor, providing just enough room for a small crane to lift wagons to this level.
[Dan Quine]

Below right: A wide view of the southeast corner of the north chamber. The chains used to move rock are the same ones shown in the Hadrill photograph from the 1930s. Lengths of flat bottomed rail litter the floor.
[Jon Knowles]

17: Gartheiniog Quarry Described

Gartheiniog Quarry stands at the confluence of the Nant Maes-y-gamfa and the Afon Angell about halfway along the Hendre Ddu Tramway. Quarrying began in 1881 when a pit was started north of Hendre Meredydd Farm. Between 1884 and December 1886, a long adit was driven from the level of Nant Maesygamfa, and two chambers were developed underground to the east of the pit; they eventually broke through into the pit.

Hendre Meredydd Pit

The quarry's initial pit was dug into the steep hillside north of Hendre Meredydd Farm, on the west side of the road. Waste carted across and tipped to the east of the road. Once the waste tip was large enough, a tramway was laid across it and a shallow incline was built down to the mill level.

By about 1889, the slate above road level had been worked out, so the pit was extended downwards. Cranes were installed to lift rock to the road, one on the southeast corner of the pit, the second to the north. Two tunnels were dug into the pit from portals 4 and 5. Tunnel 4 took rock to the mill, and waste went out through tunnel 5.

By the late 1890s, the pit floor had dropped so far that the crane on the southeast corner could no longer be used, and tunnels 4 and 5 were now above the pit floor. Ledges were left where the tunnels entered the twll, and the cranes were likely moved onto them.

Underground Workings

In 1884, Mallory and Owen started a long adit from the west bank of the Nant Maes-y-gamfa to access the vein below the pit. It reached the slate in early December 1886.

As the chamber was opened up, waste was trammed out through this adit and tipped beside the river. The tunnel was inclined slightly to the west to drain the chambers.

Where the adit met the vein, tunnels were dug at right angles and two chambers were worked towards the twll. Both eventually breaking into the pit.

The North Chamber

The north chamber is connected to the pit in two places. In the northwest corner, a steep manway runs from the chamber up to the floor of the pit, about 30ft above. There is a caban at the bottom of the manway. There is also a wide, low opening into the pit near the chamber roof in the southwest corner. Tunnels 4 and 5 cross through the rock above the chamber roof.

The South Chamber

The north chamber is a relatively conventional space; the south chamber is more unusual. It is steeply inclined to the north to reach the pit floor. The south end of the chamber has collapsed, but just before this point an inclined spiral tunnel runs into the west wall and climbs up to emerge on a working ledge near the chamber roof.

1886 Adit

The 1886 adit enabled the development of the underground chambers, and after it opened, most of the slate was removed via this adit. Unusually the adit has three portals at the south end. Portal 1 is almost certainly the original entrance – it is aligned to the bearing of the adit. By 1887, work had started on a tunnel from Portal 3, which intercepted the 1886 adit about halfway along. Another tunnel was dug from Portal 2 between 1890 and 1900. The exact reason to drive three converging tunnels is not

Looking up the incline installed during the Bowley period. The engine from the Willys-Overland locomotive powered the incline, with a pulley system to bring the haulage wires into the chamber. The pulley suspended from the roof above the end of the incline may have been part of this system.
[Jon Knowles]

Inside the main pit at Gartheiniog in May 2016, from the ledge at the end of tunnel 4. The large opening into the south chamber dominates the view. [Dan Quine]

Inside the Gartheiniog twll in 1932 or 1933. Temple Hadrill is climbing out of the south chamber. A compressed air line runs across the pit floor into the chamber: the Standard Housing Company added air-driven rock drills in 1920.
[Hadrill-McGuire family]

A collection of quarry tools found in the south chamber in May 2016.
[Jon Knowles]

The southeast corner of the north chamber, where the 1886 adit reached the vein. The tunnel continued a short way to the north before turning through ninety degrees and heading southwest. Wooden sleepers are visible in the clear water, and in the foreground, partly submerged, is the chassis of a hand winch.
[Jon Knowles]

The tunnel connecting the two chambers, in July 2020. The tunnel curves rightwards before ending in the collapsed end of the south chamber.
[Jon Knowles]

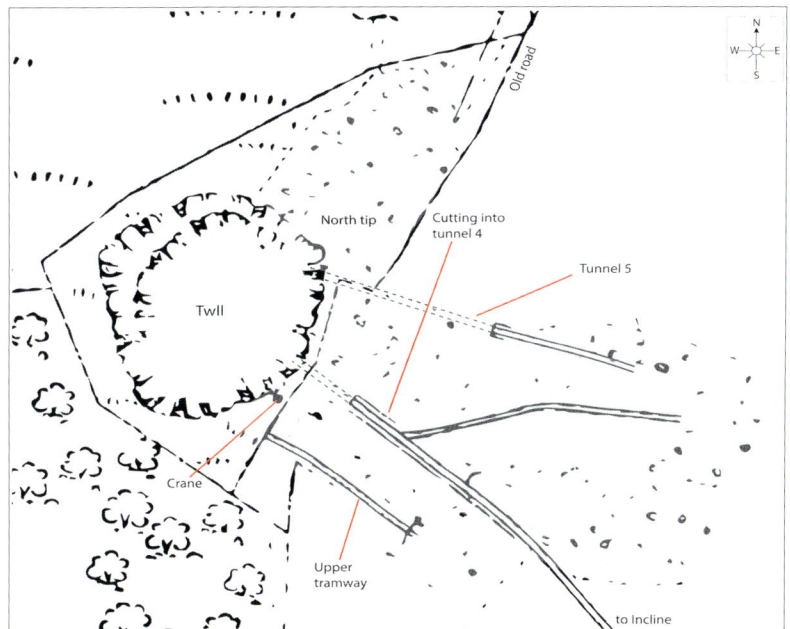

Extract from the 1901 OS Map, showing Hendre Meredydd twll. The road from Aberangell to Gartheiniog Farm had been blocked by the tips. The upper tramway ran along a tall finger tip at the level of the top of the twll, with waste lifted from the pit by crane. The tramway to the incline enters a cutting into tunnel 4 into the pit, while a short waste tramway comes out of tunnel 5.

The initials of a quarryman from August 1937, carved into the wall of the pit-end of tunnel 5. RFL is probably Richard Lewis, who worked at Gartheiniog. There is an almost identical carving underground at Ratgoed, where Lewis also worked. [Jon Knowles]

known. Aerial photography shows that Portals 1 and 2 were buried before 1948 by the Forestry Commission road from the mill towards Maesygamfa, so they cannot be surveyed.

It is clear that the ground at the south end of the tunnel was prone to collapse, and tunnels 2 and 3 were probably built to bypass roof falls. Tunnel 1 is walled off at the junction with tunnel 2, probably because it collapsed early on. The tramway leading out of Portal 1 was removed before 1900.

Mapping evidence suggests that tunnel 3 was at least started before tunnel 2 was driven. Tunnel 3 appears on the 1887, 1890 and 1900 maps but the tramway to the mill is not shown on any of them. Tunnel 2 appears on the 1900 map, but not earlier ones.

One possible explanation is that tunnel 1 collapsed near the portal shortly after it was completed. Tunnel 3 was then begun but not completed – it is relatively long and runs through hard rock, so it would have taken a year to drive. The much shorter tunnel 2 was then driven through the softer ground. Tunnel 2 also collapsed, so tunnel 3 was finally completed after 1900. Tunnel 2 may have collapsed while the quarry was idle during the First World War, with tunnel 3 being completed by SHC after the war.

The Incline

A notable feature of the surface tramway from the twll to the mill is the incline halfway along. It was probably built in 1881 or 1882 as the pit was developing. The line from the pit arrives on a low slate embankment about 3ft high. The winding house sits below this level, with the bottom of the drum below rail level and the top not far above it. One cable passes under the drum and through a trench between the rails, surfacing just before the crimp. The other cable passes over the drum and above the rails.

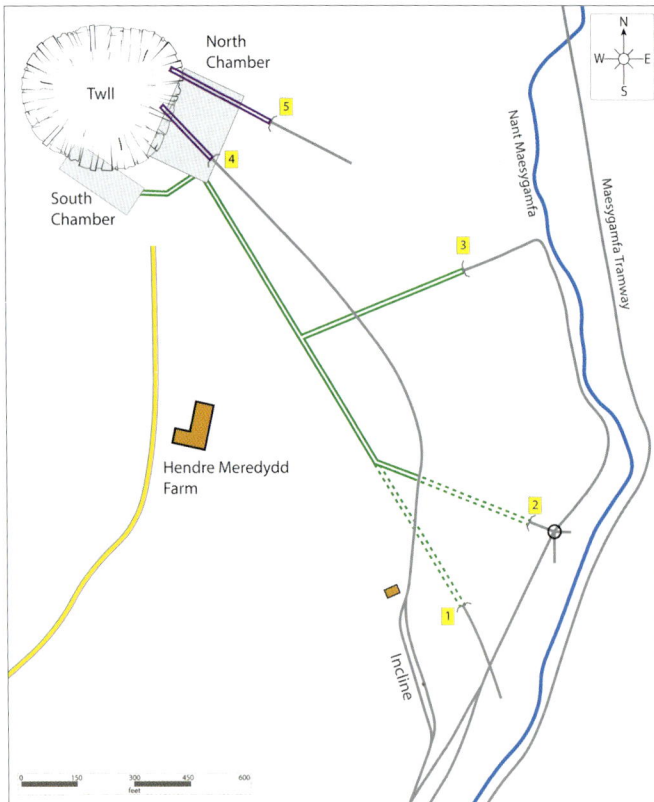

The general layout of the underground workings at Gartheiniog. Portals 1, 2 and 3 are at 390ft above sea level. The tunnels from portals 1 and 2 are collapsed at their southern ends. Tunnels 4 and 5 are at 500ft above sea level and run above the north chamber.

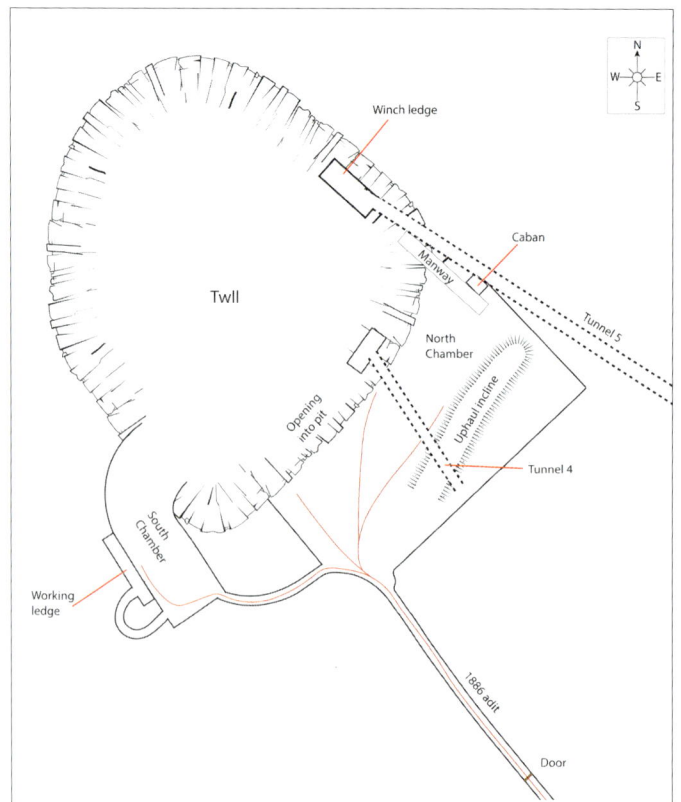

A schematic of the underground workings based on sketches by Jon Knowles. Tunnel 5 is collapsed near the portal. The approximate route of the underground tramways in the early 1930s is shown.

Right: The caban in the north chamber. Lunch would be eaten here, and it was also a shelter during blasting. The opening to the left is the manway that rises into the pit.
[Jon Knowles]

Left: Looking north west towards the two openings into the north chamber. On the right is the manway up into the pit, on the left is the wider opening at roof level. Huge fallen boulders litter the chamber floor, illustrating the dangerous conditions underground.
[Jon Knowles]

Right: Looking down into the south chamber. Above the explorer's head is the working ledge, and far below him is the chamber floor. At the left end of the working ledge is the upper exit of the spiral tunnel through the rock down to the chamber floor — its lower entrance can be seen at the bottom of the chamber near the chains.
[Jon Knowles]

The trackbed of the tramway from the mill to tunnel 3, running on a shelf of slate waste. There are walls on both sides of the tramway as it follows the curves of Nant Maes-y-gamfa. The Maesygamfa Tramway parallels this line on the other side of the stream.
[Dan Quine]

Looking north west into the deep cutting leading to tunnel 3, in May 2016. The Nant Maesygamfa is immediately behind the photographer. The portal is blocked by debris fallen from above, but the tunnel is intact.
[Dan Quine]

The remains of a Pelton wheel at Devon United Mines, near Dartmoor. The feed pipe is also held in place by u-shaped walling and there is a control valve just before the pipe joins the turbine.
[Ian Castledine]

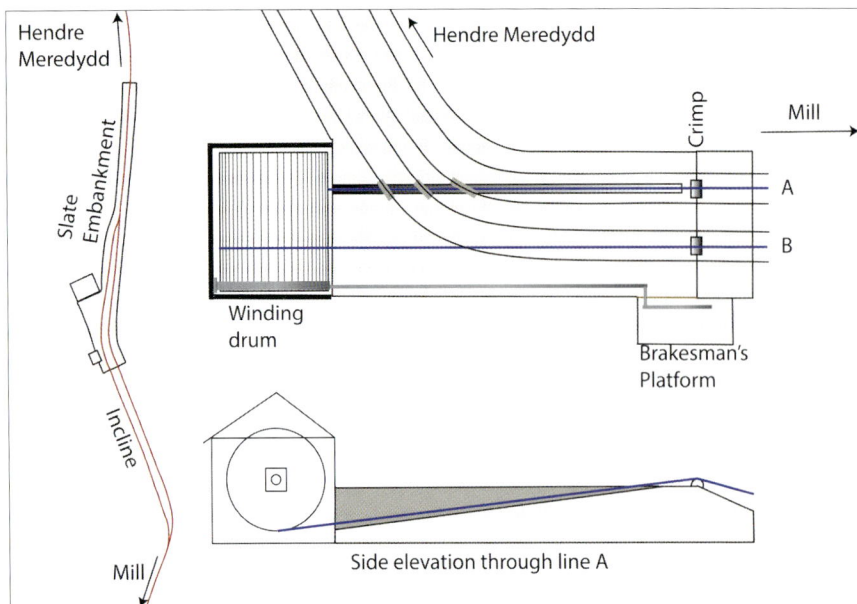

Sketch of the Gartheiniog Incline, from contemporary maps and a field survey in May 2016. The exact arrangement and measurements are not known. Loaded wagons would alternate between lines A and B.

The first phase of Gartheiniog mill, between 1881 and 1884, based on modern ground surveys and maps. The west wall of the mill was likely open with a pillar for the roof, giving access to the slab storage yard beyond.

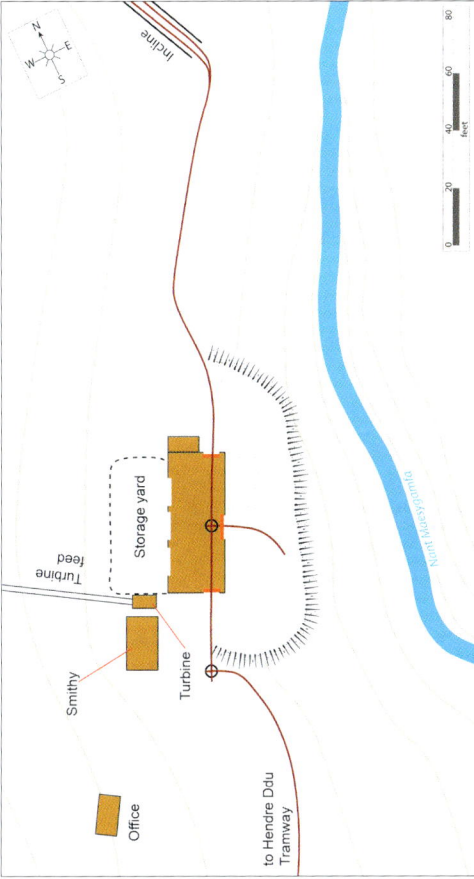

The extended mill, around 1888. The building is now about 80ft. long with a lean-to against the north wall. The waste tip to the east has grown. Tunnel 1 has been driven north of the incline but is not connected to the mill.

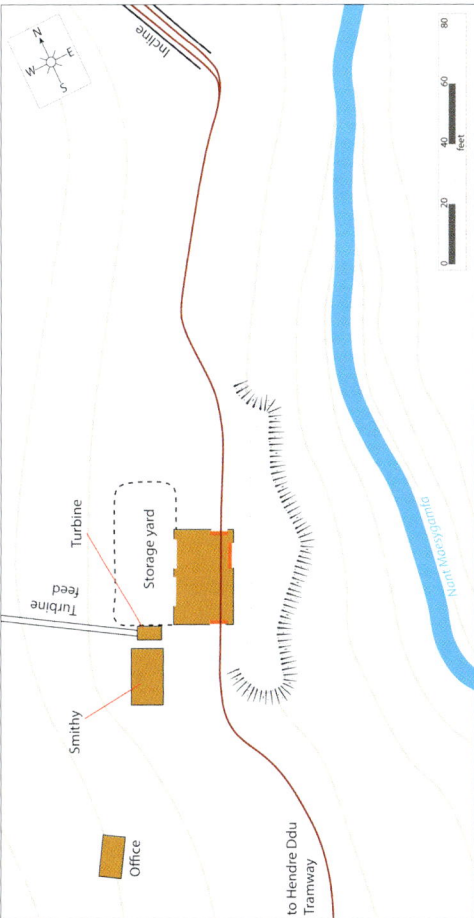

Gartheiniog Mill in 1900. The building has been expanded southwards to its full length. The main tramway has been rerouted to run outside the east wall, and there is now a tramway from adit 2. The tips have grown substantially, mostly waste from the underground chamber, and this has allowed the tramway from the foot of the incline to the mill to be rerouted to the east.

The east side of the mill in May 2016. The original 1880/81 rubble wall runs from the right edge of the nearest doorway to the second doorway. The mill was extended north and south with sawn blocks produced in the original mill. [Dan Quine]

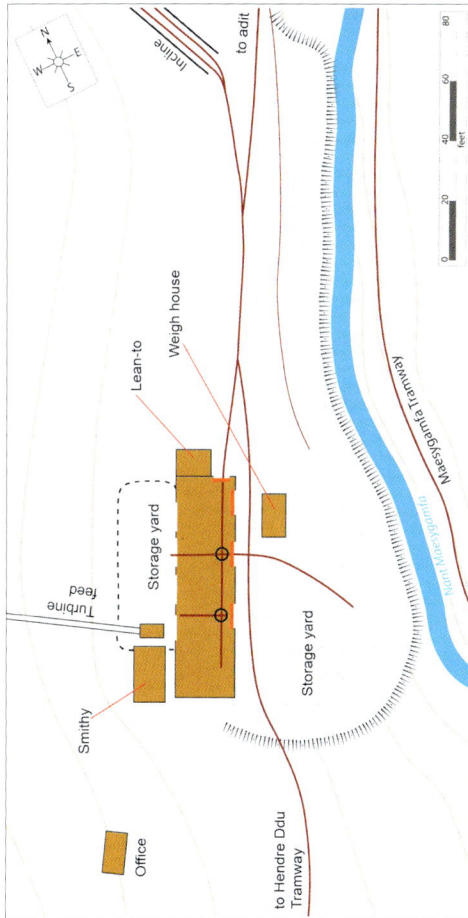

Looking north along the west wall of the mill from within the smithy. This side was originally open, with the roof supported by a series of pillars. The openings were later filled in with slate and corrugated iron. The flat area behind the mill was the original slab storage yard. [Dan Quine]

The mill from the north west in May 2016, showing the massive buttress holding up the rebuilt north wall. [Dan Quine]

The reason for this unusual arrangement is not clear. The winding house is positioned a long way behind the crimp, and a more conventional arrangement with the drum above the tracks near the crimp would have been easier to construct and operate.

The Mill

Gartheiniog Mill is a substantial construction, built in three phases. It is the only quarry mill standing in Dyffryn Angell.

The original building was about 40ft long, constructed on a flat area built up from slate waste. Its walls were of loose rubble with heavy mortaring. To the south west was the smithy, a simple slate building about 20ft by 10ft with a gable roof and a prominent chimney for the forge. Both buildings were likely erected in 1880 or 1881.

There is a reservoir on the hillside 100ft above the mill, fed by a leat from the Afon Angell. A 12-inch diameter pipe fed water to an undershot Pelton wheel next to the smithy. The Pelton wheel may have been a later replacement, though there is no evidence of an earlier water wheel. At least one sawing table was installed in this first mill, allowing the production of sawn blocks.

Sawn blocks produced in the mill were used to extend the building northwards around 1884 when Mallory expanded operations at Gartheiniog. The mill was now approximately 80ft long. The reservoir was also enlarged to provide a larger head of water. Gartheiniog struggled for water during the dry summer months and often could not operate the mill for days at a time.

A lean-to building was added against the north wall of the expanded mill, possibly a caban or storeroom. The tramway from the incline entered the mill through a door in the north wall, and ran the length of the building,

Inside the mill in 2016, showing the heavy roof trusses that span its full width and the sliding north door. There were ten of these king-post trusses along the length of the mill. The wooden pillar in the foreground was added by the Forestry Commission for extra support as this truss is suffering from rot. The door was the main access point for the tramway, bringing rock from the quarry. As slabs were moved south along the mill they were first sawn, then planed, then polished. [Dan Quine]

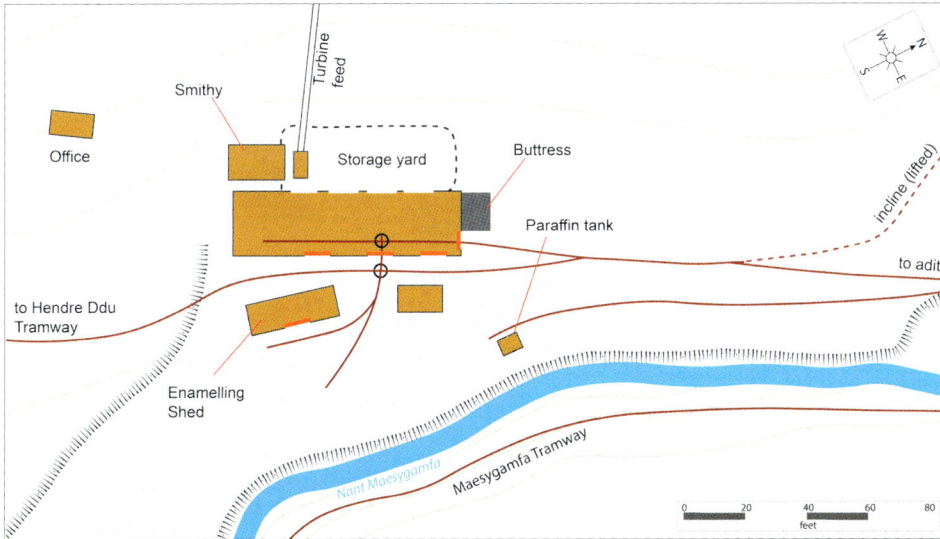

Gartheiniog Mill, during the late 1930s, based on sketch maps by Bill Breese who worked there from 1935 to 1937, and contemporary photographs.

1913 photograph in Chapter 7 shows the lean-to and a window under the gable in the north wall. It appears the north wall collapsed, most likely during the shutdown in the First World War. The wall was rebuilt without the window and with the buttress, presumably to guard against further collapse.

An enamelling shed was built east of the mill by Temple Hadrill in 1932. It was the last major building added to the site and was mostly demolished before 1946, though a section of the wall survived until the early 1970s.

During the Bowley years, most probably in 1935, a Petter oil engine was installed between the smithy and the turbine house for use when the reservoir ran low. It was mounted on a concrete base, held down by four embedded bolts. On the north side is a smaller concrete base, with two bolts, which held a bearing. The axle between the engine and the bearing had a pulley that drove the overhead line shafting in the mill via a flat belt.

South west of the mill is the Manager's Office. It is a red brick building dating from the Second World War that was used by the firewatcher when the mill stored ammunition during the war.[3] The office is on a large slate platform, with a ramp running up from the southeast corner of the mill. The platform is substantially older than the building, dating from between 1887 and 1889, and was built as a foundation for the original manager's house.

exiting through a door in the south wall. South of the mill a turntable connected to the steep line down to the Hendre Ddu Tramway. The storage yard was still on the west of the building.

Between 1889 and 1900, the building was extended south, again using lightly mortared sawn blocks. This took the mill to its final size of 143ft x 40ft. The waste tips on the east side had grown considerably by 1900 filling the area between the mill and Nant Maes-y-gamfa.

A weighbridge and weighhouse were added east of the mill before 1900. The tramway was rerouted onto the waste tip, as the south wall of the new extension did not have an exit door. This removed the need for a turntable south of the mill. The mill appears to have been re-roofed when it was extended south. The extant roof is a single gable covered with open half-slates to provide ventilation, a method called *tô brat* in Welsh. There are nine skylights in the east pitch. The roof is topped by ceramic tiles and slates cover the barge-board.[1]

A substantial slate buttress later replaced the lean-to. The

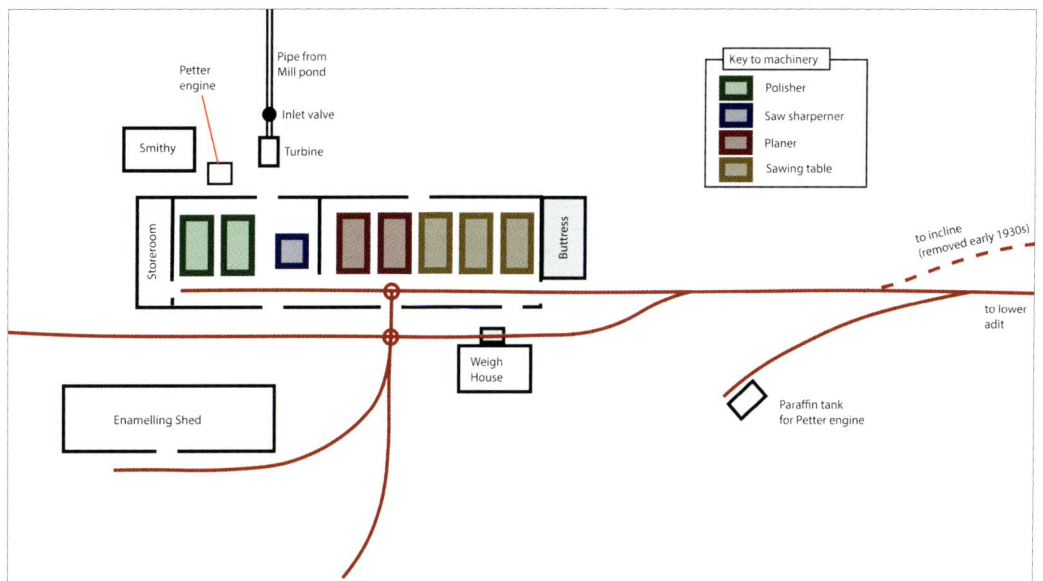

Schematic of Gartheiniog Mill interior in the 1930s, based on a sketch map by Bill Breese, notes by Ifan Meirion Edwards who worked there from 1933 to 1937[2] and contemporary photographs.

The only known photograph of the interior of the mill when operating, taken in 1932 or 1933, looking north along the east wall. The door at the end is the same one shown in the 2016 photograph. The partition wall on the left was taken down after the Second World War. In the foreground are two planers, used to give the slabs a flat surface. Beyond are the three sawing tables used to cut rock to size. All these machines are driven from an overhead shaft running parallel to the west wall – a drive pulley from the shaft can be seen on the nearest planer. The overhead crane suspended from the roof trusses was used to move slabs between the machines. On the right is a trestle wagon – shorn of its trestle – on the line leading to the enamelling shed and waste tips.
[Hadrill-McGuire family]

References

1   Celia Hancock, Gartheiniog slate mill, Report of the Plas Tan y Bwlch Study Group, 2016.

2   Lewis Cozens, R.W. Kidner, Brian Poole, *The Mawddwy, Van and Kerry Branches*, Oakwood Press, 2004.

3   Marieanne Mills, Jul. 2016.

The relatively modern Manager's Office on the slate platform. [Dan Quine]

The west side of Gartheiniog Mill in May 2016. In the right foreground is the bottom of the pipe from the reservoir which fed the Pelton wheel, held between concrete blocks. On the left is the concrete base of the Petter oil engine installed in 1935. Beyond and to the right are the walls of the smithy, a rubble-walled building dating back to 1880.
[Dan Quine]

18: Hendreddu Quarry Described

Hendreddu was the largest of the quarries in Dyffryn Angell. It began as a series of open pits where the Narrow Vein outcrops in Cwm Hendreddu. To the east of the pits, faults run across the site, displacing the vein to the north.

In 1870, James Gillart oversaw the first underground working at Hendreddu when Gillart's Level was driven into the vein east of the open pits. In 1873, a 470ft long adit was driven from the mill level northwest into the vein. A series of chambers were opened on this level. Eventually, chambers were worked on five levels as further adits were driven into the hillside.

Exit Incline and Tramway

The Hendre Ddu Tramway terminated on the east bank of the Afon Angell. From here, the exit incline rose 204ft at about 1 in 3 to 790ft elevation.[1] The winding house was set back from and above the incline crimp. It had a horizontal drum mounted on a square wooden axle with an iron band brake. The brake lever was three yards long, and the brakesman stood on a high slate platform with a view down the incline, though it was very exposed to the weather. The rear wall was reinforced with a length of grooved tram rail.

The mountain is now covered in forest, but when the incline was operating it was on an open hillside. Unfortunately, no photographs survive of the incline in use and the top and foot were lost when the Forestry Commission built roads across the trackbed in the 1960s. It had three rails, with a passing loop in the middle. Above the crimp, the tracks turned sharply east and a single-bladed point joined the lines into a regular two-rail track. There was a similar arrangement at the foot.

A tramway ran about half a mile from the top of the incline to the quarry. There was a short siding below the winding house, for loaded wagons waiting to descend.

The Mill Level

The tramway from the incline ended at a weighbridge on the east side of the manager's house. The mill level

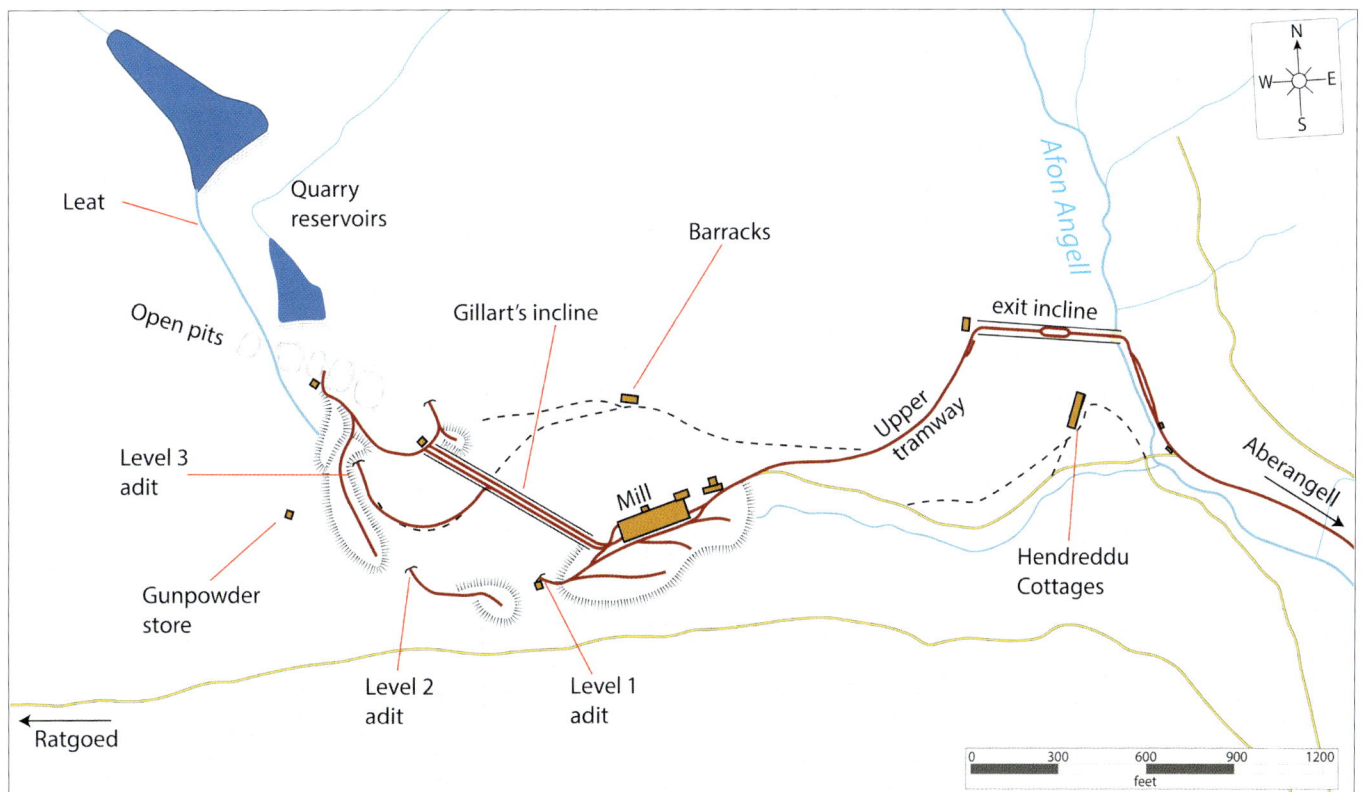

The main surface features at Hendreddu – though not all of the tramways existed at the same time. Quarrying started in the open pits which follow the outcrop of the Narrow Vein. The adits were driven to the vein from the mill level upwards. Gillart's incline, built in 1870, allowed slab to be taken down from the pits to the mill. The exit incline was built shortly afterwards.

The winding house in 2005, showing the rough stone walling and remains of the wooden drum axle. On the right end of the axle is the brake band. The brakesman stood on a platform in front of the right wall; the platform and incline crimp were destroyed when a Forestry Commission road was built along the route of the quarry tramway.

The grooved tramway rail at the rear of the winding house. It formed a strong anchor point for the band brake.
[Both Dave Billmore]

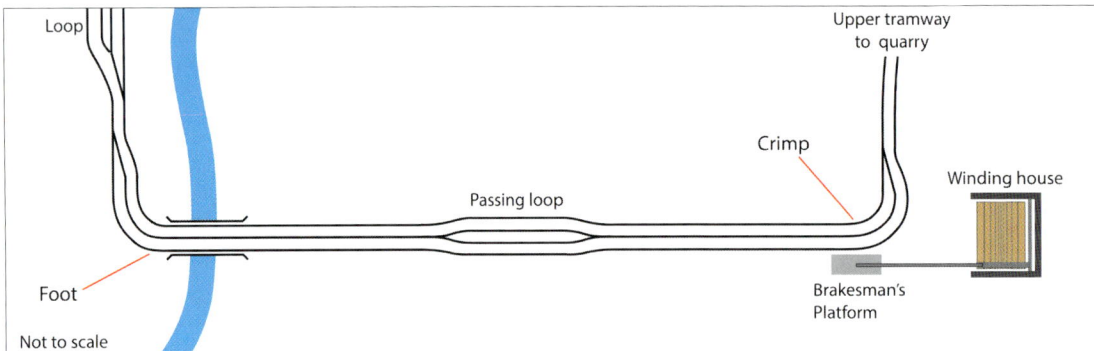

Schematic diagram showing the track arrangement of the exit incline

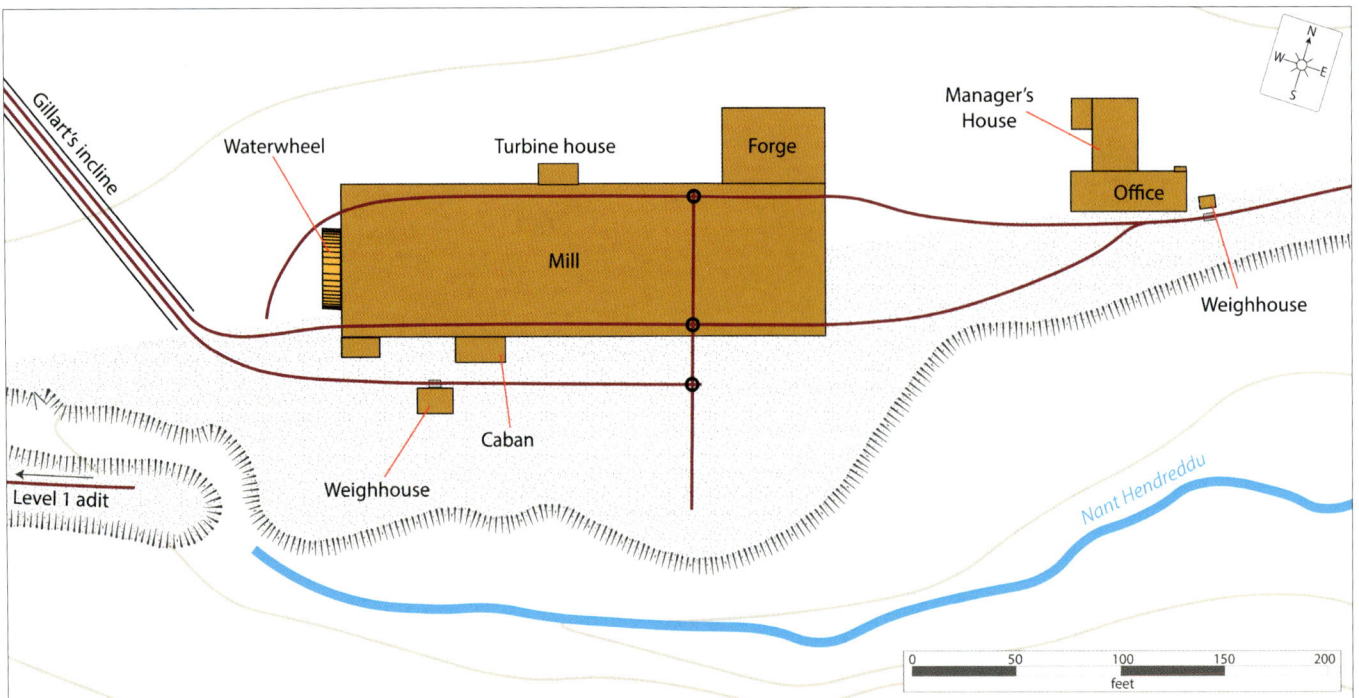

The mill level in 1887-1889 during Jacob and Dennis Bradwell's tenure. Slate arrived down Gillart's incline. The tramway from the Level 1 adit, seen bottom left, was not connected to the mill at this time. The tramway layout in the mill is speculative.

Right: The Hendreddu manager's house and office are the only mill-level buildings that survived after 1946. To the right, behind the temporary fencing, is the site of the weighbridge. From here the tramway followed the contour of the hill to the top of the exit incline – the trackbed is now a forestry road.
[Dan Quine]

Left: The manager's house, in 1925. Henry Davies, the clerk of the quarry, stands next to the office door. The weighhouse is a corrugated iron building, similar to the flour store on Aberangell Wharf. It was likely installed in 1920 to replace an earlier slate building.

Engineer's workshop

Store

Manager's house

Weigh house

Tramway

Quarry office

Below: The mill level in 1900. Gillart's Incline has been abandoned, and all slate is coming from the Level 1 adit, which is connected directly to the mill. The waste tips have greatly expanded in the previous decade, covering part of Nant Hendreddu. A carpenter's shop has been added to the side of the forge, and a stable block next to the office.

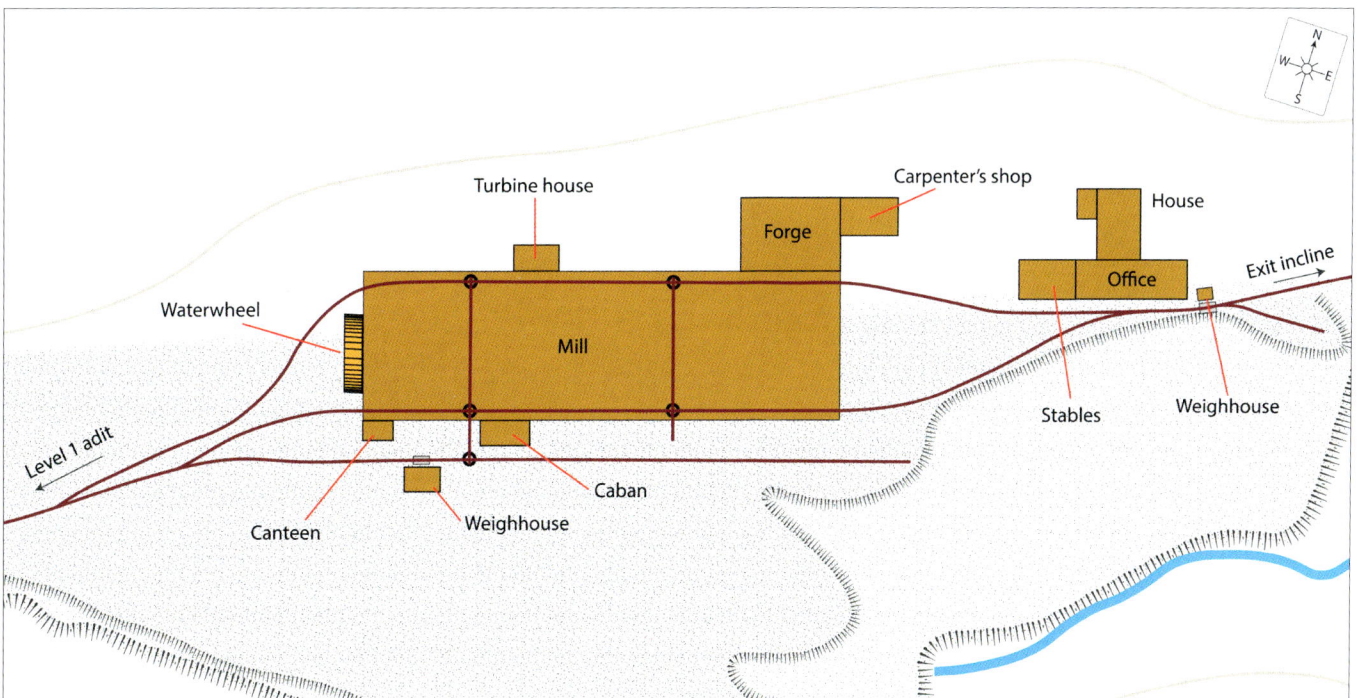

Turbine house

Carpenter's shop

Forge

House

Waterwheel

Office

Exit incline

Mill

Level 1 adit

Stables

Weighhouse

Canteen

Weighhouse

Caban

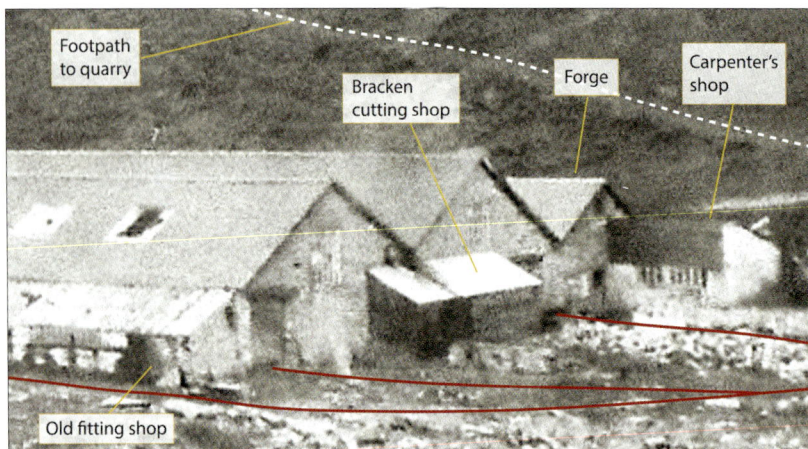

Left: The east end of the mill in 1925, showing the cluster of sheds surrounding the main building. The carpenter's shop was added after 1889. The forge was the social hub of the quarry, especially in winter when it was a haven from the cold. The forge may be the pre-1873 mill building, though this is speculation. The bracken cutting shop was used to store and dry bracken, which was used as a packing material for products going down the tramway in box wagons.

Left: The west end of the Hendreddu Mill taken in 1925, showing the Paxman Shed offset from the mill's west wall.

Below: The interior of the mill following a severe storm, probably in the winter of 1938/39. Snow was driven inside and covered everything. The middle photo is looking along the north wall. A flat wagon sits on the right, next to a wagon turntable. In the distance, barely visible, is the door into the mill store. The crane installed by Bill Milns can be seen below the roof trusses. This is very similar to the crane at Gartheiniog Mill. The right photo is looking west along the north wall, with slabs stacked for drying. In the distance is the sprung-top wagon. [Courtesy John Breese]

was built on a platform of waste from the open pits and the Level 1 adit. The tramway ran in front of the manager's house – which still stands – then entered the impressive mill building to the west. Beyond the mill, Gillart's incline rose to the level of the open pits, just above the 1000ft contour. The Level 1 adit was on the mill level, about 300 feet beyond the foot of Gillart's incline.

The original mill building was built around 1868, though little is known about it. In 1873, Buckley built a new mill at great expense. It stood, with modifications, until 1946.

The mill was a substantial building, measuring 236ft by 62ft[2] (14,600 square feet). It had a double gable roof with ten skylights in the south-facing pitch – there were further skylights in the other pitches, but the number is unknown. The mill was built in anticipation of much greater production than was ever realised. For comparison, the main mill at Maenofferen Quarry in Blaenau Ffestiniog was 330ft by 120ft (39,600 square feet). In 1901, Hendreddu produced a modest 630 tons of slate, while Maenofferen produced 11,294 tons[3] eighteen times more output from a mill just twice the size.

There were other buildings on the mill level, some next to the mill, and others by the manager's house. In front of the house was the quarry office, with part set aside as a store. An engineer's workshop was added to the west.

The mill was well equipped from the outset. The 1876 sale listed sixteen saw tables, eight planing machines, and machinery for saw-tiling and punching. The development of the mill is not entirely clear and it changed rapidly as working developed. The earliest maps show that rock

The open pits and reservoir system at Hendreddu before 1925. Not all of the tramways existed at the same time. The dashed blue line shows the approximate course of Nant Hendreddu before it was dammed; it followed one of the faults that run across the site. The discontinuity in the narrow vein caused by another fault can be seen above Gillart's Level.

Mill level from 1925 onwards, based on a Bill Breese sketch and contemporary photographs. The Paxman shed and store have been added to the west. A new turbine was installed as part of the electrical system in the 1920s. A partition wall was added next to the main turbine house. The tramway system was greatly extended, with the purchase of additional turntables, probably from Hudsons of Leeds.

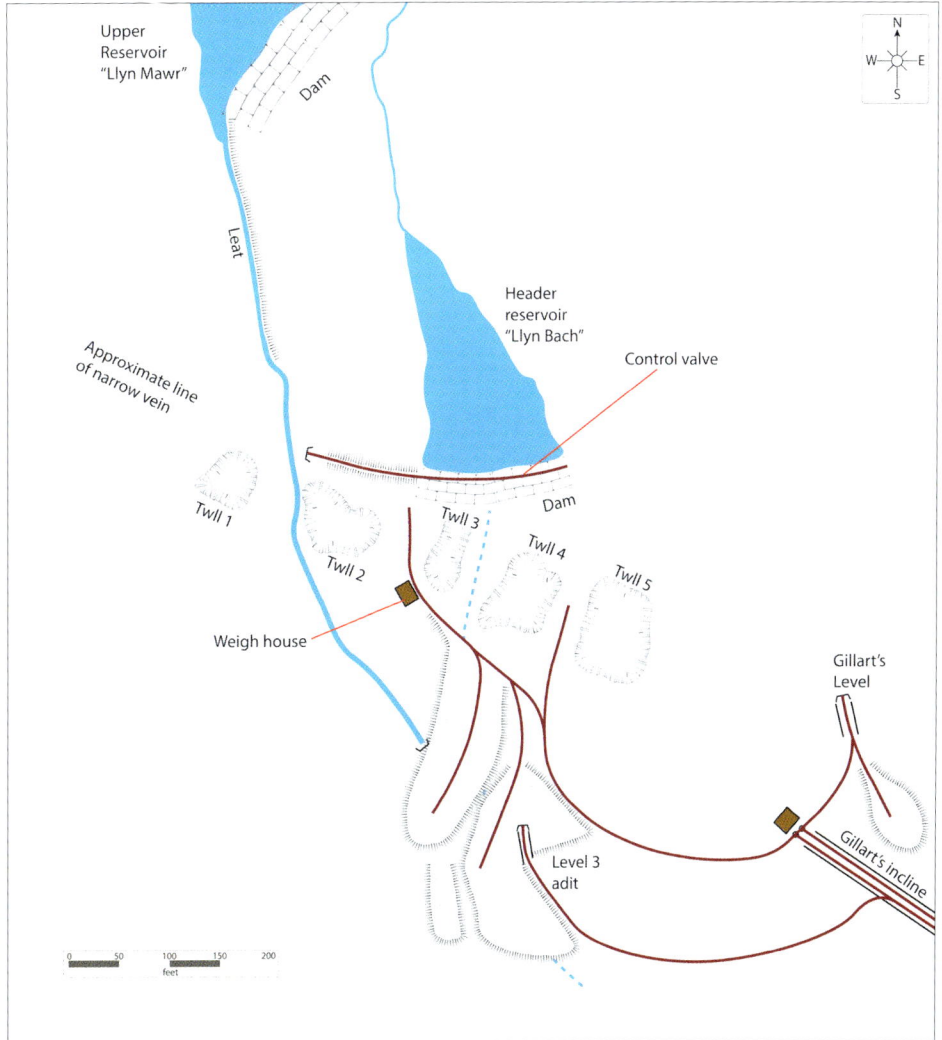

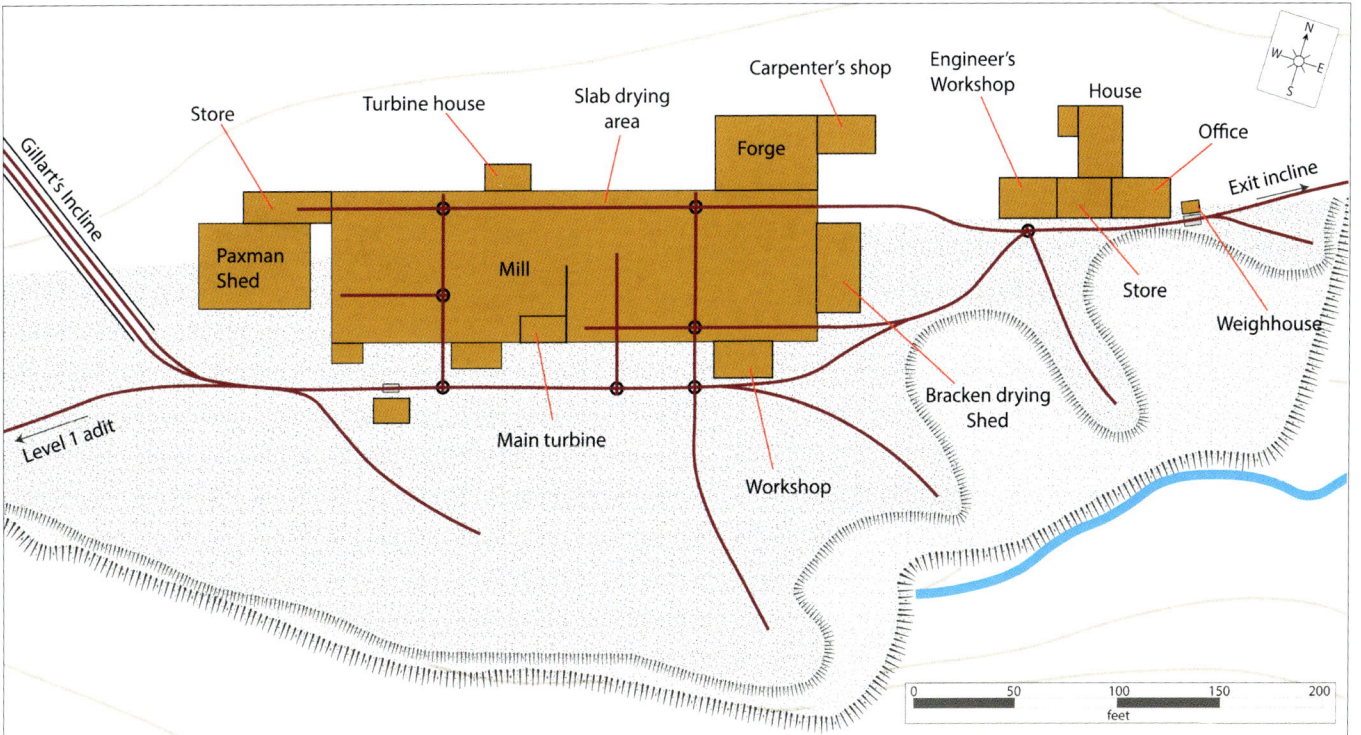

Left: The dam of the upper reservoir, looking east, with the start of the leat in the foreground.
[Chris Andrews]

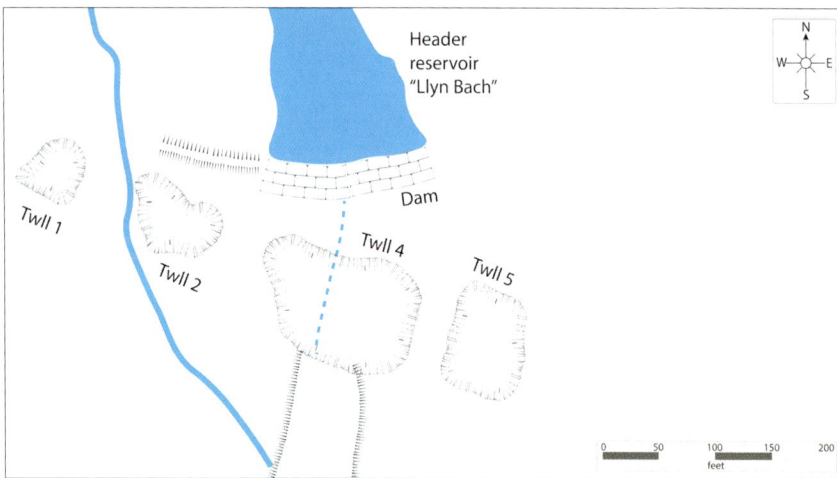

Header reservoir "Llyn Bach"

Dam

Twll 1

Twll 2

Twll 4

Twll 5

0   50   100   150   200
feet

Left: The pits after 1925, following the collapse. The rock wall between Twll 3 and Twll 4 fell into the chambers below, creating the combined Twll 4, which covers a greater area than the earlier pits; in particular, the pit has been extended to the south.

Below: The boom pulley of the 1925 derrick crane still sits in Twll 4 in 2018. The pulley sat on the end of the boom, and the lifting rope was fed over it. It appears the crane was pushed or fell into the pit after it was no longer needed. Other components of the crane can also be found here including some broken winch cogs, and the double-wheeled mast pulley.
[Alasdair Roberts]

Left: The north wall of Twll 4 in 1925, after the collapse. Rubble covers the pit floor. The lifting derrick stands on the edge of the pit. The distinctive rock formation in the centre is 'The Nose' and appears on Bill Breese's sketch maps drawn in the late 1930s. This is the remains of the wall that separated Twll 3 (on the left) from Twll 4. The level of the original floor of Twll 4 can be seen on the near side of The Nose.
[Mark Waite collection]

Right: Looking east across the top of Twll 5. The tramway to the head of Gillart's Incline ran from here, off to the right.
[Dan Quine]

Left: The bottom of the east wall of Twll 4, showing the tunnel running into Twll 5. Though untopped now, this tunnel was originally at the floor level of Chamber 3.2.
[Alasdair Roberts]

Right: Inside Twll 4 in March 2018. The person on the pit floor gives a sense of scale – the pit is about 70ft deep here. The tunnel through to Twll 5 is just to the right of the figure, while about halfway up the north wall is the northern end of the original Level 3 tunnel, just below the roof of Chamber 3.2. The Nose is off to the left.
[E.A. Lockhart]

arrived via Gillart's Incline. They also show relatively few ancillary buildings around the office and mill.

The 1876 sales list shows the mill was powered by a turbine fed from the quarry reservoirs. By 1887, a waterwheel had been added against the west wall of the mill; this was likely an overshot wheel. Whether this augmented or replaced the turbine is unknown. It may have been added by the Bradwells after they took over in April 1879.

In the early 1880s, the Level 2 adit was connected to Gillart's incline, but in the 1890s Gillart's Incline was abandoned and slate was brought out through the Level 1 adit. The tramways entering the mill from the west were realigned to suit. Two new buildings were added to the mill complex: a carpenter's shop next to the forge and what is believed to have been a stable block next to the office. This was used for the horses and donkeys that hauled wagons around the quarry and to the exit incline.

Sometime between 1901 and 1911, the waterwheel was removed and from then on the mill relied on turbines. It is unlikely that significant further changes occurred between 1900 and the First World War, as the quarry was operating at a loss.

The next major changes occurred when first National Welsh Slate Quarries Ltd and then Hendre-ddu Slate Quarries Ltd invested in the quarry. Two new buildings were added at the west end of the mill, and the office was rearranged.

A large two-storey shed was built to house the stationary engine from Davey, Paxman & Co. though it was never installed. The shed was offset from the west wall of the mill by about the width of the water wheel. They may have intended to reuse the waterwheel's gearing, driven by the new engine. Behind the Paxman Shed was a store, probably a single storey building.

The Open Pits and Reservoirs

The first pit to be developed under the Buckley regime was Twll 4[5] on the east bank of Nant Hendreddu. It is thought that Twll 3 was David Hughes's early working that predates the opening of Buckley's quarry.

Once larger-scale work started in the 1870s, new pits were dug, both east and west of Tyllau 3 and 4. When the first mill was built around 1868/69 it needed a water supply for its turbine. Nant Hendreddu was dammed just above the pits to form the header reservoir. The dam was created from Broad Vein rock extracted via a short adit to the north of Twll 2. A tramway was run out of the adit and the rock was tipped to form the dam. Water was piped across the hillside and down to the mill to drive the turbine – probably next to Gillart's Incline.

When the mill was expanded in 1873/4, a larger reservoir was needed. This was built upstream of the first reservoir. It had about three times the surface area of the lower reservoir and was 45ft deep.

A leat was run along the west side of the valley, above the lower reservoir, between Twll 1 and Twll 2 and past the tips below the open pits.

Cranes were used to remove both waste and good rock from the pits; at first, these would have been small, hand-worked derricks. A 10-ton steam crane was installed before 1876 and most likely as part of the 1873 expansion. It was located on the north edge of Twll 2 in the 1880s and 1890s and lifted rock to a tramway that ran to the head of Gillart's incline. There was a building adjacent to the tramway, most likely a weigh house. Although all five pits had been started by 1887, most early production concentrated on Twll 2, which appears to have been worked out by the mid-1890s.

The open pits were superseded by underground working, and they fell out of use before 1900. The steam crane was still in situ in 1901, but had gone before the First World War; it was most likely sold in 1908 when Jacob Bradwell's executors disposed of some of the quarry equipment.

The 1925 collapse significantly reshaped the quarry. The chambers underneath Twll 3 and Twll 4 collapsed, and the floors of both pits fell with them. Most of the rock wall dividing the two pits also fell, creating one much larger pit. The chambers below Twll 3 and Twll 4 were filled with fallen rock and the tunnels into the chambers blocked. The now much larger and deeper Twll 4 was left with a substantial amount of fallen rock in it. A lot of the rock that had formed the pillars and roof of the collapsed chambers was good quality Narrow Vein slate. This presented the company with a great opportunity, and a derrick was installed on the north edge of Twll 4 to start lifting it out. The crane appears to have been built from components of the stiff leg derrick on Aberangell Wharf, dismantled at about the same time.

The fallen slate at the bottom of Twll 4 was extracted for the next few years and appears to have been the major source of rock for the mill. The tramway from the top of Gillart's incline to the pits was relaid in 1925 and ran over the isthmus between Twll 4 and Twll 5.

By 1931, it was no longer possible to lift fallen rock out of Twll 4 using the derrick. This prompted the purchase of the steam crane from Dolbadau Quarry that was damaged on the journey up from Aberangell and never installed.

When T. Glyn Williams took over Hendreddu in 1937, he first worked the underground chambers. He also investigated Twll 4, which still contained considerable amounts of workable rock from the 1925 collapse. The slate removed between 1925 and 1934 had left the Level 3 tunnels almost exposed, and Williams was able to unblock the southern portal. He reinstated the tramway from Level 3 to the middle of Gillart's Incline and was thus able to move rock to the mill.

Gillart's Incline

In 1870, a long incline was dropped from the pit level down to the mill. This was the first major piece of civil engineering at Hendreddu and probably predates the exit incline to the Hendre Ddu Tramway. Gillart's Incline was laid in bridge rail. At various times, intermediate tramways were connected to the west track of the incline. At the head of the incline, there was a weighbridge next to the winding house. The winding house has the date '1870' carefully carved into the right-hand wall.

A tramway extended westwards from the head of the incline, running around the hillside to the open pits. At various times a tramway also led east to Gillart's Level, about 100 yards away.

The tramway from Gillart's Level was disconnected from the incline before 1887, though it still ran onto the waste tip to the east of the incline. The Level 2 adit is known to have been connected to the incline by a tramway during the 1880s. This tramway was likely lifted when Gillart's Incline was removed sometime between 1891 and 1899.

The incline and tramway to the open pits were relaid following the collapse in Twll 4 in 1925. Around 1932, and certainly by 1934, the tramway was again removed.

In 1938, two tramways were added: one connected the middle of Gillart's Incline to the Level 3 adit, the other went from the top of the incline into Gillart's Level. The chamber on Gillart's Level was worked for the first time since before the First World War and was both the first underground working at Hendreddu and also one of the last ones in use.

Underground workings

Hendreddu had extensive underground workings on five levels. No survey of the workings has survived. An abandonment plan was prepared in 1946, but it is not in the coal authority's archive. Surveying marks for the abandonment plan can be found throughout the workings.

The following account is based on modern exploration of the workings, and sketch maps left by Bill Breese. It is necessarily incomplete, and should not be treated as an encouragement to underground exploration: there are significant collapses and loose rock throughout.

The 1920 share prospectus for National Welsh Slate Quarries Ltd claimed there were 2,200 yards of tunnels at Hendreddu. The four main adits account for about 900 yards, with another 400-500 yards of known tunnels, and it is possible that there are further undiscovered workings. By 1946, there were five underground levels from Level 1 up to Gillart's Level.

A note on chamber numbering. The numbering scheme used in this section is designed to clarify the complex underground workings. The quarrymen used a different numbering scheme for the bargains they worked; there was generally one bargain per chamber. The bargain numbering scheme has only partially survived in the records written by Bill Breese: Chamber 1.1 is bargain 9, 1.2 is bargain 7, 1.3 is bargain 1, 1.6 is bargain 14, 2.1 is bargain 8 and chamber 2.3 is bargain 10.

Level 1

The Level 1 adit, completed in 1873, was the first tunnel driven below Gillart's Level. It was the main access underground for much of Hendreddu's working life. Water pipes were laid along the main adit after the 1925 collapse

to drain water entering the workings from above.

The Level 1 portal is 820 feet above sea level. The tunnel runs 157 yards northwest, meeting the vein to the southeast of Twll 5. The tunnel slopes slightly uphill, which allows the adit to drain the Level 1 chambers. The slate bed runs about 17 degrees from east-west and dips down to the south at approximately 15 degrees from the vertical. Level 1 is about 215 feet below the top of Gillart's Incline (1,035 feet ASL).

Where the tunnel meets the vein it turns west and a series of chambers have been cut on the north side of the tunnel. The vein is curving here, probably deformed by the strike-slip fault to the southeast. The tunnel follows the curve of the vein, then heads north west along its south side. The chamber closest to the portal is Chamber 1.1.

The order in which the chambers were developed in the 1870s is not known, but there is reason to believe that the Level 1 tunnel was driven west until it met the second fault, and Chamber 1.5 was the first to be developed. The chambers were then developed back towards the portal.

The chambers on Level 1 were worked from the tunnel upwards — Hendreddu used undercut working until at least 1899. In later years, certainly from 1920 onwards, the more traditional approach was used, working from a ledge at the ceiling downwards.

The chambers were accessed by short tunnels running north from the main adit. There were 6ft deep alcoves on the south side of the adit, opposite each chamber tunnel, which held winches to haul slabs out of the chambers and gave room to manoeuvre them through 90 degrees into the main tunnel.

Chambers 1.2 and 1.3 had cranes in the late 1930s.[7] Doubtless, cranes would have been used in all the chambers while they were being actively worked.

Chambers 1.2, 1.3, 1.4 and 1.5 are about the same size: 60 feet deep, 50 feet wide and 50 feet high. Chamber 1.3 was

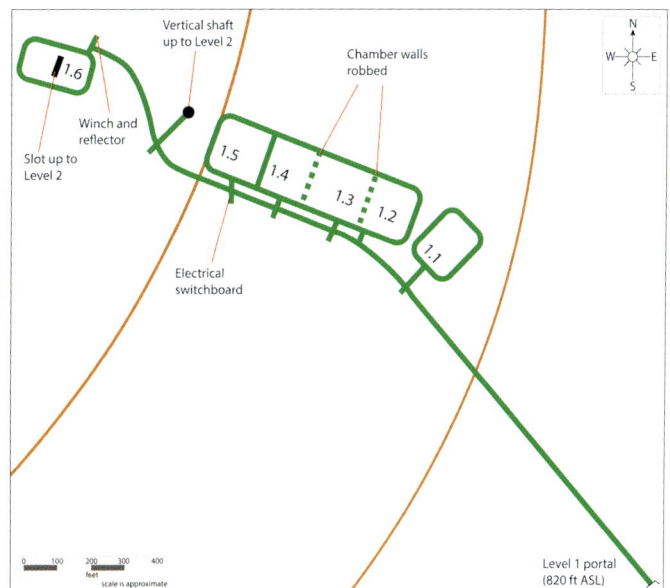

Schematic map of Level 1 workings at the time the mine was abandoned in 1946. The chambers are numbered from east to west.

THE HENDRE DDU TRAMWAY

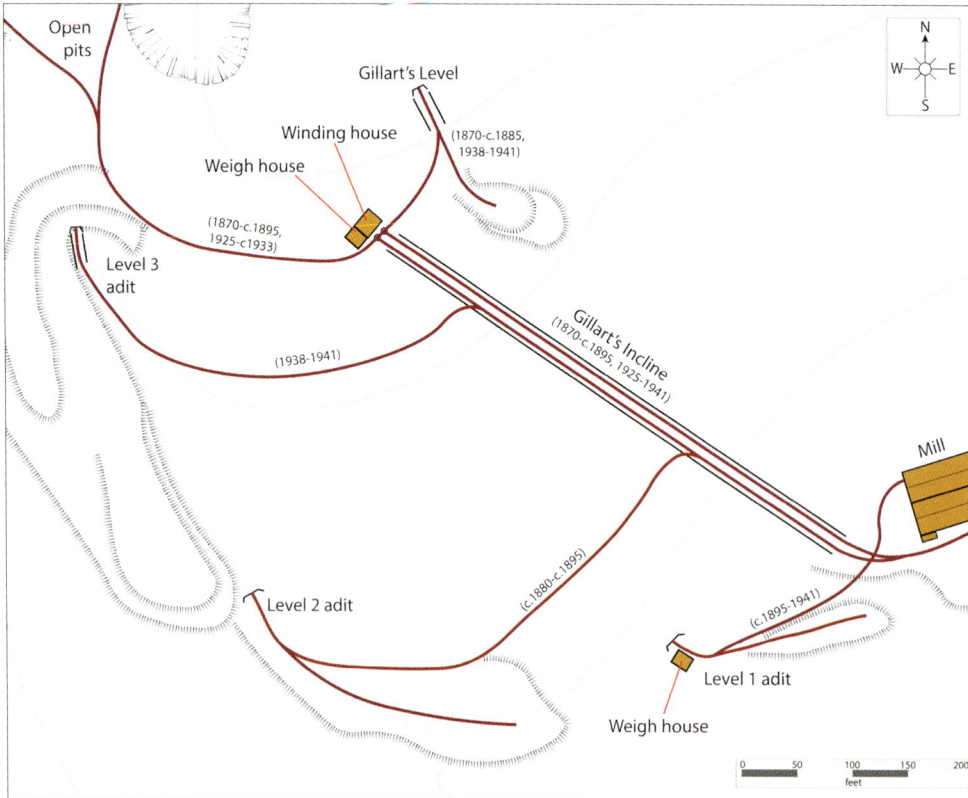

Map labels:
- Open pits
- Gillart's Level
- Winding house
- Weigh house
- (1870-c.1885, 1938-1941)
- (1870-c.1895, 1925-c1933)
- Level 3 adit
- (1938-1941)
- Gillart's Incline (1870-c.1895, 1925-1941)
- Mill
- Level 2 adit
- (c.1880-c.1895)
- (c.1895-1941)
- Level 1 adit
- Weigh house
- 0 50 100 150 200 feet
- N W E S

Left: The middle section of Hendreddu Quarry, showing Gillart's Incline and the tramways connected to the incline between 1870 and 1946. The exact layout at the top of the incline is not known and likely varied over time. The dates of operation of each tramway are shown, where known.

Below: The winding house of Gillart's Incline. The house contained a horizontal drum and there was a weighbridge on its far side. Gillart's Level is to the right, and the date of construction is carved into the nearest pillar.

Bottom right: The mill site, looking down Gillart's Incline. The roof of the manager's house is visible on the left. The mill stood to the right of the manager's house, in the grove of trees middle-left. The course of the tramway from the mill is visible between the trees at the foot of the incline. The Level 1 adit is at the bottom of the slope on the right-hand side. [Dan Quine]

Above: Bridge rail from Gillart's Incline, in 2013. The notch on the right is where the rail was spiked to a sleeper.

HENDREDDU QUARRY DESCRIBED

A schematic map showing the known underground workings at Hendreddu; the complexity of the workings is evident. Two connected faults run across the site[6] – the east one explains the offset of the chamber on Gillart's Level. The west fault is implicated in the collapse of 1925 and explains the skew of the chambers on Level 1. Special thanks to Jon Knowles, Alasdair Roberts, Steve Culverhouse, Tim Gregson, Keith Whiddon, Ken Griffiths and Mark Waite for their contributions to this and other maps in this chapter.

Approximate line of Narrow Vein at Level 3

Fault line

Fault line

Level 3 portal (1015 ft ASL)

Level 2 portal (900 ft ASL)

Level 1 portal (820 ft ASL)

Key

Levels:
1
2
2b
3
Gillart's

Chambers:
Known
Assumed

feet
scale is approximate

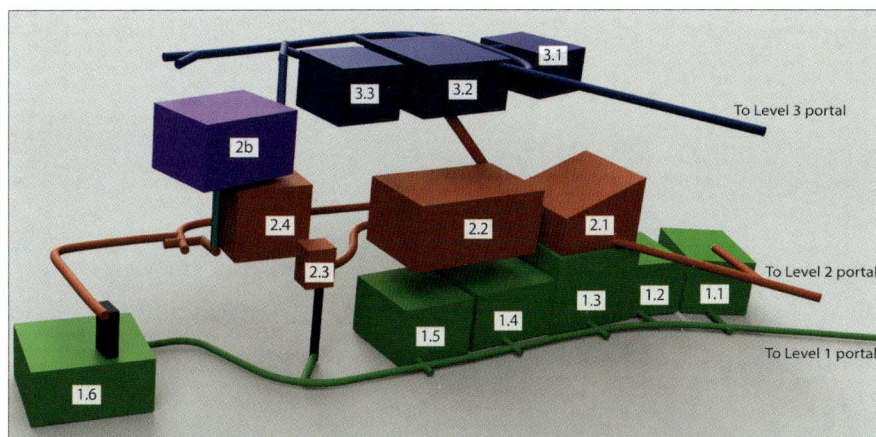

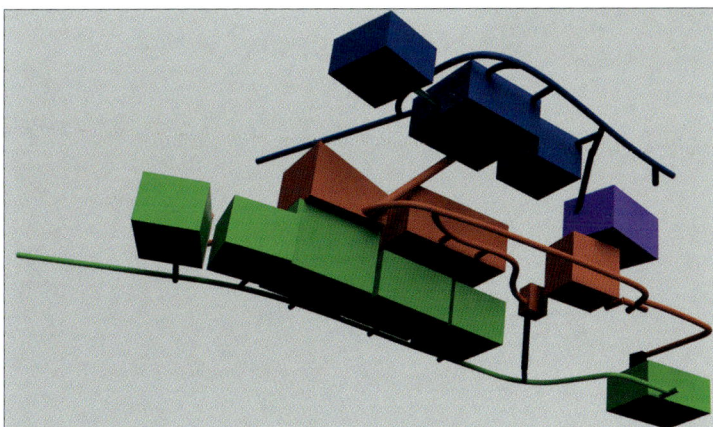

A computer model of the underground levels at Hendreddu, shown from the south (above) and the north (below). The model shows the general arrangement of the chambers on the three levels and the tunnels and shafts connecting them.

The Level 1 portal, at the point where Thomas Williams started driving the tunnel on March 5th 1872. Slate walls support the hill on both sides. [Alasdair Roberts]

14th December 1924 on the fault line running under Bala Lake to Dolgellau;[8] this may have caused the Hendreddu fault to move and led indirectly to the collapse. Chamber 1.5 is now filled with large boulders, and water flows from ground level down through it.

All of the Level 1 chambers have suffered from various levels of roof collapses since 1946. Chamber 1.4 is particularly unstable and should not be entered.

The alcove opposite Chamber 1.5 contains electrical switchgear mounted on a large slab. This was the main junction box to distribute the supply coming along the Level 1 tunnel from the mill to the chambers on this level. The Level 1 tunnel also contains the remains of compressed air pipes and a smaller diameter pipe that carried the phone lines. Iron supports with insulators line the tunnel, which carried the electrical supply. One of these is attached to a large boulder blocking the entrance to Chamber 1.5, which shows that this chamber collapsed before the electrical system was upgraded in 1927.

The tunnel continues westwards beyond the entrance to Chamber 1.5, crossing the western fault into an area of broken rocks known as 'the folds' by the quarrymen.[7] The slate vein is displaced to the north on the west side of the fault, so the adit turns right, where the tunnellers sought to find the vein.

A short way beyond the fault, there is a side tunnel leading north to a vertical shaft leading up to Chamber 2.3. This tunnel was driven to test the quality of the vein; it widens into a small chamber at the end as it enters the vein, but the rock here was too fractured to be of commercial value. In later years, a shaft was driven up to Level 2 and rock lowered

eventually worked upwards to join the Level 2 chamber above it, forming a space 100 feet high. This vast chamber is the largest at Hendreddu.

The entrances to chambers 1.3 and 1.4 have been blocked by slate pack walls, placed to hold back both rubbish tipped into these chambers and fallen rock. The walls were probably built in the mid-1920s. The walls between chambers 1.2 and 1.3 and between 1.3 and 1.4 were removed by T. Glyn Williams before 1941. Pillar robbing was a dangerous activity at the best of times, but given the collapsed chambers directly above Chamber 1.4, it was particularly perilous, a genuine act of desperation.

Chamber 1.5 collapsed in late 1924 or early 1925. This fall may have triggered the collapse of the entire space above. One theory is the fault running along the west wall of the chamber caused a weak point in the roof, and a minor seismic event caused the roof to give way, causing the floors above to collapse downwards. There was a small earthquake centred beneath Corwen on

Looking out of the Level 1 adit, to the portal. The rusted support in the right-hand wall carried electrical and telephone cables, installed in the 1920s. Just beyond the nearest support is a large mineral deposit where the east fault crosses the adit. A sleeper lies in the water in the foreground. [Iain Robinson]

down to be trammed out via the Level 1 tunnel.

Beyond the vertical shaft, the Level 1 tunnel is on the north side of the vein. It ends at a junction with a small alcove to the north and a short tunnel leading south into Chamber 1.6.

Level 2

The Level 2 portal is 900 feet above sea level. Bill Breese, writing in the 1960s, warned that the portal was full of deep water[9] and it is usually flooded to chest depth. The tunnel runs north west about 400 feet into the mountain.

Shortly before the tunnel reaches the vein there is a short side tunnel running north east. This appears to have been a trial and no chamber was developed here. It was probably a late attempt to find the vein east of Chamber 2.1 and was likely driven in the 1930s.

The main tunnel enters the combined chambers 1.3 and 2.1, about 50 feet above Level 1. The roof of this chamber is lower in the south west, where it is just above the roof of the Level 2 tunnel; in the northeast corner, it is much higher.

There is a working ledge on the south wall of Chamber 2.1, running west from the portal of the Level 2 tunnel. This was worked during the T. Glyn Williams era, and used to extract rock that could be trammed out on Level 2. There is a slot high up on the south wall of the chamber, with iron pegs for access and chains in the roof to swing slabs out. Working slots like this are rare in Welsh slate quarries and were used at Hendreddu to follow particularly good runs of slate along the natural joints and beds.

On the north wall of the chamber is a steep stairway cut into the wall, climbing from the northeast corner of Chamber 2.1 to just below the roof. The stairway starts where the floor of Chamber 2.1, once was; today it can be accessed by climbing the fallen rocks that cover the floor of Chamber 1.3. At the top of the stairs is a small caban. From here another working ledge runs west, just under the roof of the chamber.

The Level 2 tunnel continues on the north side of Chamber 2.1. A short incline was installed in 1891, running up the north side of Chamber 1.3 into Chamber 2.1,[7] and the date '1896' is carved into the wall of Chamber 2.1. The floor was likely removed between these dates using the incline to lower rock to Level 1.

On the north side of Chamber 2.1 the Level 2 tunnel continues north east, then bends round to follow the north side of the vein. This tunnel starts at a tipping point, where waste was tipped down into Chamber 1.3. There is a corrugated iron roof over the tipping point, with a wire rope running over it. The roof was installed after the 1925 collapse to protect the workers from the water coming down through Chamber 2.2.

There are the remains of a winch here and an anchor point for a larger chain. This was part of the system that controlled slabs as they were lowered from the slots in the roof. The chain took the weight of slabs as they crossed Chamber 2.1, while the thinner wire was used to guide them. The winch

Looking south and upwards across Chamber 2.1 to the south wall. The slot near the roof is an unusual form of working: men climbed up to the slot using the iron pegs in the chamber wall – visible to the right of the slot. The chain and pulley in the chamber roof were used to move slabs from the slot down to the Level 2 adit. [Tim Gregson]

was removed when this location became a tipping point.

An incline roller and axle binding were found on the waste tip in 2018. These are probably the remains of the 1891 incline between chambers 1.3 and 2.1.

North of the tipping point, there is a blocked entrance on the left, thought to be the lower end of an inclined shaft up to Chamber 3.2. This would have contained a single-track incline used to lower rock down from the Level 3 chambers. There was no other way to extract rock from 3.2, as the access tunnel there was at the top of the chambers. The inclined shaft was blocked in the 1925 collapse.

The Level 2 tunnel turns to run west, then splits into two branches. The southern tunnel runs along the north edge of the vein, with two portals to the south into Chamber 2.2. Chamber 2.2 collapsed in 1925 and its exact size is unknown. It sits partly below Chamber 3.2 and Twll 4 and above chambers 1.4 and 1.5. Water flows down into Chamber 2.2 from Twll 4 above.

The tunnel swings to the south and runs between

Right: Inside Chamber 1.1, showing the vast size of these spaces. In the top right is a chain along one of the later working ledges. The flat, angled surface in the centre is the north edge of the Narrow Vein, clearly showing the angle of dip. The chamber floor is covered with material that has fallen from the roof. [Alasdair Roberts]

Below: Looking along the Level 1 tunnel towards the portal, with the entrance to Chamber 1.2 on the left. Top-right is a surveyor's mark from the 1946 abandonment plan. The circle with a line through it is the mark itself – a plumb bob would have been hung from the centre of the mark and was sighted from the previous marked location. The '5' is the number of the survey point. [Iain Robinson]

Below right: The bottom of the shaft up to Chamber 2.3 with a skip body at the bottom. The tunnel here has been opened out, but the rock was poor and it was not worked into a full chamber. The shaft was probably driven up after the 1925 collapse. In the bottom-right corner is the rusted remains of a hooked metal pole, used to grab descending slabs and steer them onto the waiting wagon. [Ian Adams]

Right: The wall between chambers 1.3 and 1.4 showing where it was robbed by T. Glyn Williams. [Alasdair Roberts]

The electrical switchboard in the alcove opposite Chamber 1.5. This was installed in 1925 and upgraded in 1927. This was the distribution hub for all the chambers on Level 1 and was originally mounted vertically on a wooden framework. You can just see the legs of the mounting frame behind and to the right of the slab. [Alasdair Roberts]

The floor of the alcove opposite Chamber 1.6. Nearest the camera is part of the wooden base of a winch, above it is a lamp reflector. [Alasdair Roberts]

Inside Chamber 1.6, looking back towards the Level 1 tunnel. The last working ledge can be seen above the figure on the left with a compressed air pipe running along it. The access tunnel is below the chains on the right-hand wall, behind the massive fallen blocks that litter the floor of this chamber. [Alasdair Roberts]

Chambers 2.2 and 2.4, approximately along the fault line. It ends in the very small Chamber 2.3, which contains the vertical shaft down to Level 1. A wire rope hangs across the top of this shaft, with a block and tackle still in place, which was used to lower rock to Level 1.

The electrical system did not reach Chamber 2.3, and in working days there was a small pile of blue clay where the tunnel turned to the south. The men would grab a lump of clay as they passed and shape it into a ball, which they used to place their candles on the working surfaces in the chamber.[7] The lack of electrical supply indicates that this chamber was probably opened after 1927.

Ernest Price was working in Chamber 2.3 in June 1939, when he fell 100ft down the shaft to Level 1. The unfortunate Price died of multiple injuries.

The northern branch of the Level 2 tunnel runs parallel to the southern. It is not certain why they went to the expense of driving a parallel tunnel – possibly to avoid bad rock caused by the fault that crosses the site here. The northern tunnel contains an air receiver – a large tank that buffered the compressed air used to power the drills.

West of the air receiver, there is a tunnel to the south.

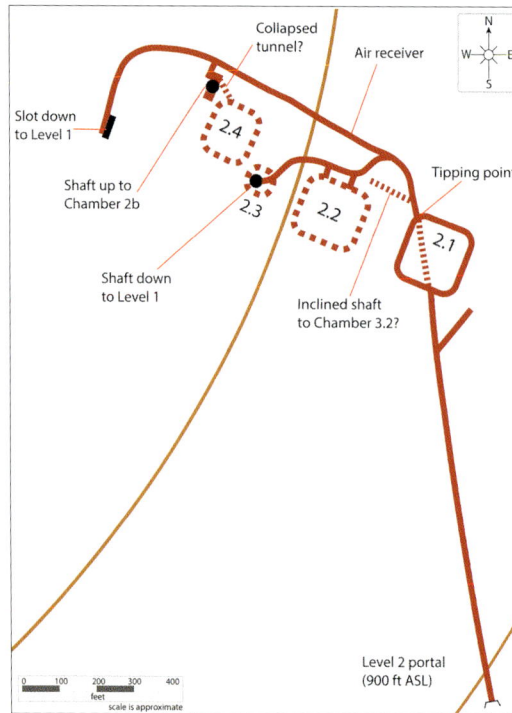

The Level 2 workings at the time the mine was abandoned in 1946.

Looking down into Chamber 1.6 through the rectangular slot on Level 2. The wooden stemple at the top and the iron bars in the walls were used by the rockmen opening out the slot.
[Alasdair Roberts]

This was probably the access into Chamber 2.3, which collapsed in 1925. Sometime after the collapse, the tunnel was extended further south and a shaft was driven vertically up into the floor of Chamber 2b, to allow slab and waste to be lowered down to Level 2.

The exact location and size of Chamber 2.3 are uncertain, and it may not have been fully developed, though there is a collapsed space of some sort.

The Level 2 tunnel continues west along the north side of the vein, before turning south across the vein. It ends at the top of a rectangular 'slot' leading down to Chamber 1.6.

Levels 2b and 3

The Level 3 portal, 1,015ft above sea level, is much further north than those of Levels 1 and 2. This level had a complex history, which is difficult to fully interpret. This account is therefore speculative and open to future correction.

From the portal, the main Level 3 tunnel runs north west for about 150ft, then enters the bottom of Twll 4.

Before the 1925 rockfall, Twll 4 was much smaller. A fault ran along its western edge, with the shallower and smaller Twll 3 to the west. The likely sequence of collapse is that the roof of Chamber 1.5 fell and brought down Chamber 2.2 above it, which in turn caused chambers 3.2 and 3.3 to collapse. These chambers were under the southern wall of Twll 4 and Twll 3 and the south wall and the south end of the dividing wall fell into the chambers below.

When the roof of Chamber 3.2 collapsed, it left Twll 4 significantly deeper. However, it also filled the bottom of the pit with rubble. The Level 3 tunnel and the inclined shaft down to Level 2 were completely blocked, and the chambers on the north side of Level 3 were cut off.

The roof of Chamber 3.1 either collapsed in 1925 or more likely was deliberately removed later, to access the good rock in the chamber roof.

With the Level 3 tunnel blocked by the collapse, there was an immediate need to restore access to Chamber 3.3 and the chamber on Level 2b. Chamber 2b seems to have been productive between 1920 and 1939, so it was probably a priority to reopen it.

It appears a new tunnel was driven to connect the Level 3 tunnel to the chambers west of Twll 4, bypassing the collapse. This detour tunnel ran through the narrow strip of rock between Twll 4 and Twll 5, starting on the south side of Twll 4 and ending on the north.

Looking south from the tipping point on Level 2 across the combined chambers 2.1 and 1.3. The floor of Chamber 1.3 is about 50ft below. On the far wall is the Level 2 tunnel leading out to daylight. To the right of the tunnel portal is a working ledge used towards the end of the quarry's life. The roof is lower on the right of the photograph: the southwest corner of the chamber. The slot shown in the previous photograph is above the top left corner of this photograph. [Stephen Thorpe]

As well as the original Level 3 tramway between Portal A and Portal C and the inclined shaft down to Level 2, three other tunnels lead out of Twll 4. Portal B is about 25ft below Level 3, at the level of the floor of Chamber 3.2. The tunnel runs eastwards into Twll 5 — though originally it would have been the connection into Chamber 3.1.

Portal D is a short tunnel leading north, connecting to the main Level 3 tunnel. This may indicate that Chamber 3.2 was two separate chambers under Twll 3 and Twll 4.

The final tunnel portal is E. This sits halfway up the face of Twll 4, above Portal D. It runs north into the Broad Vein, ending in a collapse. Its purpose is unclear, but there may have been a chamber at the end in the Broad Vein. The tunnel probably marks a floor level of Twll 3 early in the quarry's history when they were exploring the Broad Vein.

North of Twll 4, the detour tunnel turns to run almost due west and rejoins the original tunnel just past Portal C. After passing the tunnel from Portal D, another short tunnel leads south to a junction. The main tunnel continues a short way beyond before ending in a fork, with both branches ending after a few feet. These were attempts to find the vein, but either the rock was not good enough, or there was not enough capital for further exploration.

Returning to the last tunnel leading south, it too ends in a fork. The left-hand tunnel is now collapsed but probably led into Chamber 3.3. The right-hand tunnel leads to the top of a manway down to Level 2b.

The manway was described by Bill Breese as 'a horrible hole descending into the depths below'. The shaft has iron staples driven into the floor to provide footholds for the men descending into the chamber and supports in the wall to carry electric and telephone wires. It drops about 60ft into the medium-sized Chamber 2b.

The shaft is steeply inclined and was a manway into the chamber below.

There is a shaft in the floor of 2b, dropping down to Level 2. A crane was positioned over this shaft[7] and this was the only way to get rock out of the chamber. Both raw slab and waste went down the shaft; waste was taken east along Level 2 and tipped into Chamber 1.3, while raw slabs were lowered down to Level 1 using the shaft in Chamber 2.3.

Level 4: Gillart's Level

About 100 yards east of Gillart's Incline is Gillart's Level, about 200 yards long and leading to a single medium-sized chamber. This was probably the first underground level, being driven around 1870. It was also one of the last chambers to be worked by T. Glyn Williams.

The 'improvised' ironwork holding back part of the collapse at the bottom of the shaft up to 2b. Iron bars have been driven into the tunnel wall, with timbers and bridge rails laid across them, supporting a crude pack wall. Water constantly dropping through the collapse has leached iron from the bars, creating the brown stain on the rock wall. [Alasdair Roberts]

Left: The Level 2 tunnel looking south, with Chamber 2.1 beyond. There was a winch here in earlier days, and the wires are part of the winching arrangement, used to guide descending slabs from the working faces to the chamber floor. At some time after the Level 2 chamber floor was removed, the winch was moved elsewhere and waste rock was tipped from here down into Chamber 1.3. The corrugated iron roof was to protect the men while tipping the wagons, as water often flowed from the roof here, especially when the lower reservoir overflowed and large volumes of water flowed down through the collapsed chambers.[7]
[Alasdair Roberts]

Right: The southern branch of the Level 2 tunnel, looking west towards Chamber 2.3. On the left are the two entrances into Chamber 2.2. The nearest has been blocked by a pack wall to hold back the collapsed material that fills the chamber. Tramway sleepers have been taken up here and laid against the side of the tunnel. On the left wall are arms carrying the quarry's electrical system, the nearest still carries a suspended insulator.
[Ian Adams]

Left: Looking into Chamber 2.3, with track and the sheave for moving rock still in place. This chamber was worked during the T. Glyn Williams era and the shaft down to Level 1 was the main way to get rock out to the mill during this period. Near the end of the track on the right is a length of chain, which is pinned to the rock. This was laid across the track to hold wagons in position and ensure they did not fall into the shaft. A similar arrangement was used at the head of the exit incline at the end of the Upper Tramway.
[Alasdair Roberts]

Right: Looking east along the northern tunnel on Level 2. The air receiver lies on the left, held in place by a row of rocks. There are clear sleeper marks on the floor. The southern tunnel branches off to the right just past the mine explorer. [Alasdair Roberts]

Left: A closer view of Chamber 2.3. The massive pin driven into the ceiling holds the cable for the block and tackle over the shaft. Slabs would be brought to this point on flat wagons, chained up, swung into the void and lowered down. Just below the lip ahead is a small ledge that was the last working face of this very small chamber.
[Alasdair Roberts]

Right: The bottom of the shaft up to Chamber 2b. To the left is the collapsed area, with the tunnel to Chamber 2.3 behind it. On the right is the bottom of the shaft, which was driven after the 1925 collapse. The iron hook at the bottom of the shaft was used to guide descending slabs.
[Alasdair Roberts]

Left: Looking north along the Level 3 detour tunnel with Twll 4 on the left and Twll 5 on the right. The opening on the right leads into Twll 5. The hole in the floor drops about 20ft down to the east-west tunnel which now connects the two pits, but originally connected chambers 3.1 and 3.2. The floor of the detour tunnel collapsed into the east-west tunnel after the quarry closed.
[Alasdair Roberts]

Left: looking down the manway from Level 3 to 2b. The iron staples in the wall and floor were installed between the wars.
[Alasdair Roberts]

Below: Inside Chamber 2b. This was one of the last chambers to be worked. It is about 50ft deep, with a working ledge on the west wall, from where this photograph was taken. The rock was being worked downwards from this ledge when the chamber was abandoned. The manway up to Level 3 is at the far end of the chamber, above the top of the wall covered in iron oxide. The shaft down to Level 2 is in the bottom right, where the rope is curled on the chamber floor.
[Alasdair Roberts]

Above left: The Level 3 junction just before the inclined shaft down to Level 2b, looking south. The left-hand branch is collapsed but likely led into Chamber 3.3. The right-hand tunnel runs a short distance then descends via the inclined shaft, the top of which can just be seen.
[Alasdair Roberts]

Left: Looking south across Twll 4 from Portal C; the Level 3 tunnel was originally underground and crossed along the top of Chamber 3.2 and ran into Portal A, which can be seen on the far side of the pit. The wall on the left separates this pit from Twll 5. The Level 3 detour tunnel passes through this wall. The depth of the pit after 1925 can be seen, dropping significantly below Level 3. Rubble still fills the twll floor, burying the inclined shaft down to Level 2, as well as the collapsed chambers down to Level 1.
[Alasdair Roberts]

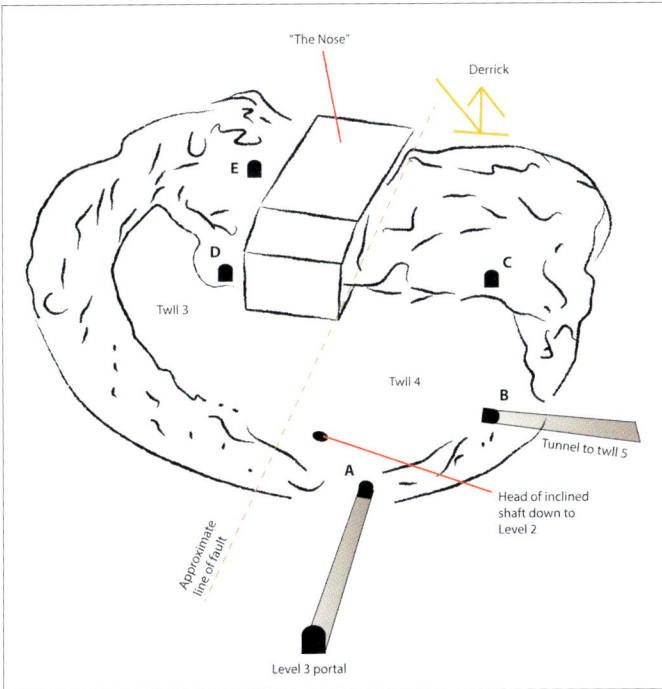

Sketch of Twll 4 in the 1930s, based on one drawn by Bill Breese. The tunnel portals in the pit are labelled A to E. The derrick used to lift fallen rock out of the pit after the 1925 collapse is next to 'The Nose' – the distinctive remains of the wall that once divided Twll 3 from Twll 4. The southern section of the dividing wall fell into Chambers 3.2 and 3.3 below.

The Level 3 portal. The piece of cast iron pipe at Mark's feet is the remains of the turbine feed pipe from the header reservoir to the mill that John Parry mentioned in his 1911 report.
[Alasdair Roberts]

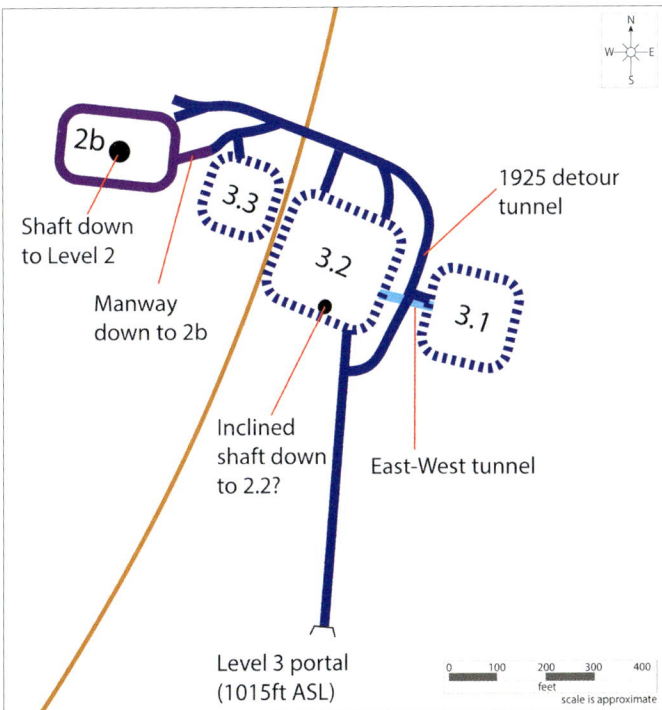

Schematic map showing Level 3 workings at the time the mine was abandoned in 1946 .

Gillart's Level portal. The vein is significantly further north here due to the fault just west, so they tunnelled into the hillside to find good rock. [Dan Quine]

Right: Cross-section of Hendreddu before the 1925 collapse. Not to scale. It is believed that Chamber 3.2 was worked downwards from the Level 3 tunnel, and most of the rock from this chamber, as well as 3.1 and 3.2, went out through the inclined shaft down to Level 2.

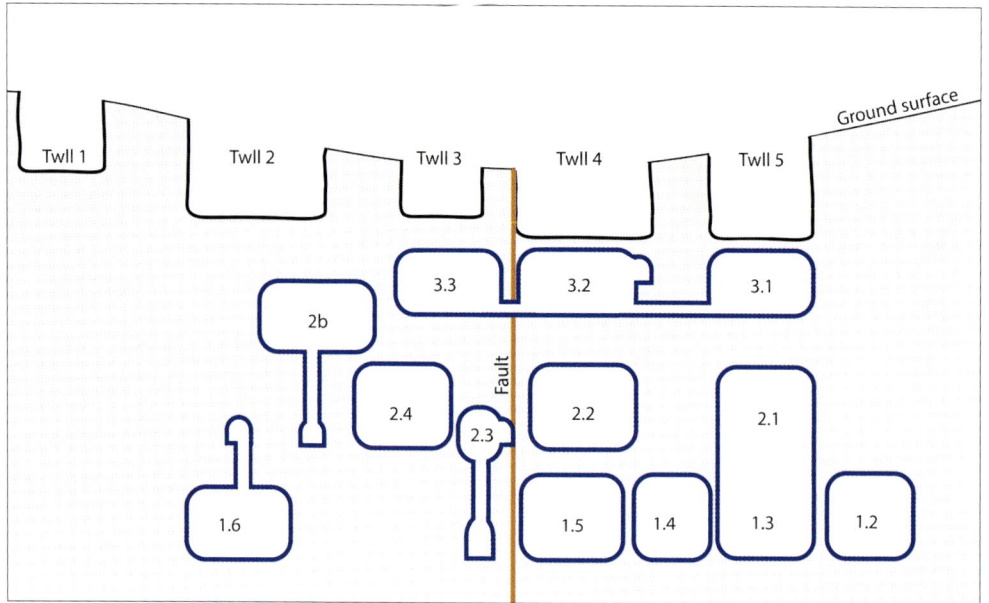

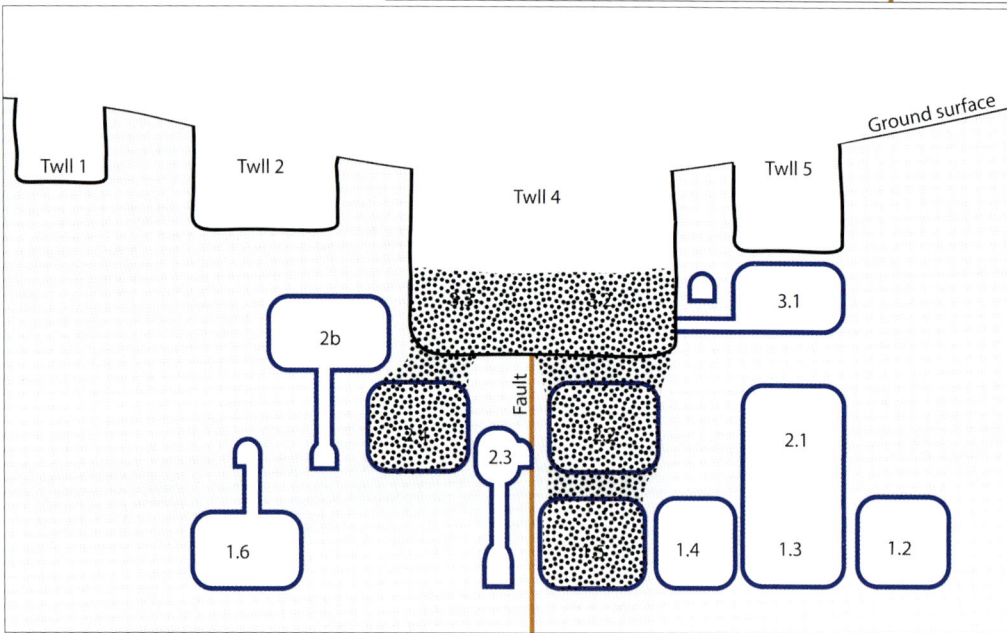

Left: Probable state of the quarry after the 1925 collapse. Twll 4 is now deeper and wider but filled with rubble. The Level 1 and 2 chambers below Twll 4 are collapsed and full of rubble. The Level 3 detour tunnel is shown running between Twll 4 and Twll 5.

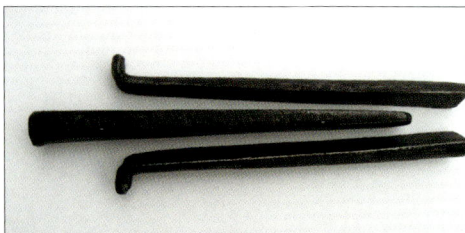

Left and Below: Quarrymens' tools recovered from Hendreddu by Bill Breese. Left: a wedge and feather set used to split large blocks. Holes are drilled into the block along the desired line of cleavage, the feathers are inserted into each hole, and the wedge is used to force them apart, splitting the rock. Bottom left: A set of dressing chisels used to split down smaller blocks and work the rock to the desired shape and size. Bottom middle: Hammers and mallets used in the quarry. Bottom right: Larger splitting chisels. [Dafydd Pughe]

Left: The chamber at the end of Gillart's Level, with the adit out to daylight in the centre. The adit turns through 90 degrees just beyond the chamber entrance. Many tools and lengths of rail remained scattered across the chamber floor in 2016.
[Jon Knowles]

Below: On the waste tips of Chamber 1.3 lies this strange object. After some research, it has been identified as an incline axle binding that holds one end of a square wooden axle in the bearings. These bindings were developed for waterwheel axles. Identical bindings remain on winding houses for the Hendreddu exit incline and the incline system at Cae Abaty quarry a few miles to the east. This binding is likely a component of the 1891 incline within this chamber.
[Tim Gregson]

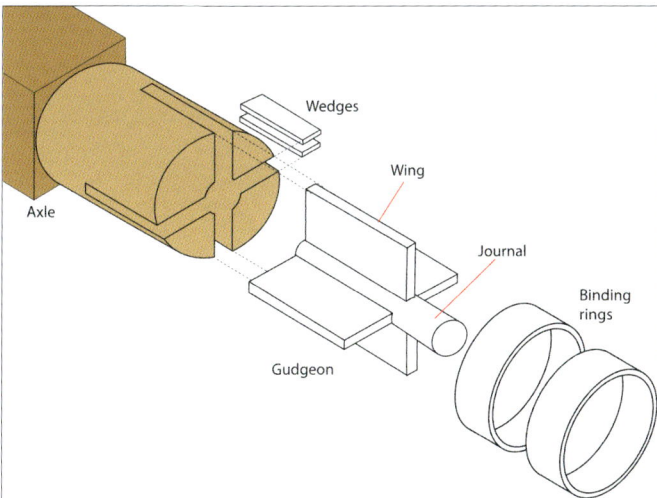

Above: An isometric diagram above shows how the components of the axle binding fit together. The journal rotated within a bearing block.

References

1   Gwyndaf Breese, The Angell Valley Tramway, unpublished manuscript.
2   Prospectus of the National Welsh Slate Quarries Ltd, *Sheffield Daily Telegraph*, p.10, Mar. 17, 1920.
3   List of Mines in Great Britain and the Isle of Man, 1901. H.M. Stationery Office, 1902.
4   Bill Breese, Snow in the Mill, unpublished manuscript.
5   Bill Breese, Notes on a sketch map of Hendreddu quarry, unpublished manuscript.
6   D. M. D. James, Depositional and tectonic relationships of Upper Ordovician and Lower Silurian strata around Dinas Mawddwy, Mid-Wales, *Geological Journal*, vol. 26, pp.307–316, 1991.
7   Bill Breese, Notebook on tramroad and local quarrying, Dolgellau Archive, no. ref ZM/6541/5, c. 1970.
8   British earthquake database, British Geological Survey.
9   Bill Breese, Sketch map of routes into the underground workings, unpublished manuscript.

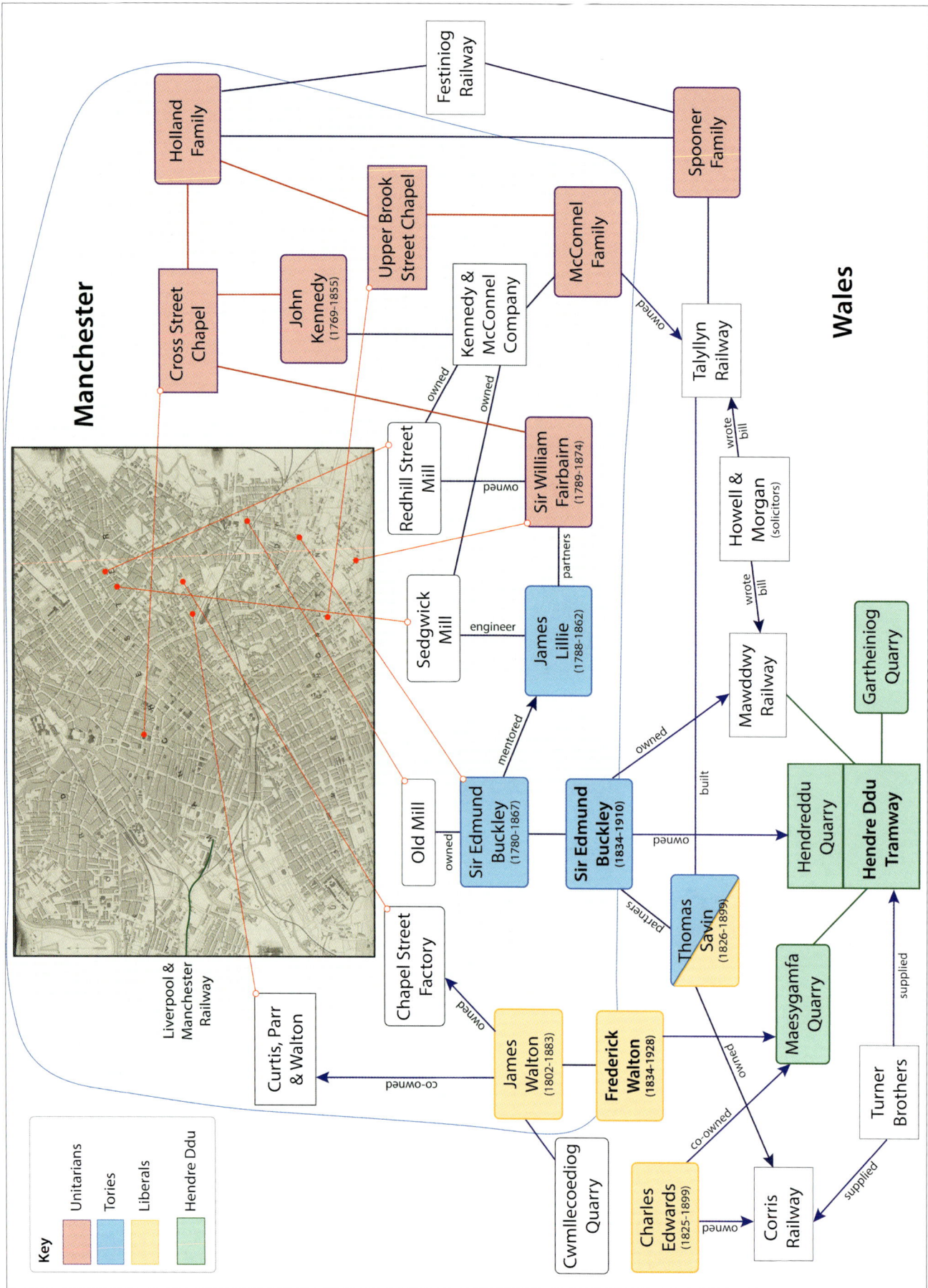

Appendix: Manchester

This diagram shows the close relationship between Manchester and the Hendre Ddu Tramway.

Unitarianism was a powerful force in Manchester. Until 1813, being Unitarian was a punishable offense, and it was decades before church members were considered socially acceptable. As a result they formed a tight-knit community and often worked together in business. The Kennedys, Fairbairns, McConnels and Hollands flourished as mill owners and engineers. The McConnels worshipped at the Upper Brook Street Chapel, while Fairbairn and Kennedy attended the Cross Street Chapel, where William Gaskell was the minister. His wife Elizabeth was the novelist Mrs Gaskell and cousin of the Hollands who founded Oakeley Quarry and promoted the Festiniog Railway. The Unitarians were strong supporters of the Liverpool & Manchester Railway. John Kennedy was a committee member of the railway and a judge at the Rainhill Trials. Sir William Fairbairn – who sold his Redhill Street Mill to Kennedy & McConnel – was a partner of Robert Stephenson and supplied a bridge to the railway.

James Walton was another notable Manchester industrialist, though he was not Unitarian. He co-owned the successful firm of Curtis, Parr and Walton with George Parr and Matthew Curtis – who was twice the Mayor of Manchester. Walton went on to purchase the Cwmllecoediog Estate, and his son Frederick was the co-founder of Maesygamfa Quarry.

Sir Edmund Buckley was a Tory grandee. He lived in Ardwick, about half a mile north of James Walton's home on Anson Road, and even closer to William Fairbairn. Buckley was extremely wealthy, owning mills in and around the city, as well as collieries and railway and canal interests. He mentored the young engineer James Lillie who equipped Kennedy & McConnel's Sedgwick Mill and became a partner of William Fairbairn, though they eventually fell out over Fairbairn's Unitarianism.

Two more influential figures are shown on the diagram. Charles Edwards was the landowner of the original Maesygamfa quarry. He was also the founder of Continental and General Tramways, which owned the Corris Railway for a crucial year in 1877. Thomas Savin was the well-known railway contractor who built many of the lines amalgamated into the Cambrian Railways. He also briefly owned the Corris Railway from 1862-1864 and is believed to have helped James Swinton Spooner construct the Talyllyn Railway. Savin suffered a spectacular bankruptcy in 1866, a not uncommon fate.

Research Sources and Thanks

This book would not be possible without the kind contributions of many others. The most significant of these was from Bill Breese, who as a young man worked at Gartheiniog and Hendreddu. Bill was fascinated with the history of the district and collected a large number of artefacts from the tramway and quarries, which he displayed in his garden at Pantyronen.[1] He was assisted in his work by neighbours Derek Jones and Ifan Price.[2]

He researched the history of the tramway, writing extensive private notes, many based on conversations with his father John. In the 1970s he published a series of articles in the *Cambrian News* based on his research. He wrote in both Welsh and English and his craft as a historian and writer is evident in both languages.

After Bill's death, his museum collection was purchased by Hugh Jones, of Llanwrin. For 40 years it was kept untouched in a shed on Hugh's farm. After his death, the family sold the collection to Dafydd Pughe, of Caeadda, who has restored several artefacts for display.

With Thanks To

Gwyndaf Breese (no relation to Bill) gave access to his work, which built on Bill's. John Lazenbury provided many photographs of the area. Brian Poole updated Lewis Cozens's work and captured many important local stories. Edryd Price described his childhood in Aberangell and his work in the Forestry Commission. Marieanne Mills talked about growing up in the village and shared memories of her family. Tecwyn Williams, son of T. Glyn, provided access to family photographs and memories of Hendreddu. Tecwyn's uncle Edwin remembered playing at Hendreddu quarry when he was a boy.

John Breese and Cyril Evans, grandsons of John Breese the locomotive driver, gave access to family photographs, documents and memories. Dafydd Pughe saved Bill Breese's museum collection and contributed many photographs to this book. Martin Shelley and Dewi Morris recalled Aberangell and its inhabitants.

Mike Cowley has long been an expert on the Hendre Ddu. He photographed many of Bill Breese's documents, and his advice, expertise and encouragement have greatly enhanced this work. I spent a wonderful afternoon in the company of Donald Sills, who gave me access to his notes and photographs of the tramway and Gartheiniog in the 1970s. Mike Shaw provided photographs of Aberangell and helped to decipher the tramway's history. John Davison accompanied me on a typically 'soft' Aberangell day when we surveyed the Gartheiniog and Cwmllecoediog quarries.

Steve Culverhouse provided photographs, encouragement and a great deal of local knowledge. He also visited the Dolgellau Archive on my behalf to copy hundreds of pages of Bill Breese's writing. Mark Waite shared his collection of photographs and his knowledge of the underground world.

MRFS helped with translations from the Welsh and proofread an early draft of this book. He found errors large and small and suggested many improvements. Scrutinising a text at that level of detail is a hard task, I was extremely lucky to have such a skilled and knowledgeable writer helping with my book. I also want to thank him for his steadfast support of the narrow gauge community generally and historical research specifically. Eddie Castellan kindly completed a thorough proofread of the second draft of the book. The quality of his work is second-to-none – his meticulous insights considerably improved the text and prompted me to clarify much; the remaining mistakes are all mine.

The late Vic Bradley contributed information about the Forestry Commission's Chirk Depot. Andrew Neale provided excellent notes on the Forestry Commission tramways. Pete Briddon shared his photographs from Gillingham Pottery and Gartheiniog. Pete Nicholson also provided photographs and details of Gillingham Pottery. Ian Doughty, Chair and Collections Manager, Congleton Museum Trust, also provided a picture from their archive.

John Webb helped identify the crane at Aberangell Station. Richard Greenhough helped with valuable information about the Corris Railway. Richard Kidner generously allowed me to use the photographs that he and his father took of the tramway. John Peredur Hughes contributed his deep experience of quarrying, foundries and wagons. Francis Stapleton and Clive Briscoe helped me identify wagons from the Hadrill photographs. Alan Keef supplied high-quality versions of some of the 1925 photographs and helped me with the history of Motor Rail No. 2059. John Rowlands was an immeasurable help with the technical details of Motor Rail locomotives.

Rod Allcock and Brian Clarke helped with matters related to the timber tramways and the preservation of Hendre Ddu artefacts. Brian kindly allowed me to use his excellent photographs. Graham Fairhurst shared his research into the tramway and reviewed early drafts of several chapters. His correspondence on many matters greatly clarified the story. A number of his photographs appear in this book.

The late Jeremy Wilkinson's indispensable *Wilkinson's Gazetteer and Bibliography of the Mines and Quarries of North Wales* is a wonderful resource. Julian Hunt's research materials on the history of Dinas Mawddwy and Sir Edmund Buckley were invaluable in uncovering the story of the wayward Lord.

Jeff Follett, his brother Terry and his father John gave me wonderful details of Maesygamfa quarry mill, which made possible a much more accurate computer reconstruction of the building. Don Newing and Malcolm Phillips of the Narrow Gauge Railway Museum helped with research and put me in touch with further Hendre Ddu enthusiasts, including the late Dave Billmore who kindly contributed his notes and recollections.

David Gwyn led an industrial archaeology group from Plas Tan y Bwlch on an exploration of the Aberangell quarries. The group let me use their field notes and surveys. David

Bill Breese's museum in the 1970s. [Gwyndaf Breese]

also assisted with translating notes from Welsh into English. Special thanks to Jon Knowles for his extensive notes and photographs of the underground workings at the various quarries. I look forward to his book on Aberllefenni.

Jonathan Clay produced the magnificent artwork that graces the cover of this book. It took a lot of back and forth and comparing notes, but the result is spectacular. Alasdair Roberts provided me access to his photographs. He was instrumental in photographing and surveying Hendreddu. Edward Lockhart, Tim Gregson and Stephen Thorpe also provided photographs and notes of the workings.

The extended Hadrill family, especially Marilyn McGuire, Varel Hadrill McGuire (Temple Hadrill's daughter) and the late Dave Bindon, helped with the section on Temple Hadrill. Kristi Dumais and Stewart Katz, descendants of William Bowley, helped untangle the Bowley family history and generously supplied several photographs.

A huge thanks to all the members of the Hendre Ddu Tramway and Slate Quarry Enthusiasts groups on Facebook for their enthusiasm, encouragement and advice. Every one of you has contributed to this study.

Finally a special thanks to my father, Simon Crow. He has always supported my passion for narrow gauge railways and helped this book immeasurably by conducting interviews, visiting the Dolgellau archives, and working with the Jones family to secure the future of the Bill Breese collection. It is fair to say that without him, this book would not have been written.

References

1   D-block GB-284000-309000, BBC Domesday book project, 1986.
2   Gwyndaf Breese, End of the line, unpublished manuscript.

Index